BUSINESS INTERRUPTION INSURANCE

BUSINESS INTERRUPTION INSURANCE
Its Theory and Practice

by Robert M. Morrison JD, CPCU
with Alan G. Miller JD, CPCU
& Stephen J. Paris JD, CPCU, CLU

A NATIONAL UNDERWRITER PUBLICATION

Reproductions of and quotations from insurance policies and forms in
this book are the copyrighted material of Insurance Services Office,
Inc., and are used with its permission.

International Standard Book Number: 0-87218-331-9
Library of Congress Catalog Card Number: 85-63188

Printed in the United States of America

"Until the time comes for the appearance of a standard treatise on Use and Occupancy, the searcher for information concerning it will find his task a tedious and confusing one. That time is not yet. For the subject itself is being standardized but slowly, either in theory or in practice. At present much of the best work in this field is being done by adjusters and others examining into the detailed features presented by typical Use and Occupancy losses and endeavoring to secure such improvements of policy form and interpretation as will promote equity by extending the scope and flexibility of this form of coverage."

Willis O. Robb, "Use and Occupancy Insurance," *Annals of American Academy of Politics and Science,* March, 1927.

About the Authors

ROBERT M. MORRISON, a graduate of Harvard College and Harvard Law School, is the founding partner of the Boston law firm of Morrison, Mahoney & Miller and currently of counsel to the firm. He has been involved in all aspects of the insurance industry since 1927 when he graduated from Harvard Law School. Since 1969, when he published *Insurance Agency Purchases and Mergers*, he has been an advisor on insurance agency management and planning for clients throughout the United States. He has written extensively on all aspects of the insurance business, has taught classes in insurance and insurance law at various universities and has lectured on those subjects throughout the United States and in various foreign countries. He is President Emeritus of the School of Insurance Inc., a member of the Board of Governors of International Insurance Seminars, Inc. and President of Affiliated Business Consultants, Inc.

ALAN G. MILLER, University of Illinois 1952, Harvard Law School 1955, is Senior Partner of Morrison, Mahoney & Miller, a law firm engaged in the practice of insurance law with offices in Boston and Springfield, Massachusetts and London, England. For over twenty five years he has served as an instructor in insurance law and has had wide experience as a speaker on insurance topics in the United States and abroad. He is the author of numerous articles appearing in insurance and legal publications including "Business Interruption Insurance," a legal primer in the *Federation of Insurance Counsel Quarterly*. His experience in the field of business interruption losses has been extensive.

STEPHEN J. PARIS is also a senior partner at Morrison, Mahoney & Miller where he has specialized in all aspects of insurance law since graduating from Boston College Law School in 1963. Mr. Paris achieved his C.P.C.U. designation in 1966 and his C.L.U. in 1973. He is Vice President of The Insurance Library Association of Boston, Past Chairman of the Insurance Institute of Northeastern University and is a Regional Vice President of the Defense Research Institute. He has taught insurance and law courses and has been a speaker and written on insurance and legal topics internationally for many years.

Contents

Part Two—Practice

Addenda

Preface

We offer this volume to the buyers and sellers of Business Interruption Insurance policies, as a guide for understanding the provisions of the contract. To that end, we draw on the decisions of both federal and state courts and those of the tax authorities, the writings and opinions of numerous authors and speakers in this field, as well as on our personal experiences. Whenever possible, we have tried to give proper acknowledgment to the source. To the extent that we may have lost track of an original source and fail to acknowledge it, we offer our apologies.

During the century since Business Interruption Insurance was first written in the United States, there have been numerous changes in the form of policy issued. Earlier forms have been largely abandoned. To the extent that the principles involved in them have relevancy to the forms of policy issued today, we shall deal with them. Moreover, some of these forms may still be used appropriately in special circumstances today and thus are worthy of record. For the same reasons, we will on occasion refer to forms of policies issued in other countries.

During the period that the present volume was being prepared, representative members of the insurance industry were working at a new policy form for Business Interruption Insurance. As this volume is being readied for publication, word is received that a new policy form has been filed in all jurisdictions. Entitled the *Business Income Coverage Form* (referred to hereinafter as the BIC Form), it is scheduled to become effective on January 1, 1986. Its use is scheduled to become mandatory on January 1, 1987.

The introduction of this new form does not materially affect the approach utilized in this book for at least three reasons. First, policies incorporating the Gross Earnings forms will obviously and necessarily continue in force for some time into the future; second, litigation involving present forms will undoubtedly continue for years to come; and third, a review of the new forms reveals that the changes accomplished are more in the nature of form than substance. Nevertheless, special chapters have been incorporated into this book dealing with the provisions of the BIC Form. In addition, readers are alerted to departures from the statements made in the text by the provisions of the BIC Form.

In general, it can be stated that while changes in wording and format are introduced by the BIC Form, few changes in coverage or concept are involved. Thus, with few exceptions, the material presented herein with respect to both theory and practice remains valid and unchanged.

It is the purpose of this book to present a broad approach to the concepts underlying Business Interruption Insurance. The discussion will sweep across all variations—regional, trade or Insurer originated—to achieve an understanding of the general principles. Differences do exist in individual policies; there are variations from the norm. It is, therefore, of utmost importance that there be a close and careful reading of the policy involved in any specific situation to ascertain its exact language.

The term Business Interruption, rather than the broader term Time Element, or the latest term "Business Income Coverage" has been utilized herein for the practical reasons that (a) it is the generic term customarily used in the insurance industry to describe all insurance contracts in this area; (b) if the long continued use of the term "U & O" is any criterion, the term "Business Interruption" will be used for many years into the future by persons who have dealt with this type of coverage under the earlier form; and (c) such terminology, being more familiar to the average reader, will have a tendency to facilitate understanding in what is commonly considered a subject difficult to understand.

Since it is our aim to serve also the needs of those not professionally conversant in insurance matters, we have chosen to couch our text, as far as possible, in nontechnical language. Where helpful, we have included examples to illustrate the precepts. It is our belief that this approach does not detract from the benefits of this volume for the professional and the technician. Indeed, it may serve to allay, in part, the feeling of insecurity with which even some insurance practitioners currently approach the entire subject of Business Interruption Insurance.

References and discussion of specific items in depth have been placed at the end of each chapter. These will be of value to those who seek a deeper understanding of various matters discussed.

In addition to exploring the past and surveying the current scene, we also, from time to time, give some thought to the future. Two paths will be followed. The first will lead to suggested changes in the text of the Business Interruption Insurance policy forms. The second will deal with possible extensions of the Business Interruption concept to new developments in business operations in general.

The larger part of the presentation is directed to what is generally termed Business Interruption Insurance. But reference will be made to other types of time element coverages, such as Rent Insurance and Extra Expense Insurance, from time to time.

We have no intention to discuss general principles of insurance law, except as may be necessary to an understanding of the final outcome of cases that have been tried in the courts. Occasionally, we diverge from this intention where we believe the principle is of fundamental importance to Business Interruption Insurance practices.

Of most significance, the method of structured analysis upon which this book is premised is entirely new and, indeed revolutionary, as the reader will discover when introduced to the "Six P's" and "Six E's."

Finally, our deep appreciation is expressed to all those whose invaluable help in preparing the final text has made it possible to bring this project to fruition; with special appreciation to Nancy Petriello whose mastery of the word processor and enthusiastic interest were most helpful.

Introduction

The Plan of the Book

The plan of this book is relatively straightforward. It is divided into two main sections. The first part is devoted to the theory of Business Interruption Insurance; the second part to its practice.

The first part deals initially with the basic concepts underlying this type of insurance—the needs which it is designed to meet. Secondly, comes a history of how these needs developed and of the steps taken from time to time by the insurance industry to meet them. Lastly, there will be an analysis of the framework of the Business Interruption Insurance policy form on two levels—the first, a simple outline of its structure; the second, a more searching probe into its interpretation.

The first part is designed to meet the requirements of those who have a need to understand—students of this subject or in general, those called upon to deal with *specific* situations that arise in business activities.

The time has come to dispose of the myth that there is something inherently mysterious about Business Interruption Insurance. We hope that goal will be achieved by the precepts set out and the simple examples used for illustration. Some issues are also raised and problems cited that should interest the theoretician in this field.

The second part represents a different approach to dealing with the issues that arise in the process of buying, selling and servicing Business Interruption Insurance policies. These issues are raised by introducing, one after another, a prototype of the characters who deal with such issues. First, the Owner or Manager of the business enterprise, who is responsible for protecting the assets of his business, will present his requirements. The term "Owner" will be used to designate the person upon whom rests the responsibility for taking adequate steps to protect against risk of loss, including the transference of risk by the purchase of insurance. In a large business enterprise, this responsibility may be delegated to an employee typically referred to as the Risk Manager.

He is followed by the Intermediary, who surveys the risk, determines what kinds of insurance coverage are appropriate and undertakes to place the insurance. The term, Intermediary, is used in the text to designate the distributor of insurance. He may be licensed as an Agent, Broker, Advisor or Consultant. After the insurance is written, he is referred to herein as the Agent. Then comes the Underwriter, who will evaluate the risk and set the price.

In the vast majority of cases, no loss will occur during the policy term and the Owner will have obtained the benefit of the protection and peace of mind that he requires; the Intermediary will have received a commission or a fee for his services and the Insurer will have gained a revenue to be used toward paying the losses of other Owners and toward earning a fair return on the risks it has assumed. This completes the first cycle of general practice and often the only cycle in which the parties are involved.

The challenging aspects of Business Interruption Insurance arise when a loss occurs. Challenging because, more than in any other type of insurance, the settlement of losses involves subjective and speculative insights as well as objective standards. Policies using such phrases as "due diligence," "probable experience," "necessarily continue," and "same quality," leave much room for judgmental conclusions. (For similar phraseology in the BIC Form see Ch. 8.) The courts have used the term "theoretical" in describing the extent of the loss an Insured has suffered.

The second cycle starts with the occurrence of a loss. The Owner is now referred to as the Insured. There follows the introduction onto the scene of what we term a Loss Manager, representing the Insured, and of an Adjuster, representing the Insurer. The procedures that the Adjuster follows in adjusting and settling the loss are surveyed, as well as the procedures that the Loss Manager must follow under the terms of the policy.

Credit must be given to the ranks of those Adjusters who over the years have taken the "theoretical" language of the policy and worked it out into specific practical terms. Since they were engaged by the Insurer, in most cases, it is not surprising that the intent of the Insurer in entering into the contract influenced their thinking. It is also interesting to note that a substantial portion of the existing literature on this subject has been written by persons associated with the claims end of the insurance business.

Much of the information with respect to the extent of the loss is derived from the Insured's financial records. The Insured may call upon his Accountant to help in preparing the necessary figures.

In most cases, the Adjuster and the Loss Manager, with the help of experts they may call in, are able to settle the amount of the loss. The closing papers are drawn up at this juncture, the claim is paid by the Insurer and the matter is closed.

Unfortunately, differences sometimes arise between the Insured and the Insurer that are not compromised and settled. At that point, recourse must be had to further procedures. These involve the third cycle of practice. They include appraisal and/or court action. The Lawyers then usually appear on the scene and take charge. There is a growing body of case law to aid the Lawyer in deciding on the course of action he should follow. Many of the cases are referred to in the text and in the notes to the text. Where more than one court has handed down a decision on the same controversy, the date of the pertinent reported decision will usually be noted.

The Lawyer's efforts are traced through the necessary legal procedures until there is a final determination of his client's rights. Since most Lawyers will want to refer to the exact text of the various court decisions, they will generally not be analyzed in depth herein.

There are six addenda. The first addendum consists of comments, which are expanded discussions of items referred to in the main text. Second is a sampling of forms currently used and of the new forms to be used after January 1, 1986. Their purpose is to present, in visual format, some of the matters discussed in the text.

For the benefit of lawyers and accountants who may seek authorities to guide them in resolving Business Interruption Insurance policy problems, we have collected and listed, in a third addendum, most of the cases decided to date involving such policies. The end of chapter notes usually will contain only a representative citation. All pertinent cases are not cited; nor are conflicting cases usually included. Fourth is an outline and example of the calculation of a claim. Fifth is a glossary of terms as used in this book. Some of these terms are new to the literature. Others are used in a different sense than is generally employed in practice. Sixth, is a general index. This index should prove of value in locating any major subject of immediate interest to the reader.

The Use of Terms

As mentioned earlier, the glossary of terms contains definitions that depart somewhat from usages of long standing currently to be found in insurance policies, text-books and court decisions. At the same time, new terms have been created. Such a step is not to be undertaken lightly. Yet it appears imperative to strike out afresh and establish some order in the practices that have grown up through a century of trial and error. Business Interruption Insurance contains elements that cannot be adequately described in definitions that are appropriate to Property Insurance. Moreover, the understanding of just what is the property insured under this type of insurance has evolved only after a number of changes in underlying concepts. New ideas often call for new language. Sharper and more descriptive terms have to be employed.

Consider, for example, the word "business," which appears in the title of this book. It is not surprising that this word has different implications, depending on the context in which it appears. There are at least four different contexts in which the word "business" may be used. They can be illustrated by these four sentences:

1. *"How's business?"*—which clearly asks whether one is making any money.
2. *"What business are you in?"*—which refers to the type of business enterprise.
3. *"Will you sell me a piece of your business?"*—where the reference is to the ownership structure.
4. *"My business is practically at a standstill"*—where the word is used to denote the operations being carried on.

These are separate and distinct meanings and are not interchangeable. Yet, as will be seen later, the courts have mistakingly used one in place of another.[1]

Another example is found in the word "loss". An examination of the underlying Property Insurance contract to which the Business Interruption Insurance form is normally attached will indicate that this word is used to express two distinctly different concepts. One use is to denote the damage to the physical structure of the property described. At times it is coupled with the word "damage," as in "loss or damage," to make the meaning clear. There is, however, a second way in which the word is used. That is to denote the financial detriment suffered by the Insured as a result of the physical damage. (See Comment #6, p. 311.)

This uncertainty of meaning has been avoided in the text. *Damage* is an event, *loss* is an experience over time under business interruption concepts. The word "damage" will be used to describe the deterioration in the physical condition of the property, while the word "loss" will be limited to the financial detriment suffered by the Insured.

One more illustration may be in order. In connection with Property Insurance, it is customary to speak of a partial loss, even when the word "loss" is used to refer to the impairment of physical property. This usage is improper. There may be partial destruction, in that only a portion of the property has been damaged, but to the extent that damage did occur, it is finite and complete. When we turn to the matter of financial detriment, the term "partial loss" becomes even more inappropriate. What took place was a partial interruption of operations or an interruption of part of the operations but, as far as the loss was concerned, there was nothing partial about it. A specific number of dollars were lost; the amount of detriment to the Insured's financial condition was specific and complete.[2]

It is unreasonable to expect that all of the misuse and abuse of terms that have crept into the field of Business Interruption Insurance can be resolved in short order. What the Glossary represents is a decision, in this volume at least, to use terms in a more clear and specific fashion. Except where direct quotes require otherwise, that policy will be diligently pursued. It is hoped that this will serve in the long run to facilitate not only greater understanding of the subject, despite the variance from current policy language, but also ultimately, a change in that language.

A lingering, although diminishing, practice that should also have a quiet funeral is that of referring to Business Interruption Insurance as U & O insurance. This practice relates back to that stage in the development of concepts when policies actually insured the "Use and Occupancy" of the described property. Formerly, there was such a thing as U & O insurance. And it has not entirely departed the scene. When the text delves into the historical development of this type of insurance and when it deals with early legal decisions, there will be occasions when Use and Occupancy coverage will be discussed. But the term and the concept have little current relevancy and should not continue to obfuscate the thinking and language of those who currently deal with the subject of Business Interruption Insurance.[3]

Current practice is to use the term "Business Interruption Value" to describe the dollar amount of Gross Earnings to which the Contribution Clause will apply.[4] While this is a useful term, it should be recognized that it is not the language used in the Coinsurance Clause which reads in part ". . . the Gross Earnings that would have been earned (had no loss occurred) during the 12 months immediately following the date of damage . . . ."

In the work sheet, which is described at some length later, the calculations refer to the "Business Interruption Basis for Coinsurance." Only in the foot-noted instructions on the work sheet does the term "Business Interruption Value" appear.

Lastly, the term "policy" is used in the text to refer to the document issued by the Insurer for delivery to the Insured. Usually it is a Business Interruption Insurance form attached to a policy of Fire or Property Insurance. In certain instances, the Business Interruption Insurance form may be attached to another type of policy. Business Interruption Insurance forms can be attached to Casualty, Inland Marine, Ocean Marine, Boiler and Machinery and various forms of package policies, among others. It is also possible to issue a policy designed specifically to insure only against loss resulting from interruption of business operations. Where the text deals not with a specific document but with the agreement between the parties, the term "contract" will usually be used. Since the agreement is normally incorporated into a written instrument, the two terms may be interchangeable up to a certain point. Where, however, the underlying Fire or Property Insurance policy contains terms that are at variance with the intention of the parties, or are incongruous with the thrust of the Business Interruption Insurance concept, the difference between that policy and the "contract" can take on significance. At times, the terms "policy" and "form" are used to distinguish the two parts of the written instrument.

The Use of Capitals

Many of the nouns denoting persons acting in a particular capacity and the terms applied to basic concepts will be capitalized. This practice has been adopted to add additional emphasis to such words where used. Such emphasis is intended to bring out more clearly the meaning of the text and also to reinforce the introduction of new terms into the literature on this subject. Also, the Insured will be usually referred to by the personal pronoun "he," while the Insurer will be referred to as "it."

From time to time, a question will be posed to which no answer is given. This often, but not always, involves a situation where, in the opinion of the authors, further legal precedent is needed before a definitive answer can be given.

Notes

1. Some early forms included a definition of "business" according to the class of property insured. See: Hartford Fire Ins. Co. v. Wilson and Toomer Fertilizer Co.

2. Currie uses the terms "interruption" and "interference." These might be appropriate to differentiate between a stoppage of all operations and a stoppage of only part of the operations because of the damage. The words "cessation" and "curtailment" would appear to be more apt. Currie's terms might represent the difference in impact between on-premises and off-premises damage; or even the difference between loss caused by fire damage and that resulting from a strike. See: Lyndesay M. Currie, *Consequential Fire Loss in the United Kingdom and Eire* (London, 1952).

3. Klein suggests that the acronym "BII" might be confusing because it might be confused with Bodily Injury Insurance under the automobile liability policy. Henry C. Klein, *Business Interruption Insurance,* 4th Ed. (July, 1960), p. 13.

4. Withers uses the term "actual cash value of income." The word "actual" means present, current, existing in truth. There can be an actual value of a piece of machinery or a building. But the future potential income of a business enterprise is at best an estimate—and can hardly be considered as existing in truth. See K.W. Withers, *Business Interruption Insurance*, (Berkeley: Howell-North Press, 1957), p. 2.

Part One

Theory

1

The Need for Income Protection

*Income derived from land and ships. No coverage under property
insurance for loss of income. Insurance on
freight, rent and profits.*

A. Income from Land and Ships

From early times, land and its ownership has been a medium for producing income—not only from the crops it produced, but also as a source of revenue when its use was turned over to another. Conversely, the obligation to pay rent, whether in the form of service, crops or money, created a burden on the tenant, continuing over a period of time. Where the land itself or the structures erected thereon were dedicated to a use that would produce income, that income was relied upon by both landlord and tenant as the source from which the rental payment would be derived.

Another early use of property for the production of income was the dedication of a ship to the transportation of goods. The building and equipping of the ship involved an investment of a substantial amount of money. The shipowner anticipated a return on this investment either by way of freight, when he operated the ship himself, or by way of charter fees, when he rented it out to others to operate.

In England, from whose experience much of the economic system of the United States has been derived, it was early recognized that not only the wealth represented by the property itself, but also the flow of income from that property, needed protection. In the same way that the risk of loss to the property itself could be transferred, the risk of losing income from the property should be similarly transferable. One way of transferring such a risk was to place the burden of loss on the tenant. Thus, at common law as administered in England, the tenant was obliged to continue paying rent for the duration of the lease, even though the leased property was destroyed by fire.[1]

The possibility of using the insurance mechanism for the transfer of risk of loss of income was probably first developed in connection with freight earned by vessels. Examples of insurance of freight charges can be found as early as 1746.[2] The flow of income to the shipowner was thus protected.

The analogy between income from maritime property and from real property appears relatively simple. If the anticipated income from the use of a ship on a voyage can be insured, why not the anticipated income from the renting of a parcel of real property? Such insurance would benefit both the lessor and the lessee.

B. No Coverage Under Insurance on Physical Property

There is no definite record of when insurance against loss of income resulting from the destruction of real property was first written. The earliest records involve cases where the Insured tried to collect for loss of income under the Fire Insurance policy he carried on property which he rented. These cases established the principle that a Property Insurance policy did not insure against loss of income resulting from the destruction of the property.[3]

The first of such cases is *Wright v. Pole*, decided in 1824. Wright was proprietor of Ship Inn at Dover, England which he rented. When the Inn was partially put out of operation because of a fire, he sued for "damages consisting in rent paid by him to his landlord, the hire of other houses while the apartments were undergoing the necessary repairs, and the loss or damage sustained by him by reasons of various persons refusing or declining to go to the said Ship Inn whilst the apartments so damaged were undergoing such repair." The Insurer maintained that the policy which insured Wright's "interest only" in the inn, meant only the interest that Wright had in the fabric of the inn. The court decided that the interest in the possible profits of an inn cannot be recovered under a policy insuring an interest in the physical buildings.[4]

The same type of situation arose a few years later in Scotland, in the case of *Menzies v. North British Insurance Company*.[5] Menzies owned certain buildings in which he operated a mill for grinding corn, a storage warehouse and a bath house with hot and cold baths. He took out fire insurance on his interest in the property. The property was partially destroyed by fire. In addition to his property loss, the Insured sought to recover for what would be the rental value of the property (had he rented it to another) during the period of shut down, the profits he would have made during the period if operations had not been interrupted, and the wages he had to continue paying to his employees even though there was no building in which they could work.

In its decision, the court described the Insured's claim as being based "on a want of occupancy." This, the court concluded, was not covered under his Fire Insurance policy.

The Wright case thus held that a tenant could not collect for rent he had to pay when the premises were not usable and the Menzies case held that the owner-occupant could not collect the value of the rent of the premises he himself occupied. In the Leonarda case,[6] brought in Louisiana in 1842, the court held that a landlord who held property for rent to others could not collect (under a Fire Insurance policy covering on certain stores and buildings) for the loss of rents suffered while the property was being repaired by the Insurer under its option in the policy.

C. Insurance on Freight, Rent and Profits

A strong reason for the decisions that were reached in these cases is the fact that it was possible to obtain an insurance policy specifically insuring income and profits.[7] As early as 1781, the decision in the case of *Grant v. Parkinson*[8] decided in England, assumed that writing insurance on profits was a current practice.

Some years later, a learned English judge, delving into the writings of foreign authors in various European countries, demonstrated that the insuring of the profits of a maritime venture was well established, although in some countries it was specifically forbidden by law.[9] The impact of economic statesmanship, as exhibited in a desire to foster English trade, can be seen in the judge's opinion (p.547): "It is surely not an improper encouragement of trade to provide that merchants, in case of adverse fortune, should not only not lose the principal adventure, but that that principal should not, in consequence of such bad fortune, be totally unproductive; and that men of small fortunes should be encouraged to engage in commerce. . . ." He cites an English case, decided in 1776, where the insurance was on "imaginary profit" on a shipment of indigo.

In *Wright v. Pole* (p.623), Lord Denham, C.J., made the statement that "the interest in question (on profits) might have been the subject of insurance."

In the course of the *Leonarda* decision, there appears the following verbiage: "In the absence of an express stipulation, *such as appears to exist in the policies of several Insurance Companies of this city*, [italics added] that during the rebuilding or repairing of a house, rent shall be paid as part of the indemnity due to the Insured. . . ." From this phrase, it would appear that Rent Insurance was available in New Orleans as early as 1842.[10] While there is no specific reference to the fact that such insurance on profits involved the element of time, it is obvious that this element was recognized, of necessity, in the establishment of any loss.[11]

The concept of providing insurance against the loss of profits from the use of ships and real estate gradually carried over to a new type of property coming into existence about the middle of the 18th century. This was the development of manufacturing establishments.[12]

Chapter 1 Notes

1. Becker v. Merchants Mut. Ins. Co.

2. Tonge v. Watts (1746).
    For definition of "freight" see: Flint v. Fleming (1830).
    Early American cases include Abbott v. Sebor (1802)—Profits Insurance—and Stevens v. The Columbian Ins. Co. (1805).

3. In a letter from C.M. Kahler of the Wharton School to E.P. Hardy of the Insurance Library of New York, the former wrote, "The first case I have been able to find in which it was definitely held that profits were not covered in the fire policy was decided in 1781. It was Grant v. Parkinson, 16 East 218." [Such a named case, found also in 3 Douglas 16, deals with the issue of profits of a voyage.]

4. Wright v. Pole. In this case the dispute was sent to an arbitrator. The court limited the right of the arbitrator to interpreting the meaning of the policy term "interest."

5. Menzies v. North British Ins. Co. The Insured's attorney relied on a statement made by Professor Bell (1 Bell, Comm. 627). But the court followed the decision in Wright v. Pole and limited the meaning of the term "interest." The court pointed out that the option of the Insurer to repair the damage mitigated against any claim that more than physical damage was intended to be covered. (It should be noted that that option has existed for many years in Fire Insurance policies, to which Business Interruption Insurance policy forms are attached). Counsel for the Insurer based his defense on the argument that the claimed loss was consequential and not included in coverage on buildings and machinery.

6. Michaela Leonarda, Baroness of Pontalba v. The Phoenix Assurance Co. of London (1842).

7. The issue of the *Policy Holder*, published in England on August 10, 1949, at page 713, quotes a letter from the Secretary of the Phoenix Assurance Company to its agent, W. Carlisle, in Hull, under date of December 3, 1849, which reads as follows:
    "In re Loss of Income by Fire 3 Dec. 1849
    Dear Sir:
    The Peculiar Insurance proposed by Mr. Wood on the future earnings of his oil mill has again had the consideration of the Committee.
    We have already had a somewhat similar application from Scotland. This in a much less definite, and uncertain form . . . and this we have declined. In fact, it would

not be safe, as a general practice, to extend the operation of our Insurance beyond its legitimate object, the reinstatement of the Property destroyed.

Mr. Wood's proposition is, however, I think sufficiently definite to be admitted, and we will, therefore, consent to issue a Policy to him in the words he has used, at the same rate as the Mill itself 10s. percent.

In doing this, however, you will be so good to understand that it is not to be construed as a precedent . . . but rather as an evidence of our desire to give what facility we can to the extension of your Agency. The policy shall follow.

I remain, Dr. Sr
Yours faithfully
TR

8. Grant v. Parkinson (1781) and cases cited. At the trial in the lower court it was found that it was common practice to insure profits.

9. Judge Lawrence in Barclay v. Cousins, (1802).

10. The court stated: "These are consequential losses for which the Insured cannot be indemnified, especially when such losses fall on things susceptible of being insured separately." (p. 132) A later American case is Farmers Mutual Ins. Co. v. New Holland Turnpike Co. (1888).

    The first known instance of consequential loss coverage in the colonies is found on p. 56 of James Logan's *Pennsylvania Journal* (1701-1710) in the files of the Historical Society of Pennsylvania in Philadelphia where there is a notation reading, *"May 6, 1703. To John Budd, for insuring the 3 tun to keep good—L 1.00";* attached to an invoice for shipping 3 tuns of beer from Philadelphia to London. Reported in *Weekly Underwriter*, Sept. 4, 1934. For a case suggesting that Profits Insurance was available at an early date see: Niblo v. North American F. Ins. Co. (1848).

11. A policy of freight insurance frequently covered a particular voyage and a loss to be recoverable had to occur during the time frame of that voyage. But the realization that such an invisible item as time could have value and that the value of time was something to be protected by insurance techniques was not achieved until a later date.

12. A number of cases already cited deal with the question of whether there is a parallel between insurance on freight and insurance on rents derived from land. See: Becker v. Merchants Mutual; Leonarda v. Phoenix Assurance Co.

2

The Value of Property

Two sources of value—static and dynamic. Income from use and sale of a punch press. The Earnings Stream: the offspring of property and time. Availability for use is necessary. Time is money when associated with use. Use must fill an economic need.

A. Two Sources of Value

It is the fact that Property *exists* which is one source of its value. Property also has a second source of value. This is its *use-value*: the fact that it can function in a particular fashion.

Use-value has two different aspects. The first is related to its existence as a physical object. Physical property has quality—depending on the materials of which it is composed, the skill with which it is designed and the workmanship with which it is constructed. In combination with its existence, this quality determines the use to which it can be put. This aspect of use-value can be termed a static aspect—it affects the value for Property Insurance purposes.

The second aspect of use-value stems from its use potential—the potential of the property being used as a tool in the production of an Earnings Stream. Through its use over the course of time, earnings can be derived. This is the dynamic aspect of use-value.[1] (A piece of property need not operate as an economic tool for the production of earnings. Property which is used or kept by the owner solely for the gratification of personal needs—such as a coat, a private dwelling or a coin collection—does not have dynamic use-value, though it does have static use-value.)

Consider a typewriter, for example. It is composed of materials wrought into a special form and designed and created for a particular purpose. It has static use-value depending on its adaptability for that purpose. But it also has dynamic use-value for an author who uses it to write a book and earn royalties.

This concept of dynamic use-value is applicable to all kinds of physical, tangible property. An apartment house designed and dedicated to the production of rents, a ship designed and dedicated to carrying goods, a clothing store's stock dedicated for sale to customers and designed for that use, a barber shop designed and dedicated to the improvement of its customers' appearances, are all examples of property which is dedicated to the production of earnings through its dynamic use-value.

Both of these aspects of an item of property are taken into consideration in our economic system in determining the market value of the property—its physical existence and condition and the use to which it can be put.[2]

B. Income from Use of a Press

Despite a widely held belief to the contrary, the way in which Business Interruption Insurance relates to use-value is not difficult to grasp. To do this, one must have a general understanding of how a business firm operates as it earns an income; but this is quite simple.

Take, for example, a small metal fabricating shop which contains a motor-driven press. This is a large piece of machinery that has a hammer-like arm which slams down intermittently with great force onto a shaped anvil or die, so that the piece of metal which has been inserted between the hammer and the anvil is formed into the desired shape. The owner of the shop has paid many thousands of dollars to buy the press, to have it installed and to have the necessary die made. He plans to use the press for eight hours a day during a five-day work week.

The press has been set up to punch out pill boxes. At each stroke of the press, the body of a box is formed. With another die, the top of a box is formed. In the course of an eight hour day, the press will stamp out tops and bodies for 3600 boxes. When completed, each box is sold for a price that is 20 cents above the cost of the materials and labor that went into its production.

Should the press stop working for a day, the stoppage would deprive its owner of 20 cents for every box it failed to produce. In a full day that would amount to $720 (3600 × $.20). A week's shutdown would produce a loss of $3600 (5 × $720).

The owner has been depending on that weekly flow of $3600 of gross profit to pay his rent, his telephone bill, his own salary, plus other expenses and still have some net profit left over. To ensure that this income flow will not cease, he purchases a Business Interruption Insurance policy which will pay him 20 cents for each box which does not get produced because an insured event shuts down production.

Whether it be a tiny shop with but one press or a huge General Motors automobile assembly plant, the same principle applies and is equally simple. Of course, the larger the operation, the more complicated the financial calculations become. What are proper costs and what is the margin of profit; which expenses can be stopped during the shut down; can the lost production be made up by working overtime—these and similar questions arise. By keeping the image of the punch press in mind, one can understand the basic theory underlying Business Interruption Insurance, no matter how complex the business operation may be.

Consider another punch press. This one is located in a job shop; one which does odd jobs for occasional customers, rather than working steadily on a product such as the pill box. The owner of the job shop earns income by the use of the press on job opportunities that present themselves. When there is no work for the press, it stands idle; when it is working, the owner charges $100 an hour for its use plus a minimum charge of $100 to cover set-up time. The customer also pays for or provides the materials used.

There is no method by which one can determine as to which hours during any day or which days during any week the press will be working. The production records for the past full year, however, demonstrate that the use of the punch press brought its owner a total income of $64,000 during the past year. He assumes it will produce the same income during the coming year. This assumption or estimate is subject to change upwards or downwards if there are reasons, internal or extraneous, to believe that the use during the next year will be more or less than it was last year.

Suppose that, because of fire damage, the press will be out of use for a full month. The amount of income lost during the month the press cannot operate would, other things being equal, on the average and based upon past history, be $1/12$ of $64,000 or $5,333. His policy is basically intended to replace the $5,333 he has lost because the press was not able to be used. If the month during which the shut-down occurred was normally an above-average month for operating hours, his estimated loss would be greater. Similarly, the loss would be a lesser amount if the shutdown occurred during what was normally a slower than average month.

Again, it makes no difference how big or how small, how complex or how simple the business operation might be; it can be thought of as consisting of one press, insofar as basic principles are concerned.

Consider another type of situation. This time the press is standing on the floor of a retailer of metal-working machinery and it constitutes his entire stock in trade. Past experience shows that the retailer sells twelve presses a year from his floor, earning $1,000 apiece, or $12,000 a year, as gross income over the cost of the presses to him from the manufacturer. On January 1, a fire damages his store and also renders the press in stock unsalable. It will take six months to repair the building. The business operation therein will be interrupted for six months. During that time, he would normally have sold six presses and earned

$6,000 of income. There is no doubt that, based solely on his normal operations, this amount will be lost if he is out of business for six months.

Fortunately, he is able to rent a vacant store across the street on a temporary basis. He moves his operation over to the other location and orders a new press, which is delivered in a month's time.

Customers for his punch presses have no difficulty in finding him at his new location across the street. They come and order presses just as they did in his prior location. During the six months before he is able to move back to his former location, there is no diminution in his sales or his flow of income. He has not suffered any financial detriment from loss of sales during the six months of dispossession and interruption that resulted from the fire damage.

The retailer did not get off scot-free, however. To set up across the street, to advertise his new location, to move a press back to his old store when it was ready, plus the extra rent he had to pay to gain occupancy of the other store, were extra expenses that he would not have incurred had there been no fire.

This extra expense was far less than the financial loss the retailer would have suffered had he remained shut down and out of business for the six month period. A retailer would normally have many more items of equipment than one press in stock. But no matter how many items he has, again each individual item can be treated the same as one press as to the basic principles involved. The typical policy pays for the out-of-pocket expenses the move required, provided they reduced the loss.

The entire theory underlying Business Interruption Insurance is as simple as one press.

C. The Earnings Stream

Approaching the subject on a different level, it can be said that Business Interruption Insurance stems from the wedding of two elements in the economic sphere—Property and Time. Both have economic value.

The offspring of such a marriage in a business venture is an Earnings Stream on which the business usually depends for the funds to cover its ongoing expenses. Without it, the health and even the viability of the business enterprise would be threatened. It is also to the Earnings Stream that the investor of capital in the business venture looks for a reward for his risk taking, in the form of profits.

It is the responsibility of the owner of a business enterprise to develop and foster the growth of an Earnings Stream and assure its continuance. It is the function of Business Interruption Insurance to serve as a replacement for the Earnings Stream should the property which produces it suffer impairment of function. The portion of the Earnings Stream that is replaced depends on the provision of the particular Business Interruption Insurance policy purchased.

D. Availability for Use

It does not necessarily follow that because an item of property possesses inherent use-potential, that this capability can be exploited uninterruptedly. Physical damage to the property could temporarily inhibit it from being used. Thus, were the point of a pencil to break off, though its inherent use-potential would continue, the pencil would not be available for use until it was repointed. Physical damage to the property is not the only reason which might defeat its availability for use. The same result would follow if the property were stolen.

Availability for use must accompany use-potential if the property is to be exploited effectively in the production of an Earnings Stream. This condition of availability for use is, by its very nature, future oriented; it considers use within a time frame that extends into the future.

E. "Time is Money"

Within his physical world, Man has created a time oriented economic system. The first step in placing a value on time was taken when Man developed tools to increase the productivity of his hours of labor. As these tools proliferated into more and more intricate machinery, Man enclosed space within structures to house his machines, further enhancing his ability to produce in the course of a working day. Thus, as more funds were invested in physical property, each unit of productive time became more valuable—the amount of product that could be produced each day vastly increased. Time took on ever increasing economic value.

Time has monetary value when associated with property that is productive. It is not the mere existence of machines in time that creates value. It is their use as tools of production within a time frame that is the source of value creation. If a machine cannot be used within a particular unit of time, the economic value of the machine for that time-unit is erased.

F. Filling an Economic Need

In the economic world, still one more factor must exist before this potential for producing an Earnings Stream can be realized. There must be a need for the goods or services produced by utilization of the property, such as orders in hand or sales in expectation. This can be described as a business need. When such a business need co-exists with use-potential and availability for use, then earnings can be anticipated from the use of the property.

G. Conclusion

Whether we are considering a large manufacturing plant operated by professional managers, a department store operation carried on by a family partnership or a shoe repair shop run by a sole proprieter, the funds generated by means of use of the property must continue to flow on through time if the enterprise is to continue to survive. This flow of future income is the Earnings Stream to which reference has been made earlier.

Should the Earnings Stream cease, whether by the absence of property capable of producing earnings or because the property is not available for use at the appropriate time due to damage or other reasons, or because there is no business need to keep the property activated, the business enterprise will ultimately fail. Management must operate, in effect, as a trustee for all of the interested parties, to see to it that the Earnings Stream is not interrupted in its flow through future time because of physical damage to the property by a peril against which insurance can be purchased. This, as has been suggested, can be accomplished in most circumstances through the device of Business Interruption Insurance.[3]

Chapter 2 Notes

1. Other theories describing the aspects of property have been proposed. One suggests three aspects:
    a. *In the physical sphere*—i.e., substance; appearance; function or purpose.
    b. *In the emotional sphere*—i.e., sentimental attachment; desirability.
    c. *In the economic sphere*—i.e., (a) worth or value in the market place; (b) usability; (c) earnings potential.

    In 1889, J. Griswold defined "value" as being of two kinds, *value in use* or the utility of an object for use; and *value in exchange* or the worth of an object in purchasing other goods. He stated further that present value may not be cost, but is the basis for payment. Insurance companies are cash customers and are entitled to the best values the market affords. *The Fire Underwriters Textbook*, J. Griswold, 2nd Ed. (1889), p. 627 [s] 1693 and [s] 1694.

2. Depreciation and obsolescence affect use-value negatively. In the case of depreciation, the usable life of the property has been shortened. In the case of obsolescence, the benefit to be derived from its usability has become lessened as it becomes uneconomical to use it.

3. In the English (Canada) case of The King v. B.C. Fir & Cedar Lumber Co. (1932), the court described the purpose of Use and Occupancy Insurance as follows:

    "In the conduct of their business they [the Insured] were exposed to the grave risk of fire, and the insurance of their premises and plant was an insurance against a possible capital loss dictated by every consideration of prudence. If the risk were not so guarded against, then by a fire sufficiently disastrous the whole operations of the respondents might definitely be brought to a close and acquisition of gain for them definitely ended. But such a fire, even if so far insured against, might still prove a hindrance more or less prolonged to the unbroken acquisition of gain from their business by reason of the fact that its continuance might not be possible during the period of reinstatement.

    "This insurance receipt therefore was the product of a revenue payment prudently made by the respondents to secure that the gains which might have been expected to accrue to them had there been no fire should not be lost, but should be replaced by a sum equivalent to their estimated amount . . ." Lord Blanesburgh.

3

Early Stages of
Business Interruption Coverage

*The Industrial Revolution and its impact. Early beginnings in
England. Chomage in France. Development of Profits
Insurance in England. The beginnings of modern
Business Interruption Insurance in the United
States. Dalton's Newton Mills policy
of 1877. The 1880 policies.*

A. Impact of the Industrial Revolution

Prior to the beginning of the Industrial Revolution, which can be set at about 1760, much of what today is called manufactured goods was the product of individual craft workers. Many of these were found among the families of farmers or villagers who, in their homes, created items which were purchased by traders for resale. Others were skilled craftsmen who, alone, or with the help of apprentices, produced items which they themselves sold to the public. This type of production required little more than hand tools or, at the most, a hand-operated piece of equipment, such as a loom for weaving. The ancient guilds were the trade associations organized by these craftsmen for their common welfare.[1]

The monetary value of the equipment used by any one family, although of importance to its owners and though the family might suffer financial hardship with its loss, was too small, in absolute terms, to be of economic significance. The guild, the extended family, or friends would raise the funds to replace tools which were destroyed or, in the most desperate cases of resultant poverty, the church would come to the support of the stricken family.[2]

With the advent of the Industrial Revolution and the development of substantial installations of machinery and of the buildings to house them and of a labor force composed of persons who had left their farms to gain a livelihood as factory workers, the situation changed. Substantial sums of money had to be invested in the business enterprise—invested by the operator and by people who became associated with him in the enterprise. Ultimately, the growth in value of the tools of production and of the inventories necessary to keep them operating required the borrowing of funds from the lenders of capital. A return on such investment was expected on the part of the lenders in the form of interest on their loans and on the part of the entrepreneurs as a profit from their venture.

The transition from craftsmen, who worked with their personal tools, to unskilled labor trained to operate machinery belonging to others created a new social phenomenon. Cut off from the land, which had formerly provided basic sustenance, the worker became increasingly dependent on a regular paycheck from his employer to buy the necessities of life.[3]

As workmen became more skilled in the use of machinery, their ability became an economic resource—measured to some extent by the value of time, effort and expense which went into their training. In the event of an interruption of operations, it was to the interest of the factory owner to retain his affiliation with the employee until operations were resumed.

At the same time, larger enterprises undertook committments of all kinds which required a steady inflow of income to meet them. As business enterprises grew in size and scope, the need to protect this flow of income became increasingly important.

B. Beginnings of Profits Insurance

The process of insuring the investment in real property against loss by fire had already been organized in England as early as 1666.[4] Extending the coverage of the Fire Insurance policy beyond the cost of repair or replacement of the damaged property was applied first to the potential loss of profits that would be suffered if goods already produced were destroyed before they were sold. (The usual Fire Insurance policy available to an Insured would not pay for these potential profits; it would only pay him for the cost of the goods to him.) So the manufacturer could insure the potential profits separately; i.e., the profits he would earn from his past endeavors.

To insure such potential profits may have been the basis for an announcement made in 1797, by Minerva Universal that "it was prepared to undertake fire interruption insurance to supplement ordinary fire cover."[5] No details of this coverage are available. It was twenty-five years later, in 1821, that the Beacon Fire Insurance Company of England offered "the insurance of a weekly allowance to Tradesmen and others during the period they are deprived by fire of the means of pursuing their usual vocations."[6] The progress of this particular offering is not known. (History records that the Beacon Fire Insurance Company failed in 1827.)

Following the practice established in the maritime trade, the British underwriters directed their attention to the profits to be made by the business venture. Another quarter-century elapsed before we find a reference to what might have been a type of Business Interruption Insurance. This was offered in a prospectus put out by the General Indemnity Insurance Company in 1853, which read "the fire department includes a new feature of considerable importance namely, insurance against loss of business profits in consequence of fire."[7]

C. "Chomage"

The first actual policy of Business Interruption Insurance of which we have knowledge was issued not in England nor in the United States, but in France. The story has often been told of the desire of an Alsatian businessman to protect his employees from loss of their income during a period when his plant might be shut down due to damage by fire. The French name given to this coverage was "chomage" which translates into English as "idleness" or "enforced idleness."[8] The amount of recovery was keyed into the amount collected under the insurance on the physical property.

The principle of basing the loss of potential earnings on the severity of the physical property damage was carried across the channel to England where, for a time, it was adapted to the concept of insurance of profits. The insurance was called Excess Fire Policy Insurance. Recovery was fixed at that percentage of the sum insured which the amount of the fire loss bore to the amount insured under the Fire Insurance policy.[9]

This was obviously an arbitrary way in which to determine the amount of profits lost, but it did serve as a specific method of establishing the insured loss. Not a very good way, however, because there were many situations where the degree of fire damage did not truly reflect the length of time during which the business operation would be suspended.

D. Development of Profits Insurance in England

In England, correction of the inadequacies of the method of chomage in determining the amount of loss was achieved through improvements in the provisions of the Profits Insurance policies that were offered. Loss of income was no longer based on property damage. Time suspension became the criterion.

In 1871, the Trade Profit Insurance Company was formed. Then, in 1875, the Crown Fire Office offered to insure "actual realized profit lost through fire."[10] There is no knowledge of what happened to these ventures; but they apparently were related to that concept of insurance on profits which exists today in the United States on merchandise produced but not yet sold.[11] Such insurance did not meet the needs of businessmen who required a source of profits from future endeavors; to replace those they would lose during the time they were out of operation.

It was not until 1899 that one Ludovici MacLillan Mann devised a scheme to measure the loss of future profits caused by interruption of business activity.[12] A new company was formed in 1900 called the Profits Income Insurance Company to write coverage on trading profits.[13] At first, most underwriters refused to write such insurance, and the new company had a virtual monopoly until 1908.[14]

The slow development of Profits Insurance in its early stages is very largely explained by the disinclination of English insurers to foster business where so much depended on moral hazard. In those days, knowledge of bookkeeping and accounting methods was not part of every man's elementary business training. It is doubtful whether the books of many firms were kept at all. If they were, they were often in unsatisfactory form. It was the growing importance of Accountancy as a profession, about the beginning of the twentieth century, with the resulting precision and standardization of accounts of commercial concerns, that helped provide Profits Insurance with a satisfactory scientific basis.

The fears of moral hazard being proved groundless, the regulars gradually joined in.[15] By 1939, a standard form of policy was adopted in England called the Standard Consequential Loss Policy.[16] This form of policy was exported to other countries that formed part of the British Empire and was adopted in Canada, Ireland and New Zealand among others.[17]

E. Early Developments in the United States

The Industrial Revolution had, meanwhile, arrived in the United States. Textile mills, operated largely by water power, developed in New England. Manufacturing and mercantile business of all kinds grew in size. Inevitably, this created the same need for ensuring a flow of income during a period of business interruption as had developed in England. It is reported that, at a meeting held in a Providence counting house in 1835, a Rhode Island mill owner said to a group of fellow mill owners: "Insurance is not the answer to our problems even when we can get it. Small comfort it is to us to be paid for a fire if the resulting shutdown costs us our customers and puts us out of business."[18]

The developments in France and England did not go unnoticed in the United States, where textile mill owners were becoming increasingly aware of their need for income protection and of what was being done elsewhere. There is a report that about 1860, Henry R. Dalton, an insurance agent in Boston, whose clientele included such mills, began agitating for this type of coverage.[19]

F. Dalton's Newton Mills Policy

Tentative steps in this direction were apparently achieved by him in 1877, when he procured a policy on the buildings and machinery of the Newton Mills, a corporation owning and operating a textile mill in Newton, Massachusetts.[20] There is a policy form appearing in the 1879 edition of C.C. Hines Book of Forms which apparently was the one used in this early policy. It covered the productive capacity of the mill and its equipment. (It was the practice of insurance agents at this time to draft their own forms of policy. This situation continued, as far as Use and Occupancy forms were concerned, until at least as late as 1916.)

The Insured was protected against the loss he might suffer if he could not deliver goods contracted for because the mill building or its machinery was damaged by fire. The amount of the policy was for $36,000, and the amount recoverable was reduced by $400 each day until the 90 day period necessary to complete the contract ran out.[21]

From the wording of the policy one would gather that the 1877 contract made no attempt to attach a label to the property right insured. Apparently, it was drawn to cover an order for seasonal goods which the insured mill would have to deliver by a certain date to be of value to the buyer. The latter had the right to refuse delivery of any part of the order which was not delivered on schedule.

From the form of the contract of insurance, it is possible to deduce that any day that production was interrupted would prevent delivery of that day's expected product. The policy that Dalton prepared provided that any diminution of a day's earnings as a result of a fire would be paid to the Insured. The measure of damages was fixed at the difference between $400 per day and the price the Insured could get for the goods ultimately produced when he was able to get back into operation and make up each lost day's production. Thus, while the maximum daily amount of loss was fixed, the loss would be limited to the actual loss sustained.

In certain respects, this 1877 policy followed the pattern for the settlement of losses that had developed under both marine and rent coverages. In case of a total loss, the valued approach was deemed desirable. In case of a loss of part of the profit—either a valued or an open approach could be applied.[22]

In the insurance magazines of that era, one finds a record of the fire losses in mills. Many were relatively minor, thanks to apparatus available at the time and the inspection procedures introduced by the Factory Mutual Insurance Companies.[23] The 1877 policy, was apparently prepared with such temporary delays in mind rather than with a fire which would destroy the mill. In that latter event, it may be assumed that the policy would be treated as a valued policy, with the daily value set at $400.

It is generally agreed that the first form of contract which falls within the mainstream of our present Business Interruption Insurance contract was also written by Henry R. Dalton. These were policies issued on March 3, 1880, to four Massachusetts mills operated by the office of B. Rodman Weld, including the Newton Mills which had been insured in the 1877 policy.

Credit for initially conceiving of such a contract is generally given to Edward Atkinson, President of the Manufacturers Mutual Fire Insurance Company.[24]

It was drawn to cover a period of one year—300 days of operation. For each day during which the mill was prevented from operating by reason of fire damage, the Insurer would pay 1/300th of the face amount of the policy until the property was rebuilt, repaired or replaced. If only part of the operation was suspended, the Insurer's liability was "for that proportion of the per diem sum which the product thereby prevented from being made bears to the average daily yield previous to the fire."[25]

It is not clear whether this particular form of wording was the only one written by Mr. Dalton in the early days. Reports at the time indicate that some variations crept in at an early date.[26]

G. The 1880 Policies

Dalton's 1880 policy on the Newton Mills represents a distinct step forward in the evolution of the Business Interruption Insurance policy of today. Two problems had faced the insurance industry from the beginning as it sought to meet the needs of the business community for a source of continuing income when the physical property which had been producing that income was damaged. The first was to decide just what income was to be continued. The second was how to measure the amount of income that had been discontinued by the damage.

Dalton related income to the amount of goods produced; in effect placing a predetermined amount of value on each unit of production. A preliminary survey of past experience would develop these figures. No change was contemplated during the policy terms. In this way, the first problem was met.

Difference in number of units of production was adopted as the way of measuring loss. It was assumed that, for each unit of production lost, the loss in income would be the same. This met the second problem.

Chapter 3 Notes

1. In Vol. III, p. 438, of his *Insurance Encyclopedia* under the heading "Chronological History of Fire Insurance in England from the Earliest Period to the Present Times," Cornelius Walford wrote:

    "The first glimmer of the principle of mutual insurance arises in connection with the ancient Anglo-Saxon guilds where the members made fixed periodical payment toward a common fund whereby they insured each other against the loss from fire, robbery or other calamity."

    See: "Use and Occupancy Insurance"–address by Frank L. Erion, Michigan Association of Ohio Farmers Insurance Co. Agents, April 9, 1924.

    For a study of the early history of insurance (prior to 1560), see reprint of article by Professor Irving Pfeffer, in *Modern Insurance Theory and Education*, Vol. I, edited by Kailin Tuan, (1972), p. 3.

2. In Volume III of Walford's *Encyclopedia*, under the heading "Fire Briefs," appears a statement about the appeals made in churches to raise money for those suffering loss. In early times, before the origin of Fire Insurance, on the occurrence of a great fire (or, indeed, any other serious calamity) in any particular locality, it was the custom to intake the aid of charitably disposed people by issue of Briefs, Kings Briefs, Letters Patent, Fire Briefs or King's Letters, as they were variously called, and which set out in more or less detail the circumstances attending the calamity, and were ordered to be read in churches and otherwise.

3. See: "Use & Occupancy Ins., Its Relation to the Accounting Profession," Lee J. Wolfe, *Journal of Accounting* (April, 1925).

4. A report on earlier attempts in England is to be found in Volume III of Walford's *Encyclopedia*. It states:

    "Beckman, in his history of inventions, mentions that in 1609 a proposal was made to Count Von Oldenburg for an insurance against fire, but he turned it down on the basis that he was under the protection of Providence.

    "In 1638 Edward Mabb, Gent. proposed a scheme of fire insurance to King Charles I. He, in turn, turned it over to his Attorney General, who reported on it favorably. The grant of a patent was ordered to be prepared. What developed is not known. Charles I was beheaded in 1649 and the plan was apparently dropped.

    "After the Restoration and the ascension of Charles II to the Throne in 1660, a scheme of fire insurance was set on foot by 'several persons of quality and eminent citizens of London.'

    "In 1667 an insurance office was set up by Dr. Barbon, who was one of the leading builders engaged in restoring the City of London after the Great Fire of 1666."

5. *Insurance on Profits.* A.G. Macken & G.J.R. Hickmott, 6th Ed. (London, 1963).

6. *Insurance on Profits.* A.G. Macken & G.J.R. Hickmott. This appears to be an early form of Unemployment Insurance. Absent any information that the amount recovered was related to the amount earned, it would fall short of being true Business Interruption Insurance.

7. *Insurance on Profits.* A.G. Macken and G.J.R. Hickmott.

8. In *The Chronicle*, Vol. XXV (1880), p. 307, the Liverpool letter describes chomage insurance being written in France as of that date. See also: *Insurance Times*, Vol. XIII (1880), p. 232.

    In the *Fire Underwriters Textbook* by J. Griswald, 2nd Ed., (1889), at page 9, [s]10, appears a statement about chomage. Originally issued to insure workmen's wages, *"it was extended in 1876 to merchants, manufacturers and others to cover consequential damage resulting from the occurrence of fire not covered by ordinary insurance, such as loss of revenue from capital, plant or machinery, etc. caused by the destruction of the property of the insured, who may hold thus a regular fire policy upon buildings, stock or machinery and another, entirely distinct, upon the same property, but based upon the productive value of such property and the average yearly income derived therefrom, upon which interest at a certain rate per cent (usually 6 to 10) is guaranteed by the policy from and after the fire, during such time, as from the circumstances attending the loss, the capital invested may remain totally or partially, yet compulsorily, unavailable to the Insured, as in rent or lease policies, which represent the principle exactly. There can be no chomage insurance without a corresponding fire insurance upon the property. The amount of chomage insurance is always limited to the existing amount of fire insurance.*

    "The principle is the foundation of mortgagee insurance, rent and lease policies, policies on profits, income, or commissions unearned, and insurance of production at mills under contract against failure to fill such contracts, when such failure was caused by fire."

    See: George Harrington, Lecturer, Insurance Society of New York, Inc., Insurance Education Courses, Fire-Part III, #15 (1934-1935). The statement is made that this type of coverage continues to be written as of the 1930's in France and in some Scandinavian countries. See: Klein, *Business Interruption Insurance*, 4th Ed. (July, 1960), p. 9. Also: *Insurance on Profits*, Macken and Hickmott.

9. According to Albert Ellis in an address to the Hull Institute, "The Origin and Development of the Modern Loss of Profits Policy", given on January 14, 1935, in England, an intermediate step in the development of policy forms in Great Britain was the adoption of the Time Loss Policy, described as "an extension of the principle embodied in the Rent Clause of a Fire Policy." The amount of insurance equalled the amount of annual profits divided by the number of working days. This form disappeared in England about 1899.

    See: Thesis by George Harrington in New York Insurance Library (1931)–filed under Business Interruption Insurance. It was also called "percentage of fire loss insurance." See: *Insurance on Profits*, Macken & Hickmott.

10. *Insurance on Profits*, Macken & Hickmott.

11. *Insurance on Profits*, O.R. Bendall, 2nd Ed (London, 1939).

12. *Loss of Profits Insurance*, Study Course–1(c)-25(d), (London, 1962). The Chartered Insurance Institute–Tuition Service.

13. A policy was issued by this company through its Glasgow office in May 1902. (See: Wylie Hill & Co. Ltd. v. Profits and Income Ins. Co.) The amount of recovery was set at 325% of the amount paid under the fire insurance contract during any interruption or interference with the business in consequence of a fire.

    In his thesis (supra), Harrington states that about 1,900 underwriters in England produced a policy to protect profits on a basis of output. Later changed from output, which is a quantitive measure of material, to turnover–its monetary equivalent–because it is easier to work in terms of value. From 1912 on, this was called Profits Insurance.

    Mr. Ellis, in his talk, quotes from a letter from a Mr. Ludovici MacLillian Mann to the editor of the *Post* magazine in 1911, which read in part as follows: *"It is true that Consequential Fire or Profits Insurance was carried on both in Europe and America for many decades prior to 1900... In 1899, the idea occurred to me that a scientifically accurate assessment could be worked out comparing (through some fixed unit or standard) the degree of activity of the business before the fire with the degree of activity after the fire... At that time Acme Insurance Company [established 1896] adopted the idea. Around 1901, Acme merged with the Profits Income Insurance, which later sold its portfolio of Profits Insurance to The Legal Insurance Company... The concept was adopted generally by 1908."*

    Address by Albert Ellis to Hull Institute, (supra).

14. See: "The Underwriting of Prospective Earnings Insurance"–address by Frank L. Erion, before the Federation of Mutual Fire Ins. Companies, Chicago, August 13, 1935.

15. In a letter dated March 27, 1928, C.M. Kahler, then of the Wharton School, wrote to E.R. Handy at the New York Insurance Library, "I have found no cases on the present form of Profits Insurance in England."

    A case on percentage of fire loss (chomage) occurred in 1904. Wylie Hill Co., Ltd. v. Profits and Income Ins. Co.

16. *Principles and Practices of Profits Insurance*, E.L. Butler, FCII (London, 1940). (See appendix in his book for earlier forms.) See: *Consequential Loss Insurance and Claims*, Dennis Riley, 3rd Ed (London, 1967). See: City Tailors, Ltd. v. Evans.

17.   For Canada and New Zealand see: *Principles and Practices*, E.L. Butler. For Ireland see: *Consequential Fire Loss in the U.K. and Eire*, Lyndesay M. Currie (London, 1952).
    Proximity to the United States has had an influence on Canadian insurance practices. Today, both Profit Insurance (English style) and Business Interruption Insurance (United States style) are written.
    Agent's Digest of Canadian Business Interruption Insurance, Alan Gregory (Toronto, 1961).

18.   American Mutual Alliance Study Course, Lesson 2D–Time Element Coverages (195-). Another source states that the idea was discussed in the United States in 1840. Insurance Society of New York, Inc., Insurance Education Course, *Fire*-Part III, #15 (1934-1935).

19.   Insurance Society of New York, Inc., Insurance Education Courses (supra). In an address entitled "Use and Occupancy Insurance," given by John H. Gray to the Insurance Society of Cincinnati on February 19, 1917, he stated that U&O Insurance was in general use in the eastern states as far back as 1860. The description that he gives of the nature and extent of the writings indicates that he has placed the date twenty years too early.

20.   See Registry of Deeds, Middlesex County, Massachusetts, Vol. 745, p. 484. This is a deed from William T. Pyle dated April 9, 1886, which indicates that the property in question was first acquired by Newton Mills in 1853. See also Vol. 633, p. 349, and other deeds referred to.

21.   *"$15,000—on all factory buildings known as Newton Mills in Newton, Mass. from damage or destruction of their buildings, or machinery, by fire, either or both, which damage or destruction may prevent the manufacture of goods. And the amount to be insured is to be $36,000 to be reduced $400 each day. This policy being reduced to its pro rata amount."*

22.   For a discussion of the difference between the approach of the English and the American courts in connection with Profits Insurance, see Canada Sugar Refining Co. v. Insurance Co. of North America at page 622 et seq.

23.   "Fire in Mills," *The Spectator*, Vol. XVI #3 (March, 1876), p. 136.
    "Insurance on Cotton Mills in America and England," *The Spectator*, Vol. XVII (Nov. 1876), p. 595. Also, *American Exchange and Review*, Vol. XXXIV (1888), p. 206. *The Index* (now the *Standard*), Vol. VII (1878), p. 374.
    Sprinklers were available as early as 1852 when a perforated type pipe was installed at the plant of the Proprietors of the Locks and Canals at Lowell, Massachusetts.
    Fire Behavior and Sprinklers, Norman J. Thompson, p. 73f.

24.   In the letter from Boston appearing in *The Chronicle*, Vol. XXV (March 25, 1880), p. 196, the correspondent states that the moving parties were "the Treasurer of the

( ) Manufacturing Company and a prominent lawyer," who worked out an arrangement with various underwriters.

In *The Insurance World*, Vol. VII (Pittsburgh, May 31, 1880), p. 59, under the heading "Profits Insurance" J. L. Bergstresser, appears an article reading: "The Boston correspondent of *The Spectator* says—the latest novelty in underwriting in Boston has been Profit Insurance. The originator of this idea was Edward Atkinson of the Manufacturer's Mutual Insurance Co...." (See also Comment #1, p. 295.)

25. See: *American Exchange and Review* Vol. XXXIV (Philadelphia: Review Publishing and Printing Co., June, 1880), p. 184. This article also contains interesting criticism of various aspects of the policy form. See also: *The Chronicle* Vol. XXV, No. 13 (March 28, 1880), p. 196.

26. In the *Insurance and Commercial Magazine* of May, 1917, there is an article by Mr. Damon, then the President of the Springfield F. & M. Ins. Co. In the 1870's he had been the Chief Clerk and in 1880 became Secretary of the Washington F. & M. Ins. Co. with offices at the corner of State and Exchange Streets in Boston. He tells of a letter he received from Henry R. Dalton, Jr. giving the history of The Newton Mills policy. In part it read as follows: "*The first U and O insurance taken out by your father was for the four mills of B. Rodman Weld's office—Webster Mfg. Co., China Mfg. Co., Pembroke Mills and Newton Mills. The rates were the same as paid annually to the manufacturing Mutuals (Boston, Arkwright) on the Plants' fire insurance ... 80[c] and 90[c] per annum. Have a strong impression that these four placings were dated March 3, 1880, but cannot verify this date. Our little office took in some premiums in the months we were placing this new kind of insurance. Mr. Dalton probably talked this form over before having any printed....*" It cannot be determined whether stock or mutual companies, I think stock. ... *From D.N. Handy, Insurance Library of Boston, I obtained copies of early U and O forms written by Mr. Dalton. They were like original forms except sprinkler clause was not in the original and the original instead of being based on average products for 30 days previous to the fire was on a "stated production of goods, say 200,000 yards."*

4

Insurance on Use and Occupation

Early Years. Analysis of Dalton's Policy. Courts define Use and Occupancy. Further Policy Developments. Adoption of Gross Earnings Form.

A. Early Years

The success which Dalton experienced in getting a stock company underwriter to insure the Earnings Stream which would result from the fulfillment by the Newton Mills of its order, if not interrupted by a fire, must be attributed to the strong desire on the part of the stock companies to recapture the mill business which was being taken over by the mutual companies.[1] It must have opened his eyes to the possibility of recapturing much of the mill insurance business if he could offer mill owners a type of protection they had long desired—protection against the loss of future earnings. However, several road blocks stood in the way of his making a frontal attack on the problem. The greatest one was the unanimous opposition expressed by the stock companies associated with the National Board of Fire Underwriters to writing Profits Insurance on mills.[2] This was interwoven with the growing antipathy toward valued policies which had been stimulated by the adoption of valued policy laws in a number of states.[3]

The adoption by Massachusetts of a Standard Fire Insurance policy in 1873 and the proposal to make it mandatory had stirred up a storm of controversy, particularly on the part of the National Board of Fire Underwriters, which sent a committee to the Insurance Commissioner of Massachusetts and to its Governor to protest.[4] Given the inflamed atmosphere, one can understand why Dalton would hesitate to propose an entirely new type of fire insurance policy. Atkinson would be similarly influenced. Instead, he drafted an endorsement to be attached to the newly enacted Standard Fire Insurance policy. It was an incongruous marriage.

An insurance policy deals only with the second stage of loss suffered by an Insured when his Property is damaged or destroyed, namely the stage which considers the monetary measure of the loss that an Insured has suffered as a result of his deprivation. Underlying it must be a first stage—a philosophical concept as to the nature of the deprivation that an Insured suffers when his Property is damaged or destroyed.

The concept underlying the Fire Insurance policy is well established. It is based on the materiality of the Property. The material which the Insured holds after the damage is not as good as it was before. The Insured has been deprived of that difference in "goodness." The monetary value of the deprivation is the difference in value of the material Property before and after the damage. (See Comment #6, p. 311.)

The problem facing Dalton was to find a concept that would describe the deprivation in use-potential and still would be acceptable under prevailing conditions. As stated earlier, he could not define it in terms of Profits and instead adopted the concept of Productivity. The damage deprived the Insured of the productive capacity of his Property. This capacity was actually specified in the early mill polices. It was conceptualized as the ability of the mill to turn out products. Each unit of production had a monetary value measured by the difference between the selling price of its products and the cost of their production. The monetary loss resulting from the damage suffered was the sum of the value of the profit on all lost units of production.

This approach tracked nicely with the underlying Fire Insurance policy. The deprivation of both kinds takes place when the damage occurs. However, in the case of the Fire Insurance policy the monetary loss can be measured immediately, while under Business Interruption Insurance the monetary loss is prospective—it is measured through future time. It starts with the time of damage and continues until the previous level of productivity is restored.

To combine a policy in which loss is to be measured at a specific point in time with an endorsement providing coverage for a loss which can be measured only over a spread of time created a large amount of inherent inconsistency. Was Dalton aware of the problems he would be creating? Looking back to conditions existing at the time, one can be sympathetic with the problem that Dalton faced in finding an Underwriter who would write this coverage.

Some format had to be found to write it without the Underwriter becoming an outcast in the industry; hence, the approach taken. In theory, this would not be an insurance of profits; it would be an insurance of productive capacity. The drop in productivity from normal standards due to fire damage would be the basis for measuring loss. The Insurer agreed to pay a fixed sum per day for the loss occasioned by the prevention of the entire production of goods on that day and such percentage of that sum as the product prevented from being made bore to the average per diem product yield previous to the fire. The loss would be measured from the moment of damage until productivity was restored to normal.

The matter of value could not be avoided. However, value was to be determined by what had been the past experience of the particular mill. But how was its dollar amount to be set? In most cases, this would have to be a matter of speculation. So the parties agreed in advance on a dollar amount for each period of suspension of operations. They included this projected figure in a valued policy. The experience of the Insured, past and prospective, would be taken into consideration in establishing this figure, so as to minimize the moral hazard.

It must be borne in mind that, at this time, the New England mills were the property of the leading citizens in their respective communities. Business was flourishing and profitability was great. Looking at just this single segment of industry, which is what Dalton was doing, much of the danger of moral hazard could be discounted.

Instead of announcing that the new contract would be a Profits or Chomage or Productions Insurance policy, Dalton treated it just as fire insurance. He based his insurance on the Use and Occupancy of the physical property. The words "Use and Occupancy" were not new. They were already a part of the Fire Insurance policy.[5] True, they had been inserted in that policy to control the hazard implicit in the way in which the property was being used, or the purpose for which it was occupied. So he stretched the meaning a little. After all, "use" came from the Latin word "usufruct" which meant "the fruits."[6] And the fruits of productivity were produced goods.

The shift in Dalton's contract was a subtle one. He used the same words. But now they referred to the *ability* of the Insured to manipulate the described property. That became the subject of the insurance. Inserted in a form attached to a fire policy, where similar words appeared, they were easily accepted. One can ask whether in the employment of such innocuous words, the real purpose of the contract was adequately described. Of what purpose to the mill-owner was the ability to use the property? It must have been to enable him to take advantage of a business opportunity which required the use of the property, and by the use of which an Earnings Stream could be established.

Despite Dalton's subterfuge, the insurance industry of the time regarded it as both a type of Chomage and as Profits Insurance.[7] It was so described in the insurance press. Writers and speakers dwelt on the moral hazard that its issuance would create.[8] Once the ice was broken, however, the benefit for all parties of this type of coverage must have been apparent to some Underwriters, as witness the statement that $100,000 of premium had been written in the month of April, 1880.[9]

The practice of writing Use and Occupancy Insurance in the valued form continued for many years. As its use grew, the care with which Underwriters had policed the Insured's estimate of the appropriate amount of coverage was gradually relaxed. By 1916, it appears that the Insured could write as large an amount of the Use and Occupancy Insurance as he desired on a valued basis without careful investigation by the Underwriter. Nor was there any standard form of Use and Occupancy policy.[10]

Numerous attempts have been made to attach an implicit meaning to the phrase "Use and Occupancy" in connection with time element insurance. They have no *implicit* meaning in that frame of reference.[11] A meaning would ultimately be bestowed upon them by the provisions of the contract and by the practices of the trade.[12]

B. Analysis of Dalton's Policy

In the 1877 Newton Mills policy, Dalton had established the passage of a day as the time unit to be employed in measuring a loss. Dalton apparently took a day as the smallest unit of time within which it was practicable to measure the amount of loss. To a large extent, that unit is used today in settling losses. Some industrial plants are of sufficient size and keep sufficient records, however, so that it is possible to break down productivity results into shifts, or even into hours of production time. (Query: what hours should be applied to a day of production when the Fire Insurance policy runs from noon to noon?)

Under the Per Diem form, as this type of policy gradually came to be known, the amount that the Insured could collect for any one day of interruption of operations came to be a fraction of the face amount of the policy. For a plant that operated seven days a week throughout the year, the fraction was 1/365th or 1/360th. When a five day week was later introduced into industry, the appropriate fraction per day would be 1/250th.

The concept of paying for a partial interruption of operations had long been established. As early as 1802, in *Barclay* v. *Cousins*, the court had stated "if there be only a partial loss, the assured (sic) will only be liable to pay for the expected profits on the goods lost."[13]

What was new in Dalton's approach to determining the amount of the loss due to partial interruption was that he keyed it into production. The percent of loss was the proportion of the production lost when compared to the average daily production previous to the fire. It should be noted that there was no attempt to relate the amount produced to the amount for which the manufacturer had a market. Probably this was no problem in the case of the textile mills which Dalton insured. However, as this type of insurance spread to other business enterprises, it opened the door for abuse. As one writer stated, "this paid a premium to the poorly or improvidently conducted business which might be producing more than it could sell."[14]

Dalton's decision to write the 1880 policy for a period of one year must have been an arbitrary one, adopted as providing a base for setting rates.[15] Fire insurance on property was being written at the time both on an annual basis and also for three and five year terms. (It is suggested that in subsequent years, Dalton essayed to secure a three year policy of Use and Occupancy Insurance.)[16]

The acceptance of Use and Occupancy Insurance by all Insurers continued to be slow. There was a genuine distrust of its legitimacy in insurance company circles.[17] On the part of Agents and Insureds, there was a lack of understanding of what it was intended to accomplish. It has been suggested that this was due to it being offered to the public as insurance on profits rather than as protection for the dividends of stockholders and for the salary of valued employees.[18]

One effect of setting a fixed daily limit to recovery was to impose upon the Insured the obligation to buy an adequate amount of insurance if he wanted to collect in full for any interruption of operations that he might suffer. This was appropriate where the business operation was uniform throughout the year. However, many types of business experienced substantial fluctuations in activity depending on the day of the week or the season of the year. In order to recover the full loss, should he be shut down during his best day of the year, the Insured would have to use that day's figures as the per diem amount provided for under his policy. The result would be that he was fully insured for that day but over-insured for the balance of the year.

The problems arising from fluctuations in the production from day to day or from period to period was ultimately met in two ways. First, the span for a unit of time was extended from a day to a week and, later, to a month. The weekly policy provided that 1/52nd of the face amount of the policy was to be paid for any week of interruption and a proportionate amount was to be paid for a period of less than a week. The monthly policy divided the face amount of the policy into twelfths, with similar provisions.

This arrangement evened out some of the daily fluctuations. But operations that were highly seasonal were still not properly insured. So special provisions were built into policies to take care of such seasonal fluctuations. But each of these changes was effected only because some Insureds complained that they were not properly served by the form of the contract in existence, often a realization that developed only after they had suffered a loss. Such experiences built up an atmosphere of dissatisfaction with this type of coverage.

Another type of complication developed by virtue of the fact that most business interruptions did not last for an entire year. The face amount of the policy was, therefore, in excess of the probable loss that the Insured could be expected to suffer. To force him to carry insurance equal to the loss he would suffer if shut down for an entire year was an unfair burden. This problem was ultimately met by the introduction of a coinsurance clause into the policy.

C. The Courts Define Use and Occupation

The lack of clear understanding of the intention behind the employment of the term "Use and Occupation" by Dalton and the failure to define it in the policy contract resulted in a shocking surprise to the insurance fraternity some twenty years later. In 1902, the Court of Appeals of New York put its own interpretation on those words.[19]

It becomes apparent from a reading of a series of New York court decisions, handed down at the beginning of this century, that, despite the basic disapproval of Profits Insurance, this was the concept upon which such insurance was regarded by the insurance industry. As a result, George Richards, an acknowledged authority in the law of insurance, took the case of the Buffalo Elevating Company all the way up to the New York Court of Appeals,[20] basing his defense to the Insured's claim on the theory that a contract transferring a portion of the Insured's right to profits violated the provision of the underlying Fire Insurance policy in which the Insured had warranted that he had sole and unconditional ownership of the subject matter of the policy. Richards took the position that it was similar to insurance on freight. This brought directly into focus the question of what was the subject matter of a policy of Use and Occupancy Insurance—what was the interest that was insured?

The case arose out of a fire at the property of the Buffalo Elevating Company that operated a grain elevator and that carried Use and Occupancy Insurance. The Insured had entered into an agreement with other grain operators to set up a pool into which they put most of their earnings and out of which each drew a share of the group's earnings, at the end of the season. Although the Insured was shut down for part of the season, its economic loss was buffered by its share drawn from the pool. Nevertheless, the Insured filed an insurance claim for the full per diem amount for the 250 days that its elevator was put out of operation as a result of the fire.

It was accepted by the court that freight or profits on a voyage could be the basis of a valid contract of insurance. Moreover if "Use and Occupancy" was correlative with earnings, or affected them in any way, the Insured may well have violated the terms of his policy by having entered into the pooling arrangement. But both the intermediate court and the Court of Appeals held that while the term "Use and Occupancy" was broad enough to include the concept of profits, it could not be interpreted to refer specifically to the profits to be derived from the use and occupancy of the property. If that narrower interpretation were intended, it should have been specifically so stated. Absent any words of limitation, the term was ambiguous and was to be interpreted as providing an indemnity (at a valued amount) in the event that the property should not continue, as a result of fire, in the same condition of availability to the Insured to use for any purpose to which he may be able to devote it. It made no difference whether or not the Insured was using the property and whether or not such use was profitable.[21] In effect, the court held that the insurable interest of the Insured rested on the right and opportunity to use and occupy the structure—on availability for use in general and not for use to produce an Earnings Stream. In the Michael case, the court was not required to decide how the loss should be measured, because of its ruling that the policy was, in effect, a valued policy.[22]

At this late date, one can only wonder at the inability of the court to recognize that the purpose of the policy was to protect the value of the business opportunity provided by the continued existence of the property. This opportunity had an economic advantage; it could be expressed in terms of dollars of value based on what it could produce in earnings. It was something that the operators of a grain elevator would consider of sufficient value to justify the payment of an insurance premium. The fact that they "hedged their bet" by entering into the pooling arrangement did not change the underlying business purpose. The mere right to use and occupy could have an emotional value but hardly a monetary value sufficient to support an insurance contract.

It would also be strange if, during the period of twenty years from the issuance of the Newton Mills policy to the issuance of the policy to the Buffalo Elevating Company, losses had not been suffered and adjusted under such policies. The practices of the business should have played a role in the court's decision.

Within a year, a lower New York court, taking its lead from the Michael case, followed the same line of reasoning in the two Tannenbaum cases.[23] Both were suits by an insurance Broker against clients for loss of commission resulting from breach of a contract to buy Use and Occupancy Insurance through him. In neither case was there a policy or a fixed value. In the Freundlich case, the court held, that, in determining the amount of insurance which the defendant should have taken out, i.e., the market value of the Use and Occupancy, evidence of the net yearly profits earned by the business operated by the Insured was irrelevant. "The profits of the business were quite another insurable risk, and not at all covered by the phrase 'Use and Occupancy.' "

The Simon case went even further and, in addition to following the two earlier cases, stated, "nor in the case at bar, do the fixed charges mentioned in the statement of facts constitute the market value of use and occupancy." The court then threw a roadblock against any type of Use and Occupancy policy other than a valued policy by stating, "Profits of a business are always an uncertain element and speculative to a certain extent and market values ought not to be fixed upon a basis so doubtful and unreliable. In the absence of such a provision (valued amount), it is incumbent upon the plaintiff (the Broker) to show by definite and certain testimony what the market value of the use and occupancy of the defendant's premises was during the time covered by the contract, and what the character of its testimony shall be is for the plaintiff to elect, and the court to determine when presented."[24]

In the Michael case, the court allowed that the words "Use and Occupancy" may assume, within their general scope, the expectation of profits and earnings. But the two Tannenbaum cases appeared to close the door on that possibility. Absent specific definition, Use and Occupancy was not to be considered a term denoting the aspect of property as an income-producing entity, but rather as the right to use and enjoy the property for whatever purposes its owner wished.[25]

One would have hoped that a new form of contract, one more descriptive of the intent of the coverage, would have been promptly adopted. Such was not the case. Instead, a definition of the term Use and Occupancy was inserted in the contract; the subject of the insurance was stated to be "net profit and continuing expenses."

The words Use and Occupancy continued to be used for many more years. They can be found in standard forms printed as late as 1954. (Business Interruption Insurance Form No. 1–Two Item Coinsurance Form– Mercantile and Non-Manufacturing Form 505, September, 1954.) Their employment finally ended as the Gross Earnings form gradually became the form in general use.

D. Further Policy Developments

By its valued policy approach, the Newton Mills policy had provided a fixed amount of recovery for each day of total suspension, no matter what may have been the true loss. This departure from the principle of indemnity, one of the basic foundations of insurance theory, had much to do with the early fear that it involved too high a degree of moral hazard. Shortly after the turn of the century, however, the principle of indemnity had been reinforced by the development of an "open" or non-valued type of policy form where recovery was limited to "actual loss sustained." By 1922, Use and Occupancy Insurance had been generally put on an indemnity basis.[26] The use of the valued form of policy was not entirely eliminated, however, and its use extends to the present time in special situations where it is appropriate. The forms are new and more innovative. There is no coinsurance, no pro rata clause and no definition of gross earnings. It can be written on individual merits and not on a standard form. There is also a special form for mining risks. See Ch. 8 for further consideration.

Pressure from Insureds and the problems created by World War I created an atmosphere for change. Even though the United States did not enter the War until 1917, it had, from the beginning of hostilities, become the arsenal of the Western Alliance. Not only munitions of war, but all types of civilian goods that the Allies could not produce for themselves had to be supplied. Productive capacity and inventories of goods in the United States expanded rapidly. Manufacturers and merchants made unprecedented profits.

When, in April of 1917, the United States did enter the war, the situation intensified. Materials of all kinds were in short supply and the time that it took to repair damage or replace damaged equipment stretched out into many months. On top of that, freight embargoes were imposed by the government, giving priority to the shipment of war supplies, which further extended the period before operations could be restored to normal in damaged plants and retail enterprises which were doing civilian work.[27]

During the war, while business was booming, moral hazard was not a major concern. But with the cessation of hostilities, many businesses found themselves overextended. The unlimited amount of Use and Occupancy coverage that an Insured could buy and on which he could collect in case of total loss, proved very tempting to the unscrupulous.[28]

This combination of factors resulted in an increased demand for Use and Occupancy Insurance and the market grew very tight. The insurance industry had to stop and carefully re-examine the contracts which they had been offering to the public. Immediately, the need for a uniform contract became apparent.

Dissatisfaction with the results experienced under the Per Diem form led to the adoption of what was called the Two Item Contribution form. First suggested about 1925, it was available on both the East and West Coasts by 1927. (*The American Agency Bulletin* of January 16, 1925, has a story by W.S. Foster in which he refers to a series of joint meetings held by Eastern and Western U & O Insurance committees.) By 1929, it was the form generally in use in most states.[29]

While the Two Item Contribution form was an improvement over previous forms, it did not quite meet the needs of the buyers of the coverage. Special interest groups devised more acceptable contracts and threatened to take business away from the mainstream companies. The chief complaint was that the contract was too complicated. Agents had difficulty in advising Insureds how much insurance to carry and Adjusters had difficulty measuring the amount of loss.[30]

E. Adoption of the Gross Earnings Form

To meet the demands of businessmen, an inter-regional conference open to all Underwriters was convened in Atlantic City in 1935 by the Eastern Loss Executives Conference. Out of its deliberations there finally evolved, in 1938, the Gross Earnings form. Since this form will serve as the basis of later discussion in this book, no analysis of it will be made at this point.[31]

In 1939, the Gross Earnings form was offered to non-manufacturing risks only. The argument then developed that there was no reason to make a distinction between mercantile and manufacturing risks.[32] So, in 1944, it was made available to manufacturing risks as well.

The onset of World War II in 1939 brought back some of the problems experienced during World War I. Even though the United States did not enter the War until December, 1941, a great deal of manufactured material was being sent to Great Britain and later to Russia. Materials became scarce and priorities were established by the government, with preferences being given on the basis of importance in carrying on the war effort. This was implemented, after the entry of the United States into the war, by the War Production Board's Conversion Order L-41 issued in April, 1942. The effect of this order was to prevent or delay the repair or reconstruction of property which was not engaged in war work. This had the direct result of extending the period of interruption in civilian-oriented businesses and thereby increased the amount of loss they suffered. There has been discussion from time to time during the past few years of establishing a controlled economy in the United States, funneling economic assets to designated industries. If established, such controls could well affect the time required to restore operations after an interruption. An example would be restrictions on the availability of gasoline for private automobiles.

This disruption of normal procurement practices for materials necessary to deal with property damage caused by insured perils continued on even after the end of World War II. A whole series of shortages, brought about by unusual conditions, led to government intervention and extended delays in reconstruction.[33]

In the face of these changing conditions, Insurers, as early as 1941, developed various endorsements, limiting the total length of interruption for which they would be liable, or increasing the premium charged if they didn't so limit their liability but agreed to be liable during the full period of interruption. There was a constant effort to balance the needs of Insureds for protection and the needs of the Underwriters to protect themselves in an unprecedented and unexpected situation. Ultimately conditions returned to normal and these special clauses were removed.[34]

A special problem that developed during the period of World War II and that continued after its end was the provision for renegotiating the amount of a government contract after its completion—whereby the Insured would be obliged to disgorge any excess profit he might have made in carrying out the contract. This renegotiation concept confronted adjusters with the necessity of determining just what was the "experience of the business."[35]

The year 1946 saw changes in Use and Occupancy Insurance contracts. Many different forms of contract were being offered. It was stated that on the east coast there were 48 choices of policy forms for manufacturers and 40 for merchants; while on the west coast, there were 1022 choices for merchants and 1037 for manufacturers.[36] Gradually the number of forms was reduced to the limited number available today.

By 1959, the use of the Two Item form finally came to an end and the era of the Gross Earnings form began.

Now, after a quarter of a century, a new form, the BIC Form, is "waiting in the wings" to supplant the Gross Earnings form. Some of the specific aspects of what this will entail are set forth in Chapter 8 and Chapter 16. However, as a general matter, it can be said that the BIC Form is designed to meet the mood currently in vogue, which fosters "simplifying" insurance contracts so that Insureds can better understand them. Whether this goal will be accomplished by the forms that have been filed remains an open question for the future to determine.

F. Summation

The changes that have taken place in the form of Business Interruption Insurance since the issuance of the original Newton Mills policy reflect a growing understanding on the part of Underwriters of the type of protection which such a policy should offer. During the same period, pressure for change was brought to bear by Adjusters and Insureds who had to deal with actual loss situations. Finally, the courts, by their decisions interpreting various policy provisions, have had an impact on the language of the policy form.

Such changes did not occur everywhere at one time. An innovative provision would be adopted by a particular company or in a particular region. If it proved useful, it would gradually be adopted generally.

There have been three basic steps in the evolution of today's contracts. To summarize the previous history, the first step was taken in the Newton Mills policy of 1880, which was based on the concept that during each time-unit of operations a certain contribution was made to production. Cessation of operations for a unit of time would result in the loss of the contribution to production that would have been made by that unit. The loss was measured by the number of units of shut-down time on a valued basis.

A second step was taken with the adoption of the Two Item form. This contract considered the period of interruption as a whole, and compared the actual experience during that period and its contribution to the Earnings Stream with what would have been the experience had no damage taken place. In so doing, it divided the subject matter of coverage into two parts—the net profit and the necessarily continuing expenses other than ordinary payroll—on the one hand, and, as an option, ordinary payroll on the other. In processing a claim, the procedure was to add up the individual items of continuing expense to reach a total of that part of the claim. This total was added to the amount of profit lost.

The third step came with the adoption of the Gross Earnings form. Loss is determined by what would have been the gross earnings of the business (as defined) during the period of interruption had no damage occurred. The expenses which do not necessarily continue are deducted from these gross earnings. Ordinary payroll employees are no longer segregated as a separate item. Their payroll is covered to the extent that their continued employment is "necessary to resume operations of the Insured with the same quality of service which existed immediately preceding the loss."[37]

In essence the new BIC Form is an earnings form. It is the Earnings Stream that is regarded as the subject of the coverage. Despite the various changes in format and in wording, its basic philosophy is the same as that of the Gross Earnings form.

The preceding brief overview of the three general types of Business Interruption Insurance policy forms that have developed over the course of the past one hundred plus years represents merely the tip of the iceberg. Multitudinous changes, endorsements, supplementary coverages and specialized forms of Time Element Insurance policies have been introduced during that period of time. Some have faded out of use, as have the Per Diem and Two Item forms to a large degree, while others are in current use, often as an adjunct to the Gross Earnings form. At the cutting edge of the industry, new types of coverage, sometimes incorporated in manuscript contracts, are constantly being introduced.[38]

An example of the expansion of the business interruption concept is found in Tax Interruption Protection Insurance. Municipalities which depend to a large extent on sales tax receipts from a limited number of businesses to meet their budget take out insurance against the interruption of such income should a particular business stop operating. The same concept is applicable to so-called "company towns." The City of Miami took out Contingent Business Interruption Insurance against a football strike diminishing the return from concessions operated in connection with a sports stadium. Insurance protecting product integrity or against bomb threats by both employees and outsiders is still another example.

In the second half of this volume, consideration will be given to such developments. However, in light of the extensive literature describing the provisions of current forms and their application, the approach adopted herein will tend more to an analysis of the handling of the various coverage areas than to the impact of specific provisions in individual forms.[39] The major exception to this approach will be in the consideration of court decisions.

Chapter 4 Notes

1. Klein, *Business Interruption*, p. 9.
   In 1835, Zachariah Allen organized Manufacturers Mutual Fire Ins. Co. because his insurance company would not reduce the rate on his carefully constructed mill. He cut rates by almost two-thirds. *The Able Man of Boston*, York Dane (Boston, 1950).

2. *The Index*, Vol. VII (1878), p. 374; *Weekly Underwriter*, Vol. XVII (Nov. 1876), pp. 594, 595; *The Index*, Vol. XI (1880), p. 204 and p. 311.
   Weekly Underwriter, Vol. XXIII (September 11, 1880), p. 115. A resolution against Profits Insurance originally contained such language as "subversive of one of the fundamental principles of underwriting and introducing a serious moral hazard and encouraging incendiarism."

3. One writer referred to it as "the epidemic of the valued policy (which) is spreading like small pox." He was referring to the spread from state to state (starting in Wisconsin in 1870) of proposed legislation declaring that in the event of a total loss the fire insurance policy on the property should be treated as a valued policy with the Insured collecting the face amount of the policy. At the time, the amount of insurance included the value of the land on which the building stood. As one writer put it, "Insurance has been continued upon buildings long after material value has gone from them yet such worn out structures as occupy valuable situations are productive of income and are, therefore, properly insurable..." *The Index*, Vol. XII (1881), p. 5. See also: *Weekly Underwriter*, Vol. XXIII (1880), pgs. 115, 149, 227, 155.
   The report of the Committee on Valued Policy Laws to the 14th Annual Meeting of the National Board of Fire Underwriters held in N.Y. on April 28, 1880, contains the following language: "... that some course must be adopted by companies which will prevent those seeking insurance from obtaining a guarantee of indemnity in case of loss beyond sixty percent of the value of the property insured...." They suggested that the Board "oppose the valued policy law before the New York legislature." *American Exchange & Review*, Vol. XXXIV (1880), p. 152.

4. Commonwealth of Massachusetts, Chapter 331 of the Acts of 1873. Its use was made mandatory on January 1, 1881. See *Weekly Underwriter*, Vol. XXV (July 23, 1881), p. 49.
   The Standard Fire Insurance policy amended form, approved in Massachusetts on April 7, 1880, read in part: "The amount of said loss or damage to be estimated according to the actual value of the insured property at the time when such loss or damage happens." *American Exchange & Review*, Vol. XXXIV (1880), p. 183.

5. For example, Policy #1347086 of the Liverpool, London, and Globe Insurance Company issued on March 14, 1882, by its general agent in Boston, George W. Gordon, covering property of the Hampshire Manufacturing Company reads in part: "or if the above-mentioned premises shall be *occupied or used* so as to increase the risk. . . ."; Policy #1732108 of the same company issued by Charles E. Guild, General Agent, at Boston on September 23, 1873, contains the language "if during this insurance the above-mentioned premises shall be *used* for any trade, business or vocation. . .or if the *occupation* of such premises be changed." The actual phrase "use or occupation" appears in Policy #638 of the Home Insurance Co. issued on May 25, 1887, which reads in part ". . . in case the *use or occupation* of the above-mentioned premises. . .shall be changed so as to increase the risk thereon. . . ."

    In these fire policies, the words "use" and "occupation" referred to the manner in which the Insured manipulated the property described. They related to a change in the physical employment of the property in such a way as to increase the risk of loss and related solely to the materiality of the property.

    These policies and others are to be found in the archives of the Insurance Library of Boston.

    In a talk before the Fire Insurance Society of Philadelphia entitled "Use and Occupancy Insurance" delivered on November 18, 1912, W.N. Bament commented, "In adopting a name for U&O Insurance, the originators probably had in mind the occupancy of the buildings as a manufacturing plant and the use of the machinery and tools therein." Quoted in *Weekly Underwriter*, (December 7, 1912), p. 18.

6. The court states at p. 132: the fire policy "has never been understood to extend to the profits or fruits the assured was drawing, or might have drawn from the thing insured." See: Arcadia Bonded Warehouse Co. Inc. v. National Union F. Ins. Co.

7. In Vol. XXXIV, p. 123, of *American Exchange and Review*, published in Philadelphia in April, 1880, appears the following statement: "Boston now begins the practice of income insurance, something after the patterns of the French *assurance contre le chomage*; that is, production being suspended by fire in mills, etc., a daily compensation is allowed for such suspension of work. In Boston such provision is part of the fire insurance contract."

    In the article in *The Insurance Times* of April, 1880, p. 232, entitled "Damage" appears the following statement: ". . . we notice that its practice has begun in this country, though in somewhat different form (than France) but amounting in practical results to the same thing. . . ."

    Typical of other attitudes were the words of the editor of *The Chronicle* published in New York in March 25, 1880: "*The Chronicle* does not believe in chomage as described in the Liverpool letter . . . chomage or profits insurance certainly and distinctly means the increase of [moral hazard] to an indefinite extent. Wise underwriters will have none of it. It is a business only for gamblers and speculators." Vol. XXV, p. 306. See also the quoted "Boston Letter" in Comment #1, p. 295.

8. In Volume XXXIV of the *American Exchange and Review* of June, 1880, at page

184, the editor writes: "it will be seen that the contract cited above makes the policy virtually a valued one . . . . On the whole, this matter should be carefully considered by all agents and companies who are asked to embark on it to the end of determining whether it is not calculated to increase the moral hazard. . . ."

The Bulletin of The Fire Insurance Society of Philadelphia is quoted to the effect that "there exists sufficient danger of the creation of moral hazard, to say nothing of the lack of knowledge of the subject, to make Use and Occupancy a subject to be avoided in insurance circles. "Use and Occupancy Insurance," address by John H. Gray, February 19, 1917 (supra).

As late as 1924, a speaker could state: "The Insured used to have a stake in avoiding fires because he could not recoup all his loss. Now with Property Insurance, Use and Occupancy Insurance and/or Profit Insurance, the moral hazard is greater."

"Side Lines and Loss Ratios," address by Wm. J. Greer. Western New York Field Club, College of Ins. Library N.Y.C. (General File U.S. 010), March 7, 1924.

9. In *The Spectator* of May, 1880, the editor adds: "The line is considered a novelty and risky outside of Boston."

10. "Use and Occupancy Insurance," address by John A. Eckert before Insurance Society of New York, Nov. 14, 1916. Pamphlet located in Library of College of Insurance, New York City (General File U.S. 010).

In the course of his address, Eckert said: "There is a speculative element associated with Use and Occupancy insurance when written under a valued form . . . . Under the present underwriting methods an insured is at liberty to carry as much Use and Occupancy insurance as he is willing to pay for. This permits an insured, knowing that he has a plant subject to a probable total destruction, to carry insurance in excess of all probable loss."

In his address, Eckert stated: "most all large agencies have their own form and most every large brokerage office has its own form, with the result that we rarely see two forms alike, and by this is meant alike as to application and coverage."

The 1873 statute, establishing a form of Standard Fire Insurance policy in Massachusetts, contained no provision concerning riders that might be attached thereto. Neither the amended form adopted in 1880 nor that of 1881 included any provision about securing the Insurance Commissioner's approval of any proposed attachment, though there were some requirements as to its form.

In 1917, steps were taken to produce a uniform Use and Occupancy form. Various Underwriters Boards also adopted regulations concerning the wording of the form.

See: Unton v. London, Liverpool & Globe Ins. Co. A policy can be partially valued and partially open: Lite v. Firemen's Ins. Co.

11. Cf: "The name 'Use and Occupancy' Insurance, while cumbersome in a way, really conveys the intent of the coverage. This name is derived from the fact that the insurance is designed to protect the insured against the loss of use or occupancy of the physical property entering in and necessary to the conduct of his business, and the consequent loss of earnings which through the use and occu-

pancy of the physical property the business produces . . . . This form of coverage is often referred to as Business Interruption Indemnity, or Loss of Earnings Insurance or Prospective Earnings Insurance."

Outline of Use & Occupancy Insurance, C.D. Minor. Director of Education. Pamphlet issued by Royal Liverpool Groups (1941).

Thrasher Hall writes in *Use and Occupancy, Excess Floater and Betterments Insurance Enclaircised* (Indianapolis: Rough Notes, 1920), p. 57.: "The term 'on the Use and Occupancy of' . . . means nothing. Mr. White, now of the Hartford Fire Ins. Co. has coined a better term to express what is meant, and his idea in this respect has been adopted by the author in the form suggested for Mayer Bros. of Chicago, i.e. 'loss due to interruption of business by fire.' "

By 1919, the term had not yet found its way into the dictionary. *Use and Occupancy Insurance or Business Interruption Indemnity. How & Why*. Pamphlet, Insurance Company of North America (1919), p. 7.

12. Hartford F. Ins. Co. v. Wilson & Toomer, Fertilizer Co.; Arcadia Bonded Warehouse Co. Inc. v. Nat'l Union F. Ins. Co.

"The term 'use and occupancy' is generally used interchangeably with the term business interruption (West, 1968)—indeed they are both used somewhat interchangeably in this contract. The terms both go to coverage of losses sustained when for one reason or another the operation of the business is interrupted. Business interruption insurance generally put the insured into the monetary position it would have been in but for the interruption of its business. Use and occupancy insurance provides the same type of coverage but tends to focus on the business use which the property was capable of prior to the loss." Stephenson, Circuit Judge. U.S. Ct. of Appeals 8th Circuit (1979) in Omaha Paper Stock Co. v. Harbor Ins. Co. See: Nickals v. Ohio Farmers Ins. Co.; Miner Edgar Co. v. North River Ins. Co.; Appleman 4 Ins. L. & Prac. §2329, p. 323.

13. Barclay v. Cousins, p. 551. Barclay acted as agent for Richard Wells, who shipped a cargo for his own account on his own ship. He insured the profits to be made from their sale and he ultimately disposed of the goods. It may be that Barclay had assumed responsibility to Wells in some fashion.

See: Buffalo Elevating Co. v. Prussian Nat'l Ins. Co.

14. *Use and Occupancy Insurance—A Historical Review*. Charles A. Erickson, August, 1945. Article in files of College of Insurance Library, New York City (General File U.S. 010).

15. "The Role of the Accountant in Business Interruption Insurance," address by Ambrose B. Kelly before National Accountants Association, Portland, Maine (May 17, 1962).

A later writer, with the benefit of subsequent developments, wrote: "One year is logical: Taxes are paid on an annual basis, salaries and bonuses, insurance rates, interest and all are figured on an annual basis; so are subscriptions. . . ." *Consequential Coverages*, W.S. Foster (Indianapolis: Rough Notes, 1936).

A rent insurance policy form in the archives of the Insurance Library of Boston was issued from March 17, 1878 to March 17, 1879, a period of one year: Policy

#5012 of the American Insurance Company of Philadelphia on rents of a four story and basement brick and stone building situated No. 167/169 East Madison St., Chicago.

16. *Insurance and Commercial Magazine* (supra).

17. Gradually the legitimacy of this type of insurance was established. Speaking on March 18, 1926, Frank L. Erion stated, "Does Use and Occupancy create a moral hazard? No—neither does a display of diamonds in a store window create a thief— but it may prove a temptation to a weak or biased mind—so the question of moral hazard in Use and Occupancy risks is important. There is no justification for the valued form—which does offer a moral hazard if the Insured is earning no profit ... In the history of nearly fifty years there was not a single case on record where Use and Occupancy insurance was even suspected of causing an 'arson' fire."

18. See: *Use and Occupancy Insurance—An Educational Primer*, Percy Ling, Insurance Federation of Pennsylvania (1947).

    Harrington analyzes the problem as follows:

    "Perhaps the difficulty of visualizing and describing just what this type of insurance was upon delayed its development.

    "First, the idea was stated as a stipulated sum as part of the probable trading margin no longer available when the plant had burned. This was arbitrary, inadequate and inadaptable.

    "Then it was stated as damage preventing manufacture.

    "Then as loss resulting when business was 'prevented from producing goods' and 'proportionately as the product thereby prevented from being made bears to the average daily yield.'

    "Then as part of a 'fixed sum per day.' Arbitrary sums per day and valued forms violate the basic principle of indemnity and when production was qualified by 'finished goods', the result was disastrous."

    "Use & Occupancy Insurance," Paper by George Harrington, Lecturer (August, 1929).

19. In Michael v. Prussian National Ins. Co., the plaintiff was a trustee in bankruptcy of the Insured, the Buffalo Elevating Company, which had gone into bankruptcy since first instituting suit in a lower court.

20. Buffalo Elevating Co. v. Prussian Nat'l Ins. Co.

21. In the Menzies case (1847) the Scottish Court referred to the claim for lost rents, profits and for continuing charges as claims based "on a want of occupancy." To that court, occupancy clearly meant the opportunity for creating earnings as well as the mere right of physical possession to use it as one wished ... to occupy it for the purpose to which it had been dedicated. Still it says nothing about it being a profitable dedication.

22. As soon as the decision was handed down, the attorneys for the Insurers sent out a letter to their clients suggesting that the intention of the Insurers at least be

clearly defined "by adding a definition in the standard (sic) form of policy as follows"—1) Use and occupancy, to wit: estimated net earnings from the business described, valued at $ per year, or 2) Use and Occupancy, to wit: estimated profits from the business described, valued at $ per year."

23. Tannenbaum v. Freundlich;
Tannenbaum v. Simon

24. In 1917, Leo Levy, Esq., a leading member of the New York insurance bar said: "In the absence of express language clearly indicating the contrary, I am inclined to the belief that a policy upon Use and Occupancy as such would be held to be valued and that, if it be sought in practice to avoid such a construction, there should be clear language of exactly what measure of damage is to be applied and that the intent to leave the ascertainment of damage as under an open policy should be made unmistakably clear." Address to Insurance Society of New York, entitled "Use and Occupancy: Profits and Commission; Rents and Leasehold Insurance," January 30, 1917. This pamphlet in the N.Y. College of Insurance Library (General File U.S. 010) contains an excellent bibliography.

For example of valued policies see: City Tailors Ltd. v. Evans; Flaxlinum Insulating Co. v. Commissioner; Jacksonville Oil Mills v. Stuyvesant Ins. Co.

25. In a much later case, where the question was raised as to whether an insurance policy on Use and Occupancy was insurance on property, it was held that Use and Occupancy is property. The term property "generally includes the use and enjoyment of physical property which is an essential quality or attribute of absolute property." Thorrez & Maes Mfg. Co. v. American Central Ins. Co.; Cf: Hudson Mfg. Co. v. N.Y. Underwriters Ins. Co.

26. "Understanding and Selling Business Interruption Indemnity Insurance," William A. Riordan, *The Eastern Underwriter*, Vol. 23, no. 49 (December 24, 1922), p. 2.

27. Flaxlinum Insulating Co. v. Commissioner.

28. "Side Lines and Loss Ratios," address by William J. Greer to Western N.Y. Field Club (March 7, 1924).

29. "Use and Occupancy Insurance," Nat'l Retail Dry Goods Ass'n Inc. Insurance Bulletin: (April, 1925).

"Use and Occupancy," Clarence T. Hubbard, *Insurance Age Journal* (January 5, 1927).

"Use and Occupancy Insurance," Address to Insurance Board of Cleveland, Roy E. Julian (December 18, 1929).

Address to N.Y. Ass'n of Local Agents by Lawrence E. Falls. Reported in *Underwriters Review*, June 5, 1930. See: "Origin and Development of Business Interruption Insurance," manuscript dated 1948 by George S. Jones in New York Insurance Library (General File U.S. 010).

30.   "Losses were not settled according to the contract. They were 'horse–traded' ",
      Charles A. Erikson (supra).
         A letter written by a Boston agent to a customer on June 21, 1918, states in
      part: "... adjustments of losses of this nature by a compromise...." Quotation
      from paper by a Mr. White of the New York Underwriters reads: "In my opinion
      a crystal clear mathematical partial payment clause will be extremely necessary at
      least until such times as our adjusters (speaking generally, for of course there are
      exceptions) have a better conception of the scope and purpose of Use and Occu-
      pancy contracts."
         Use and Occupancy, Excess Floater and Betterments Insurance Enclaircised,
      Thrasher Hall (Indianapolis: Rough Notes Co., 1920), p. 38.

31.   Gross Earnings Endorsement is not an extension of coverage underlying fire pol-
      icy but insures against a new type of loss. Victory Container Corp. v. Sphere Ins.
      Co.

32.   "Drug stores not only buy manufactured goods but also process material which is
      then sold. Not infrequently manufacturing concerns supplement their 'line' by
      adding a product manufactured by another firm." *Use and Occupancy Insurance,*
      C.A. Erikson.

33.   "Underinsurance and Material Shortages Face the Use and Occupancy Field,"
      Eastern Underwriter (April 26, 1946). p. 1.

34.   For a description of the various problems and the endorsements drafted to meet
      them see: Klein, *Business Interruption Insurance* pp. 196-205.

35.   "Effect of Renegotiation in Use and Occupancy Coverage." *The Management
      Review* published by American Management Association (September, 1943), p.
      354.
         Renegotiations on the average resulted in the government getting a rebate of
      from 11-19%. The problem existed where a loss occurred before the contract was
      renegotiated, as to whether adjustment should be held open until renegotiation
      was completed, or should be consummated with recognition of the potential rene-
      gotiation or should advance payments or loans be made to the Insured. Another
      question was whether an Insured should be penalized under a Coinsurance Clause
      if the amount of insurance was inadequate on the basis of paper profits but ade-
      quate on a renegotiated basis. See article in *National Underwriter*, July 15, 1943, p.
      1.

36.   "What's New in Business Interruption Insurance," H.C. Klein, *Rough Notes*, Vol.
      91, no. 6 (January, 1947), p. 32.

37.   See: "Following Development of U & O Forms: Step by Step," W.S. Foster.
      Rough Notes (May, 1937).

38.   See: *Developments in Business Interruption Ins. Coverages.* Randolph S. Christian-

son, V.P. Reciprocal Manager, Inc. (April 16, 1955). College of Insurance Library, New York City (General File U.S. 010).

39.   Among the sources of information available:

Henry Charles Klein, *Business Interruption Insurance*, 4th ed. (Indianapolis: Rough Notes Co., Inc., 1960).

K.W. Withers, *Business Interruption Insurance Coverage and Adjustment* (Berkeley: Howell-North, 1957).

John D. Phelan, CPCU, *Business Interruption Primer*, 6th ed. (Indianapolis: Rough Notes Co., Inc., 1966).

Frank S. Glendening, C.P.A., *Business Interruption Insurance: What is Covered* (Cincinnati: The National Underwriter Co., 1980).

Edward C. Bardwell, *New Profits—Business Interruption Insurance*, 2nd ed. (Indianapolis: Rough Notes Co. Inc., 1974).

5

The Contract in
Business Interruption Insurance

---

*Structural analysis of contract. Six P's and six E's. Introductory view
of the six P's. Introductory view of the six E's.*

A. The Structural Analysis Approach

Various techniques have been employed to pierce the aura of mystery
which has grown up about the Business Interruption Insurance policy. Writers
and jurists have sought to deal with this problem by composing definitions of
the policy function. A rather simplistic definition, of which there are numerous
variables, is that "this insurance is designed to do for the Insured, in the event
of business interruption caused by an insured peril, just what the business
would have done if no interruption has occurred—no more."[1] A more elaborate
definition reads: "Business Interruption Insurance is a form of insurance
designed to indemnify the Insured against losses arising from his inability to
continue the normal operations and functions of his business, industry or other
commercial establishments or, in other words, the total or partial suspension of
such business due to the loss, or loss of use of, or damage to all or part of the
buildings, plant, machinery, equipment, or other physical assets thereof, as a
result of a peril or hazard insured against."[2]

A different approach has been taken in this book. Cutting through the
wording of the policy, it is possible to determine just what are its basic structural elements. It would appear that they are twelve in number—that every contract of Business Interruption Insurance is built up on a dozen fundamental
elements. Six of them play a role in determining the Insurer's liability and six
of them affect the Insured's ability to collect in the event of a loss.

As a mnemonic tool, each of these elements has been labeled herein with a

49

single word. Such simplification can be achieved only by the sacrifice of completeness and sharpness of definition. However, if the method employed succeeds in achieving a satisfactory technique for understanding the subject, it is well worthwhile. Its deficiencies can be overcome as the exposition proceeds.

B. The six P's and the six E's

The first six elements can be represented by six words each starting with the letter "P". These are **Parties, Property, Perils, Productivity, Period** and **Profit**. Obviously these are symbols.

In the same way, the second six factors can be represented by six words each starting with the letter "E". These words are **Extent, Experience, Exclusions, Effort, Extras** and **Enough**. These latter six words do not describe as sharply as do the six P's the exact nature of the element they represent. However, as symbols they serve their purpose. With an understanding of these twelve words and their application to a fact situation, anyone can acquire a firm grasp of the structural nature of the Business Interruption Insurance policy. A preliminary and brief explanation of the meaning of these words will precede their study in depth.

To prepare a Business Interruption Insurance policy the persons who are *Parties* to the contract have to be named; the physical *Property* which produces the earnings must be described and located; the particular *Perils* against which protection is provided must be stated. Then, to constitute a loss under the contract, there must be an interruption of *Productivity* of products or sales; this interruption must continue for a measured *Period* of time and it must result in a diminution of *Profit* which otherwise would have been earned. (The word "Profit" is used to designate the Earnings Stream.)

The essence of this aspect of the Business Interruption Insurance policy can be captured in a single sentence reading: "It is a contract which insures a *Party or Parties* against loss resulting from damage to *Property* caused by an insured *Peril* which results in an interruption of *Productivity* for a *Period* of time with a resultant diminution of *Profit*."

The second six elements, each beginning with E, can similarly be briefly introduced at this point. *Effort* refers to the requirement that the Insured must use his best efforts to shorten the period of interruption and reduce the amount of loss. *Exclusions* refers to the elimination of liability for any increase in the amount of loss that might be caused by certain specified collateral factors; *Experience* is the actual past and potential future Earnings Stream as defined in the policy; the *Extent* of the Insured's recovery is limited to the actual loss sustained except in the case of a valued policy; *Extras* refers to expediting expenses incurred to reduce the loss; while *Enough* refers to the Coinsurance or Contribution Clause, which requires the Insured to carry enough insurance, if he does not want to bear part of the loss as a coinsurer.

These six elements, which deal with the amount the Insured may recover, can also be summarized in a single sentence which would read: "An Insured can collect to the *Extent* of the loss *Experienced*, not resulting from *Excluded* causes, and also for *Extra* expenses incurred, provided he exerts the proper *Effort* to reduce loss and carries *Enough* insurance." To indicate graphically the skeletal nature of the Business Interruption Insurance policy, the chart at the end of this chapter has been prepared, which presents in visual form the six P's and the six E's (page 63). There is no special significance to the relative position of the various elements.

By understanding these twelve key words and using them as a check list, the vast majority of all special matters that must be considered in connection with writing Business Interruption Insurance and in dealing with a loss under such a policy will be covered.

The point that is sought to be made is that there is nothing mysterious about the contract. True, there are several areas in the contract that are so worded that they call for the use of judgment. The Business Interruption Insurance contract is quite unique in that, contrary to most insurance contracts, it calls for value judgments (e.g. did the Insured use due diligence and dispatch?) and also for what must be partially subjective opinions (e.g. what will be the *probable* experience of the business in the twelve months following the damage). (To compare wording of BIC Form; see Ch. 8.) Moreover, as has been mentioned, the fact that the insurance industry has seen fit to write this coverage usually in the form of an endorsement attached to a Fire Insurance policy has created a fertile area for controversy, because some of the provisions of the Fire Insurance contract are not compatible with the design of Business Interruption Insurance. The wording of the requirements of the Fire Policy for filing a Proof of Loss is one example in point. (See Ch. 16.)

However, in the hundred or so years that Business Interruption Insurance has been written in the United States, most of these areas of potential conflict have been explored and the issues resolved by able adjusters, who have contributed greatly to the methods of computation to be applied, and by various federal and state courts that have decided about two hundred cases arising out of this type of insurance. The sum total of their collective efforts has been utilized in preparing this volume. It must be kept in mind that much of what other authors have written as well as many of the court decisions are based on policies different in form from those in use today. Care must be taken to account for such differences. In addition, there have been opinions written which depend on some particular local statute or situation that must be taken into consideration. Finally, some of the opinions appear to be incorrect.

Another way to look upon the six P's is as constituting the *Expanding Provisions* of the contract. The first three lay out boundaries for determining that a loss has been suffered by the Insured under the policy, the second three P's create the basis for measuring how much loss was caused by the damage. In the same vein, it is possible to look upon the six E's as the *Limiting Provisions* in that they tend to limit the amount of the loss which has been suffered for which the Insured can collect.

C. Introduction to the Six P's

The first "P" of a Business Interruption Insurance contract is **Parties**. An insurance policy is a contract between an Insurer and one or more Insureds. With the exception of policies issued by syndicates at Lloyd's, most Business Interruption Insurance policies today are issued by a corporation, chartered by one of the several States or by a foreign country, and authorized or approved by each state to engage in the business of issuing such policies therein.

There are few problems that arise with regard to the Insurer insofar as this "P" is concerned. When a claim requires action in a court, the matter of the proper jurisdiction for bringing suit can be an issue. On the whole, however, there is little concerning Insurers as a Party that requires consideration in connection with this type of insurance.

The Insured is the Party to the contract concerning whom problems are likely to arise. Such Party may be an individual, a partnership, a joint enterprise, or a corporation.[3] There may be more than one Party included as an Insured either expressly or by description as a member of a group, e.g., subsidiaries of the named Insured. The named Insured may represent his own interest, or the interest of others, or both.

As are other contracts of insurance, the Business Interruption Insurance policy is based upon the principle of indemnity. This requires that the Party insured have an insurable interest in the subject matter of the policy—a financial stake that would be adversely affected were such subject matter to suffer as a result of damage. (See Comment #2, p. 299.) Under the Business Interruption Insurance policy that subject matter is the Earnings Stream produced by the use of the Property.

The second "P", **Property**, presents a much more complicated situation. This develops primarily because of the early lack of understanding of just what was the purpose to be served by Business Interruption Insurance. The problem has its roots both in the wording of the Business Interruption Insurance policy form and in its relation to the underlying Fire Insurance policy.

As demonstrated earlier, Property can designate the physical material that composes the fabric of an object and it can also designate the intangible property right that results from the dynamic use-potential of that physical object. In connection with this element, the term Property is used herein in the former sense—the physical material. (The dynamic asset aspect is considered under the element of Profit.)[4]

Physical property can be real property, which includes land, buildings and other structures attached to the land which become part of the real property. These are composed primarily of material which encloses space and thereby renders it useful for certain purposes.

In this context, Business Interruption Insurance deals largely with space that is enclosed. Houses, stores, theatres, warehouses and factories are examples of this type of property eligible for Business Interruption Insurance coverage. Even an oil storage tank would qualify as being space contained by materials put together by labor according to a design and dedicated to a use. Bridges, telegraph lines, and railroad tracks probably would not be considered as enclosing space—though they occupy space and meet other criteria. Such structures are also eligible for Business Interruption Insurance coverage and are included within the element of Property. The usual exclusion of underground installations from coverage under a Fire Insurance policy may not be appropriate for business interruption coverage. An interesting question arises in connection with a large chemical installation erected in the open with little, if any, enclosure; is it a building, a structure or just machinery?

Physical property can also be personal property. From the point of view of Business Interruption Insurance, personal property can be divided into three main categories—tools dedicated to production; instruments employed in performing services; and goods designed for ultimate sale. All three types are employed by business enterprises to create an Earnings Stream. All three can constitute the described Property on which the Business Interruption Insurance policy is based.

The third "P" is *Perils*. This refers to the active cause which resulted in the damage to the Property and thereby created financial loss for the Insured.

To be compensable, the Peril must be one covered by the insurance contract. It must be specifically mentioned in the policy or must be reasonably implied as being included therein. It cannot be a Peril which is specifically excluded by the terms of the policy.

Because of the general practice of attaching the Business Interruption Insurance policy form to a policy of Fire Insurance, it is to that contract that one usually looks to see what Perils are covered. The Standard Fire Insurance policy covers "direct loss by fire, lightning and by removal from premises endangered by the perils insured against". Such Perils would apply to Business Interruption Insurance coverage as well. (See Comment #8, p. 315.)

Various extensions of the Perils covered by the basic Fire Insurance policy can be achieved by the addition of supplemental forms to that policy. Among these, the ones which impinge most frequently on the matter of Business Interruption Insurance, is the Extended Coverage Endorsement and various forms of so-called "All Risk" covers.

As has been mentioned earlier, instead of the underlying insurance policy being one against the Peril of fire, it may be a Boiler and Machinery policy, an Inland or Ocean Marine policy, a Multi-Peril or Package policy, or a policy of a different type.[5] The Perils named in such policies may differ from those named in the Fire Insurance policy.

Whatever the nature of the underlying policy and the forms attached thereto, the basic point to remember is that the Perils covered therein are applicable to the Business Interruption Insurance coverage. If a Peril is not covered by the underlying policy, it is not covered by the Business Interruption Insurance policy. (The BIC Form uses a Declarations page; see Ch. 8.)

The first three elements which have been considered up to this point—*Parties, Property* and *Perils*—are necessary ingredients in the formation of a Business Interruption Insurance contract. The next three elements bring into consideration the question of whether a loss has occurred under such a contract.

The fourth "P" stands for *Productivity*. That term indicates that the Property described must possess the following characteristics:

(1) It must have been designed by Man or Nature for a use;
(2) It must have been dedicated to the use for which it was designed or another use;
(3) It must be in a condition to be used;
(4) It must be in a position to be used;
(5) There is a demand or need for its use—and
(6) Through its use, products would have been produced or sales made had no interruption occurred.

If all these characteristics co-exist, the Property is usable for creating an Earnings Stream. It is capable of Productivity.

Termination of Productivity could result, either from the destruction of all of the Property, or from destruction of a part of it vital to any production being carried on by the balance; in either event putting the entire Property out of operation. *Curtailment* of Productivity, on the other hand, could result either from only a part of the Property being put out of operation while the remainder continues to operate normally, or from the slowing down of the entire operation due to damage to part of the Property; in either event, permitting part of the productive process to continue. The total or partial interference with Productivity forms a basis for claim of loss if caused by an insured Peril.

The fifth element is *Period*—this is the time factor, which is the particular hallmark of Business Interruption Insurance. Not that time is an element foreign to the Property Insurance policy, which serves as the base for Business Interruption coverage, since that policy has an inception date when coverage starts, and an expiration date, when coverage ends. For a loss to be recoverable, the damage must occur between those two dates. This provision applies with full force to the Business Interruption coverage as well.

In the case of Property Insurance, however, the damage and the loss both occur at the same time—the loss has been brought into being by the time the fire is extinguished. It may take some time to determine just how much damage was suffered. There may also be continuing repercussions that keep adding to the physical damage after the fire is extinguished; e.g. deterioration of remaining Property, but all of the factors that go into determining the amount of loss are present at the time that the damage occurs.

In the case of a Business Interruption Insurance policy, on the contrary, the physical damage acts merely as a trigger which sets into operation a continuing situation, extending for a Period of time. During this time-span, loss keeps mounting. While the date of the physical damage that triggers the running of time can be fixed with accuracy, the Period over which loss accumulates is much more difficult to determine.

The Business Interruption Insurance policy supplies guidelines that tend to place a time frame around the accumulation of loss. The starting point is obvious—it is when physical damage to Property interrupts the Earnings Stream. If no physical damage occurs—time does not begin to run. Also, if no interruption of the Earnings Stream is caused by the physical damage, time does not start to run. Both physical damage and resultant interruption of the Earnings Stream must be present before the element of Period begins to play its role. The special provisions of the Civil Authority Clause bring into play physical damage to adjacent property. (See Comment #4, p. 305.) Also see Ch. 8 for provisions of BIC Form.

The policy then defines how long a Period of time will be taken into consideration in calculating the loss. Basically, it is the time necessary to rebuild, repair or replace that part of the Property which has been damaged or destroyed using due diligence and dispatch, so that its former productive capacity is restored.

The period of interruption could run beyond the expiration date of the policy.[6] Under a policy which expires on December thirty-first, a fire may occur on December tenth which causes interruption of operations until the middle of June of next year, well after the expiration of the policy term. The policy provides for this contingency by stating: "... not limited by the date of expiration of this policy." In other words, as long as the physical damage occurs within the term of the policy, a loss will be covered even though the Period of loss accumulation runs beyond the expiration date. Nor is it necessary that the policy be renewed for the following year for this result to occur. The obligation of the Insurer to pay all consequent loss is fixed when physical damage occurs within the term of the contract.

The sixth "P" is *Profit*; it is also the third element involved in the calculation of the amount of loss. Under the Gross Earnings form, for the purposes of this text, the word, "Profit," is used to indicate the dollars entering the Earnings Stream (i.e., the money earned by the Insured's operations) over and above the cost to the Insured of the goods sold or the materials which went into the product manufactured. It is the source of the funds out of which to pay labor, the overhead and administrative costs and to produce a surplus after taxes.

This surplus may be kept in the business enterprise as retained earnings or may be distributed in whole or in part to the investors as dividends on their investment.

Withers (p.2) introduces the term "Actual Cash Value of Income." The concept apparently is to parallel the term Actual Cash Value as used in the Standard Fire Insurance policy. Actual Cash Value of property is a measure of one of its attributes—its material value. It states a formula for expressing that attribute in terms of money. The other attribute of property—its Earning Potential—is already expressed in dollars. The term "Actual Cash Value of Income" translates into "the dollar value of dollars received" and appears to be redundant.

Under certain conditions, the business operations may not have produced enough Profit to show such a surplus or, in still more adverse circumstances, not enough to cover all of the overhead and administrative costs incurred in the operations. While it may be that the business enterprise was operating at a loss in an accounting sense, this loss had been reduced by the amount of Profit that the business operations was able to produce. If operations were interrupted by damage to the Property, even this limited Earnings Stream would dry up and the Insured would be financially damaged to the extent that the limited Profit was no longer available to offset continuing expenses.

If no Profit at all would have been earned by the continuing business operation during what becomes the Period of interruption caused by the damage, then there is, by definition, no loss of Profit for which the Insured can make claim. Such a condition could exist if it would have been necessary, absent any damage, to sell goods at less than the cost of materials. It could also have resulted from an absence of sufficient orders to warrant the manufacture of any products by the factory. An absence of necessary materials or labor to carry on operations would also create a no Profit situation.

The subject of just what items are to be included in determining whether Profit was lost will be considered at length later in the text.

D. Introduction to the Six E's

Just as the six P's are necessary elements in perfecting a loss under a contract of Business Interruption Insurance, so the six E's have an effect on the amount that the Insured ultimately collects. And just as the P's are sub-divided into two groups of three each, so the six E's are similarly subdivided. The first three—**Extent**, **Experience** and **Exclusions**—are outside of direct control by the Insured; while the second three—**Effort**, **Extras** and **Enough**—do involve, to some extent, action by the Insured.

The first E is *Extent*. This refers to the extent to which the number of dollars to be collected by the Insured for his loss may be limited by the provisions of his policy.

Such limiting provisions are found both in the underlying Fire Insurance policy and in the Business Interruption Insurance policy form. The basic Fire Insurance policy is written for a stated amount of dollars. That puts a ceiling on the amount of money that may be collected in the event of a loss. In some cases, the underlying policy form contains a specified number of dollars applicable to the Business Interruption Insurance coverage; in such cases that amount becomes the ceiling.[7]

Besides the ultimate ceiling, the Fire Insurance policy has certain subsidiary restrictions. One of them limits recovery to the actual cash value of the property. Obviously, this has no relation to a Business Interruption policy where the loss can exceed the actual cash value of the property damaged.

The second is an exclusion from recovery of consequential loss resulting from business interruption. Of course, the purpose of the Business Interruption Insurance policy form is to supplant this limitation. (See Comment #11, p. 325.)

The third limits recovery to the insurable interest of the Insured. This invokes the basic insurance principle of Indemnity. (See Comment #2, p. 299) This limitation extends to all coverages under the policy, including business interruption. A fourth limits recovery to the amount of the loss. This is where this E—Extent—fits into the picture vis-a-vis Business Interruption Insurance.

In practice, the determination of the Extent of loss sustained by the Insured under the business interruption coverage is usually the product of informed judgment based on experience. What the Earnings Stream would have been had no interruption occurred can be estimated, but absolute accuracy is not obtainable. This situation is aggravated when the Insured does not restore the Property to its former condition because, then, even the Period of interruption must be estimated without the benefit of experience.

The one fixed point in this sea of uncertainties is the requirement that the Insured must establish the amount of the loss that he has sustained; he has the burden of proof.

The second "E" is *Experience*. This focuses in on the fact that the bases for determining the amount of loss are to be drawn from the Experience of the Insured's own business operation. Academic theory, government figures, industry statistics and similar guidelines may serve as a background against which to compare facts alleged to represent the Insured's Experience but, in the last analysis, it is his own Experience, as finally established, which must prevail.

Two aspects of Experience are to be considered. The first is "the experience of the business before the date of damage or destruction." Although the loss suffered will accumulate *after* the time of the damage, past history must serve as a jumping-off place. That is because the past experience of a business supplies a basis of historical fact from which a projection into the Period of interruption can be made. If a graph were to be constructed showing the development of the Earnings Stream in past years, and if the assumption can be made that no changes would be introduced, then the graph showing past results can be trended into the future as a continuing line, a simple straight line projection.

However, things are rarely this simple. In the first place, it is to the past Experience of a similar period of the year that our attention is directed by the reference to past Experience. Moreover, past Experience must be examined to see whether the conditions of the past under consideration had been similar to those of the Period of interruption with which the loss calculation is concerned.

The discussion to this point has been based on the assumption that business conditions would remain static and that, at the time of damage, it could reasonably be expected that the future would be a duplication of the past. Given the dynamism that usually accompanies business enterprises, however, such uniformity of operations and results often is not present. The business enterprise is either expanding or contracting, gaining or losing profitability. The Earnings Stream during the period of interruption may not be comparable to that of the similar period in the past.

This fact is recognized by the policy in its second reference to Experience, which is to the "probable future experience of the business had no damage occurred." Here, again, is an example of the "speculative" nature of Business Interruption Insurance that makes the subject most challenging.

Without attempting at this stage to discuss the many ramifications that are inherent in the language employed in the policy form, suffice it to say for now that there are limitations on the Insured's recovery imposed by the Experience, past and future, of the business. (For change in language in BIC Form see Ch. 16.)

The third "E" is *Exclusions*. These are certain named types of damage and certain causes of damage or of loss for which the Insurer does not assume liability even though they may directly or indirectly result from damage to the described Property and even though they may create or add to a diminution of the Earnings Stream.

Some of these exclusions or limitations appear in the underlying Standard Fire Insurance policy; some are contained in the riders and forms usually attached to a Fire Insurance policy; while others are peculiar to the Business Interruption Insurance form, itself. Examples of the latter type of Exclusion include the increased amount of loss that results from the enforcement of a building code, or the action of strikers or from the acts of third persons which deprive the Insured of a business opportunity he otherwise would have enjoyed; an opportunity created by orders, contracts, leases or licenses. A business opportunity would result from the concurrence of the need of a third person for the product of the Insured's operations and the Insured's ability to meet that need through the productive capacity of the described Property, which concurrence has already led or is expected to lead to an order for such products. (See Comment #7, p. 313.)

There are other types of specific Exclusions and of limitations on recovery that are in the nature of Exclusions. These will be discussed later in the text.

It should be apparent that the three "E's", so far mentioned—*Extent, Experience* and *Exclusions*—while affecting the amount of loss which the Insured may recover, are basically matters over which the Insured's actions can exert little or no influence following the damage to the described Property. Not so, with the next three "E's".

The fourth "E" is *Effort*. With this item we leave the area of restrictions or the putting of parameters around the amount paid and move into the area of how the acts of the Insured may affect the amount he can collect.

Effort refers to the obligation placed on the Insured to mitigate the loss—to reduce the amount of loss. In effect, this is an application of the fundamental principle requiring good faith on the part of both parties. The Insured is expected to act just as he would have acted if he had no insurance protection; as if it were his own money that was being lost every day that the interruption continues.

To back up this principle, current Business Interruption Insurance policy forms recite certain specific tasks the Insured must undertake to the extent that they are possible. Pressure on the Insured to use his best Effort to shorten the period of interruption is created by the inclusion of a provision that the Insurer will be liable for loss of Gross Earning(s) during only such a period of time as it would have taken the Insured to repair the damage had he acted diligently. The Insured himself must bear any additional loss suffered because he had not acted with due diligence and dispatch, thereby lengthening the Period of interruption.

This same measure of time-loss is applied arbitrarily where the damage is never repaired. The measure is the theoretical time it would have taken to make the repairs if the Insured had acted diligently and had made the repairs.[8]

Similar pressure is put upon the Insured by the Resumption of Operations clause. This, in effect, reduces the amount of recovery by the savings that could be achieved by the use of alternate means of production if the Insured made the Effort to take advantage of them. (See Comment #5, p. 309.)

The fifth "E" is *Extras*. This word is used to describe expenses incurred by the Insured in an attempt to reduce the amount of the ultimate loss. These are out-of-the-ordinary expenses. The ordinary expenses to repair and replace the damaged property are covered by the Fire Insurance policy. If the Extras do, in fact, result in a reduction of the loss, the Insurer will reimburse the Insured to the extent that the loss was so reduced.

These Extras are often referred to as "expediting expenses." They fall into three categories: those that speed up the resumption of operations, those that continue operations during the period of interruption but at a higher than normal cost, and those incurred, after operations are resumed, to refill inventory.

An example of the first category would be the use of air freight to bring in a replacement machine, where normally a rail shipment would be used. To the extent that the extra cost of the air shipment is offset by the savings to the Insurer due to the resultant shortening of the period of interruption, such cost should be and is recoverable.

An example of the second type would be the hiring of temporary quarters in which to carry on business operations while the damage to the described Property is being repaired. Extra rent, cost of moving back and forth, extra advertising and similar expenditures could be justified as a way to maintain the Earnings Stream flowing during the interruption.

Some types of business must be kept going at all costs; banks, newspapers and laundries are frequently cited as examples. For such businesses a type of contract known as Extra Expense Insurance has been devised. The requirement that a savings in the amount of loss must be achieved in order to secure reimbursement has been removed in this contract.

The third example of expediting expense is applicable where normal inventory is depleted during the period of interruption to maintain sales.

It should be noted that the risk is on the Insured. He may pay out the extra expense and not reduce the amount of the ultimate loss. Such would be the case where the replacement machine brought in by air could not be put into operation, due to a lack of electric power, until after the railroad would have delivered it anyway.

The Insured may pay out more for Extras than the amount by which the loss is reduced and thus be able to recoup only part of the Extras. The desire to maintain operations as close to normal as possible or to restore normal operations as soon as possible would be the motivation behind the Insured's actions. From the Insurer's point of view, there is everything to gain and nothing to lose in encouraging the Insured in undertaking such Extras. (For handling of Extra Expense under BIC Form see Ch. 16.)

The sixth E is *Enough*. This is an oblique reference to the fact that the Insured must carry enough insurance if he wants to collect his loss in full. Its focus is not the obvious fact that the face amount of the policy must be as great as the amount of the loss if the Insured is to collect fully. Rather it is the provision found in most Business Interruption Insurance policy forms called a Coinsurance Clause, which penalizes the Insured if the face amount of the policy does not equal an agreed percentage of the total amount at risk—the amount of money that the Earnings Stream would have produced in a period of twelve months if no damage had been suffered—referred to as the Business Interruption Value.

If, for example, the policy provides that the Insured shall carry a face amount of insurance equal to fifty percent of the Business Interruption Value and he fulfills the obligation, then he will be paid his loss in full up to the face amount of the policy. If he fails to do so, then he is penalized and must go uncompensated for part of his loss. The percentage of the loss that the Insured cannot collect is determined by a fraction; the denominator being the amount that should have been carried and the numerator being the amount of deficiency. For that part, he is considered to be a coinsurer.[9]

This completes an enumeration and brief examination of the six E's—those items which may limit the amount that an Insured may recover in the event that there has been an interruption of the Earnings Stream as a result of damage to Property insured under an existing policy of Business Interruption Insurance.

E. Summary

Early in the text it was stated that there was no mystery to the subject of Business Interruption Insurance. The assertion is now made that the nature of the coverage and the basic structure of the contract can be grasped by anyone who is prepared to learn the six P's and the six E's. Once these elements are understood, their application becomes a matter of simply ascertaining the facts in any given situation.

Undoubtedly, the way in which certain contract provisions are phrased—the subjective and even speculative input required for vital calculations—makes the determination of the facts more difficult than is usually the case under a Fire Insurance policy. There is more room for possible differences of opinion. Nevertheless, the guidelines for determining the facts are set forth fairly clearly in most instances. The second part of this volume will be devoted to an analysis of their application in practice.

STRUCTURE
OF THE BUSINESS
INTERRUPTION CONTRACT

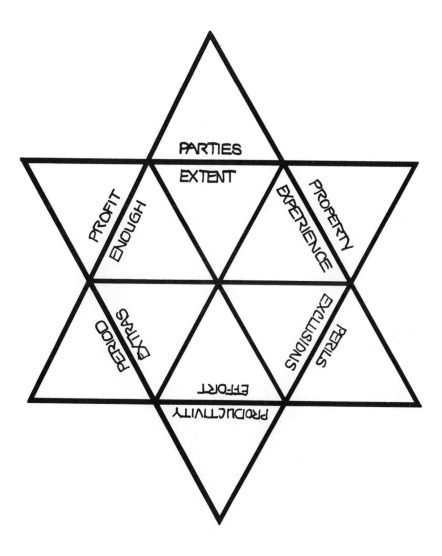

There is no significance to the position of the items.

Chapter 5 Notes

1. National Union Fire Insurance Co. v. Anderson-Pritchard Oil Co.

2. Manufacturer's Mutual Fire Insurance Co. v. Royal Indemnity Co. (dissenting opinion)
    The oft-repeated statement that the function of Business Interruption Insurance is to do for the Insured what his business operation would have done had no damage occurred has its limitations.
    One of these involves the loss of future income which would have been earned by additional productive capacity which was in the process of being developed at the time of the damage. If the date when this additional capacity was scheduled to come on stream was later than the date when operations are restored, no recovery is allowed even though the damage caused a delay in the schedule for starting up the additional productive capacity. The financial loss suffered by the Insured as a result of the delay is not covered. Great Northern Oil Co. v. St. Paul Fire & Marine Ins. Co. citing the cases of General Ins. Co. of America v. Pathfinder Petroleum Co., Fidelity-Phenix Ins. Co. v. Benedict Coal Corp. See: *Adjusting Business Interruption Losses*, Walter Boston, College of Insurance Library, New York City (General File U.S. 010) October, 1953.

3. A voluntary association of a group of utilities was named as Insured in New England Gas & Electric Co. v. Ocean Accident and Guarantee Corp.
    See also: National Union F. Ins. Co. v. Anderson-Pritchard Oil Corp.

4. "Popularly speaking, the thing to which the damage is apprehended is said to be the thing insured, or that on which the insurance is; and the cause of damage apprehended is said to be the thing insured against. But, strictly, the matter insured is, that the assured shall sustain no damage, the thing insured against is, that the event shall do no damage to the assured because he shall be compensated. Here the thing to which the damage was apprehended was the goods and, the cause of damage apprehended, was the perils enumerated affecting them or the ship. If the goods are uninjured, no damage was apprehended to the profits." Pollack C.B. in Smith v. Reynolds (p. 1186).

5. For examples see: Hartford Steam Boiler Insp. & Ins. Co. v. Schwartzman Packing Co.; Anderson & Middleton Lumber Co. v. Lumbermen's Mut. Cas. Co.; Manufacturers Mut. F. Ins. Co. v. Royal Indemnity Co.; National Children's Expositions Corp. v. Anchor Ins. Co. Great Northern Oil Co. v. St. Paul F&M Ins. Co.

6. See: Harper v. Phoenix Ins. Co.

7. Victory Container Corp. v. Sphere Ins. Co.

8.   See: Anchor Toy Corp. v. Am. Eagle F. Ins. Co.
              General Insurance Co. v. Pathfinder Petroleum Co.
              First Investment Co. v. Vulcan Underwriters.

9.   Cf: Industro Motive Corp. v. Morris Agency, Inc..

6

The P's Revisited

Parties. Property. Perils. Productivity. Period. Profit

A. Introduction

Before closing Part I of this book, the part dealing with theory, it may be well to take another look at the six P's and the six E's, this time in somewhat greater depth. An examination of the application of broad concepts to particular issues and situations will provide a broader base for the practical application of theory to the daily work of selling and servicing Business Interruption Insurance policies, which will be undertaken in the second part of this volume.

B. Parties

1. As stated earlier, in order to have rights under an insurance policy, the Insured asserting such rights must establish that he has an insurable interest in the subject matter of the policy—a financial stake that would be adversely affected were such subject matter to suffer because of physical damage to the described Property.[1]

As we have seen, an owner can have several kinds of insurable interest in a single piece of Property. He has an interest in the physical fabric of the Property: an interest which is insurable under a Property Insurance policy. He has an interest in the availability of the Property for the owner's use: an interest insurable under the early types of Use and Occupancy policy and under some types of valued Business Interruption Insurance policies. Also, he has an interest in the Earnings Stream produced by the use of the Property: an interest insurable under a Business Interruption Insurance policy.[2]

Where several persons have an insurable interest in the continuation of the business operation, thought should be given to naming all of them as Insureds under a single policy. This is particularly the case where a large business enterprise divides its operations among several subsidiary units or even separate corporate entities. The business enterprise should be insured as a whole regardless of the arbitrary election of the Insured to recognize profit at any given facet of the enterprise. This principle has not always been recognized by the courts.[3]

One who is not an owner may have an insurable interest. So, a lessee of machinery or a tenant conducting business on the real estate could properly be named as Insured under a Business Interruption Insurance policy.

A Party who has invested time, effort and money, or any of them, to gain for himself a direct share of the income developed by the use of Property also would have an insurable interest therein. Thus, a salesman, whose commission is payable only when merchandise has been shipped to fill the order that he has secured, has an insurable interest in the continued availability of the plant and equipment to produce the goods ordered.

Where vending machines or laundry equipment owned by a third person are located on the described premises under an agreement to share the money collected with the Insured, the latter has an insurable interest in the earnings derived by the use of such equipment under a Business Interruption Insurance policy. So, too, a patent holder, who is paid royalties by his licensee when the latter produces items under the license, has an insurable interest in the continued availability of the equipment used in such production.[4]

2. An extension of this principle is present in what is known as Contingent Business Interruption Insurance. This involves the insurable interest which a Party would have in the continued flow of goods from a supplier's plant, where the availability of such goods is vital to the continued operation of his own business. The supplier's plant is considered a Contributing Property. The reverse situation is equally the basis for an insurable interest—where the continued need for goods by a customer in the operation of the customer's business is the source of the orders which keep the Insured's business operating. Such are called Recipient Properties. Under such a Contingent Business Interruption Insurance policy, the physical Property which is described in the policy is that of the supplier or the customer. The subject matter of the insurance, however, is the Insured's own Earnings Stream. In this respect, a Business Interruption Insurance policy differs from a policy of Fire Insurance in which the Property described and the subject matter of the insurance are the same. (Contingent Business Interruption Insurance has been available since 1927.)[5]

C. Property

1. At an earlier point, three examples were given of the loss that might be suffered as the result to damage to a piece of machinery. In each case the use-potential of the press was different. In the first instance it was regarded as a tool of production in manufacturing; in the second, as equipment used to serve

customers' needs and in a third, as merchandise held for sale. From the description of these situations, it becomes clear that the use-potential of a piece of Property bears a relationship to the use to which it is has been dedicated by its owner. While it is equally true that the design of the Property exercises a restraining influence on its possible use, the loss suffered by its owner, if for any reason it cannot be used, relates directly to the use to which that particular owner has dedicated the Property. Not that a piece of Property must necessarily be put to the use for which it was originally designed; it may be dedicated by its possessor to another use. Thus a drumstick may be used, in an emergency, as a baton by a band leader.[6]

In the Business Interruption Insurance policy there are two ways in which the term "Property" is used. It sometimes refers to the Property which produces the Earnings Stream and other times to the premises at or on which such Property is located.

Insofar as the underlying Fire Insurance policy is concerned, no doubt can arise as to which application is involved. Although different terms are used— such as "the property," "the property insured," "the building described," and "the premises"—no difficulty should be encountered in determining to which variety of Property the term is applied.

The situation is not as clear with the Business Interruption Insurance policy forms currently in use. A careful reading of the forms will indicate that in about one-half the instances where the term "Property" is used, it refers to the geographical location where the Property exists. (See: Gross Earnings Form #3, clauses 1,3,7,9, and 15.)

At other places in the policy form, the term appears clearly to refer to the Property which is producing the Earnings Stream. (See: Gross Earnings Form #3, clauses 2, 3, 17 and 18. Clause 13 contains the phrase, "the occupancy as described herein." This would appear to have no connection with occupancy in the phrase "use and occupancy," but appears to relate back to the Fire Insurance policy where the nature of the occupancy was important.) While the proper application can be made in each case, it does indicate the need for care in reading such policies.

2. How exact does the description of the Property have to be? Normally, the geographic location will be described by street name and number. A number of cases have been brought to court to extend a geographic description to cover Property added as an additional structure after the policy was issued, or to minor structures used in the business operation in conjunction with the major buildings that were described.[7] While such questions might revolve about the issue of increase of risk rather than of adequacy of description, they do point out the need to make the description of location as specific as possible.

A full statement of all locations is advisable if later problems are to be avoided. Sometimes an Owner will give his mailing address when asked for the location of the Property, even though production may be carried on elsewhere.

Raw materials, dyes and molds, goods in process, computers and other kinds of property, which are vital for continuing operations may be stored off-premises. The garage which stores the specially equipped delivery vehicles may be at a different location. Buildings once separate may have been joined together, as a practical matter, for operating purposes.[8] Also, interruption of operations may stem from damage to a minor building not included in the description, but used in connection with the business operation.

Interruption of operations may result from damage to Property temporarily away from the described premises. In one case, a machine sent out to be repaired was further damaged at the repair shop. In a more complicated situation, skins purchased by the Insured abroad had been delivered to the plant of another firm for processing, prior to ultimate delivery to the Insured to be made into fur coats. The skins were destroyed at the processor's plant. The damage was to the Insured's Earnings Stream in the course of his business operations but the physical damage did not occur to Property on the described premises, as set forth in the Gross Earnings form.[9] So, too, a business interruption loss due to the interruption of foundry operations in Building #1 (specifically described in the policy) when dyes and patterns used in the foundry operations stored in Building #2 (20-feet away) were destroyed by fire, was not covered.[10] Such situations should be provided for in the policy.

The Owner may be in the process of building another plant in the same community. While "additions" and new structures on the described premises added after the inception of the policy would automatically be covered, a new structure located on different premises would not be so insured.

Under the Business Interruption Insurance policy form, the same conditions apply to buildings protected by automatic sprinklers as is provided in the Automatic Sprinkler Clause. The addition of an Alterations and New Buildings Clause is wise before reconstruction or enlargement of such a building is undertaken, otherwise protection will not be extended to the new construction beyond 15 days time. This probably would apply to operations to be carried on in the new construction.[11]

While the term "Property" extends to include intangible or inchoate rights in physical property, it does not extend to any goodwill which may emanate from the operation of the business enterprise through the use of the physical property.[12]

3. A description, listing all of the individual instruments of productive Property that function in unison to carry on a particular manufacturing operation, would not normally be feasible. A statement of the business or occupation in which the Property is used has to suffice.

Tools of production are usually machines employed to produce goods. They can be described in a policy by the use for which they have been designed, such as drill presses, screw machines, canning machinery or power lifts. They can also be described by the use to which they have been dedicated, such as paint mixing equipment, coal mining equipment, or saw mill equipment. It is possible, further, to describe them in connection with their ownership, such as, "the machinery and equipment of Antique Furniture Manufacturing Corporation and used in connection with its business."

The category of "instruments" covers a wide range of objects from the scissors used by a barber to the computer used by a bank. They are service-oriented tools and equipment rather than product-creating equipment. Hand tools used by workers, laboratory equipment and office equipment are other examples of such instruments. Automotive repair equipment would also belong in this group. A reference to the instruments and equipment used in connection with the business would certainly remove any doubt of their being included in the property described.

4. Goods related to the manufacturing process can be divided into two subclasses. The first sub-class relates to the products being produced in a factory. There are usually three kinds of such products depending on the stages of preparation which the materials have undergone—raw materials, goods in process and finished stock.

The first kind—raw materials—were purchased by the factory for processing into finished goods. Without raw material to put into production, the manufacturing process would grind to a halt. Over the years, various provisions have been incorporated in Business Interruption Insurance policies in an attempt to compensate the Insured for the interruption of production resulting from the damage to or destruction of raw materials. In some cases, the raw materials alone may have been damaged, as in the case of the destruction by fire of seasoned lumber that was to be used for furniture manufacturing. In others, both the raw material and the tools of production may have been damaged.

At the time in history when Underwriters were focusing their attention on the process of production, they sought to draft policy form provisions which would limit their exposure to such period of time as the raw materials, which were available prior to damage, would enable the plant to keep operating. This could be a lesser period than the time required to restore the tools of production to operating condition, and would thus reduce the Insurer's liability. Or it could be a longer period and increase the loss. For example, if at the time of a fire there were only enough skins to run a leather factory for two weeks, that was the limit of time for which the Insurer would be liable, even though it took four weeks to repair the damaged machinery. Even if there had been no fire, the production line would have been shut down anyway after two weeks, due to lack of raw material with which to operate.

This type of provision is no longer necessary, now that it is the Earnings Stream that is being insured. The forms that have been in general use contain a definition of Raw Stock, namely, "material in the state in which the Insured receives it for conversion by the Insured into finished stock." (The raw stock may be some other producer's finished material.)

The second kind is stock in process. In most manufacturing processes, some period of time elapses from the time raw stock enters into the production process until it emerges as a finished product. Sometimes raw stock has to be conditioned before it is ready to enter the manufacturing process—skins have to be tanned before they can be turned into shoes; wool cloth has to be sponged before it is cut for suits. If the once raw stock is damaged while undergoing such processing, the procedure has to start over again when replacement raw material is available.

Also, during the various stages of manufacture, there may be processes which involve the passage of time. The aging of whiskey and alcoholic products is an example of such intermediate processing. In the BIC Form, this commodity is specifically included as Finished Stock.

It is obvious that the value of the raw stock is enhanced as time and labor are added to it. During this period of processing, the stock is known as "stock in process." This, too, is defined in the manufacturing form, as "raw stock which has undergone aging, seasoning, mechanical or other process of manufacture at the location(s) herein described but which has not become finished stock."

Finished stock is the third kind. It is "stock manufactured by the Insured which in the ordinary course of the Insured's business is ready for packing, shipping or sale." Finished goods have thus moved out of the productive process and have become part of the stock of merchandise that the factory has for sale. (Only finished stock is defined in the BIC Form.)

There are occasions when stock is transferred from one department to another, and even from one corporation to another, as it moves from the raw to the finished state. To the first unit, the product that it passes on to the second is its finished product, while the second unit takes it in as its raw material upon which to apply further manufacturing processes.

With respect to finished stock, any profit above the cost of replacing it cannot be recovered. Gross Earnings Form #4—"Manufacturing", for example, provides that, "This Company shall not be liable for any loss resulting from damage to or destruction of finished stock nor for the time required to reproduce such stock."

This exclusion is based on the fact that finished stock represents the product of *past* activities. In this respect, it must be differentiated from the thrust of the Business Interruption Insurance concept which considers what would be the consequences if, at some time in the future, finished goods were not coming off of the production line. If the manufacturer wants to insure the difference in amount between replacement cost and the ultimate sales price of the goods already manufactured, he can do so under a type of Profits Insurance policy known as Selling Price Insurance.

A second sub-class of finished goods is the stock of finished merchandise that is held for sale by a distributor, wholesaler or retailer. No special problems arise as to it. The non-manufacturing form of Gross Earnings provides that the selling price is the basis for loss determination.

Side activities carried on by the Insured which produce earnings but do not require the use of the premises would not be covered unless specifically mentioned.[13]

D. Perils

1. A question often raised is whether, in order for a loss to exist under a Business Interruption Insurance policy, the interruption of business must result from actual physical damage caused by an insured Peril to the described Property or whether there also will be coverage for a loss resulting from the threat of damage from such a Peril, even though no physical damage ever occurs.

If smoke emanating from a fire in an adjacent building penetrates the Insured's premises and permeates the stock of men's clothing held for sale, the loss of business during the period in which sales are suspended in order to remove the smoke odors from the clothing forms the basis for a claim under a Business Interruption Insurance policy. But what if smoke from the adjacent building merely frightened customers and employees so that they fled the premises, and no physical damage to the stock resulted? Or what if the acrid odors of burned debris permeated the restaurant next door to the fire damaged property so that patrons could not be accommodated?

In the Princess Garment case, where the described Property was not physically damaged by the insured Peril, the Insured's employees were in the process of moving a stock of goods from the basement of the Insured's building to a higher story to salvage them from threatening flood waters when they were ordered out of the building by the fire department, which feared that the building would become involved in the fire which was sweeping through the neighborhood at the same time. The fire never actually reached the Insured's building, but the flood waters did, and they damaged the goods remaining in the basement. The actual case where this situation arose involved only a Fire Insurance policy. There was only a threat of fire, but the court allowed the Insured to collect under his Fire Insurance policy for the water damage to his abandoned goods.[14] Had there been Business Interruption coverage as well, should the Insured have been allowed to collect for any loss of income resulting from the delay in replacing the damaged goods?

This type of problem, which might appear somewhat far-fetched, became pertinent in the 1960's and the early 1970's when outbreaks of rioting and looting in a number of communities resulted in the imposing of curfews and other restrictions over wide areas, well beyond the site of the actual rioting. Restrictions on the sale of liquor in such remote areas interfered not only with the business of package liquor stores but also cut down on the business of restaurants, whose clientele stayed away when they could not buy a drink with their dinners. There had been no damage to the physical Property described caused by an insured Peril, i.e., rioting and civil commotion.

However, it was claimed that this type of loss was covered under the Civil Authorities Clause, which applied to an interruption of business brought about by an order of civil authority denying access by the Insured and others to the Insured's Property because of the threat to life and limb posed by the dangerous conditions of Property (other than the Insured's) which had been damaged by a Peril named in the Insured's policy. The classic example, often cited, involves the danger of the collapse of the wall of a nearby building which has been damaged by fire where, to prevent injury to passersby should the wall fall, the police or fire department has closed off traffic on the street leading to the Insured's place of business and will not allow anyone to enter his building. There has been no physical damage to the Insured's Property. The power of civil authority is being exercised primarily to avoid physical injury to members of the public. (See Comment #4, p. 305.)

To cover such situations, protection against the Perils expressly mentioned in the underlying Property Insurance policy had been extended by a specific provision of the Business Interruption Insurance policy form to include loss resulting from action of civil authorities which results in loss due to the interruption of access to the Insured's premises. On the surface, this extension would appear to apply equally to the curfew cases where, because of distant riots, civil authorities limited the availability of access to the Insured's premises. This argument served as the basis for some of the claims made against Insurers in the curfew cases.

The position taken by Insurers was that there still had to be damages on the described premises despite the language of the Civil Authority Clause.

A number of cases involving Business Interruption Insurance claims resulting from such curfews have reached the courts. The results have not been uniform. Some state courts found the Insurer liable for the resulting business interruption loss; while others did not. The issue has yet to be finally resolved.[15]

The adoption in 1968 of an amended wording to the Civil Authority Clause was designed to resolve any ambiguities in this regard. It reads, ". . . resulting directly from an interruption of business as covered hereunder, . . . when, as a direct result of damage to or deterioration *of property adjacent* [italics added] to the premises herein described by the peril(s) insured against, access to such described premises is specifically prohibited . . . ." Bardwell (p. 51) points out that the new wording requires that the "order of civil authority must be the *direct* result of damage rather than the existence of a peril." Now actual damage must be suffered by "adjacent" property; the order must result from such damage and only loss from interruption of business is covered. The new language undercuts previous arguments on both sides—that the damage has to be suffered by the described premises or that the fear of injury is sufficient to give rise to a cause of action under the policy, however remote the scene of actual damage.[16] (The word "adjacent" is omitted in the BIC Form.)

Some minor questions are not solved by the present wording. How close is "adjacent"?[17] As of what moment in time does the two week period commence— the day of the damage or of the order? Must denial of access be complete, or can denial limited to certain people—e.g., customers—while employees are admitted, result in a partial loss?

It should be kept in mind, however, that this discussion pertains only to those situations where there has been no physical damage to the Insured's property. Thus, if there is damage to the *described* Property and, because of the action of civil authorities repairs are held up, the two week limitation would not apply. Here due diligence and the period of interruption will be the issue. What if the curfew is lifted in three days, but the period of interruption is extended beyond two weeks because of additional damage to the described Property resulting from the fact that the owner could not gain access to prevent its deterioration. Should the period of extension be limited to two weeks so that suspension or operations after that time is not covered? How "direct" is the further damage?

2. Any threat advanced as the basis of a claim must be related to a Peril covered under the Property Insurance policy. Some years ago, a serious interruption of business occurred in Philadelphia when an outbreak of Legionnaire's disease frightened away potential guests of the Bellevue-Stratford Hotel.[18] Since the hotel's Property Insurance did not insure against this type of Peril, the Insured could gain no relief under the attached Business Interruption Insurance from the financial loss it suffered. (Steps have been taken to remedy this deficiency.)[19]

In our complex society, there exist many such threats which adversely affect the successful continuation of an Earnings Stream. Violence by strikers; questions of the safety of certain airplanes; the danger of hijacking or bomb threat; the derailment of tank cars carrying dangerous chemicals; accidents at nuclear plants; looting which occurs during blackouts; power failures or power slow-downs because of inadequate fuel supplies, and plant closure due to air and water pollution from operations—all are sources of loss of income that have occurred within recent history.

The use of sources of nuclear energy, albeit under greater safety regulations, creates not only the potential for loss because of the physical contamination of Property caused by the leakage of radioactive materials from such installations, but the even greater potential of loss due to extended periods of government-ordered non-accessibility to use the Property in an area which has been contaminated.

The normal form of Fire policy currently offered to the public by the insurance industry excludes perils that result from nuclear reactors and also excludes from the definition of the word "fire" any nuclear reaction or nuclear radiation or radioactive contamination. This would carry over to the Business Interruption Insurance coverage.

In some cases, damage to physical property may underlay the financial loss. In other cases, it can be fear of bodily injury alone. The providing of insurance against business interruption developing from such causes is a problem with which the insurance industry is attempting to cope.

E. Productivity

1. Various characteristics of Property were earlier mentioned as prerequisites for Property to possess the necessary element of Productivity. Further discussion would now seem appropriate.

Before it is possible for Property to create an Earnings Stream, it must be in existence. Yet, for the purposes of Business Interruption Insurance, Property which is not yet fully operational at the time of damage can be the source of loss. Such would be the case with Property which is in the process of being built or constructed. It raises the interesting question of when Productivity must exist to establish a claim.

There is a provision in the Alterations and New Building Clause found in the Gross Earnings form which bears specifically on the question of new or additional facilities. It states that "the length of time for which this Company shall be liable shall be determined as otherwise provided herein but such determined length of time shall be applied and the loss hereunder calculated from the date that business operations would have begun had no loss occurred." Similar language appears in the BIC Form.

Such would be the case where an insurance policy is issued on a building in process of construction or where, within the insured plant, equipment for carrying on a new process is being installed at the inception of the policy. Productivity has not been established when the policy is issued because the Property is not in a condition to be used. If, however, by the time damage occurs, Productivity has already commenced, a compensable claim could be established for the interruption of such Productivity. Taking the situation a step further, suppose that Productivity had not started up at the time of the damage, but would have started up during the Period of interruption, had no loss occurred. Claim can be made for the interruption in activity during so much of the Period of interruption as Productivity would have existed. Thus, if a machine scheduled to be in operation by June 1 is damaged on May 15, so that it cannot be put into operation until June 15, a claim may be made for loss of Productivity from June 1 to June 15.[20] Conversely, if production had not started up at the time of the damage and was not scheduled to start up prior to the date when the damage can be repaired, no loss can be claimed.[21]

For further example, suppose work on new equipment was expected to be completed in four months time. Repair of fire damage stopped the work on the new equipment for two months. There is no basis for a claim because there would have been no Productivity from this new equipment during the two month repair period. The fact that the time when the equipment will come on stream and become productive has been delayed for two months is disregarded under the terms of the contract unless specifically provided. (See Part I, Ch. 8 for discussion of impact of wording of BIC Form.)

Where actual construction of a new structure has not as yet started, but the design has been drawn and the components have been ordered and the production schedule calls for the structure to be operating and producing income before the time when the fire damage to the building can be repaired, the Insured should be entitled to recover for lost income from the time that anticipated productivity would have started up on the theory that the new structure is "under construction."

2. As stated, Property which has not been designed in a usable form, either by Nature or by Man, cannot be used productively. Conversely, it is necessary that the design be one which provides for usability in the production of income. History is replete with examples of machines that did not work because there was something wrong with their design. A coin-operated coffee dispensing machine is taken off of the market because it overfills the cups of customers. Cans, designed to be packed under a high vacuum, leak air along the side seam. The design plans must go back to the drawing board and, in the meantime, the Property intended to produce income stands idle because it cannot be used productively.

If a stock of medical supplies had been condemned by the health authorities because it was contaminated prior to the time the fire occurred, any financial loss resulting from the curtailment of sales of such medicines after a fire until the stock was replaced would not be the basis of a business interruption claim, because there could have been no Productivity from such merchandise. If, on the other hand, it was the fire that caused the contamination, a valid claim could be made for the loss of Productivity that was caused.

3. Not only must the Property exist and be adequately designed for producing income but the person in control of it must actually have dedicated that Property to an income producing role to bring it within the context of a Business Interruption Insurance policy. Thus, a person who buys a sewing machine, not for the purpose of making goods to sell and not in the course of a business trading in sewing machines, has not dedicated the machine to produce income. Obsolete machinery in a factory, put aside as no longer economically usable in making the product for which it was designed, is not dedicated to producing an income.

The Insured may have dedicated the Property to the use intended by its designer or he may have adapted it to some other use. The use to which it has been dedicated or adapted is usually specifically or indirectly mentioned in the policy in connection with a description of the nature of the Insured's business or the process in which the Property is to be used. It is possible that after the issuance of the policy, but before damage was suffered by the Property, its use in the productive process was changed by the Insured. It is its potential for producing income in its dedicated new use that must be considered in calculating the amount of loss. It is also possible to make claim where there was an established plan at the time of the damage to dedicate it to a new use effective during the time of interruption. Proving the facts may be difficult.

4. Machinery which cannot be used because it is located in a zone where such use is prohibited cannot be productive. An interesting example is that of the railroad engine which was marooned on an island when the connecting bridge to the mainland was destroyed by fire. The actual case raised the question of whether there was a constructive total loss under the Property Insurance policy, since it would cost more to rebuild the bridge than the engine was worth. Had there been a Business Interruption Insurance policy in effect on the engine, the loss of Productivity of that piece of equipment could have been the basis of a claim; the loss being what the engine could have earned during the time required to secure a replacement. If the time to replace the bridge were shorter than the time to replace the engine, the shorter time period would be applied.

In some respects, the underlying basis for a claim under a Contingent Business Interruption Insurance policy might be said to rest on the fact that the Property described is located at a place where its Productivity cannot be utilized for the Insured's benefit because the other location has been made unusable. Also, claims made under the Civil Authority Clause are based on the interruption of Productivity due to the location of the described Property—it is in a location to which access is prohibited because it is deemed to be dangerous by the civil authorities.

5. A stock of merchandise or a machine product that nobody needs and nobody wants, lacks a characteristic essential for Productivity. Even though the storekeeper has laid in a heavy stock of such merchandise or the manufacturer has planned a heavy production schedule of such product, unless it can be shown that the goods or the product would have moved through the channels of commerce, there can be no claim of loss of Productivity due to they or the equipment having been damaged.

There need not be an immediate need or demand for the goods at the time of the damage. There need not even be a need or demand during the Period of interruption. Such would be the case of a manufacturer producing goods in the off-season for storage until the time for shipment arrived.

Damage to the machinery, which prevents production of goods to be held in storage, can result in a claim of loss if the goods will not be available for shipment when scheduled. Thus, a manufacturer of Christmas cards, whose operations are interrupted in July for eight weeks, would have a basis for claiming a Business Interruption loss if he could not make up for the lost production in time for making required deliveries in October.

6. Lastly, even though all of the other characteristics co-exist, there may not be present the final necessary characteristic of Productivity. That result could be based on the plans of the Insured not to operate his plant and not to create an Earnings Stream. This introduces the matter of subjectivity—what thoughts existed in the mind of the Insured at the time that the damage occurred—which plays so interesting a role in the entire matter of Business Interruption Insurance. The Insured may have made his decision because of his assessment of market conditions, because of problems with help, because of the state of his health and for innumerable other possible reasons. The Insured may have planned to curtail or even to shut down operations during a particular period of time, which includes the period of interruption. It might be to provide a two-week vacation in July for his employees, while his plant is undergoing its annual reconditioning. Conversely, the Insured may be anticipating an increased demand for his product and may have set in motion the wheels to double his production during the approaching manufacturing season.[22]

Productivity must take into consideration what actually would have been the use to which the Property would have been put during the time that operations were terminated or curtailed due to damage caused by an insured Peril. Evidence of this projected course of action is often largely subjective in nature.[23] Objective tests also exist such as the size of orders placed for raw materials, advertisements for extra help or negotiations at the bank for increased credit. In the last analysis, however, it is the intention of this Insured about his Productivity which must control.

Assuming that all of these six characteristics co-exist, then the requirements of Productivity have been met, and the basis for a claim of loss is created should this Productivity be interfered with by an insured Peril.

7. Before leaving the subject of Productivity, it may be useful to point out that Productivity may be affected by some outside influence which may not be covered under the policy. If the major store in a shopping mall is put out of business by a fire, the smaller stores in the same mall would undoubtedly lose income, as the traffic falls off. So would the landlord whose rental income depended in part on a percentage of the sales made by the magnet store and the balance of the store in the mall.

F. Period

1. The element called Period throws light on the concept upon which Business Interruption Insurance has developed in the United States. The coverage is tied into the productive ability of Property. Once the damage has been repaired or the destroyed Property has been replaced, productive capacity is re-energized to recreate the Earnings Stream. This capacity, rather than the actual

restoration of earnings, is the controlling factor by which the loss is stopped from running. As discussed elsewhere, this basic approach is not universal and it can be amended by endorsement in the United States. Such additional coverage or "Lag Insurance" does not begin to take effect until "time to repair" has been exhausted, even though operations start up earlier. This coverage is included in BIC policy. (See Ch. 8.)[24]

The Business Interruption Insurance policy provides a rule for determining when the productive capacity has been restored. It is when it is possible "to resume operations of the Insured with the same quality of service which existed immediately preceding the loss." (By the word "loss," the policy refers to the physical damage, not the financial loss which the Insured has sustained. Due diligence and dispatch are implied. See Comment #6, p. 311.)[25] Until the potential for such resumption of operations comes into being, the period of interruption continues. The extent of the interruption, whether of all operations or only a portion of them, will depend on the circumstances in each particular case. But while it continues, the amount of loss continues to accumulate.

2. While the language of the Business Interruption Insurance policy form does provide a measure for the time frame into which the accumulation of loss must fall, it is not always easy to determine its boundaries.[26] In a situation where the determination of the amount of loss and the payment thereof does not arise until productive capacity has actually been restored, it is relatively easy to decide just when the accumulation of loss did terminate. In practice, that is what often happens. But there is nothing in the contract which says that payment can be so delayed. Recovery based on hindsight is not specified under the policy. (See Comment #9, p. 317, and the provisions of BIC Form in Ch. 8.) In the case of an interruption of extended length, the Insured needs the cash inflow replacing the Earnings Stream to keep himself financially viable while repairs are being made. A refusal to settle the loss and/or make advance payments prior to the time that operational capacity is restored could well defeat the purpose of the insurance and lead to the collapse of the Insured's business enterprise.

Moreover, the Insured may not be able or willing to restore operational capacity as speedily as it could reasonably be achieved and thus keep the interruption to a minimum. The Insurer cannot force him to do so. While the Insured may take all the time he wants, the liability of the Insurer is limited by the provisions of the "due diligence" clause, to be discussed later. This may be somewhat different under the BIC Form. (See Ch. 16.)

The Insured may decide that he will not repair, restore, or rebuild the property in the form in which it was prior to the damage. Or he may decide not to rebuild at all, but to go out of business. There is no obligation under the contract for the Insured to recreate productive capacity to the status it was in prior to the damage. Under such a factual situation, the only available method for determining the end of the time frame for accumulating loss is a theoretical one—what would have been the time required to rebuild, if productive capacity had been restored.

3. The period of loss calculation includes any time that might be needed, even after repairs have been completed, to resume operations with the same quality of service which existed preceding the damage. It is fairly clear that, if the time for repairs is of considerable duration, the re-establishment of the ability to produce as before may not immediately turn on the Productivity stream with the same quality as before the damage. There are conditions that linger after the Period of Interruption has come to an end. Employees may have wandered off to other jobs, in which case time and effort is needed to train their successors. And even when they have stayed on, the employees may have to adapt themselves to new machinery. Nor can the delay have failed to upset temporarily any team spirit that may previously have been built up. To the extent that such developments take place, the "same quality of service" may not be immediately attainable. Suppose, for example, that the business venture is a new one and the described Property has never had a "quality of service." What limitation, if any, would the policy language have on the Period of loss under such circumstances?

Even where such adverse developments do not occur and the full flow of the Earnings Stream could start up with the restoration of operations, conditions sometimes exist that render such return to the *status quo ante* impossible or impracticable. In a chemical plant, for example, experimental batches must frequently be run before the restored product is up to specifications. This situation is often aggravated if new pieces of equipment have been installed in the production line to replace damaged equipment. Such additional time as is necessary to restore the quality of service is included in the Period over which the loss is calculated.[27]

It must be kept in mind, however, that the Period is not to be extended, after the physical Property has been restored, merely because the volume of the Earnings Stream has not been restored to its prior condition. Such extension of time is not provided for under the Gross Earnings form of Business Interruption.[28]

4. The contract of insurance may contain specific time limits on the Period of recovery for certain types of loss. Thus the Gross Earnings form places a limitation on loss resulting from damage to media for electronic data processing. Also, an increase in the Period of interruption due to the acts of third persons may be specifically excluded from coverage. Other policies may provide a waiting time before the loss begins to accumulate.

5. Assume that the expiration date of the policy is December 31, 1980, and that damage suffered on April 1, 1980, delays the expected start-up date of new facilities from July 1, 1980 to September 1, 1980.[29] The loss to the Earnings Stream from July 1 to September 1 would be covered.

If, with an expiration date of December 31, 1980, the damage occurs on

November 1, 1980, and delays the start-up date from the scheduled February 1, 1981 to May 1, 1981, the loss from February 1 to May 1 would be covered. This would also be the result if the start up date was pushed back from February 1, 1981 to May 1, 1982.

Some question might exist on how to measure the loss if, because of damage on November 1, 1980, start-up scheduled for February 1, 1982, was delayed to May 1, 1982. On theory, however, such loss should be recoverable. Obviously if the damage occurred on January 2, 1981, there would be no coverage under the expired policy.

Three other provisions of the Business Interruption Insurance policy, which make reference to *time*, will be considered elsewhere. One deals with establishing the amount of gross earnings, by taking into consideration the Experience of the business during a period of time before the damage and the probable Experience during a period of time after the damage. Another deals with the Contribution Clause where the probable gross earnings (had no damage occurred) are to be calculated for a period of twelve months immediately following the date of the damage. The third deals with the time, within which, notice of loss and proof of loss must be furnished to the Insurer. (With reference to provisions of the BIC Form, Ch. 16.)

The element of Period can be summarized in the words of one court: "this contract provides a theoretical as opposed to an actual replacement time as the basic time standard for computation of business interruption loss . . . . It seems obvious that the Insurer wanted a standard of potential replacement time which was amenable to computation in advance and which was not subject to vagaries like owner indecision, strikes or failure of lease negotiations which might affect the actual building time."[30]

G. Profit

The term "Profit" is used as a word of art in the context of the six P's. It is synonymous with the subject matter of the contract as defined in the particular policy. Thus, in the Gross Earnings form, it is "Gross Earnings less charges and expenses which do not necessarily continue. . . ." (See Comment # 10, p. 323.) In Item 1 of the Two Item form it was the "net profit which is thereby prevented from being earned and such charges and other expenses, including payroll expense of Group I employees but excluding payroll expense of Group II employees. . . ." (In the BIC Form, "Business Income" is defined differently. See Ch. 8.) In general, Profit represents that part of the costs and expenses of operational activities which necessarily continue during the period of interruption and which would have been earned had there been no interruption, plus any net profit that would have been earned during the same period.

To establish a claim under a Business Interruption Insurance policy, an Insured must prove that some amount of gross earnings would have been earned during the period of interruption had no damage occurred. But it is not necessary to show that some *profit* would have been earned or even that *all* of the overhead and administrative costs and charges would have been earned.

2. Before the present forms were put in use, a problem faced manufacturers who bought Business Interruption Insurance. It involved the profit that could have been made on the ultimate selling price of finished goods that were never produced because of the interruption.

To overcome this problem a fiction was created. This fiction held that, when the raw material was turned into Finished Stock, the tools of production had finished their duty and had fulfilled their contribution to the Earnings Stream. This gave rise to the concept of the "Sales Value of Production," which holds that the income from Finished Goods is earned upon their being completed. In other words, the Insured would be entitled to include in the amount of loss recoverable under his Business Interruption Insurance policy the amount of Profit that the Finished Goods which were not produced, would have earned if they had been produced.[31]

Further discussions of the element of Profit will be deferred to the second part of this volume.

Chapter 6 Notes

1. See: Consolidated Laws of New York 1909 (Annotated), c33, §75. Art. VII, §148.
    "Insurable interest shall be deemed to include any lawful and substantial economic interest in the safety or preservation of property from loss, destruction or preliminary damage." Citing: Feinman v. Consolidated Mut. Ins. Co.

2. "To be an *insurable* interest the interest must be of financial significance—not emotional, historical or otherwise. The Insured must stand to lose financially if the property is damaged. The insurable interest in the right to use and occupy property is an inchoate right based on the potential of the property producing income, even if there is no requirement that it actually be producing income. The insurable interest in Gross Earnings lies in the right to receive the benefit of the Earnings Stream being produced or capable of being produced by the property."
    Gordon Chemical Co. Inc. v. Aetna Cas. & Surety Co.

3. Where several separate corporate entities are named as Insureds in the same policy, it is necessary that their separate operations be interrelated for a loss to one Insured to be the basis for a claim by other Insureds.
    National Union F. Ins. Co. v. Anderson-Pritchard Oil Corp.
    New England Gas & Elec. Assn. v. Ocean Accident & Guarantee Corp.

4. National Filtering Oil Co. v. Citizens' Insurance Co. A reading of this case suggests that at the same time that Dalton was developing his concept of a business interruption rider to be attached to a fire policy to ensure the continuance of an Earnings Stream, other techniques to achieve the same end were being explored. In this case, the patent license itself was attached to a Fire Insurance policy.

5. See: "Use and Occupancy," Clarence T. Hubbard. *Ins. Law Journal* (January 5, 1927). "Blueprint for a New Package," Alfred I. Jaffe, *National Underwriter* (March 28, 1975), p. 18.
    A lessor was named as coinsured under a tenant's U&O policy covering a bowling alley, so as to ensure payment of rents. A&S Corp. v. Centennial Ins. Co.
    For an insurable interest in property not owned see Womble v. Dubuque F & M Ins. Co. 1941 (squatter in premises of an allied organization). Feinman v. Consolidated Mut. Ins. Co. (liability imposed by law).
    See: Riggs v. Commercial Ins. Co. A holding company does not have an insurable interest in the earnings of a wholly owned subsidiary. Even if named as a coinsured, it can not collect as Insured for a business interruption loss suffered by its subsidiary. Unijax v. Factory Insurance Ass'n.
    The English case of Wilson v. Jones held that the Insured's interest as a stockholder was an insurable interest and likened it to an insurance on profits. In Riggs

v. Commercial Mutual Ins. Co., the court used the Wilson case as one springboard for its own direction.

A mortgagee has no insurable interest entitling it to share in the proceeds of a Business Interruption Insurance policy even though the underlying Fire Insurance policy is made payable to it as its interest may appear. Citizens Savings and Loan Ass'n v. Proprietors Ins. Co.

6. Property itself, in a legal sense, is nothing more than the exclusive right of possessing, enjoying and disposing of a thing which, of course, includes the use of a thing.

   "The value of railroad property, outside of advantage of location and amount of business it controls, consists in the strength, permanancy and durability of its structures and its adaptability and capacity of doing railroad business." Chicago & WIR Co. v. Englewood Connecting Ry. Co.

7. See: Studley Box & Lumber Co. v. National Fire Ins. Co.

8. See: Lewis Food Co. of Calif. v. Milwaukee Ins. Co.

9. See: Swedish Crucible Steel Co. v. Travelers Indemnity Co.

10. Pacific Coast Eng. Co. v. St. Paul F & M Ins. Co.

11. See: Charles Dowd Box Co. v. Fireman's Fund Ins. Co.

12. Washington Restaurant Corp. v. General Ins. Co. (dissenting opinion)

13. See: O'Brien v. North River Ins. Co.
    Omaha Paper Stock Co. v. Harbor Ins. Co.

14. Princess Garment Co. v. Fireman's Fund Ins. Co. See also: Cleland Simpson Co. v. Fireman's Ins. Co., of New Jersey; Simpson Real Estate Corp. v. Firemen's Ins. Co. (rental ins.). See also Hillier v. Alleghaney County Mutual Ins. Co.

   Is the air inside a building a part of the described property? Suppose a fire in an outside source spreads noxious fumes inside the building, contaminates the air and forces an evacuation of the building and suspension of operations until the fumes are cleared out? On balance, it would seem that the space enclosed by the structure is part of the property. If so, it would seem that we have damage to the described property by an insured peril.

   The Cleland Simpson Co. case points out the two possible meanings of the term "Peril": (1) A specific type of misadventure, e.g., a fire; (2) An impending danger, e.g. a threat of fire. The majority adopted #1; the dissent adopted #2.

15. Bros. Inc. v. Liberty Mutual Ins. Co.; Southland Bowls, Inc. v. Lumbermen's Mutual Ins. Co.; Sloan v. Phoenix of Hartford Ins. Co.; Two Caesars Corp. v. Jefferson Ins. Co.

16. See: Article by H.P. Polk, Esq. in *Nat'l Underwriter* (September 29, 1967), p. 1.

See: "Riot, Curfew and Business Interruption," Robert M. Morrison, *CPCU News* (November & December 1967 and January, 1968). See: "Business Interruption Revision Clarifies Riot Coverage Condition," Roy E. McCormick, *Rough Notes* (December, 1967).

17.   Suppose an explosion in a railroad tank car caused the spread of poisonous fumes and resulted in a police order to vacate an area of a dozen blocks. How many feet from the tank car would the line be drawn as to which were "adjacent" properties and which were not?

18.   See article in *Business Insurance* by Marie Krakowiecki, (December 13, 1976), p. 4.

19.   "Son of Consequential Insurance," Alfred I. Jaffe, *National Underwriter* Vol. 83 #14 (April 6, 1979), p. 43.

20.   General Ins. Co. v. Pathfinder Petroleum Co.

21.   Great Northern Oil Co. v. St. Paul F & M Insurance Co. (1975)

22.   See: Eastern Associated Coal Corp. v. Aetna C & S. Co.

23.   In Eastern Associated Coal Corp. v. Aetna C&S Co., the Insured had contracted to sell all of its production of a certain type of coal to a particular customer at a fixed price. It so happened that the prevailing market price for that type of coal during the period of interruption was higher than the contracted sales price. In effect, there was a contractual obligation to sell the product at less than would be its "sales value of production," which measured the price the Insured could have got for it in the open market. The production department would have produced the potential profit, if there had been no damage; it was the sales department which lost that profit by its contract.

When the Insured had to go out into the market and pay the prevailing price to fill its delivery obligations, the amount, paid in excess of the price received from the customer, was not an extra expense due to interruption of production, but a loss that had been undertaken under a sales contract. Therefore, it was not a loss due to lost production for which the Insured would be liable. This would be a sounder basis on which to reach what was a correct decision than the basis used by the court, viz; that this was a newly created expense produced by the interruption and hence not recoverable under the terms of the policy.

24.   See: "Indemnity Principle is Hollow," Marvin Milton, *National Underwriter* (April 8, 1983), p. 11.

25.   The Gross Earnings form in its Definition of Gross Earnings uses the language "had no loss occurred." This is not a correct use of language. A loss does not "occur"; damage occurs. A loss is "incurred" by the Insured.

26.   A question arises as to whether the diminution in Gross Earnings must actually be experienced during the period of interruption to be recoverable or whether it will

suffice that a diminution in anticipation, or in "embryo," was created during that period. Has the fact that a diminution in future Gross Earnings, can now be anticipated due to what was the situation during the period of interruption, bring that diminution within the coverage of the policy?

An example can be found in the case of a seasonal goods manufacturer. As a result of a fire, his operations are shut down for eight weeks. During that time, he fills orders for customers from inventory produced in advance of the season. During the period of interruption he normally would have been producing goods to fill re-orders. He cannot accept such re-orders. He loses the sales value of the additional goods he would normally have sold after the date of restored operations. Here there is no cancellation of a contract, but the inability to accept contracts which he could have performed and which would have improved his Earnings Stream.

For cases involving loss beyond expiration date see: Harper v. Phoenix Ins. Co.; Becker v. Merchants Mut. Ins. Co.

27.   The term "quality of service" is one more example of language which is open to various interpretations. In the case of a manufacturing plant does it mean "quality of product" or "quality of efficiency"; i.e., the production cost per unit based on the restored efficiency of manpower employed?

28.   In an early Rent Insurance case, it was held that completion of physical restoration, not retenanting, was the cut-off point in loss accumulation. Chronicle Bldg. Co. v. New Hampshire F. Ins. Co.

29.   The Period of interruption begins with the day the damage was sustained, even though the fire occurred in the early morning and the underlying Fire Insurance policy runs from noon to noon. See: Maple Leaf Lodge Inc. v. Allstate Insurance Company. Query: would there have been coverage if the damage had occurred before noon on the *inception date* of the policy?

See: *Consequential Coverages*, W.S. Foster (1936), p. 49. Also, Beautytuft Inc. v. Factory Ins. Ass'n. (1970)

30.   The Appellate Court in the 1913 Amusement Syndicate case said that "since no reconstruction took place, the arbitrary rule of the policy must be given effect (instead of actual facts). This arbitrary rule gives no effect to date of fire, season of year, etc.—only to shortest time to rebuild the building on a theoretical basis.

See: Amusement Syndicate Co. v. Milwaukee Mechanics Ins. Co.; Anchor Toy Corp. v. Am. Eagle F. Ins. Co.

31.   See: Withers, *Business Interruption Insurance Coverage and Adjustment*, p. 114. For a contrary opinion see Miner-Edgar v. North River Ins. Co.

Defined in Eastern Associated Coal Corp. v. Aetna C. & S. Co. See: Travelers Indemnity Co. v. Kassner: Net Sales Value of Production includes shipments to company stores shown on company books as transfers.

7

The E's Revisited

Extent. Experience. Exclusions. Effort. Extras. Enough.

A. Extent

1. The element of Extent is closely controlled by the terms of the policy. A brief comment may be in order on the introduction into Business Interruption Insurance policy forms of the words "Actual Loss Sustained."

Dalton did not use the phrase in his early policies. Those were valued policies and there was no need for such language. There is no indication in the Michael (Buffalo Elevating) case that such a phrase was present in the contract. As suggested by the court in *Tannenbaum v. Freundlich* in 1903, Use and Occupancy policies were still being issued mainly in the valued form.[1] And the suggestion of the court in *Tannenbaum v. Simon* was that the Insurers add some definition of coverage in their policies.[2]

No solid evidence is at hand to indicate when the phrase was first employed. There is an indication that it was first inserted in the form of Use and Occupancy Insurance proposed by the New York Board of Fire Underwriters some time before May, 1918. Comments on such proposed form quote from Section 4, in which the following language appears, "This Company shall be liable under this policy for the actual loss sustained of net profits. . . ." The critical nature of the comments with regard to the use of this phrase strongly suggests that it was a novel proposal.[3] It was probably proposed in connection with the attempt to adopt a standard Business Interruption Insurance form. When the Two Item Form was adopted in 1929 this phrase was retained.[4] And it was retained through all further changes in Business Interruption Insurance policies up to the present time.

It is likely that the adoption of the language of this phrase for use in the

Business Interruption Insurance forms was a conscious attempt to parallel the phrase, *actual cash value,* that appeared in the underlying Fire Insurance policy. In view of the problems that have resulted, it may be well to examine in some depth the language used.

In the Fire Insurance policy the phrase, *actual cash value,* is used as part of the insuring language relating to the liability which the Insurer assumes: "does insure ... to the extent of the actual value...." Its employment there serves two purposes. First, it places a sub-ceiling on the amount of liability assumed, notwithstanding the face amount of the policy. In his dissenting opinion in *Phillips v. Home Insurance Co.* (1908) Justice McLaughlin states that the words *actual cash value* were inserted in the Fire Insurance policy to limit the liability of the Insurer. Second, it indicates that the policy is an open and not a valued one: "actual cash value at the time of loss," not some previously agreed upon amount.

In the Business Interruption Insurance form, the phrase *actual loss sustained* can be read as a statement of the assumption of liability: "shall be liable for the Actual Loss Sustained by the Insured...." As so used, it parallels one purpose of its counterpart phrase in the Fire Insurance policy defining the policy as being open and not valued.

It should be noted, however, that neither in the Fire Insurance policy nor in the Business Interruption Insurance form does the phrase operate to establish a basis or method for measuring the amount or limit of loss resulting from any *particular* incident of damage. The typical Fire Insurance policy does this by the provision, "but not *exceeding* the amount it would cost to repair or replace, etc." Those words set only the *maximum* for any particular event. In parallel fashion, the Business Interruption Insurance form reads, "but not exceeding the reduction in Gross Earnings, etc."

While not spelling out in detail the yardsticks to be used in measuring a particular loss, the Fire Insurance policy, by reference, makes that process quite clear. The measuring technique is the cost of material and labor necessary to restore the condition of material value that formerly existed. This objective test is also fairly well pinpointed in time: "within a reasonable time after such loss" (i.e., damage).

Even if the word "amount" is to be interpreted as meaning "amount of such actual cash value," no difficulty arises. There is an objective test by which actuality is to be determined. Even if no repairs are ever made, bids can be secured from third persons for doing the work. "Actual" adds no additional dimension to an otherwise objective test for measuring loss.

Nowhere in the Business Interruption Insurance form can the basis for a similarly objective test be found. Certainly not in the phrase, Actual Loss Sustained. The word "actual" cannot be used in this context, as purporting to supply a yardstick for measuring a particular loss.

To the extent that a dictionary definition carries any weight, Webster defines "actual" as meaning "acting or existing; timely and objectively; real; now existing; present; current." As suggested, for purposes of the Fire Insurance policy, the present value of the physical property can be objectively determined; it has a current market or replacement value that exists. So it was quite proper to use "actual" in the Fire Insurance policy.

But there is no such objective test that can be applied to the amount of loss sustained when operations are interrupted. There can never be a *real* determination of the amount of the Earnings Stream which the Insured's operations *would* have produced had no loss occurred. No one can say what might have happened had operations continued. A fire due to the same spontaneous combustion that created the present interruption, if it had not occurred when it did, might have broken out three weeks later during what became the shut-down period. A machine could have become disabled; the plant manager might have been killed. No one knows for certain and know one can ever know. It must, at best, remain somewhat speculative. One can only make assumptions and come up with an answer which for practical purposes will be accepted by both parties as coming as close to the truth as is possible under the circumstances. As it has been said, forecasting is always difficult.

Writing at an early date, Percy Ling posed the question, "Is it possible to accurately determine what would have happened in the future if some casualty had not occurred?" To this he gave a very practical answer, one that has no doubt operated well in most loss situations. He said, "It is a matter of agreement. Assuming honesty of purpose on both sides, a satisfactory adjustment should be possible."[5]

In those situations where the interruption will be of long duration, the loss is often settled by such measures long before operations are resumed or advance payments are made. A projection can be made on the basis of known facts as to what is likely to be the loss which will be sustained. Settlement can be made on the basis of "*Probable* Loss Sustained" or rather on the basis of "Probable Loss That May Be Sustained." ("Sustained" is a word that describes something which has in fact been accomplished; it does not readily fit in with "probable.")

2. The Extent of recovery could be affected by the Loss Reinstatement Clause. This could happen if there was a second loss while the policy was in force. The clause provides that any payment previously made does not reduce the amount recoverable under a subsequent loss. Coverage is restored to the full face amount of the policy and this amount would be available to pay a second loss during the policy term.

If the second damage occurred while the first damage was still being repaired and resulted in prolonging the period of restoration, the first claim would run until the theoretical time when, with due diligence and dispatch, operations could be renewed. Then, if the second damage did not extend to other property, the claim for that damage would start when the claim for the first damage had run its course. However, if the second damage brought into existence suspension in additional areas of the Insured's operations, the loss would start on those additional areas from the time of their damage. *Local Agents Manual*, N.E. Insurance Exchange (September 14, 1917), contained the following provision under Use and Occupancy Rules–5(d) "... liability under the policy for total suspension of business for an entire year shall be the same whether such suspension be caused by several fires occurring at different periods of the year or by a single fire."

3. Different limitations on the Insurer's obligation are found in the Resumption of Operations Clause. This calls upon the Insured to resume operations of the property described in the policy, whether damaged or not, to the full extent that it can be used. "Do as much as you can do, just as you would have done if you had no insurance" would appear to be the thrust of this provision. And, further, "you might just as well, because we will only pay for the loss that you would have suffered had you done so." This clause is a controlling factor on the Extent of recovery. (See Comment #12, p. 327.)

B. Experience

1. The element of Experience plays a role in determining the amount of loss that has been suffered. It is, without doubt, the most challenging aspect of the Business Interruption Insurance policy. A knowledgeable and imaginative insight into the Insured's business operations is critical and is required to deal with it adequately.

One challenging issue arises as to the time when the amount of the Insured's loss is to be determined. As a practical matter, most losses are not finally settled until after the interruption has ceased and the Insured is back in operation. At that time, it is possible for both parties to determine by hindsight what events—both internal and external—that have occurred since the time of the damage would have had an impact on the Earnings Stream during the period of interruption. The conclusions reached on the basis of knowledge of those events is still an estimate since no one can know what other internal developments might have occurred had operations been carried on. However, the risk of such unknown possibilities is one that the parties are willing to disregard as they settle the loss.

It is also a matter of general practice, when a loss is settled before the interruption has ceased, for the parties to take into consideration those events, internal and external, that they know about which have occurred since the time of the damage. The parties then accept the risk of not knowing about the other events which might occur before the Insured is back in operation, which might affect the amount of the Insured's ultimate loss.

Where the Insured does not restore operations, the parties again, in practice, take into consideration those events that have occurred since the time of the damage which would affect the amount of the loss and of which they are aware at the time of settlement.

It is easy to understand such action of the parties when a settlement is agreed upon. Events subsequent to the damage may have increased or decreased the potential Earnings Stream that would probably have been earned. With the knowledge of that probability, each party would seek to gain the reward of events that favored its position in a settlement. As a practical matter, it would be hard for the other party to refuse to recognize the reasonableness of such a position. If taking those events into consideration brings the final amount closer to the best guesstimate of the probable amount of loss, it is a fair basis for a settlement.

So much for the practical aspects of the matter. But it leaves unanswered the basic question of what the contract says. What is the risk that was transferred under the terms of the policy? It is strongly felt, by one of the authors, that in theory, the wording of the policy indicates that the risk assumed by Insurer and Insured alike was the risk inherent in using foresight and not hindsight. What represents the "probable" loss is the amount that appears probable at the time of the damage. The risk that is transferred by the policy is measured by the facts that are known or should be known at the time of the damage; the parties accept the risk that later events may bring about a change that might benefit either one.

The alternative position would require a reading which said that, in the absence of a settlement by agreement, the Insured must wait until he is back in operation before he can establish the amount of his loss; because only then could the measure of the risk he had transferred be determined. As discussed in Comment #9, p. 317, a strong argument can be advanced against such an interpretation. Going all the way back to the Buffalo Elevator case for a precedent and an example, had the parties intended such a reading of the policy, they could have adopted language that would have set out this position clearly. Adding the words "actual loss sustained" does not achieve that goal.[6]

It may be that this theoretical approach to a solution of the problem has little practical significance. It does, however, suggest that a rewording of this portion of the policy may be in order. The same suggestion is applicable to the BIC Form.

2. Consideration of past experience can serve as a good starting point in every case. Where the Earnings Stream has set a uniform pattern in times past, it offers a relatively reliable foundation upon which to base projections. It may also be necessary to go back for several years to determine whether there have been trends on which a projection can be based. This would be the case, for example, where Experience shows that every Christmas season for the past five years sales volume increased about ten percent above the previous year. The trending must take such past experience in the business operation into consideration.

Frequently, such a simplistic evaluation fails to deal adequately with the

facts of past Experience. Special circumstances, both within the business operation and external to it, may have distorted results during those similar periods
in the past that are being examined. An investigation in depth, probing into all
of the surrounding facts, is mandatory before past Experience can be accepted
as a reasonable guide upon which to base calculations.

3. The reference to the "probable" future Experience of the business gives
rise to all kinds of questions. (The word used in the BIC Form is "likely". See
Ch. 16.) Some consideration has already been given to the pertinent sources of
information that shed light on what probably would have happened to the
Earnings Stream during the Period of business interruption had the damage not
occurred. Both the plans of the Insured and the climate of the general business
environment must be taken into consideration. This makes considerable speculation possible and, in some cases, even necessary.

A case in point was that of an art goods store in Miami which doubled its
floor space and tripled its stock of merchandise in preparation for the coming
winter season. Just as the enlarged store was about to open for business, it was
damaged by fire with a resultant loss of the entire season's sales. As it turned
out, it was an unusually cold winter in Miami that year, which reduced the
number of winter visitors. Upon the facts as given, the probable Experience of
the business during the Period of the business interruption cannot be determined with any large degree of certainty. At best, a conclusion can be achieved
only by a substantial amount of speculation.

4. From what date is the probable future Experience of the business to be
measured? A theoretical argument could be advanced that it is the date when
the policy took effect. Practically, however, the question is answered by the
language of the Business Interruption policy form which reads "probable experience *thereafter* [italics added] had no damage occurred." This leaves little
doubt that the date of the damage is the date when the "future Experience"
begins to run.

5. For how long a period after the damage occurs is the probable future
Experience to be measured? Again, there seems to be little room for doubt. It
includes events which could occur in the period during which the interruption
continues. The diminution in the Earnings Stream during that span of time is
the measure of the Insured's loss under his policy. It is quite possible that, as
a result of the interruption of operations, the Insured lost a business opportunity that would have developed substantial profits in the Period following the
repair of the damage; profits that he will not now be able to earn. However,
such lost future potential is probably not a factor in the Earnings Stream
during the Period of interruption and is not covered by the policy.

C. Exclusions

1. Reference was made earlier to specific items of expense or loss which

will be excluded from the amount which the Insured can collect under the provisions of the Gross Earnings form. An examination into such Exclusions is necessary.

In the first instance, liability is excluded for certain matters which may delay the restoration of operations. One such matter is the extra time required to restore the physical premises to a usable condition because of the enforcement of a local or state ordinance or law regulating the construction, repair or demolition of buildings or structures. Such laws and ordinances fall mainly into two classes—building laws and zoning laws. The former regulate the materials that can be used in buildings and how they are constructed and maintained. The latter, while they sometimes involve matters of construction, deal primarily with how the building is used—whether its use conforms to the standards set for the particular area in which the building is located. The application of such laws has been a matter of several court decisions.[7]

The New York Standard Fire policy contains a provision excluding any compensation for increased property loss resulting from such laws and ordinances. The basic endorsement normally attached to the Massachusetts Standard Fire policy contains a similar exclusion. The exclusionary provision in the Business Interruption Insurance policy form tracks closer with the Massachusetts wording, because it includes the necessity of demolishing any undamaged portion of the building before it can be rebuilt or repaired.

Suppose a plant utilized for light manufacturing work is located in an area zoned for dwellings only, but cannot be restrained from carrying on its operations because it has been in place since before the zoning ordinance was passed. If it suffers a substantial loss by fire, the right to restore operations could be barred by the zoning ordinance. This would extend the period of interruption indefinitely into the future. As a result of this exclusion, the loss is calculated as if the law or ordinance did not exist.

The New York Standard Fire policy provides in (lines 49-52), "No . . . waiver of any provision (shall) be valid unless granted herein and expressed in writing added hereto." If a demolition clause and waiver is attached with reference to Property damage insofar as *materiality* (the physical loss) is concerned, does it extend from the damage to *usability*? In cases where the property can be physically rebuilt if it is made to comply with the law, the only problem is the extension of time involved. But where further use is denied completely, the problem becomes more sticky.

2. A second Exclusion refers to delay in restoring operations due to the actions of strikers or other persons. Two types of situations are dealt with: first, interference by strikes with the process of rebuilding, repairing or replacing the damaged Property and; second, interference with the resumption or continuance of business. Both of these interferences must take place at the described premises for the Exclusion to take effect. In other words, a strike at the plant of a supplier resulting in a delay in the delivery of equipment, materials or mer-

chandise required to start up operations would not be excluded. On the other hand, a delay in starting up due to the fact that the Insured's employees are out on strike, whether the strike started prior to the damage or during the period of interruption, would be excluded. So, too, a strike by the workers engaged in the work of repair certainly would be excluded.[8] (Also see Comment #11, p. 325.)

This exclusion also covers the action of other than strikers. Environmentalists protesting the operation of a nuclear plant, for example, would fall within this exclusion if they delayed the making of repairs necessitated by a covered Peril.

The Exclusion refers to interference. It is not entirely clear whether this term requires an ongoing activity or whether a single incident would suffice to bring the Exclusion into operation. A case in point would be the destruction or theft by vandals of equipment or materials required for the repair work. The delay resulting from the necessity of replacing this equipment or materials could well increase the amount of loss. A strict interpretation would relate the words "other persons" to "strikers" and would require the kind of organized or ongoing interference that is associated with strikers. A liberal interpretation could result in excluding the increase of loss due to a single, non-continuing act.

It should be noted that the Exclusion covers both a total shutdown by use of the word "resumption," as well as a partial shutdown, by the use of the word "continuation."

3. A third Exclusion applies to acts of third persons which increase the loss otherwise due to the interruption by depriving the Insured of the business opportunity to recreate the Earnings Stream after repairs are completed.[9] The Insured can be deprived of this business opportunity in several ways. First, the withdrawal of an order or the cancellation of a contract placed by the third person is a clear example. Such a cancellation could result because, in the opinion of the third person, the Insured will not be able to make delivery in time, which causes the customer to seek another source for the products he needs. It can also result from the refusal of the third person to accept goods delivered after the contracted delivery date. (See Comment #7, p. 313.)

Another way in which an Insured can be deprived of the business opportunity is by loss of the capacity to produce, even after the physical property has been restored to its predamaged condition. This can be brought about by his loss of the right to use the premises on which production has been carried on as a result of the cancellation of the lease under which he occupies the premises. Many written leases contain a clause giving the lessor the right to cancel the lease if the rented premises or building of which it is a part is damaged by fire or other cause beyond a specific percentage. (This percentage can be described in terms of the building's value, its materiality, or the time it would take to repair the damage.) Where a lessor exercises his rights and terminates the lease, the lessee may be delayed from starting up operations until he can find new premises to occupy. A similar provision in the lease of machinery or equipment, if exercised by the lessor, could also result in additional loss during the period when the lessee is trying to find substitute equipment.

Still another way is by the loss of rights under a license given to the Insured which authorizes him to carry on the particular operation in which he is engaged. This could be a license under a patent held by a third person. Such a license frequently requires a certain level of production if the licensee desires to retain it. Failure to live up to the requirements of the license may result in its suspension or cancellation. Another type of license is that given by a public body to use the premises for a certain purpose. A license to manufacture potentially dangerous products on the premises would be still another example. The failure of the licensee continuously to maintain operations under the license, or the shut down of operations for a specific period of time, may result in a lapse of the license. Or a plant explosion might result in a cancellation of the license by the public body that had granted it. Of course, the lease or license involved should have a relation to the operation of the business and the production of an Earnings Stream.

4. Another Exclusion applies to loss resulting from any other consequential or remote loss.[10] A recent analysis of the contents of the phrase "remote or consequential loss" lists the following items: expense of preparing the claim; loss of trade or market; effect of loss on a secondary location; increase of operating costs after loss for any reason; deterioration of stock through inability to use it; loss from cancellation of lease, contract, etc.[11]

5. Some of the coverage provisions found in the Fire Insurance policy with their limiting provisions are incorporated into the Business Interruption Insurance policy form with the appropriate change in language to make them applicable to business interruption losses. They include the Electrical Apparatus Clause and the Alterations and New Buildings Clause.[12]

6. The Gross Earnings form contains a number of special exclusions. One deals with loss resulting from damage to metal smokestacks by windstorm and hail. An Insured, with property subject to such Perils, requires a special endorsement if loss from such Perils is to be covered. In the case of mining risks, buildings which do not contribute to the production of the mining plant are excluded from the coverage.

D. Effort

1. Reference has been made to the provision that the Insured's recovery is limited to the amount of loss that would have resulted had he used due diligence and dispatch in an Effort to keep loss at a minimum. This requirement of due diligence has been a part of the contractual provisions from an early day in Business Interruption Insurance policy forms.[13]

The wording of the forms heretofore in use provides that the Period during which loss can be claimed is limited to the time it would take "with due diligence and dispatch to rebuild, repair or replace such part of the property as has been damaged or destroyed." The terms used in the BIC Form are "as quickly as possible" and "with reasonable speed." (See Ch. 8.) Here is another example of the use of elastic words. What constitutes due diligence and dispatch is a fact not always easy to establish. Different people can have substantially different opinions as to what meets the test under a particular set of facts.

The origins of the phrase shed little light on the matter. In early Rent Insurance policies appeared the words "with ordinary diligence and dispatch." It may well be that "due" carries on the concept of "ordinary." Other early rent policies used such a phrase as "in as short a time as the nature of the case will permit."

Another question presents itself. Is there any difference between "diligence" and "dispatch"? From the dictionary definitions, one senses that diligence includes the aspect of planning, while dispatch tends to emphasize action in carrying out plans.

It still comes down to what is appropriate action to expect the Insured to take. The fairest measure would be what a reasonable man in the Insured's position would do if he had no insurance.

2. There are many factors which typically tend to extend the time before the repair or restoration can be completed. Where a large building has been severely damaged, for example, a great deal of preliminary work must be done before actual construction can commence. The damage must be inspected, debris removed, plans drawn (if none exist which can be utilized), financing arranged, permits received, specifications issued, bids received and evaluated and materials ordered and received before actual work can start. The time necessary for all these steps is included in the Period of loss.

External factors also play a role. Weather conditions can have an important bearing on when and how fast the work can be done. The availability of labor and materials are factors to consider; the latter was a particularly critical item during both world wars. Natural disasters, affecting a great amount of property, such as the hurricanes which hit the east coast in the 1930's and 1940's, can create a shortage of manpower and materials and delay the making of repairs.

The Insured may decide that the type of construction of the destroyed building no longer meets his needs and he may plan the construction of a different type of structure. If the planning and construction require more time than would a duplication of the earlier structure, the question arises as to whether his loss should include the additional time. One New York state court answered the question as follows: "It is beyond the bounds of reasonable contemplation to expect that a replacement structure would ignore all progress in the art and slavishly retain any proven disadvantage.... Doubtless, if any extraordinary additional time would be required to include improvements or innovations, these would not be included."[14]

This approach is helpful up to a point, but it still leaves open the question of when the additional time required would be "extraordinary." Certainly the Insurer should not be held liable for the time necessary to build a six story office building on land in Baltimore where the structures which were destroyed were three two-story dwellings.[15]

Sometimes there is a question as to whether it is necessary for the Insured to demolish the remaining structure and rebuild totally to restore it to its former condition; it may have been just as effective and less time consuming to repair the damage. If the facts so indicate, the Insurer should only be liable for the shorter period.[16]

3. Since the question of due diligence is a question of fact taking into consideration surrounding circumstances, it may be well to mention one type of situation that does arise and which, in some cases, ends up in the courts. Some policies of Business Interruption Insurance extend the Period of loss to include the building of a plant at a new location if it is not possible to rebuild at the described location. This sometimes results from the inability to get a permit to rebuild at the same location. Zoning laws, which prevent rebuilding of nonconforming use structures when more than a certain percentage in value of the original structure is destroyed, would be an example. The development of environmental restrictions could well create a parallel situation.

In the case of a refusal of the authorities to grant a permit to repair or rebuild, the Insured has two options. He can file a lawsuit to try to force the issuance of a building permit. There is a duty on the part of the Insured to exert every reasonable effort to obtain the necessary permits.[17] In one case, when the Insured failed to do so, it was successfully argued by the Insurer that he had such an obligation. The court, however, permitted the Insured to collect for the time it would have taken to repair because it found that the time required to repair would be less than the time required to get a decision from the court on his writ on mandamus against the authorities.[18]

The second option is to wait, hoping for a change in the official climate. One Insured had an explosion in his chemical plant, which killed employees and caused damage to a nearby school and houses. He felt that the resulting adverse public attitude would, as a practical matter, prevent him from promptly securing a renewal of his permit to carry on his operations at the same location. As a result, he delayed the seeking of a permit to rebuild his plant (which would be useless without a permit to operate it), hoping that community tension would abate and that it might be possible, after a while, to get the necessary permit from the local board of selectmen. After four months, he gave up hoping, found a new location and built there. While the case was compromised without court action, it was agreed as part of the settlement that the Insured could collect for the loss resulting from the four month delay. It is the course of action a reasonable businessman would have taken.

Where disasters such as conflagrations, floods and earthquakes result in an ordinance ordering a lengthy delay in the issuance of building permits until the authorities decide how to rezone or redevelop the stricken area, the extra time required for rebuilding is not included in the loss.[19]

A more difficult question is presented where, even though a permit is issued, the Insured decides not to rebuild. If it could be shown that the decision not to rebuild was taken immediately after the damage occurred, it would seem that the extra time needed to get a permit should not be included in the loss. On the other hand, if it were the limitations in the permit that led to the Insured's decision not to rebuild, the extra time should be included. Due diligence would have included waiting for the permit to issue.

4. A question left open by the Gross Earnings form is who must use due diligence and dispatch. Obviously, it is the Insured who must. But how far must he succeed in expediting repair or replacement? What if he is not in complete control of the decision making process?

A plastics manufacturer immediately called in the equipment maker after the fire to see if damaged reactors could be repaired on his premises. When it was determined that they had to go back to the equipment maker's plant, the Insured was advised that the latter would not work his men overtime to make the repairs nor put on a second shift for that purpose. Since the Insured could not force the equipment maker to work longer hours, he could not be charged with lack of due diligence.

In another case, the Insured successfully contended that he was not required to employ outside workers, who were unfamiliar with the intricate machinery he used. Moreover, working his repairmen only ten hours a day was found to be within the requirement of due diligence. If they worked longer hours, it was argued, their efficiency would drop and they would be more likely to make costly mistakes.[20]

A situation that frequently arises involves an Insured who is a tenant in a building owned by another person. The landlord takes his time in making the repairs that are necessary to render the tenant's area usable. For example, a delicatessen, occupying a store in a block of stores, was without electricity and could not operate until the landlord finally compromised his dispute with the local building department which was insisting that a new wiring system be installed in the entire building. The extra delay of several months was included within the Period of loss.[21]

5. Sometimes it is the Adjuster handling the Property loss who holds up all action aimed at getting repairs under way until he has adjusted the loss under the Fire Insurance policy.[22] In one case, the error of the adjusting company in ordering needed replacement equipment was the basis for part of the unwar-

ranted delay.[23] Where arson is suspected, the fire marshall may hold up the making of repairs.[24]

Where damage repair must be put out on bid, as in the case of public buildings, the low bidder who gets the job may not be able to perform the job as rapidly as one of the higher bidders. In such a case, could it be argued by the Insured that the difference is an expense to reduce loss and hence the extra time is justified?

The sole issue is whether the Insured has exerted the required Effort—has done all that he reasonably could do to expedite the restoration of the physical condition that would permit him to renew operations. If he has, then no penalty is imposed upon him by the due diligence requirement.

6. Another area in which Effort must be used by the Insured is provided by the Resumption of Operations provision found in the Gross Earnings forms. He can collect for only so much of the financial loss that he has suffered as could not have been avoided by compliance with the requirements of that clause. Since this subject is discussed elsewhere, only a mention of its impact will suffice at this point. (See Ch. 8.)

7. There is another relevant provision to be found in the requirements in case a loss occurs. This is to "protect the property from further damage that might result in the extension of the period of interruption." This provision, like the similar ones to be found in the underlying Fire Insurance policy, deals with the materiality of the described Property.

Both the New York and the Massachusetts Standard Fire Insurance policies contain a provision excluding recovery for any loss resulting from the neglect of the Insured to use all reasonable means to save and preserve the Property at or after a loss. In the New York policy, but not that of Massachusetts, there is an additional provision requiring the Insured "to protect the property from further damage." Such measures would, in most cases, require an expenditure of funds and could involve a stoppage of operations. There is no specific provision under the Fire Insurance policies to reimburse the Insured for such expenditures, except expense incurred in removing the Property to a place of safety. It would seem that time lost due to interruption of operations incurred for such purposes could be included in the amount of loss under the Business Interruption Insurance coverage.

8. The issue of Effort is raised in connection with the archaic provision, long existing in the underlying Fire Insurance policy,[25] which provides that "it shall be optional with this Company to . . . repair, rebuild or replace the property destroyed or damaged . . . on giving notice of its intention to do so within thirty days after the receipt of proof of loss herein required." (In Massachusetts, fifteen days.) There is nothing in the Business Interruption Insurance form specifically overriding this provision. (It does not appear in the BIC Form.) This would apparently bring it within the opening statement that "all provisions and stipulations of this . . . policy shall apply separately to each such

item." If the option provision were to be considered applicable, it would create an impossible situation in that technically, no repairs could be undertaken until the option period had expired.

Yet, before dismissing this concept out of hand, it should be realized that the option provision was, in fact, applied by the Kansas Court in 1913 to a Business Interruption Insurance policy loss in deciding that since the Insurer had this 30 day option, the Insured was not at liberty to proceed to let contracts for reconstruction until 30 days after filing proof of loss.[26]

E. Extras

1. The introduction by Business Interruption Insurance of a time element into the calculation of the amount of loss made it desirable from the point of view of the Insurer that the Insured truly exert himself to reduce the time required to restore operations. This led to the inclusion of a special provision in Business Interruption Insurance policy forms encouraging the Insured to take such action by agreeing to reimburse him for certain expediting expenses.[27] Although incorporated into the form itself, this provision really represents a supplementary contract. It would not only apply to expenditures made to comply with the due diligence and resumption of operations provisions, where appropriate, but would also extend to expenditures made beyond the requirements of those provisions.

From the point of view of the Insurer, no additional burden was being assumed. The payment for such expenses in no event would be more than the actual savings achieved and hopefully, a small expenditure could achieve a substantial savings in the loss sustained.

From the point of view of the Insured, there could be a risk if no savings were actually achieved. However, he is under no obligation to make such expenditures beyond those required by "due diligence and dispatch" and normally would do so only if he considered it to his benefit from an overall business consideration to hasten the resumption of business activities.

There is pressure imposed on the Insured by the Resumption of Operations Clause to take specific steps to maintain operations and maintain his Earnings Stream as far as possible if thereby he can reduce the amount of the loss he will ultimately suffer. If, as a result of taking such steps he incurs expenses, they will be reimbursed to him by the Insurer in addition to the amount of his resultant business interruption loss provided they meet certain criteria.

2. While the concept of expenses to reduce loss is not difficult to comprehend, its application under the wording of policy forms now in common use is not so easy. The difficulty arises from the wording of the policy forms.

For example, the Gross Earnings forms set up certain criteria. They require that the expenses be both "in excess of normal" and be "necessarily incurred." The use of the word "normal" at this juncture is undoubtedly controlled by the definition of "normal" elsewhere in that form, i.e., "the condition that would have existed had no loss occurred." (Again, "loss" should be read "damage.") It would appear, under this wording, that not only must the expenses be such as would not have been made had there been no damage, but also that within the framework of the extraordinary efforts which were undertaken, these particular expenses must have been necessary.[28] The Business Interruption Insurance policy form does provide for reimbursing the Insured for such expense if the required criteria are met.

But, one question is left unresolved—how to determine between when expenses were incurred under the terms of the underlying Fire Insurance policy and when they can be attributed to Extras under the Business Interruption Insurance policy form. A situation in point involved debris removal. By using his own workmen and working normal hours, the Insured could have cleaned up the debris left by the fire in three weeks' time. The cost of this work could be recovered under the Fire Insurance policy. However, by bringing in outside contractors and working around the clock, the work was completed in one week's time but at additional cost. Most of these additional costs are not usually recoverable under the Fire Insurance policy. The Insured, however, could make claim for this as extra expense under his Business Interruption Insurance policy to the extent it reduced the overall business interruption loss.

3. Inserted in the Business Interruption Insurance policy form is the limitation that it does not cover expense incurred to extinguish a fire. This may have been inserted to avoid a duplication of expenses that would also be compensated for under the underlying Fire Insurance policy.

4. It should also be noted that, in the application of the expediting expense provision, a different timing approach may be taken than in the case of the basic business interruption loss. In the case of expediting expense, hindsight must be used because only *after the fact* is it possible to determine whether or not there was an actual savings and how much it is. This should create no problem because the two compensation provisions have entirely different purposes and each stands on its own feet.

5. It would appear from the language of the expense to reduce loss clause that there must be a specific intention on the part of the Insured to incur the particular expenses "for the purpose of reducing loss under the policy." To what extent this purpose must be expressed and to what extent it can be implied is not clear.

The minimum requirement for an expression of purpose would be a declaration by the Insured *after* the expenditure; the language seems sufficiently broad to permit the declaration to be made in connection with the filing of a claim. Clearly a declaration made before incurring the expense would be more desirable. This is just another example of the subjective aspects of this policy.

6. Under the provisions of the Gross Earnings Form there are two types of expediting expenses that can be incurred by the Insured and be reimbursed by

the Insurer—those that speed up the resumption of business and those that continue operations at a higher cost during what would otherwise be a period of total or partial suspension. It is the "aggregate" of all such expenses that constitutes the limit imposed by the provision that recovery cannot exceed the amount by which the loss is reduced.

The reduction must be in the amount payable by the Insurer, not in the amount of loss suffered by the Insured. When added to the reduced amount of loss, the total can never exceed the face amount of the policy. For example, if the Insured with a $50,000 policy, succeeded by expediting expenses of $12,000 in reducing the loss from $60,000 to $40,000, the Insurer's payment under this clause would be limited to $10,000 since $40,000 + $10,000 equal $50,000—the face amount of the policy. (See Comment #3, p. 303.)

The limitation on recovery to that period when operations could have been restored with due diligence and dispatch does not conflict with the expense to reduce loss provision. Where the exercise of due diligence involved expediting expense which succeeded in shortening the Period of interruption, such expense would be reimbursable as having been incurred "for the purpose of reducing loss under the policy."

The final sentence of the clause found in the Gross Earnings Form provides that expense which reduced loss is not subject to the application of the contribution clause. (For examination of the provisions for expenses in the BIC Form, see Ch. 8.) This will be considered under the heading of "Enough."

Under certain policies, the consent of the Insurer was required before extra expenses could be undertaken if reimbursement was to be recovered.[29]

F. Enough

1. The adoption of the Contribution or Coinsurance Clause in connection with Business Interruption Insurance was motivated by the same factors that led to its introduction in Property Insurance policies. "Coinsurance Clauses are designed to compel the Insured, either as self-insurer or in the policy, to carry insurance on the risk in an amount equal to the percentage of its value fixed by the particular clause."[30] It has also been called "reduced rate contribution clause," "reduced rate coinsurance clause," "reduced rate average clause," and "percentage coinsurance clause."

However, Business Interruption Insurance introduces the additional factor of time—of future time starting after the damage has been caused. For this reason, the thrust of the Coinsurance Clause in Business Interruption Insurance is directed to the insurable value that will be created in the future; not the insurable value that existed when the policy was written nor the insurable value when the damage occurred. Moreover, the value considered is not related to material value, as in the case of Property Insurance, but to the value of the Earnings Stream that would have been produced. The common practice is to fix the period used as a basis for calculation to the twelve months following the date when damage occurs. That is the period set out in the Coinsurance Clause of Gross Earnings forms. If the interruption turns out to be of more than one year's duration, no separate calculation need be made of the value in each future year. In other words, the determination of whether the Insured carried the agreed upon percentage of coverage is recalculated, starting with the date of the damage that caused the interruption and extending one year from that time. That recalculated amount becomes the denominator of the fraction that determines whether an Insured is a coin-surer. The numerator is the amount of the policy covering business interruption.

2. To reduce the likelihood of being underinsured, a work sheet has been prepared for use by Insureds. This is a form on which the amount of present and future insurable value can be calculated. The filling out of such a work sheet will be discussed in Part II but it should be kept in mind that when prepared, it represents a projection of one year from the date of its calculation. As one speaker put it when discussing an earlier form of policy, "The coinsurance form makes it unnecessary for the Insured to guess how his business will be divided between the various seasons of the year. The weather bureau cannot predict the weather infallibly and yet under the 300 day form we ask an Insured dealing in women's wear or dry goods to make the same prognostication. We penalize him if he guesses incorrectly. On the other hand, the burden was now shifted to the Insured to anticipate what his future income would be and what loss he could suffer if that income stopped. He was forced to put a price tag on his judgment when he had to decide how much insurance to buy and how large a premium to pay. Human nature being what it is, the tendency was to guess too low."[31]

Since it is possible, under a policy expiring on January 10th, to incur a loss on January 9th and the calculation of insurable value would start at that time and run for another twelve months, it becomes obvious that the Coinsurance Clause constitutes a possible pitfall for unwary Insureds who are not farsighted enough to look at least two years ahead, or alternatively, who do not verify or recalculate their potential insurable value from time to time during the life of the policy. (For the change introduced by the BIC Form, see Ch. 8.) In a business firm where the Earnings Stream is flat or dropping, that is no problem. But, in a business firm where the Earnings Stream is growing because of inflation or otherwise, there could be a serious problem; the Insured might find himself an inadvertent coinsurer.

In practice, coinsurance penalties are imposed in a great many loss settlements. There are various reasons for the inadequacy of insurance that brings about this result. They include (1) the reluctance of the Insured to pay premiums in the absence of solid facts, (2) the inability of the Insured and the Agent to accurately determine what amount is required, (3) the reliance upon book figures (compiled for tax purposes) for underwriting purposes and then shift to actual figures in the event of loss.

3. A practical question is raised as to what should be used as the Business Interruption value in the case of an Insured who has changed his method of calculating the value of inventory from FIFO to LIFO. In a period of inflation, the effect of such a change is to lower gross earnings. (The higher cost merchandise is sold first.) The reverse is true when cost of merchandise is going down. This could affect the amount of insurance required under the Coinsurance Clause; especially if the change takes place during the term of the present policy. Such a change, then, should trigger a re-evaluation of the amount of insurance carried.

4. The provisions of the Coinsurance Clause do not apply to expenses incurred to reduce loss. In the case of a $50,000 loss where the Insured was a 40% co-insurer, the Insurer would normally pay only 60% or $30,000. However, if by an expense outlay of $10,000, the loss was reduced to $40,000, the Insurer would pay 60% of $40,000 and 100% of $10,000 or a total of $34,000.

Despite its complexity, the Coinsurance Clause has been determined to be not ambiguous, nor is it inconsistent with the Pro Rata Clause.[32]

Chapter 7 Notes

1. See: Buffalo Elevating Co. v. Prussian Nat. Ins. Co. On appeal: Michael v. Prussian Nat. Ins. Co. Also see: Tannenbaum v. Freundlich where Justice Clarke states, "It is usual for such policies to be valued . . ." (p. 294).

2. Tannenbaum v. Simon (1903).

3. "Comments and Suggestions on the Uniform Rules and Clauses for Use and Occupancy Insurance," Fire, Marine & Liability Brokers Ass'n of the City of New York (May, 1918). To quote from the above-referenced article: "The limitation of the insurance company's liability to the 'actual loss sustained' meets with objection, as it would not be possible under that phrase, to adjust a loss until the plant resumed operations and the actual loss sustained was determined. The reason for this wording is not apparent and would lead to confusion in adjustment."

4. See Klein, *Business Interruption Insurance*, p. 12.

5. *Educational Primer on Use and Occupancy Insurance*, Percy Ling, Series 5, Vol. I (Insurance Federation of Pennsylvania), p. 7 (Undated).

6. "The measure of loss is based on either of two criteria: (a) loss of gross earnings for a limited period of time as estimated or (b) actual loss, inferring an *actual* resumption of business. Actual loss sustained is meant to apply only when there is an actual resumption of the insured's business." Di Leo v. USF&G Co. (1969). While indemnity is an underlying basis for insurance recovery, the parties can agree on another basis. Northwestern States Portland Cement Co. v. Hartford F. Ins. Co.

7. Amusement Syndicate Co. v. Milwaukee Mechanics Ins. Co.; Palantine Ins. Co. v. O'Brien; First Investment Co. v. Vulcan Underwriters; Heim v. Alliance Ins. Co.; World F&M Ins. Co. v. Palmer.
    Paragraph 10(c) of the Gross Earnings Form #4 refers to laws affecting the "construction, repair or demolition of buildings." No reference is made to the use of buildings, as governed by zoning laws. Suppose that in the case of a plant manufacturing a dangerous product, the appropriate department issued a permit to rebuild the damaged structure but the licensing body would not issue a license to carry on the operation. Would the resultant loss of an Earnings Stream fall within the exclusion? Probably not.

8. For cases involving strikes at customer's plant see Buffalo Forge Co. v. Mutual Security Co.; Standard Printing & Publishing Co. v. Bothwell.

9. Rogers d/b/a Elmer's Plaza Bowl v. American Ins. Co. See: Fleet-McGinley Co. v. Bothwell; Port Murray Dairy Co. v. Prov. Wash. Ins. Co.

10. Pacific Coast Eng. Co. v. St. Paul F&M Ins.; Co.; See: Fleet-McGinley Co. v. Bothwell.

11. "Business Interruption Basics," James W. Douglas, *Underwriters Report* (April 1, 1982), p. 28.

12. See Simon v. Girard F&M Ins. Co.

13. See: Earlier discussion about Dalton's 1880 policy. Also 1900 policy in Michael v. Prussian Ins. Co.

14. Anchor Toy Corp. v. American Eagle F. Ins. Co. (1956).

15. Palatine Ins. Co. Ltd. v. O'Brien.

16. Congress Bar & Restaurant, Inc. v. Transamerica Ins. Co. The court refers to time necessary to restore building to former condition.

17. See: World Fire & Marine Ins. Co. v. Palmer.

18. World Fire & Marine Ins. Co. v. Palmer.

19. Palatine Ins. Co. Ltd. v. O'Brien.

20. Anderson & Middleton Lumber Co. v. Lumberman's Mut. Cas. Co.

21. Cf. Harper v. Phenix Ins. Co.

22. Eureka-Security F & M Ins. Co. v. Simon.

23. Omaha Paper Stock Co., Inc. v. Harbor Ins. Co.; Eureka Security F & M Ins. Co. v. Simon.

24. Saperston v. American & Foreign Ins. Co. of N.Y. (Rent). Cf. Bradford v. Canadian Fire. Ins. Co.

25. It apparently was used by the Insurer in the Leonarda case.

26. Amusement Syndicate Co. v. Milwaukee Mechanics Ins. Co.
    Cf: Leonarda case where Insured made the repairs. A similar provision appears in the case of Menzies v. North British Ins. Co. (1847).

27. In the early case of Hartford Fire Ins. Co. v. Northern Trust Co. (1906), where no such provision was contained in the policy, the court ruled that since the expediting expenses had reduced the loss to zero the Insureds did not have a claim.

28. The policy provision speaks of "expenses as are necessarily incurred for the purpose of reducing loss." This provision could be interpreted as referring back to paragraph 3 and to include only those expenses necessarily incurred in carrying out the requirements of that paragraph; in other words, it could refer back to the reduction of loss mentioned in the Resumption of Operations Clause and only to such activities. This does not appear sound. The Insured could also meet the requirements of paragraph 4 by using other equipment not at the premises during what had been his normal hours of operation, or by working overtime and thus incurring extra labor costs. Replacement parts which might be ordered in by rail could be flown in by air freight at extra expense. These are actions which fall outside the requirements of paragraph 3.

    The problem with thus extending the application of paragraph 4 arises from the words "necessarily incurred." Actions are necessary if a certain course of action is decided upon but may not be necessary if normal procedures are used. It would seem that the discretion as to what is the course of action to be taken must be left to the Insured, and what are expenses necessarily incurred would follow his decision.

29. See: Ocean Acc. & Guar. Corp. v. Penick & Ford, Ltd.

30. See: Home Insurance Co. v. Eisenson (2nd Case–1950).

31. Talk by Laurence E. Falls to N.Y. Ass'n of Local Agents. Reported in *Underwriters' Review*, June 15, 1930.

32. Apparel City Sewing Machine Co. Inc. v. Transamerica Ins. Group.

8

The Business Income Coverage Form

In General. Policy Format. Outline of Form. Provisions of Form.

A. In General

1. New Forms Submitted for Approval

After years of preliminary work, the Insurance Services Office (ISO) has submitted in all of the United States jurisdictions a whole new series of property insurance forms, among them new forms of Business Interruption Insurance. In some states, they have already been approved and are to go into effect as of January 1, 1986. In others, the matter of approval is still pending as these lines are written. In some jurisdictions that have approved them, their use is scheduled to become mandatory on January 1, 1987. Among these is Massachusetts. The discussion that follows will be based on the forms filed in that state. They are typical of those filed elsewhere.

2. Its Name

The particular forms that will be analyzed herein are those designed to replace some of the Business Interruption Insurance—Gross Earnings Forms heretofore in use. A useful change has been made in the name—the title—given to the new forms. Objection has long existed in many circles to the use of the name Business Interruption, a title that suggested that it was the interruption of the business that was insured. In truth, it is the earnings of the business that are protected by this coverage. Hence, "Business Income Coverage Form," the new name, is an appropriate title and, therefore, an improvement. For purposes of convenience it will continue to be referred to here as the BIC Form. If past experiences with changes in forms is any criterion, it will continue to be called

Business Interruption Insurance for years to come, maybe even U&O Insurance.

3. Language used

Following the general practice that has been developing in the wording of insurance policies, a use of ordinary language is employed. Indeed, this shift to the simplified wording is probably the original motivation for the new forms. In addition, the particular form analyzed contains extended examples illustrating just how the policy provision would be applied to specific sets of facts. Accordingly, some of the traditional and well-litigated terms, in use for most of a century, have been replaced by more "every day" words. (One difficulty which accompanies a shift in wording is the "trashing" of generations of legal decisions which interpret the language discarded. This can be good or bad but does have the effect of undermining whatever certainty had been created by court decisions.)

The structure and provisions of the BIC Form represent substantial improvements over the forms heretofore in use. By providing full coverage in its initial form and requiring that any limitations be added thereto, it reduces the likelihood of an Insured being left with inadequate coverage as a result of oversight at the time the policy is written. This should eliminate a great deal of the unhappiness that has sometimes developed after damage has been suffered and it is found that items of coverage that should have been included were left out.

It is to be assumed that the hiatus of one year between the time that the BIC Form goes into use and the time when its use becomes mandatory, is to provide an opportunity for it to be tested and examined in the market place. With the thought of suggesting possible improvements in the BIC Form, various criticisms of its language and provisions are included in the discussion contained in this chapter and Chapter 16.

Undoubtedly, the drafters of the form knew what they meant by the language used. The questions raised are intended to show that to an Insured the language used may not represent a clarification or simplification that is free from uncertainty.

4. Definitions and examples

For purposes of clarification, some of the terms used in the BIC Form appear in quotation marks, which indicates that they are defined in the definitions section of the policy. Other terms are defined within particular provisions, without such special designation.

B. The Policy Format

1. A Single Policy

The BIC Form has been designed to stand on its own as an independent policy—there is no need for an underlying Fire Insurance policy. When all of the various parts that together form a complete contract are assembled, all the pertinent provisions hitherto borrowed from the underlying Fire Insurance policy will have been included. Unless there is a statutory provision that the use of such a Fire Policy is required, its use will no longer necessary. In Massachusetts, there was such a statutory requirement. Legislation has been passed eliminating this requirement.

2. Various Parts

Among the parts that normally will be necessary for writing coverage, on a manufacturing plant for example, will be the following:

a. a Common Policy Declarations Page;
b. a Common Policy Conditions Form;
c. a Commercial Property Conditions Form;
d. a Commercial Property Declarations Page;
e. a Business Income Coverage Form;
f. a Causes of Loss Form.

3. Common Policy Conditions

The Common Policy Conditions contain, among others, such familiar provisions as those for cancellation, amendments and assignment. A new provision gives the Insurer the right to examine the Insured's books and records during the policy period and up to three years thereafter. A limitation is placed on the assumption of liability by the Insurer when making surveys and inspections.

4. Commercial Property Conditions

The Commercial Property Conditions Form includes provisions about fraud, other insurance, time for bringing suit and subrogation, as well as a liberalization clause. A major issue, as yet unresolved, involves the question of whether the liberalization clause in the Gross Earnings form in a policy issued and in force is applicable to the provisions of the BIC Form. See attached form ISO.

5. The Covered Causes of Loss Forms

There are three such forms: Basic Form, Broad Form and Special Form, listing the perils insured against together with limitations and exclusions.

Amendatory endorsements on these forms, as on other forms, are included in the total package that has been filed. They lie outside the scope of this book.

These forms, in addition to listing the perils that may affect the physical property, also contain a special section setting out special exclusions applicable to the BIC Form as well as to the new Extra Expense Coverage Form.

6. The BIC Form

The discussion and analysis of policy provisions that will be undertaken herein will be devoted primarily to those found within the four corners of the Business Income Coverage Form—Commercial Property. This form is six pages long and deals primarily with the type of matters to be found in the Gross Earnings forms #3 and #4. Where appropriate, a comparison of the parallel items in the two approaches will be undertaken.

In the process of simplification, the words "you" and "your" have been substituted for Insured and the words "we," "us" and "our" for Insurer. There have been other changes in wording as well, all intended to make the Insured feel at home in the contract. How important that is for the type of Insured who buys this type of coverage is an open question. How successful it will be is still another, given the amount of reading matter that will be included in one policy. There have also been some changes in the rights and duties of the parties. In addition, there has been an opening up of the types of coverage that an Insured can purchase using this new form.

C. Outline of the BIC Form

1. Coverages

The form begins with a recital of what may be called a *basic* coverage. This parallels the six P's with which the reader is now familiar. Then, four *additional* coverages are set forth. These are Extra Expense, Civil Authority, Alterations and New Buildings and Extended Business Income. Next follows a coverage *extension* applicable to newly acquired locations. Finally, there are four *optional* or modifying coverages. These are: (a) Maximum Period of Indemnity, (b) Monthly Limit of Indemnity, (c) Agreed Value and (d) Extended Period of Indemnity which applies to the time limit in the regular Extended Business Income provision.

2. Exclusions

Exclusions which are the next item considered are not set forth in the form itself; the attention of the Insured is directed to those exclusions specifically applicable to this form set out in the various Causes of Loss Forms.

3. Limits of Insurance

The applicable limit is set forth in the Declarations.

A 10% additional limit, not to exceed $100,000, is provided in the Coverage Extension. It does not apply to the additional coverages.

4. Loss Conditions

In addition to the those set out in the Common Policy Conditions and Commercial Property Conditions, additional conditions are set forth in the BIC Form itself. They apply to such matters as appraisal, duties of the insured in the event of loss of business income, a special limitation applicable to electronic media and records, the process of loss determination, the time for loss payment and a resumption of operations condition.

5. Additional Condition—Coinsurance

Provisions regarding Coinsurance are set out separately as an additional condition.

6. Optional Coverages

These have been referred to above under Coverage.

7. Definitions

As stated above, certain terms appearing in quotation marks in the text of the form are defined.

D. Provisions of the BIC Form

1. In General

A review of the new BIC Form reveals that no fundamental changes have been made in the traditional concepts underlying its provisions. This will become apparent when the six P's and six E's are applied to its provisions. Neither are the loss determination and settlement provisions seriously disturbed. Nevertheless, all parties dealing with this new contract, when it comes into general use, will have to be aware of those changes that have been made in specific details.

Coverages written in the Gross Earnings form which are in force on January 1, 1986, will continue in force until their expiration. Disputes on policies written in that form will undoubtedly continue and be under consideration by the courts for the next several years. However, it will be important in the years ahead to check carefully as to the form on which the policy has been written. Statements made heretofore concerning certain items under the Gross Earnings form may not be applicable to the new form. Reference to changes has been incorporated in the text where applicable.

The BIC Form is developed around a basic contract to which are added certain options. They are three in number. The first option is to replace that part of the basic contract that contains a coinsurance clause with what is similar to the old Earnings Policy. The second changes the provisions for loss calculation and payment by substituting an arrangement for monthly payments of indemnity within certain limits. The third incorporates the provisions of the agreed value type of policy to predetermine by agreement the amount of loss involved in each time-unit of total or partial suspension of operations.

The Declarations Page indicates which of these alternative options the Insured has selected, if any.

The basic contract itself has been automatically extended to include the additional coverage previously provided by Lag Insurance. This is a significant improvement and should answer many of the complaints Insureds confronted with a loss experience have expressed as a deficiency in the coverage.

2. Applying the Six P's

In order to focus in on those changes which have been introduced by the BIC Form, its provisions will be organized in the format used earlier in this book to uncover the framework of the contracts insuring against loss resulting from interruption of business operations. It is fortuitous that the BIC Forms came out as this book was being written. It provides an opportunity for the analytical methodology (the 6 P's and E's) to be used. That method is useful in analyzing any Business Interruption cover including these new BIC Forms.

Not surprisingly, the opening paragraph of the BIC Form, entitled COVERAGE, parallels the six P's, though with somewhat different wording, in the following way:

P's	BIC FORM
Parties	*We—you*
Property	*Property at premises described*
Peril	*Covered Cause of Loss*
Productivity	*Suspension of Operations*
Period	*Period of Restoration*
Profit	*Business Income*

a. Parties. As stated, the words "you" and "your" are used to refer to the Named Insured and the words "we," "us" and "our" to refer to the Insurer.

An exception to this practice is found in the Common Policy Conditions Form where "first Named Insured" is employed in the cancellation provisions and in the provisions about payment of premiums and return premiums. Care should be taken in writing a policy to name the party who should receive notice of cancellation as the first Insured.

The Commercial Property Conditions Form specifically provides that the coverage does not apply to bailees.

b. Property. The physical property whose damage results in a suspension of operations is referred to as "property at the premises described in the declarations, including personal property in the open (or in a vehicle) within 100 feet . . . ." There is no specific indication anywhere in the BIC Form that the property has to be the property of the Insured, or that the Insured has to have an insurable interest in it. However, as a matter of logic and law, an Insured cannot collect insurance proceeds unless he has an insurable interest to support the type of coverage involved, and then, only to the extent that such insurable interest has been diminished by an insured event. There is a strong inference in some of the later provisions of the form that the Insured must have control over the property but again, nothing specific—except for paragraph D.4.b.(1)(a) where the amount of Extra Expense is to be reduced by the salvage value of property *bought* [italics added] for temporary use.

A similar problem arises, in connection with the resumption of operations provision. The form reads, "by using damaged or undamaged property (including merchandise or stock) at the described premises or elsewhere." If the position is taken that the word "property" in the provision about "property at the described premises" refers to property of the Insured, then it might well be argued that in the requirement to use other property to resume operations, the word "property" can refer only to property of the Insured, in the absence of such language as "belonging to the Insured or others."

The term "premises described" plays an important part in the implementation of the BIC Form. It becomes necessary that the description in the Declarations be properly drawn. Just how this is done would depend on the meaning given to the word "premises." The advisory form of declarations page has space to insert under description of premises: *Prem. No.; Bldg. No.; Location, Construction, and Occupancy.*

Where an address describes a property devoted exclusively to the Insured's operations, the use of a proper street address would appear to be adequate. But the problems under the older forms where an Insured shares the occupancy of a building with a dozen other firms persists. If only the street address of the building is given under "location," has the coverage of the policy been enlarged to cover loss to the Insured resulting from damages to any part of the entire structure? Or, turning to the Civil Authority Clause, is the damage to the property of another tenant in the same building included within the meaning of the clause which refers to "damage to property other than at the described premises"? If the description is more limited, e.g., "The premises of the Union Club on the 50th floor of the building known as and numbered 50 Union Street in San Francisco, California," would there be coverage if a fire destroyed the controls in the basement of the building so that the elevators could not be operated and patrons could not gain access to the Union Club?

It should be noted that in the Commercial Property Conditions, a different expression is used. Instead of "property at the premises described," the term used is the "covered property." Conceptually, we have already concluded that the covered property under this type of insurance is the inchoate property right to receive a flow of income from certain physical property. This, then, is lost sight of in the Commercial Property Conditions which reads in part "prior to the loss of your Covered Property or Covered Income." The physical property is *described*, it is not *covered*. The language used could be improved.

The BIC Form contains a paragraph entitled "Coverage Extension" which extends the coverage to apply to property at any other location that the Insured may acquire other than fairs and exhibitions. There are restrictions in the amount that can be applied at such other locations and a requirement of notice to the Insurer in order to continue the coverage beyond 30 days.

A traditional alterations and new buildings clause is also included. If the damage delays the start of operations, the "period of restoration" begins on the date operations would otherwise have begun. Of significance is the fact that this provision now applies to new machinery, equipment etc., which was not the case previously.

For example, if damage on December 10 to a building under construction delays its scheduled opening and start up of operations on February 10 to May 10, then any loss of Business Income incurred from February 10 until May 10 will be recoverable. Of course, if repairs could be completed before February 10 and operations recommence, there is no loss.

The operations must occur at the described premises. Suppose that the executive offices of a business enterprise are located at the described premises and contain the computers and programs whereby the operations at a number of subsidiary plants located elsewhere are directed and controlled. Damage to the computers will affect operations at the other plants. Does this constitute operations at the described premises? If so, then the financial activities at the other non-described premises may have to be included in calculating the business interruption value under the provisions of the coinsurance clause, which covers "operations at the described premises." The same problem arises when the damages are at a show room where orders are taken that are executed at the plant in another area.

c. Productivity. "Operations" is the key word used in the BIC Form to deal with productivity. It is defined as meaning "the type of your business activities occurring at the described premises." This definition serves as a gateway into more questions.

What is "type" of business activity? Presumably, it is intended to refer to such diverse activities as manufacturing, merchandizing or service-oriented operations. For persons informed about business interruption practices, this meaning comes naturally to mind. This unifying approach eliminates the need for special forms for those different kinds of business activity. However, the work sheet for use under the options has columns for manufacturing and non-manufacturing operations.

The verb "occurring" refers to a present time. While this could be either the time when the policy was written or the time when the damage occurred, it is undoubtedly the latter because the coverage statement refers to "suspension of operations." This puts it in a time frame. A change in the nature of the operations between the two times would not, however, affect liability. Whether any provision for increase of risk is made is not known. However, traditional precepts would seem to protect the Insurer where an Insured has materially increased the risk of loss between the time the policy is written and the time of the damage.

d. Period. "Period of restoration" is another term appearing in quotation marks in the BIC Form. As defined, it ends on the date when the physical premises "*should* [italics added] be repaired, rebuilt or replaced with reasonable speed and similar quality." "Similar quality" would appear to incorporate the extended period provided by the built-in "lag insurance." As in the past, the exclusion of any increased period of interruption due to the operation of zoning or building laws persists.

Again, as in the old forms, the period is not cut short by the expiration date.

These provisions raise a number of questions. The first is semantic. It involves the word "should." The word could connote that there is some standard that must be met; the Insured is under obligation to meet this standard. The Insured was under no obligation to get back into operations under the Gross Earnings Form. His loss was measured by the time it *would* have taken him had he used due diligence and dispatch. Does the change to the word "should" indicate that this leeway is now being eliminated; that the Insured is obliged to proceed with reasonable speed? Probably, not—this new approach in wording does not appear to have any intent to make a substantive change.

If one checks the duties imposed upon the Insured in the event of loss under the BIC Form, the last one listed is to "resume all or part of your 'operations' as quickly as possible." This does, indeed, impose upon the Insured a positive obligation to act promptly.

Since the form further provides that the Insurer will pay the loss if "you have complied with all of the terms of this Coverage Part," failure to proceed promptly might serve as a basis for denying liability because of a breach of the policy terms. This constitutes a change in the contract and imposes a new burden on the Insured. Certainly, it restricts the limits of discretion formerly allowed the Insured on how he should proceed. The reasoning behind this change is found under Extent, where a change in the handling of extra expense is discussed.

In the "period of restoration" definition, the substitution of "reasonable speed" for "due diligence and dispatch" is of little consequence. Both terms are dependent on speculation for their interpretation. All that was written on the subject earlier would still seem to apply. The same comment can be made about the change, in the definition, of "same quality of service" to "similar quality." Note, however, that in the loss determination provision the old phrase "quality of service" is used.

"Cut short," in the final sentence of the BIC Form, is another attempt to popularize the language. Its use does not materially affect the intention of extending liability for loss resulting from damage occurring within the policy term to beyond the expiration date of the policy.

This language does not change the concept that it is the ability to restore operations that forms the termination of liability. However, there has been introduced into the BIC Form, as a basic coverage, what previously was securable only as Lag Insurance. Under the heading "Extended Business Income," liability for actual loss sustained between the date when operational ability is restored and operations start and the date when the Insured could restore his business with reasonable speed to the condition that would have existed had no damage occurred is assumed. This is a meaningful liberalization of the coverage.

There is a provision in the Commercial Property Conditions Form that coverage applies to "loss or damage commencing during the period shown in the Declarations." This puts a time frame around the period during which the damage causing the loss must take place.

Under the same extended business income provision appear the words "restore your business." Just what this means could raise a question. It could mean restore the volume of production, or the volume of sales, or the amount of gross income or the amount of net income, as well as the reduction of expenses to what was normal before the damage. Hardly the latter, because that development is otherwise dealt with in the resumption of operations provision. It probably refers to retention of net income. There is however, a thirty day limit on this extension; although, a lower extension period may be purchased with the policy.

e. Profit. The term "Business Income" replaces "Gross Earnings" to describe the subject of the insurance. It is defined as: "Net Income (Net Profit or Loss before income taxes) that would have been earned or incurred, and continuing normal operating expenses including payroll, incurred." This is a return to the type of calculation required under the old Two Item form.

By including the word "loss," it clarifies the fact that, even though the Accountant's financial statement shows a loss, this negative figure does not eliminate the possibility of a compensable business interruption value. The expenses incurred are treated as a positive figure and if, when added to other-wise negative operating loss, results in a positive figure—that figure represents the Insured's business interruption value. Should a negative figure result, then there was no such value. Here the word "loss" represents the result of the Accountant's normal calculations and could be a different amount from that reached if techniques required by the policy were used.

The new wording calls specific attention to the fact that it is income before income taxes that should govern the amount of insurance bought.

The words "continuing normal" exclude new expenses necessitated by the damage. "Normal" is carried over from past policies. However, there is in this form no definition of what is normal. Presumably, it means normal for this particular business enterprise.

Reference has already been made to the additional period over which profit is calculated provided by the extended business income provision. What if a fire sale is held right after operations start up and produces a substantial profit in the first 30 days—the lag period—does this reduce the Insured's loss under his policy? Arguably it should, at least with respect to the lag period.

3. Applying the Six E's

a. Extent. There are a number of provisions in the BIC Form which deal with the number of dollars available for paying a loss. It is not dealt with in the Common Policy Declarations, but the declarations page of the Commercial Property Coverage Part, under "coverages provided," has space for noting the limit of insurance on each of the coverages shown in the appropriate place on the page. This applies to what has been called the basic contract to differentiate it from the various options. For them a separate place to note the amount is provided.

The policy limit, however, does not represent the maximum amount that an Insured can collect. Within the BIC Form is provision for an additional amount, in excess of this limit, that the Insured can collect. This derives from the coverage extension to newly acquired Property.

Provided that a coinsurance percentage of 50% or more is shown in the declarations, the Insured can, for a limited time, apply 10% of the limit of insurance, but not more than $100,000 to such other property. The BIC Form states, "the limit applicable to the Coverage Extension is in addition to the Limit of Insurance." It is stated to be additional insurance. In 30 days from acquisition, the coverage ends unless additional values are reported and the appropriate additional premium, if any, is paid.

However, an increase in the limit is not applicable to the other policy provisions which provide additional coverage, including alterations and new buildings, the extra expense, the civil authority or the extended business income provisions.

There are a number of provisions applicable to the Extent of recovery in the event of loss which will be discussed in the second part. One notable change is the replacement of the capitalized phrase ACTUAL LOSS SUS-TAINED by the words "actual loss of Business Income you sustain." The downgrading of emphasis appears to be some recognition of the impossibility of determining actual loss. While it is a move in the right direction, it does not seem to go far enough.

The coverage provision goes on to state that "the suspension must be caused by direct physical loss of or damage to property . . . ." It is difficult to conceive of indirect physical damage. It would seem that the "directness" applies to the causation and not to the loss or damage. In other words, the reference is to a suspension *directly caused by physical damage*.

Another change is the elimination of the right of the Insurer to elect to repair the property.

New wording is introduced in the BIC Form concerning the limit of insurance. It states that the applicable limit is the most it will pay "in any one occurrence." There is no statement in the form about automatic reinstatement of coverage. But the per occurrence wording is to the effect that the full limit remains available for subsequent losses during the policy period.

The civil authority provision in most respects follows the approach of the Gross Earnings form. However, the comparatively recent additional requirement in the Gross Earnings form that the damage must have occurred in "adjacent" property has been removed. The wording clears up one question—from what date do the two weeks start to run—it is from when the authorities act. There is no requirement that there be damage at the described premises.

b. Experience. Substantial change has been made in the prior language about experience before and probable experience after. Again, it can be said that the change in wording does not make a change in basic concepts.

The amount of loss will "be determined based on the Net Income of the business before the damage." No guide is offered as to how long before. What has been written herein about calculations under the Gross Earnings Form is still applicable.

Instead of "probable future experience," the BIC Form reads, "the likely Net Income of the business if no loss or damage occurred." There does not seem to be any substantive difference between the two as far as the effect is concerned.

c. Exclusions. These are Exclusions specifically applicable to the Business Income Coverage Form to be found in the Causes of Loss Form. They are five in number. The Insurer will not pay for:

1. Any loss caused by or resulting from damage or destruction of "finished stock" or the time required to reproduce the same. This exclusion does not apply to extra expenses.
2. Any loss caused by or resulting from damage to radio or television antennas.
3. Increase of loss caused by or resulting from strikers or other persons whose

actions at the site of the rebuilding, repairing or replacing causes a delay in restoring operations.

4. Increase of loss caused by suspension, lapse or cancellation of any license, lease or contract unless such extra loss results directly from the suspension of operations. In the latter case, it will pay for loss experienced during the "period of restoration." Also, there is no payment for extra expense beyond that period.
5. Any other consequential loss.

Additionally, the BIC Form contains a limitation of the length of time for which the Insurer will be liable for loss resulting from damage to electronic media and records.

d. Effort. Mention has already been made concerning the obligation of the Insured to minimize his loss by curtailing the period of suspension of operations. One area where such effort is dealt with specifically is the provision concerning resumption of operations. While not mandating any specific action on the part of the Insured, the BIC Form states that the Insurer will reduce the amount of the Insured's business income loss to the extent he can resume "operations" in whole or in part, by using damaged or undamaged property. This parallels the provision in the Gross Earnings form discussed earlier.

An area where specific effort is required of the Insured is found in duties in the event of loss of business income. Again the pattern of the fire insurance policy sets the pattern for the details.

These duties include the taking of all reasonable steps to protect the property from further damage. In the Gross Earnings form, this duty was tied into preventing extension of the period of interruption. This limitation has been eliminated in the BIC Form. As written it has more relevance to property insurance contracts.

There are some positive additions to the list of duties which have always existed in practice but which were never spelled out in previous forms of policy. One is the keeping of a record of expenses for consideration in the settlement of the claim. Another is a statement that the Insured must cooperate with the Insurer in the investigation or settlement of the claim. One wonders whether liability could be denied for breach of contract, if the Insured took an arbitrary stand in settlement negotiations. Could this be considered lack of cooperation? Specific mention has already been made of the duty to resume all or part of the Insured's "operations" as quickly as possible.

Other duties listed will be considered in Chapter 16.

e. Extras. An extensive rearrangement of material in the BIC Form involves the matter of extra expense. In this regard, a new approach has been incorporated in the BIC Form. This represents one of the major departures from the approach taken under the Gross Earnings form. In the latter form, expediting expenses incurred by the Insured which speeded up the restoration of operations were recoverable only to the extent that they reduced the Insurer's loss. In addition, an Insured could purchase Extra Expense Insurance which picked up costs beyond normal ones incurred by him to maintain service to his customers.

The BIC Form provides both of these coverages under the heading of Extra Expense and includes them automatically in the policy. They are divided into three classes—the first two in connection with property. In the first two classes, there is no longer a requirement that the expense result in a reduction of loss to the Insurer. The sole limitation is that they be "necessary." Only in the third class is this requirement maintained.

The typographical set-up of Section A.3.a. is most unfortunate. A reader, accustomed to the provisions of the Business Interruption Insurance policies, readily assumes that the limitation at the end of (3) applies to all three classes, limiting recovery of expediting expenses to amounts reducing the Insurer's loss, as in the past. It takes close observation, preferably with the help of a straight-edge, to determine that the printed type of the limitation does not extend out beyond (3); it is not positioned so as to be associated with "3. a., Extra Expense," at the beginning of the provision. Furthermore, a close reading of the language indicates that the pronoun "it," appearing in the limitation, grammatically refers back to the word "expense" in (3). In the new Extra Expense, coverage form however, the word "expense" does not appear at the beginning of (the equivalent provision in Section A.1.c.), nor of (1.a.) or (1.b.), so that the pronoun "it" could well be related to the word "expense" in "A.1."; thus raising the issue as to what the limitation applies to under that policy. (By way of caveat, it is possible that the form used by your authors was incorrectly printed and that the intent was to make the loss reduction requirement applicable to all three elements of extra expense.) As a result, an Insured who needs the protection of traditional Extra Expense Insurance should clarify the question with his Insurer.

It may be that it is this increase in liability assumed by the Insurer that supports the express requirement, listed as (i) under Duties in the Event of Loss, making it mandatory for the Insured to "resume all or part of your 'operations' as quickly as possible." The Insurer is now paying for the extra expenses incurred until operations are resumed. Therefore, the Insurer is justified in putting the burden on the Insured to resume operations.

The third class of extra expense, where the requirement of loss reduction clearly prevails, is divided into two sub-classes: (1) extra expense to repair or replace any property and (2) extra expense to research, replace or restore the lost information on damaged valuable papers and records. The requirement that they be "necessary" still applies.

Extra expense is carried as an additional item of payment, subject to various limitations. It does not increase but rather is subject to the applicable limit of insurance. It is also subject to reduction by the salvage value that remains of any property bought by the Insured for temporary use and by the amount of any extra expense paid for by other insurance not of the same character. Extra expense loss payment will be limited to the amount paid out before "operations" *can* be returned to normal by the actions of the Insured in compliance with the resumption of operations provisions. ("Could" would express the intent better than "can.")

The Coinsurance Clause, as in the Gross Earnings form, does not apply to extra expense.

f. Enough. As used in this book, Enough refers to the operation of the Coinsurance Clause. The same general discussion devoted to the Gross Earnings form is relevant to the BIC Form with one exception. The 12 month projection period is not counted from the date of the damage but, instead, from the inception or last previous anniversary date of the policy, whichever is later.

This is a significant change in favor of the Insured who calculates his coinsurance requirements on the same basis and at the same time that he decides upon the limits of insurance that he buys. This will decrease the possibility of a coinsurance penalty arising out of increases in the Insured's business subsequent to policy inception. Of course, if he has a policy running for more than one year, he still has to make a new calculation on anniversary date. Three quarters of an entire page of the six pages constituting the BIC Form are devoted to describing the operation of the coinsurance clause and giving examples of how it would operate in the event of a loss under specific circumstances.

The provisions of the BIC Form in connection with the handling of a loss are discussed in Ch. 16.

9

Summary

In the first part which now comes to a conclusion, the theory underlying the Business Interruption Insurance contract has been explored.

The preceding analysis involved a discussion of the gradual evolution of a contractual arrangement whereby that group of persons who were involved in a particular type of business activity might make limited contributions to a money pool out of which payments could be made to those members of the group who were not able to develop the Earnings Stream that they had reasonably anticipated, because their tools of production had been damaged or destroyed by a specified peril. From the early involvement of the persons engaged in shipping who wished to ensure the receipt of anticipated freight and profits, to the lessors of real estate whose flow of rental income might be interrupted, the concept spread to those who had invested large sums of money in manufacturing and mercantile enterprises. Ultimately, the continuing flow of funds to those engaged in what are known as servicing functions became the object of similar concern.

The drafting of a satisfactory contractual arrangement was not an easy one. The chapters dealing with history and development graphically indicate the groping that took place over the years for adequate conceptualization and appropriate language with which to meet the needs of persons in each group.

Many changes have been made in the original concept of protecting the Insured's net profits from production on a daily basis—the amount of profits to be established, in advance, under a valued policy. Periods of time were lumped together in weekly and monthly units and then, with the introduction of coinsurance, were eliminated. Recognition of the need to discharge ordinary help in case of a long interruption resulted in the development of the two-item form. Final eradication of the term "Use and Occupancy" and the problems it created arrived with the adoption of the Gross Earnings forms. With them, came the recognition that it was the potential of the physical property to produce an Earnings Stream, that was the interest which this type of contract was intended to protect.

The potential for improvement, in the contracts in general use up through 1985, has been indicated. So, too, has been the need to develop new contracts which will meet the needs of those engaged in business in the age of nuclear development and technological break-through which is upon us.

The Business Income Coverage (BIC) Form scheduled to go into use nationally on January 1, 1986, grapples with some of the subjects for improvement so indicated. Without changing the basis nature of the contract or of the inchoate property interest which is insured, it does make changes in some fairly substantial concepts, incidentally cutting the contract loose from an underlying Property Insurance policy.

As indicated in Chapter 8, there are still some matters that would benefit from improvement, among them some questions created by the new form. No doubt, further consideration will be given to the entire subject before the form becomes mandatory in 1987.

In the course of the discussion, tangential reference has been made to the fact that special forms have been designed for persons with special needs. So, Period of Indemnity or "Lag" Insurance and Contingent Business Interruption Insurance have been mentioned, also Strike Insurance and Profits Insurance.

Extra Expense Insurance has been developed to reimburse those who must undertake extra expediting expenses without regard to whether the ultimate loss will be reduced. A form of Earnings Insurance has been developed for persons operating smaller enterprises who, for one reason or another, do not want to become involved with the requirements of the Coinsurance or Contribution Clause.

Endorsements have been promulgated whereby ordinary payroll can be excluded from the calculations of the Gross Earnings form. Others are available to cover off-premises damage which causes on-premises interruption of operations.

Copies of a few of the forms in current general usage as well as a copy of the BIC Form for Commercial Property will be found in Addendum II. To some extent, there will be a consideration later of the employment of these forms. On the whole, however, the frequent changes in wording of such specialized applications of the underlying theory have suggested that their analysis and application be left to current writings about these various forms as they develop rather than discussing these forms here.

Through the analysis of the current Gross Earnings form, a skeletal structure of a contract of Business Interruption Insurance has been exposed. There are twelve component parts. They have been designed as the six P's and the six E's.

The skeletal structure has been fleshed out to some extent in this first part. More detail will be supplied as the discussion moves from theory to an examination of practice in later chapters. But no discussion, however lengthy, can attempt to explore the unlimited number of possibilities that can arise.

The practitioner must bring to his work an understanding of how business enterprises operate, so as to develop a practical approach to issues, and must also possess a flexibility of thinking capable of dealing with the subjective framework within which many decisions have to be made.

That is why Business Interruption Insurance presents such an exciting challenge to the practitioner.

Part Two

Practice

Introduction
to
Part Two

History. Organization. Procedure.

A. Past History

The history of the development of today's Business Interruption Insurance contract and the conceptual framework on which it is built were dealt with in earlier chapters. During the more than one century that has elapsed since this type of insurance was first made available in the United States, great strides have been taken in composing a contract to meet the needs of the insuring public. The road to today's Gross Earnings form is strewn with the debris of contracts that inadequately served that purpose. It took time and the experience of many loss adjustments to develop a clear understanding of the exact nature of the coverage that should be offered.

There is still room for improvement. New types of exposures are being created. Because of the vast size and complexity of many of today's business enterprises, the establishment of the amount of loss often involves a tremendous amount of calculation and very heavy costs for Accountants. Imagination and innovation on the part of Agents and Underwriters will still be needed in the future.

As discussed in Chapter 8, a new form will soon be in use. Its provisions will bring about some changes in practice in order to meet its requirements. By and large, these will be minor, as indicated in the earlier discussions. Fundamentally, the practices that have developed over the years will continue to be pertinent. Those that have proven useful will continue to apply.

For that reason, the Gross Earnings form will be used herein for purposes of analysis and discussion since most readers are familiar with it and since, with a few exceptions, the anticipated changes are more a matter of form than of substance. Where deemed appropriate, a reference to the BIC Form will call attention to materials contained in Ch. 8 and Ch. 16. However, the reader is again cautioned to take into consideration the exact wording of the particular policy that may be involved in any given situation.

B. Organization of Part Two

The second part deals with practice; how a policy of Business Interruption Insurance operates in the real world. Consideration will be given to the kind and amount of insurance an Owner should purchase and the reimbursement of loss he can reasonably expect to recover.

In exploring these areas of concern, an innovative technique will be employed. The usual method of analyzing the language of each policy provision and applying it to a series of fact situations will not be followed. Business Interruption Insurance will herein rather be considered through the activities of the people involved in its functioning in a business setting. It could be called a *Sequential Approach.*

Five processes have been identified as the steps taken in the development of the usual fact situation. They are described in the text as the processes of insuring the risk, of adjusting a loss, of settling the claim, of dealing with differences of opinion, and of the ultimate recourse to the courts.

They constitute the subject matter of Chapters 10 to 15. Chapter 16 deals with the provisions of the BIC Form and the related provisions in other forms specifically referred to therein. Then it considers the duties of the Insured in the event of loss, and the basis on which the amount of loss will be determined and paid. Chapter 17 examines briefly various other types of time element insurance.

C. Procedure to be Followed

Conceptually it makes no major difference as to the type of business organization that is taken as the prototype—a self-proprietorship, a partnership or a corporation. The basic applicable principles are, in large part, the same. For purposes of unity in exposition, it will be assumed that the business enterprise operates as a corporation, unless a specific fact situation requires a different approach. The third party singular pronoun will still be used to refer to the Insured.

The names of the types of parties involved at various stages of the sequence of events will be capitalized for emphasis. These parties will include the Owner, the Intermediary and the Underwriter as the main characters in the process of insuring the risk; the Loss Manager, the Adjuster and the Accountant in the process of adjusting the loss and settling the claim; and the Lawyer, the Appraisers and the Judge in the process of confrontation. Other parties such as

Engineers, Public Adjusters and others will also be introduced. It is planned to bring these various characters onto to the scene one by one as the action of writing and dealing with a Business Interruption policy develops. Types of insurance policies will also be capitalized.

The six P's and the six E's, where mentioned, will be relegated to lower case treatment.

The notes in the second part will consist largely of references to reported cases. The exact citations are listed in Addendum III. These references are designed to assist the reader who desires a broader understanding of the matter under discussion. The decision of the court in each case, may or may not conform with acceptable principles today. They are presented as illustrations, not as authorities. They deal primarily with policies of Use and Occupancy, Business Interruption and Rent Insurance; a few involve policies of Fire Insurance.

10

Process of Insuring the Risk

Owner. Intermediary. Underwriter.

A. The Owner

The term "Owner" is used herein to denote the person responsible for determining the overall program of the business enterprise. It includes the salaried person who is employed to manage a business for its stockholders. It also includes employees charged primarily with the handling of the insurance programs, such as the Risk Manager.

1. Determine the Extent of Exposure to Risk

It is the responsibility of the Owner of a business enterprise to maintain the integrity of the physical assets that produce its Earnings Stream. To that end, he must apply the traditional principles of risk management. As a final stage in that process, insurance in a certain amount must be procured as a source of funds to repair or replace those assets should their materiality be damaged by specified perils. This is accomplished by Property Insurance. It is also the responsibility of the Owner to maintain the financial integrity of the business enterprise by the continuity of the Earnings Stream during the period when the physical assets are being repaired or replaced.[1]

The term "Disaster Plan" is coming more and more into use in connection with avoidance of loss. It encompasses those steps that have been prearranged to maintain operations in the event of damage.

The concept is not entirely new. Having spare parts on hand has always been a way of limiting suspension of operations. So has been the provision of standby equipment that can be brought into use quickly, and the division of operations into separate units not all subject to the same exposure.

But, recently, industry has found it desirable to carry planning much further. Reciprocal contracts with other companies to make their facilities available in the event of damage are being executed. Arrangements with banks, schools and other computer owners for shared time in the event of computer shut-down are proliferating. The planning even extends to such matters as the transportation, housing and feeding of employees in the event that the contingency arises and other facilities must be used.

To date, it has primarily been large companies that have taken the necessary steps to arrange a full Disaster Plan. Apart from any considerations of insurance, this would appear to be a step that is highly desirable for every operating company.

Suspension of operations takes a toll that no insurance can completely eliminate. There also remains the very practical consideration that, if by the adoption of an adequate Disaster Plan, a cap can be put on the extent of the loss that is likely to be suffered, an Insured may be able to buy a lesser amount of insurance than would otherwise be required—enough to cover the residual loss anticipated after the Disaster Plan has been put into operation.

Whether or not the Owner does establish a specific Disaster Plan for continuing operations, much of the thinking that such a plan would entail is involved in the process of providing Business Interruption Insurance for his business. Beyond these brief remarks, the process is too specific to a particular enterprise to be susceptible of further rewarding discussion.

a. Use of Asset Schedule. The Owner's responsibility is met, in part, by means of the schedule of assets maintained by the enterprise. This normally contains the name and description of each of the capital assets, its source, the date purchased and its cost or value. If properly maintained, the schedule will also be updated from time to time to reflect the increased cost of replacements due to inflation. This type of schedule should be used for buildings, machinery, tools, furniture and also for a stock of merchandise. By referring to it, the Owner can readily determine the values at risk and can use this as the foundation for his decision about the amount of Property Insurance that should be purchased. But that schedule is not adequate as a basis for forming a judgment regarding the amount of Business Interruption Insurance that should be purchased. Even the loss of a relatively inexpensive item of equipment could, if not readily replaceable, cause an extensive interruption of business.

Time is a major element in the amount of business interruption loss that may be suffered. It is the value of the time required to restore the property to its former quality of operations that is the basis of a loss. Therefore, time as well as value must be taken into consideration by the Owner in deciding how much Business Interruption Insurance to buy. This requires that he have information which does not usually appear on the schedule of assets. The schedule statistics must, therefore, be expanded to show the time it would take to replace each item of physical property involved in the creation of the Earnings Stream, should it be destroyed.

b. Bottlenecks. The purpose of such expansion is to bring to the Owner's attention any "bottlenecks" that might exist. This term has generally been used to describe any situation or condition which would extend the period of replacement beyond the time span that might normally be expected. A number of circumstances could bring about such a result.

With respect to a factory building or other structure, a bottleneck could exist in the unavailability, through ordinary channels, of special materials used in its construction; in the necessity to comply with local zoning or building laws; in the need to secure the cooperation of others in the process of rebuilding; in the terms of a lease that may force a move to other quarters; in the peculiarities or "flow" of the manufacturing process itself; in the seasonal weather conditions of the area where the property is located, as well as in other circumstances which might affect the timing of its repair or replacement.

Where the manufacturer of machinery or equipment used by the Insured has discontinued the regular manufacture of the item, or will produce it only on special order and only when time permits, a delay can be encountered. This is particularly the situation where specially designed machinery has been manufactured abroad. A classic case is that of the Scott Paper Company mill which had to wait more than eighteen months before a major piece of equipment could be manufactured by the one company in the world that could build it and whose employees were on strike. Almost $4,000,000 was reported to have been paid by the business interruption Insurer.

Such extraordinary situations as those brought about by war, boycott, extended strikes at the suppliers' plants, government restrictions on the use of materials and the like may not always be anticipated in buying Business Interruption Insurance. But the Owner who has been sensitized to the factor of time will be more alert to these possibilities and will make necessary adjustments as conditions develop.

Materials used in the course of manufacture sometimes require a lengthy preconditioning period. If they are destroyed midway through the period, production must wait until new materials have gone through the process of preparation.

Normally, stocks of merchandise can be readily replaced, but such action is not always possible. Where a stock of embroidered tablecloths made by hand in Italy by farmers' wives during the winter months were destroyed by fire, the importer had to wait until after the following winter before he could replace his stock in trade. In another case, an explosion in a factory laboratory destroyed all of the control samples of colors used by the manufacturer in the dyeing of threads, together with all of the books in which the formulas were recorded. The delay encountered before these could be replaced was extensive.

It is not possible to list all of the "bottlenecks" that might exist in the operation of a particular business. (Klein lists a considerable number of examples, though from the point of view of an Underwriter and not of the Owner.)[2] In the majority of cases, no "bottleneck" of great magnitude exists. But in fulfilling his responsibilities, the Owner must conduct a full investigation. This requirement will grow increasingly important as robotics and computerized equipment as well as sophisticated products are introduced into the operation of business enterprises.

Another possibility exists where a manufacturer produces several products which, while not integrally related, do constitute a "line" that his customers generally buy from one source. For example, a manufacturer and distributor of supplies for a particular type of business operation (such as hotel, hospital, or auto body repair shop) may find that his inability to supply one major item of those supplies substantially impacts on his sales of the other items of his "line" which were unaffected by the physical damage.

c. *Expansion of the Schedule.* One technique used to meet this requirement is the addition of another column to the usual schedule of physical assets. This contains an estimate of the time required to replace the particular item should such action become necessary. As a practical matter, only those that might prove to be bottlenecks need to be so treated. The list should be reviewed once a year to bring it up to date. As suggested earlier, the development of extraordinary outside conditions should also trigger a review.

For such a survey to be effective, structures and machines must be broken down into their component parts. The observation that "for want of a nail, a kingdom was lost" has application here. Parts may have been built to individual specifications; additions or modifications may have been made in the process of installation; special installation materials may be required. Often, this type of specialization is where a "bottleneck" lurks and should be disclosed by an adequate survey.

It is hardly necessary to add that, in a business enterprise of any size, it will not be the Owner himself who will conduct the survey. It will be done by the production, the engineering and the procurement personnel. But the Owner still remains responsible for designing a program that will ultimately bring to him the information necessary to determine what might, "in worst case," be the period that operations may be shut down, in whole or in part. This will assist the Owner to make the final determination as to the amount of Business Interruption Insurance that is required to meet the amount of possible loss he has decided to cover by insurance.

d. *"Off-premises bottlenecks."* In addition to any "bottlenecks" which may exist on the Owner's premises, there may be external "bottlenecks" that exist off-premises, which may equally affect the timing of restoration of operations. One type of external "bottleneck" would slow down the inflow of materials upon which operations depend. Thus, an interruption of goods or supplies needed by the Owner, brought about by damage to the productive facilities of the producer of such goods or supplies, could bring about an interruption in part or in whole of the Owner's operations. Such goods or supplies might be made by a separate plant belonging to the Owner or by a plant belonging to someone else.

Where the same company owned both a factory making a special type of electric bulb and a separate factory using that bulb in producing Christmas ornaments, the destruction of the bulb factory could result in a shut down of the ornament factory. Similarly, a store selling factory "seconds" would have no supply of goods to sell, if the factory were destroyed by fire.

The possibility of "bottlenecks" existing in the flow of incoming goods and supplies by damage to the supplier's plant must be investigated by the Owner. If alternate sources of the necessary materials are not available, a need exists to seek protection by insurance against interruption resulting from such damage to the property of others.

In a mercantile operation, the destruction of a warehouse or distribution center may have drastic effects upon the availability of a product for sale at retail outlets. In the case of the grocery chain, where the central warehouse was destroyed, the local store managers were faced with extra expense in shopping for, stocking and handling the merchandise they needed. Even if the product can be obtained from alternate sources, the mix of goods at retail level may be affected with resultant loss in profitability.

Conversely, an external "bottleneck" may exist where the continued operation of the Owner's production depends upon the ability of certain customers to accept and pay for the goods produced. In the case of Christmas ornaments mentioned above, the bulb manufacturer could have found himself with no place to sell his bulbs if his ornament-making factory was out of operation. It might be possible for him to find another buyer, but not if the product was specially designed for the needs of his particular ornament factory. Further, there may be adequate business reasons why the Owner of both factories would not to want to sell his special bulbs to competitors.

Where a service organization depends for a major part of its income on the continued operation of a customer's plant or place of business, an external "bottleneck" normally exists. The Owner is thus presented with a challenge—to determine if any such "bottlenecks" exist in connection with Buyers and, if so, to take measures to protect his company's Earnings Stream against loss due to damage to the property of his customers.

Goods and supplies are not the only items whose uninterrupted flow is vital for the continuous operation of the Owner's business. Electric energy, as a source of power, light, cooling and other uses, is almost universally required by every type of business operation. Where such energy is purchased from outside sources rather than being produced in-house, any damage to the source at which the energy is produced can adversely affect the Owner's production. The

Owner should also examine the channel of supply of such electric energy to determine whether any possible "bottlenecks" exist in the transmission lines to his own premises. The need for an adequate inflow of water can also be the source of a possible "bottleneck."

One more possible external "bottleneck" that it would be wise to investigate is that of outside services which are needed to keep an operation running. These could exist, for example, in the transportation of items into and out of the place of business.

Where the business enterprise does not own the building in which operations are being conducted, but merely occupies all or a part of the building as a tenant, there exists the strong possibility that damage to the building, without any damage to those premises occupied by the business enterprise, could interrupt operations in part or entirely. Such could be case with the Owner of a leased department in a department store or the Owner of a small factory operating in a large multi-purpose manufacturing building. A related situation would exist for the Owner of a small retail store in a large shopping mall to which customers are attracted by the presence of a large "anchor" store. In each of the above situations an Owner must be alert to the possibility of a diminution in the Earnings Stream of his business enterprise by damage to the property of others without any damage to his own property on the premises occupied by his own activities.

The increasing dependence of many business operations on computers, which may often be located off-premises, presents an Owner with another area of concern. Damage to the computer itself or to stored information can seriously impair the ability of the enterprise to continue in its usual fashion and can reduce earnings. Transfer of information via satellite, if interrupted, could stop operations. The development of a Disaster Plan to go into operation when damage occurs in large properties, particularly where computers are involved, is . become increasingly a duty of management.[3]

e. Owner's Precautions. With the results of the survey in hand, the Owner should return to his application of risk management techniques, particularly to the efforts to reduce risk. These should now be re-examined in light of their impact on a possible business interruption loss. How great is the residual risk that cannot be reduced and should be covered by insurance? In this connection, certain concerns should be considered.

The first concern is what might be called "defenses"—the aspects of the physical set-up that mitigate against a total shut-down of operations. The major question to be answered is whether there is such a physical separation of production facilities that not all are likely to be exposed to a single disaster. More specifically, do parallel facilities exist for every stage of operations and are they carried on in separate plants or buildings so as to be properly considered as separate risks? Careful judgment must be exercised here. For example, one storage company felt secure because it used ten separate buildings for storage purposes. Unfortunately, one fire destroyed five of them.[4]

The second concern involves what might be termed "reserves"—standby equipment and supplies that can be thrown into the breach if primary facilities are put out of commission. A standby boiler and an auxiliary gasoline-operated generator of electricity would be examples of such reserves. So would be the spare and replacement parts and equipment that are maintained on hand. An excess inventory of manufacturing or packaging materials would be another such reserve. A secondary cache of computer records, of laboratory records or of building and machinery blueprints and specifications are other examples.

Lastly, is the matter of "alternatives." These would include alternate facilities or alternate sources of acceptable materials by means of which operations can be carried on in whole or in part while repairs are being made.

The extent to which the presence of such precautionary measures have reduced the risk of loss will be taken into consideration by the Owner in determining how much Business Interruption Insurance he needs.

2. Determine the Amount of Business Interruption Value

The next step to be undertaken by the Owner is to translate the matter of risk into dollars; to determine the amount of the Business Interruption Insurable Value; to attach a dollar figure to the Earnings Stream that might be involved. In carrying out this part of his responsibility, the Owner will co-opt the services of the financial personnel associated with the enterprise, including the Treasurer, Comptroller and Accòuntant.[5]

It should be clearly understood that while the calculation of the Business Interruption Value is based on the financial figures and records maintained in the regular course of business, such figures serve only as the raw material out of which the calculations are developed. They must be adapted and adjusted to meet the provisions of the Business Interruption Insurance policy. These provisions do not parallel ordinary accounting procedures in all respects. (Gross Earnings are usually called "Earnings from Operations" by Accountants.)

a. Work Sheet—Column 1. To assist Owners in their calculations, a form has been prepared and is available known as the Combination Business Interruption Work Sheet. It is a structured outline of the steps that an Owner should take. The work sheet issued in connection with the Gross Earning forms will serve as the basis for the discussion that will follow. A copy of this work sheet is to be found in Addendum II. No matter what form of policy is involved, preparation of some type of work sheet by the Owner is necessary to determine the Business Interruption Insurable Value. It becomes almost mandatory when a Coinsurance Clause is included in the policy.

As a result of historical development, a distinction is usually drawn in policy forms between enterprises engaged in manufacturing and those engaged in mercantile and nonmanufacturing activities. This separation is reflected in the work sheet where differing techniques of calculation are applied to the differing nature of the operation. The work sheet is broad enough, however, to cover a business enterprise engaged solely in one type of operation or in several.

The line of separation between a manufacturing business and a mercantile business is not always a sharp one. Manufacturers, to fill out their line, will frequently list in their catalogues products produced by another manufacturer but sold under their own name. On the other hand, firms engaged in the sale of products will sometimes apply labor to their merchandise to meet a customer's needs. Thus a seller of fabrics may convert material into finished curtains, or a seller of kitchen cabinets may undertake to install a kitchen for a customer. The Combination Work Sheet—Gross Earnings Form—eliminates the difference in approach between manufacturing and non-manufacturing operations. (For a discussion of the work sheet used in connection with the BIC Form, see Ch. 8.)

An overview of the work sheet indicates that it calls for two series of calculations. The first, listed as Column 1, consists of financial figures derived from the experience of the enterprise during the past twelve month period. While not specifically so stated, the period should run to a cut-off date close to the inception date of the Business Interruption Insurance policy. This suggests that it is preferable and convenient for the inception of coverage to be made to coincide with a normal accounting period.

The second, listed as Column 2, consists of estimated figures based on what is expected to occur during the twelve month period following the same cut-off date. The individual items considered in the two series are the same.

The usual bookkeeping records maintained by the typical manufacturing firm do not include a figure for "sales value of production." A record of sales during a particular period is kept, but such sales may include products manufactured before the beginning of the period. Also, goods manufactured during that period may remain unsold in the manufacturer's warehouse at the end of the period. Compliance with the requirements of the Work Sheet therefore requires a series of calculations unfamiliar to the usual business management.

The work sheet refers to the "inventory—priced at sales value." It is reasonably clear that the term "inventory" refers to the written year-end inventory taken as a part of usual accounting practice. The dollar amount applied in normal accounting practice to the items listed in such inventory is their cost, not their sales value. A Business Interruption Insurance policy takes a different approach to financial details than does an income tax return or a profit and loss statement. It is a document with its own separate characteristics. Therefore, the Owner must avoid the tendency to transfer his normal accounting practices to this instrument.

The waters may be muddied even further. It is not an unknown practice for an Owner to reduce the value of the inventory so as to reduce the amount of profit shown on his operating statement for the tax period. By so doing, he can reduce the amount of income tax that has to be paid currently. Conversely, an Owner may have inflated the value of the inventory so as to strengthen his balance sheet and improve his financial standing with lenders and creditors.

Moreover, there are numerous situations where items in inventory that may have sales value some day are carried at no value. Such would be the case of a manufacturer called upon to produce a definite quantity of an item to the customer's specifications. It is normal practice to schedule an overrun to take care of rejects or defective products. Such an overrun may result in production of a surplus of the item, which then remains in the manufacturer's possession. It is customary to carry such inventory as having no value, though it may some day be sold to the purchaser as part of a repeat order and, therefore, has value.[6]

It is necessary for an Owner under such circumstances to reevaluate his inventory for purposes of the work sheet. In the case of standard items for which the sales price is well established, this is not difficult. But what about a seasonal or specialty item whose ultimate sales price may be a matter of conjecture at the time of inventory? There certainly is some room here for subjective judgment.

An unusual situation exists in the case of the scrap dealer or the buyer of second hand machinery. The inventory figure for such items is usually extremely low. But let a buyer come along who needs that item and the sales price skyrockets. This reality must be considered when completing the work sheet and during the term of the policy.

The Owner must use judgment in calculating the sales value of finished goods for purposes of this work sheet. He may use the same values that appear in his tax return though, as will appear later, he is not bound by those values, nor any other figures used in the course of his business activities. Without suggesting what techniques the Owner finally uses, it does appear obvious that it should be the same he would want to use should he seek to recover for a loss sustained. If this calls for a wide deviation from the manner in which the financial records of his company are set up, a record might well be kept of the basis for the difference. Under some circumstances, it might be wise to bring the facts to the attention of the Agent or the Insurer, if the insurance is placed directly, at the time insurance is being considered.

Looking at the dollar value of the various materials as shown on the inventory may not be enough. In the case of each item, it is necessary to check if any price fluctuation had occurred during the year and to make adjustments accordingly. This is not for the purpose of calculating the dollar value of the merchandise damaged or destroyed, but rather to calculate the amount of earnings received from operations.

This process is not usually followed by Accountants in normal accounting practices, where dollar values alone are considered in determining tax obligations. Nor is the matter of the obsolesence of items in inventory always treated objectively in preparing financial figures. In other words, the process of preparing the work sheet for Business Interruption Insurance purposes may well require a review of the way in which the inventory values were achieved and of proper adjustments being made.

The procedures that are followed in completing Column 1 all refer to past events. They form a record of past financial events in the operation of the business. To this extent, they give due consideration to the experience of the business before the issuance of the policy. This is not the same as the policy provision which calls for giving due consideration to the experience of the business before the date of damage or destruction. In the case of a loss, all of the calculations are usually recomputed using the date of the damage as the end of the period for which calculations of past events are made.

b. Work Sheet—Column 2. Guidance for the Owner in calculating the amount of insurance to buy is provided by Column 2 of the work sheet. As indicated, it is a listing of the "Estimated" values for the coming year. The items on which the estimate is made are usually identical with those in Column 1. The dollar amounts listed under each item, rather than being historical facts, call for the very best judgment of which the Owner is capable. (In those situations, where an Owner operates his business on a day-to-day basis without a long or even short range game plan for the future, preparing the work sheet presents an excellent opportunity for him to adopt a better technique for the management of the business undertaking.)

There may be situations where the amount of gross earnings for the coming year can be automatically fixed with a high degree of mathematical accuracy; long range programs are in place which will substantially control what takes place during the coming twelve months.

In most cases, however, an Owner will have to base his judgment on his plans and on anticipated conditions. A margin for error probably has been built into his plans—a deviation upwards or downwards due to unpredictable events. Query: should the upper or lower margin of such possible deviation be built into the figures in Column 2 of the work sheet or should some number in between be used? This is a decision the Owner must make. It will depend on the extent to which he is ready to assume risk.

Column 2 figures parallel to some extent the provision of the policy which refers to the "probable experience of the business" which is to be given due consideration. Again, it should be noted that there is a difference in timing—the year contemplated in Column 2 begins with the date of the work sheet, whereas in case of damage, it is the date of the damage that starts the twelve month calculation running.

Thus, while the work sheet is a helpful tool for use when insurance is being procured, the Owner must always keep in mind that changing conditions in his business operation or in the general business climate can render his conclusions obsolete. It is necessary to make periodic reviews during the term of the policy to determine whether the projection on the work sheet is still valid. It must be remembered that in case of loss resulting from damage suffered toward the end of a one year policy term, the projection of future experience can extend almost two years beyond the time when the work sheet was completed.

It is this extended period that becomes of so much importance in deciding whether or not the Owner will find himself bearing part of the loss, as a coinsurer under the terms of the Coinsurance Clause described in the first part. One of the anomalies of Business Interruption Insurance is that after Column 2 of the work sheet has been completed with the greatest of care, the Owner may still find himself a coinsurer if a loss should occur as a result of the decision of the drafters of the contract as to the particular 12 month period that is used in connection with the Coinsurance Clause.[7] (For changes under the BIC Form, see Ch. 8.)

c. Retention of Employees. One area of decision facing an Owner is what he would do with his employees in case of a business interruption. As to key employees there is no question. They must be retained if the business is to be able to operate in a healthy fashion when operations are resumed. But what about ordinary help—clerks in a store, laborers in a construction crew or machine operators in a factory? If the period of interruption promises to be a short one—of two or three days duration—the Owner will want to keep his help in place. At the other extreme, if it will take many months to repair or replace the destroyed property, it could be poor judgment to retain ordinary employees and to continue to pay them wages until the plant is rebuilt.

What makes good sense in between the extremes? There is no pat answer. It depends on the ease with which ordinary help can be replaced when operations start up again. Does the present help have skills it would be hard to replace? How long would it take to train replacements? How tight is the labor market? These and similar questions must be considered by the Owner, and a decision made as to which ordinary employees would be kept on the payroll and, if so, for how long a period of interruption.

An item of considerable importance to Insureds with a substantial payroll involves the impact of unemployment compensation penalties. In some cases these have amounted to hundreds of thousands of dollars. Such impact will be felt for years. This extra cost of doing business should be taken into consideration in estimating the amount of potential loss. In some cases, it was found possible to make a deal with the state authorities to accept a flat, agreed-upon sum to avoid such penalties. Some Insurers are prepared, as part of the policy coverage, to insure the amount of such a contribution.

3. Limitations on Protection Provided

As useful as a Business Interruption Insurance policy is in providing a continuation of the anticipated Earnings Stream, it has obvious limitations in at least two areas. The first is where the Owner cannot afford to have his business operations interrupted: no matter what the cost, the "show must go on." This situation exists primarily in service organizations—laundries that serve large industrial or business clients, banks, newspapers and local dairies are examples of such organizations. It may be very expensive for them to continue to provide service through alternative facilities; it may even cost more than the amount of earnings they would lose because of the interruption, but they must keep operating. This type of extra expense is not covered by the ordinary contract of Business Interruption Insurance, which pays for extra expenses incurred only if the extra expenses actually reduce the amount of the ultimate loss payable and only to the extent of such reduction. If the Owner is of the opinion that he must continue to operate no matter what it costs, he must also procure a different kind of insurance protection—Extra Expense Insurance. (For comparison with provisions of BIC Form see Ch. 8.)

The second limitation of the ordinary Business Interruption Insurance policy is keyed into its basic concept that once operational capacity has been restored, the obligations of the Insurer cease. But, frequently, the start-up of operations does not immediately restore the full flow of the former Earnings Stream. Customers may have shifted their patronage to competitors during the shutdown; or it may take time to build up to pre-interruption level the productivity of employees, who have been away from the job or who are new.

Once more, the Owner must examine the nature of his own business enterprise to determine whether any such possibility applies to it. If his decision is in the affirmative, he must consider steps to close this gap in the protection he needs. Mention was made earlier of an endorsement to cover this retardation in the restoration of the flow of gross earnings to their pre-damage state. It is referred to as "Lag Insurance." It covers restoration of the Earnings Stream instead of the physical property. Provision is made for such a situation in the BIC Form.

Before leaving the consideration of the Owner and the need for an in-depth analysis by him of the specific needs of his particular enterprise, mention might be made of types of business activity that have peculiar needs and for which a special type of policy may be necessary. One is the real estate operator whose Earnings Stream is derived from rents collected from tenants in his property. A second is the operator of a school or similar enterprise where tuition fees are collected in advance for services to be rendered during a future period. A third is the independent sales organization which takes orders from customers for future deliveries of merchandise from a factory that it represents, and which collects a commission only when delivery of the order is made.

Since the passage of time is an element in determining the amount of loss that would be suffered were the property producing the Earnings Stream to be damaged, the protection needed would be furnished under a type of "time element insurance." The ordinary Business Interruption Insurance contract is not worded to match the special needs of a business enterprise of such special type.

For these, special policies are available. The Owner must make sure that his special needs are covered by the policy that he buys.

B. The Intermediary

The term "Intermediary" is used to include the independent Agent and Broker, the employee of the direct writer, the independent Risk Manager, a Consultant or any other person who serves as an intermediary between the Owner and the insurance company which will write his insurance.

1. Prospecting

a. The Approach. Every Owner of a business enterprise is a prospect for Business Interruption Insurance. Most of them have a need for that type of insurance if they are to retain their financial integrity in the face of severe damage to the property which is producing the Earnings Stream from which their income and profit flows. Property Insurance and Liability Insurance protect balance sheet integrity, while Business Interruption Insurance protects the integrity of the income or profit and loss statement. A business interruption seldom stops the drain of ongoing fixed expenses. Absent the ability to restore operations at another location to fill the gap in sales or production and thus maintain earnings, a business enterprise must live on its fat, its assets, during the period when earnings have ceased. Given enough assets, a business enterprise could remain viable indefinitely, but such is rarely the case. Sooner or later, the consumption of liquid or liquidable assets weakens the working capital status of the business enterprise. The records show that most business enterprises which suffer an extended interruption of business and do not have insurance to make up the loss of earnings, suffer such a weakening of their working capital situation that they do not have the financial strength to start up anew; and even when they can get going again, it is on a much reduced scale.

If the Owner decides at the completion of his investigation that he needs Business Interruption Insurance coverage, he normally calls upon his insurance Agent or Broker to obtain it for him.[8] In the case of many Owners, this happy situation does not exist—the Owner is not aware of his needs in this area. It is the responsibility of the person handling his insurance affairs to bring this need to his attention. In the past, at least, there has been an excellent opportunity for a competitor to step in and, by dint of superior technical knowledge and superior selling strategy, become the Intermediary for the providing of Business Interruption Insurance coverage.[9]

A strong, positive attitude should characterize the approach of the Intermediary to an Owner prospect. There should be no room for doubt as to the responsibility of the Owner to protect the Earnings Stream. If any doubt does exist, the burden of proof is on the Owner to show that he can survive the financial shock of an extended interruption rather than on the Intermediary to prove that the Owner needs this type of insurance.

If successful in being given opportunity to quote, the Intermediary would be well-advised to qualify the prospect at this point. This calls for a positive commitment from a person with authority to order the insurance that, if a better or a less expensive proposal can be offered, the order will be given to the Intermediary.

b. The Coverage Must Be Sold. A survey taken in May, 1982, indicated that only about 50% of smaller businesses carried Business Interruption Insurance.[10] Most Business Interruption Insurance is not bought—it is sold. Some of the reasons for this have been discussed in Part I. There is no external pressure on the Owner from lenders to buy such insurance, as is the case with Property Insurance; although lending institutions should be more favorably inclined to extend credit to an Owner who has purchased Business Interruption Insurance. Claimants and lawyers do not lurk in the wings ready to pounce on the unprotected Owner. Nor has he been adequately educated by media stories or the insurance fraternity as to the dangers of operating without such coverage. Even where an Owner has heard of the coverage, it has often been in connection with its failure to meet the needs of an Insured who suffered a loss.

There is another, more subtle, but equally difficult hurdle to overcome in the case of an Owner who is aware of the existence and benefits of this coverage. This lies in the fact that the Owner is called upon to reveal to the Intermediary some of the secrets of his business activity including the volume of his sales and the amount of his profits. These are sensitive matters that the average small businessman often wants to keep to himself.

2. The Task of the Intermediary

a. Establishing Confidence. The first challenge to the Intermediary—to convert a prospect into a potential buyer—is undoubtedly the most demanding. It requires an approach quite different from that which can be followed in selling better known property and liability coverages. Coverage and price alone are not the leverage points for promoting a sale; included are the confidence and trust of the Owner in the knowledge and understanding by the Intermediary of the workings of the Owner's operations and of his financial situation; plus his confidence in the Intermediary's regard for confidentiality. The Intermediary must position himself to meet these requirements.

b. Establishing Credibility. How can a Intermediary establish credibility for knowledge and understanding? First, by having at his command an understanding of how Business Interruption Insurance functions. Knowledge of the six P's and the six E's, previously discussed is sufficient background at this prospecting stage.

Second, and more important, by demonstrating—in a general way at least—his understanding of the particular needs for protection that face his prospect. This calls for the Intermediary to do his homework in advance. Not only must he acquire as much information as possible about the general aspects of the line of business in which the prospect is engaged, but also its special characteristics. Among the areas of inquiry might be the following: How unique are the materials and services used and what alternative methods of providing them is available to an Owner? How important is continuity of product or service to retain customer loyalty? How important is location to maintaining business operations?

Also, what has been the general history of growth and profit in the industry? How tight are profit margins? How severe is competition? What are business prospects for the next couple of years? In a general way, what types of "bottlenecks" exist in this type of operation? What expertise is needed among employees?

Questions should also be considered about the prospect's individual business activity. How is his operation organized to deal with damage to a part of it? How dependent is he on specific sources of raw materials? How wide a market does he have for his product or services? How dependent is he on his computer? Does he have a Disaster Plan? In general, the Intermediary should understand the Owner's needs and the pitfalls that may exist, as discussed in the preceding section, and be prepared to address them intelligently.

One source of the type of information that the Intermediary needs is other persons in the same line of business. A prior reading of articles in trade magazines can supply a knowledge of terms and industry developments that makes meaningful inquiry possible. There may also be printed material that can be researched as to the specific prospect. A Dun & Bradstreet or similar financial report can help. Examination of ISO rate cards can add some information as to exposure to external sources of damage.

Armed with such background information, the Intermediary is in a position to establish rapport with the prospect. One successful executive in a national brokerage firm recalls the advice given to him by his sales manager when, as a neophyte, he first started out to sell Business Interruption Insurance to auto parts dealers. "The first thing you say after you introduce yourself is, 'Are you having much competition from the wagon jobbers?' From then on you're in like Flynn. Your prospect will accept you as being on his side and having sympathy for his aggravations and problems."

Success in the selling of Business Interruption Insurance requires the establishment of such mutuality of interest. As pointed out earlier, the Intermediary is going to ask the prospect ultimately for financial information that is normally only available to his Accountant and sometimes to his Banker. In some cases, it will be necessary to go behind published financial reports to get at the true state of facts. No wonder prospects frequently shy away from getting involved in such revelations unless they have complete trust in the Intermediary.

One way to ease such a situation is to place the responsibility for preparing the work sheet solely in the hands of the prospective customer and his Accountant. Otherwise, the Intermediary may find himself advising how much insurance is needed without having an adequate fact basis for his opinion. Provided the Owner has a clear understanding of what the work sheet requires, the Intermediary can withdraw from the compilation of the figures and accept the Owner's calculations as the basis for setting the dollar amount of the policy. The Intermediary should protect himself by a letter stating the facts.

To meet such reluctance on the part of Owners, a form of Business Interruption Insurance called Earnings Insurance has been devised. This does not contain a Coinsurance Clause. The value type of policy also avoids the problem of coinsurance. Both of these policy forms will be discussed later in this volume.

What does evolve from the foregoing is the understanding that an Intermediary who undertakes to sell Business Interruption Insurance cannot go about it as impersonally as one who is selling a Homeowners or an Automobile policy. Even the providing of a Commercial Package policy that does not include Business Interruption Insurance is a much less demanding undertaking.

It follows that the sale of such coverage must be important enough to warrant the time and effort required. For an existing client, there is no question; he is entitled to this service. A new prospect, on the other hand, must either be large enough in his own right or belong to a sufficiently large class of prospects to involve commission income adequate to justify the effort.

The real challenge for an Intermediary lurks in the situation where the size of the potential commission is so small as not to warrant such extensive preparation. It is the policy sold under such circumstances that usually creates the headaches of coinsurance penalties or improper coverages. The responsibility stemming from the promise of protection against the interruption of the Earnings Stream requires better treatment than that. Besides, each satisfied client opens the door to other prospects.

3. Three Step Program

At what level should the first approach be made by the Intermediary? Where there is an inhouse Risk Manager or Insurance Buyer, communications must naturally flow through him. Where no such internal Intermediary exists, it is suggested that the first approach should be to the person in charge of finances. Even in a small business enterprise where the Owner is the "boss," he should be wearing his hat as Treasurer when the matter of Business Interruption Insurance is first broached. Of course, in cases where the Treasurer is nothing more than a bookkeeper with a fancy title, contact should be made with the person who has ultimate decision making authority in matters involving finances. It is the financial health of the business enterprise that is at stake.

a. Step One—Survey. If the Intermediary succeeds in getting an opportunity to quote on Business Interruption Insurance coverage, he should ordinarily follow a three step program. Step one is to guide the Owner to determine the amount and types of coverage the Owner needs; step two is to formulate a package or proposal for such coverage; and step three is to find the best market in which to place the insurance. These steps may be modified to some extent by special circumstances but, in essence, they must be taken.

The result of step one should be the establishment of an amount of insurance which would eliminate the Owner becoming a coinsurer for not having enough insurance to cover a loss. The amount of coinsurance exposure that the Owner may ultimately be willing to accept under his program of Risk Management is left for later discussion with him.

There are times when the Owner calls upon the Intermediary for assistance in making a survey. If the latter is willing to accept the responsibility, he should not hesitate, when necessary, to request the services of engineers, architects or other technical personnel to help him in the undertaking and keep his errors and omissions exposure as small as possible.

The second element would take into account all the different kinds of property, the destruction of which could cause a stoppage of operations. It would also include the measures already taken, or which might be taken after damage occurs, to provide alternate or substitute facilities for carrying on operations. It is in this area that the matter of "bottlenecks" becomes pertinent.

The physical survey can itself be divided into two sections. The first section of the survey can be referred to as inside operations and covers the actual operations being carried out on the described premises. It requires a physical examination of the operating plant—whether it be a men's store, a machine shop, or a chemical plant.

The entrance of the Intermediary into the plant to help in such examination should be under the proper auspices, so that his inquiries are met with respect and a full response. This introduction should come from the highest authority he can secure. In most business enterprises, this may be the person who is in charge of operations. In such a case, the Owner should be present, at least at the initial entrance. If the actual operating process is under the supervision of a plant or store manager, this individual should take over the actual support of the Intermediary in the making of the survey.

It is quite important that those persons who are intimately involved in supervising the day-to-day operations be interviewed. They are one of the best sources of information about "bottlenecks" that may exist with regard to the equipment, supplies or merchandise. Resistance is sometimes met at the lower level of supervision to the effort necessary to make a schedule of the components of an operating installation and, yet, no better way for uncovering "bottlenecks" exists.

The in-house physical survey is aimed, as indicated earlier, at securing a determination, first as to the extent to which damage to any part of the property could precipitate either a partial or a total curtailment of operations, and second, how long it would take to repair or replace the damaged property. These are considerations seldom addressed by a plant or store operations manager. They must be educated to looking at their operations from this point of view for purposes of proper Business Interruption Insurance coverage. To a large extent, the same lack of consideration is given by the manager of operations of a service business, but there is a greater likelihood that a "seat-of-the-pants" answer is available from him. At the close of the in-house operations survey, the Intermediary should have in hand a list of the bottlenecks that possibly exist and a rough estimate of the delay that would be caused if certain items were destroyed and had to be replaced.

The second section of the survey is to explore potential sources of loss arising from off-premises damage. Again, this subject has been examined at some length under the discussion of the Owner's responsibilities. And again, the Intermediary should stress the desirability of a survey of how to reduce the loss potential should damage occur. If nothing else is accomplished, such an effort should establish an awareness on the part of the Owner of the service aspect of the Intermediary's efforts. It cannot fail to create a closer relationship.

A growing area for investigation has developed from the installation and use of computers in every business of any size. Damage to the hardware and to the software, whether in-house or off-premises, has been referred to earlier. The extent of the consideration that must be given to this item of equipment was pointed up in a recent article which called attention to the need for a continuing source of water as a coolant for the computer.[10] The Intermediary should seek help; probably from the manufacturers of the equipment in the case of a large installation. The interlinking of computers, often via satellite, for firms conducting international operations can be a special area of concern.[11]

A different aspect of the survey is the checking with the Owner about his decisions on the matter of risk handling. To what extent would the Owner prefer to spend money to reduce risk of loss by improving the physical capacity of plant and inventory to absorb damage to its component parts. Again, to what extent is the Owner able to survive an interruption of operations and does he prefer to self-insure for that aspect of any financial loss.[12]

With some responsible officer of the Owner, the matter of contractual obligations should then be explored. This would involve contracts of employment, including labor union contracts, which may require the maintenance of personnel on the payroll even though operations are shut down, leases, licenses, advertising contracts and similar obligations that may or may not continue even though operations are suspended, and contracts for the purchasing of goods or the delivery of products, etc.[13] Such contracts can have an impact on the ultimate amount of loss that the Insured could suffer in the event of an interruption of the Earnings Stream. This is probably also the appropriate time to make inquiry about existing zoning and building laws.

b. Step Two—Exposures to be Covered. The next task of the Intermediary is to extract from the results of the survey those exposures to risk that require insurance coverage, and then decide what kinds of insurance should be procured for that purpose.

At the conclusion of his survey, the Intermediary is in a position to sit down and talk intelligently with the Owner about the nature of his operations and provide a preliminary or general statement as to how a Business Interruption Insurance policy or one of the other types of time-element coverages would meet the Owner's needs. This is the vital stage of the negotiations that converts a prospect into a client. Before discussing an underwriting program to meet the needs of the Owner, the Intermediary should, of course, be acquainted with the forms and endorsements available in his jurisdiction and also of the general nature of changes and amendments which Underwriters are willing to incorporate therein.

Discussion about the underwriting of the risk is carried on with the person who is knowledgeable about the financial affairs of the business concern. Since this is usually the person who is the final authority on whether Business Interruption Insurance will be purchased, the Intermediary may again want to "qualify the prospect" and determine whether the prospect is still a prospective customer. If this possibility does not exist, no further time or effort should be expended on this prospect.

In order to develop a proper underwriting proposal, the Intermediary has to acquire certain information that will be incorporated in a policy, if, when, and as one is issued. At some point in the negotiation, the Intermediary is going to ask for the opportunity to examine any policies which may be currently in force. One reason for such examination is to ascertain whether they adequately cover the Owner's needs. It is suggested that before the Intermediary examines the existing policies he should make his own determination of the needs. This will avoid the danger of being drawn into the trap of following the pattern set by existing policies.

The determination should follow the pattern set out in the first part—particularly an exploration of the Six P's. The first of these would be the parties named as Insureds. As pointed out in the first part, a party must have an insurable interest to be named an Insured; but it is up to the Intermediary to make certain that everyone who has an insurable interest is so named. Often the Owner of a business tends to overlook the full details of the ownership situation and his attention must be directed to them.

The matter of parties is one that has to be probed by the Intermediary. A common situation would be where the Owner owns the real estate in his own name and leases it to the corporation, of which he is the sole stockholder, and which carries on the business operation. In such a situation, there are two different legal entities involved, each of which has a separate insurable interest—the corporation in the continuance of its Earnings Stream and the individual in the continuation of his rental income.

Mention was made earlier of the practice, in large business enterprises, of dividing the various parts of the operations among different legal entities, sometimes by establishing a parent company with a number of subsidiary companies or affiliates. One corporation may supply the crude oil, another operate the pipeline that conveys it to the refinery and a third own and operate the refinery. The normal practice would be to name all three corporations as Insureds in a single policy, either specifically or by a blanket description, since the Earnings Stream of all could be adversely affected by a break-down in the operations of any one of the corporations.

An example of such a division of operations was experienced under a policy of Business Interruption Insurance which named four corporations as Insureds. Company A secured orders for sweaters from department stores. Such orders covered a spectrum of styles and sizes. According to trade practices, the complete order had to be delivered by the stipulated date or the order could be cancelled. Company B manufactured yarns for the sweaters and shipped them to Company C. Company C scheduled the manufacture of the parts of the sweaters on its looms. It operated twenty-four hours a day, seven days a week. It would run the right sleeves of the blue sweater size 30, then those for size 32, and through all the sizes, before running left sleeve sizes. The various parts of the sweaters were then shipped to Company D which assembled the parts into completed sweaters and shipped them to the customers to fill the orders. Company A then billed the customers, collected the payments and distributed the proceeds between the various companies.

An off-premises power failure shut down the operations of the looms at Company C for 5 days. This represented a loss of $37,500 to it on the basis of its bookkeeping system. When power was restored, it took up operations where it left off, but could in no way make up for the time lost or replace the sweater parts that would have been produced in that time. So there were no left sleeves for green sweaters sizes 32 through 38 available by the end of the scheduled run. As a result, Company D could not complete those particular sweaters by the time scheduled in the orders for delivery. Exercising their option, the department stores cancelled their entire orders and refused to accept and pay for any of the sweaters. Their position was influenced, no doubt, by the fact that prices in the sweater market had fallen since the orders were placed.

The impasse was settled finally by Company A agreeing to accept a lower than contracted price for the sweaters it was able to deliver. A joint claim was then filed by these companies against the Insurer, based on the smaller amount earned at the end of the total business cycle. The claim was finally compromised for over $200,000.

A word of caution. If more than one legal entity is named as an Insured, and the interests of all are to be covered, the calculations for the coinsurance clause should include the Gross Earnings of all those named. The same practice should be followed if the Insurer is carrying on more than one business activity with the described property.[14] In one case, the Insured carried on four distinct businesses on the same premises. One of them, a bakery, was destroyed. The Insurer argued that the earnings of all four businesses represented the Business Interruption Value. On the facts, the court held that it was not proper to include the income of all four in the calculations for coinsurance purposes.[15]

The second step is to agree with the Owner on a description of the property broad enough to cover all items whose damage would affect the Earnings Stream. Again, reference to Part One will provide the basic essentials of such a description. The Intermediary should inquire concerning the existence of the various types of property in the Owner's operations.

The location and the description of the nature of the business operations being insured should be fully and carefully described. Since most Underwriters will accept a broad description, it is best to follow that technique. Where questioning discloses no property located other than in the Owner's hometown, a description can be used such as, "All of the property of ABC, Inc., used in connection with its business and located in the City of Troy, New York."

A narrower description may be quite adequate. Thus, "located at 10 Oak Street, Malden, and usual to the operation of a retail shoe store," would be sufficient in most cases. Where the Owner conducts two distinct operations at different locations, the writing of a blanket policy is most important. In such a blanket policy, there should not be separate limits for the different locations.

The physical survey may not have disclosed the fact that plans are already in the works for extending or adding to the plant or for adding new lines of activity. If these will come on line during the proposed term of the policy and within twelve months thereafter, they may be factored into the figures of the future sales that are being computed, rather than waiting until after they have been completed and then amending the calculations.

The question of which perils should be insured against has undoubtedly been considered by the Owner in connection with his Property Insurance. Usually the Business Interruption Insurance policy follows the same track. Nevertheless, presentation of this new coverage offers an opportunity to explore once again the sources of damage to which the property may be exposed, especially those affected by the exclusions.

It is essential that the Intermediary educate the Owner as to the type of peril to which the property described may be exposed and to propose every type of available coverage. It is the function of the Owner and not of the Intermediary ultimately to decide which perils will be insured against in the policy.

Since cost is not being discussed at this juncture, it is not relevant to the decision as to what coverages would cost. Later, the injection of budgetary considerations may force the Owner to reduce his preferred insurance protection.

When Contingent Business Interruption Insurance is involved, attention should be focused on the exposures at the other locations. Attention should also be given to goods in transit, goods in storage, goods on consignment, etc.

The element of period normally enters into the picture after a loss occurs. It has, however, one vital preliminary application. That is in connection with the maximum time that the Earnings Stream might be interrupted in the case of damage to or destruction of the described property. This information, of course, stems from the survey and particularly from the disclosure of any "bottleneck." If, for example, the possibility exists that an interruption of as long as eighteen months could develop if certain items were destroyed, then a policy amount based on the gross earnings of a single year may not be adequate. Once this fact is developed, the responsibility then rests on the Owner to decide what dollar amount of coverage he wishes to buy.

A retail store Owner, who has a franchise to sell a certain line of "name" products, is frequently obliged by contract to maintain his operations and sell a certain volume of merchandise in order to retain his franchise. Nor is there always an escape clause from such loss of franchise in the event of an interruption due to an external peril. The Intermediary should explore this area with the Owner, even to the extent of requesting an opportunity to examine the written franchise agreement. An overly long interruption in the sale or use of such products could result in substantial future loss were the franchise lost.

A similar result could materialize from cancellation of a license for failure to operate. The policy exclusion of loss caused by the cancellation of a license would block recovery not only for the loss experienced after the period of interruption ended, but also for the loss in future income resulting from losing the license.

The other two P's—productivity and profit—are tied into preparation of the work sheet. Where this work is carried out solely by the Owner and his financial staff, the task of the Intermediary is to verify that all proper factors have been taken into consideration. If a policy is ultimately delivered, it should be accompanied by a statement in the covering letter that the calculations in the work sheet are the responsibility of the Insured. In the more usual case, where the Intermediary participates in the actual preparation of the work sheet, it is most important that he direct the Owner's attention to the statistical data and other facts that he must consider in order properly to complete the work sheet. The material discussed under the heading of Owner can serve as a guide to these areas of inquiry.

The Intermediary should challenge the figures produced to the extent of establishing the fact that they are complete and meet the requirements of the form. A copy of the work sheet showing the calculations on which the various figures are based together with the backup material should be maintained by the Owner with a copy to the Intermediary.

In determining the amount of insurance that the Owner needs, the Intermediary should keep in mind that that amount refers to the Gross Earnings before taxes, not the after-tax profits from operations which show up on the profit and loss statement. It might be said facetiously that Uncle Sam's insurable interest in the earnings before taxes should be included. But the real reason is that the Insured should be left with the same net amount of profits out of any loss recovery that he would have had were there no damage.

In large part, the matters covered by the six E's come into play only after a loss has occurred. The matter of exclusions should be borne in mind by the Intermediary, since it may be possible to secure coverage other than that provided under the usual Business Interruption Insurance policy for loss otherwise excluded. Extra Expense Insurance comes to mind immediately. Strike Insurance is another example. So is insurance to cover loss from cancellation of license or franchise. While expensive and limited in protection, bomb threat insurance is available at this writing in certain markets to cover losses sustained by reason of a bomb hoax.[16] The matter of exclusions in the standard forms creates a challenge for innovative and imaginative underwriting to overcome both exclusions and gaps in coverage in those forms.

The possibility of insuring pure business risk was raised as far back as the 1880's.[17] In recent years, trapping of barges on the Mississippi River during 1976 because of abnormally low water conditions resulted in the inability of mid-west farmers to ship grain with resultant loss of earnings. The loss of contact with communications satellite III, created a loss of $27 million in revenue. Such happenings create a challenge to the ingenuity of underwriters.

The E element which is entitled "enough" brings into play the operation of the coinsurance clause. The percentage normally used is 50%, i.e., the amount of insurance required to be carried is one-half of the Business Interruption Value. If the survey shows that an interruption could take place that would last more than six months, the Intermediary should advise a sufficient amount of insurance to extend for the full duration of the potential interruption. In other words, the 50% figure is the minimum that the Insured has agreed to carry. It need not be the maximum amount. It is based on an estimate that the maximum period of interruption would be six months. If the facts indicate that a nine month interruption is possible for this particular business operation, it would suggest purchasing more insurance and agreeing to a 75% coinsurance requirement.

Despite the emergence of the Gross Earnings form as the dominant vehicle for insuring against business interruption, valued forms are still being used in specialized situations. The use of a valued policy in Use and Occupancy Insurance was barred in the 1940's by underwriting rules.[18] By 1960, its use had been restored and it has served as the basis for many innovative types of contract.[19]

For a while, great interest was aroused in its use by the 1960 decision in the Shakertown tax case; but the effect of that decision has not been followed by later internal revenue rulings. A valued policy certainly should be considered in any situation where the business has not yet established a track record, as in a newly opened enterprise or one recently purchased. (In the case of a purchase, the records of the predecessor company should be obtained if a valued policy is not desired.) Some Intermediaries favor a valued policy for small businesses where adequate records are not usually maintained.[20]

In essence, the valued policy eliminates any hassle in the event of a total loss. Whether the established value is a fixed sum of money per se, or is tied into units of production or dollars of sales or any other standard, much of the need for examining financial records in the course of settling a loss is eliminated. It is the avoidance of proving many aspects of a loss that undoubtedly appears attractive.

Some Owners like the concept of a valued policy in connection with Business Interruption Insurance because it eliminates a lot of mathematical calculations. The Insured knows just how much he will receive for each day of full interruption. Also, it is simple to file interim claims for advance partial payment as the period of interruption continues. Nor is there any room for argument about coinsurance.[21]

Business Interruption Insurance for a power plant, attached to a Boiler and Machinery policy, has been written on a valued form. Rent Insurance policies are another example, as are Leasehold and Profit Insurance policies. While the results are not as accurate, the trade-off is considered acceptable. An Insured who buys a valued policy does assume the burden of calculating the amount required.

The disadvantages are still those which led to the abandonment of the per diem policy in the first place. Specified amounts of value attached at the beginning of the contract may not coincide with what may develop during the life of the policy. Also the amount of loss, when only a part of the operation is interrupted as a result of damage, may be hard to determine. Nevertheless, where the Intermediary believes that a valued form of policy might be appropriate, he should bring it to the Owner's attention with all the pros and cons.

Whether the Intermediary be licensed as an Agent or a Broker, or even act as a Risk Manager or Advisor, he is acting on behalf of the Owner and owes the latter a standard of performance that matches the expertise that he claims. As pointed out earlier, to the extent that he fails to live up to that standard and the Owner ultimately suffers from that failure, the Intermediary may be held responsible for any damages that ensue. Not only does this responsibility suggest that care be taken by the Intermediary, but also suggests that if he is not fully qualified to do a professional and thorough job, he should get adequate advice.[22]

To the extent that the Intermediary has left matters of judgment to the discretion of the Owner, a copy of a letter confirming this fact should be maintained in the Intermediary's file. This applies equally to recommendations which the Intermediary has made and which the Owner has seen fit to turn down. An uninsured, underinsured, or coinsured loss is a great cause of "amnesia" on the part of an Insured; the only cure for which is a properly documented Intermediary's file.

Considerable thought has been given to the question of whether a consideration of the various types of policies and of forms and endorsements affecting coverages should be undertaken in this part of the book. A negative conclusion has been reached. One reason is that excellent books exist which deal with provisions in the policies hitherto in use.[23] Moreover, new forms of contract will soon be issued by individual Insurers under the BIC Form and will create a broad area for examination and discussion.

The Intermediary should keep a current list of all the available forms and check each client's needs against it. (He should consider endorsements which "buy-back" exclusions.) Insurance Companies frequently draft their own form of basic contract. Manuscript forms can also be drafted to cover situations that do not fit into the ordinary mold. The Intermediary should be knowledgeable as to what is available from time to time in the market place.

With the necessary information at hand, it is the task of the Intermediary and of the support people in his organization to draw up the program of insurance which they believe will best provide the Owner with the protection he needs. Their freedom of action may, in some instances, be hampered by preferences which the Owner has expressed. The question of whether the Intermediary's duty to the Owner ceases when the latter expresses a strong opinion about some aspect of the coverage he desires is one to which no final answer can be given. At the very least, the Intermediary should express his own preferences and the reason for them. As suggested earlier, a written memorandum should be made in every situation where the Intermediary's recommendations have been overridden and a copy of the memo should be sent to the Owner. While some Intermediaries object to this practice on the ground that it is "defensive" and might adversely affect the relationship, it is clearly a necessary precaution. It may also have the beneficial effect of alerting the Owner to just how important the matter appears to the Intermediary and cause a reconsideration of any decision.

Under normal circumstances, there should be no need for the Intermediary to get back to the Owner during the preparation process. On the other hand, that process may disclose the absence of certain information that is needed by the Underwriter. While the initial underwriting program should contain the maximum of protection for the Owner, fall back positions with less protection can be prepared to meet cost considerations that may develop.

c. Step Three—Marketing the Risk. The underwriting process comes to an end normally when the Owner has authorized the Intermediary to proceed to secure the agreed upon coverages. The process of marketing the program—finding a market that will write it at a quoted price—is the next step. In a small agency, this is another function of the Intermediary. In larger organizations, a specialist is assigned to this task.

Underlying the whole concept of marketing is the question of the breadth of the market that must be surveyed. How wide a selection of Insurers need the Intermediary approach to fulfill his duty of investigating competitive pricing? In the case of the sales representative of a direct writer, there can be no doubt that he is offering the products of just that company. For the Intermediary who is holding himself out as a Broker, i.e., the agent of the Insured, his inquiries should not be confined to those companies which he represents as an Agent without disclosing that fact to the Owner.

In many cases suggestions can be made by the Insurers approached as to improvements in the program that has been drafted. Although the growth of quotation via computer (in fact, actual interfacing) appears to foretell tomorrow's method of doing business with markets, it would seem that one of the last areas in which to use such a mechanical approach would be in the case of Business Interruption Insurance coverages, where so many nuances of possible procedure are present.

All other things being equal, there are imperative reasons for placing the business interruption coverage with the same Insurer that writes the Property Insurance policies. Not only may price considerations become a factor, but even more important is the avoidance of conflicting positions in the event of a loss. The Adjuster handling the property damage aspect should work in tandem with the Adjuster for the business interruption loss. Preferably it should be the same person or, at least, the same adjusting firm. A distribution of the dollars of loss can sometimes be achieved, to the benefit of both parties, when the same Insurer is involved.

A danger lies in the fact that if there is a delay in putting into the hands of the Insured sufficient funds to enable him to undertake the process of rebuilding, the period of interruption covered by the Business Interruption Insurance policy may be extended. A dispute as to the amount of the loss under the Fire Insurance policy thus can have repercussions of serious proportions to the business interruption carrier. Where both coverages are in the same company, the Insurer is motivated to advance part of the property loss and part of the business interruption loss (within the amounts of admitted loss), which together will provide the Insured with funds to rebuild promptly. This should be done just as soon as possible, so as to expedite the reestablishment of operations.

In the course of seeking a market for the proposed underwriting program, an Intermediary may find that the full coverage cannot be secured from markets with whose financial soundness the Intermediary is satisfied, within the premium range of the Insured's present policies or within the premium range that the Insured is prepared to pay.

It is the responsibility of the Intermediary to disclose to the Owner any doubts about the financial standing of a proposed market of which the Intermediary knows or should know. In marginal situations, usually involving price, it is for the Owner to make the decision as to the risk in the security of the market. Again, a memo in the Intermediary's file is important if an insecure market is selected.

There are two courses that the Intermediary could follow. One is to make the decision as to which of the three elements should give way—coverage, quality of market or premium limit—and then sell the result to the Insured. The other is to sit down with the Insured and let the latter make the decision. The choice will largely depend on the characteristics of the Insured and his relationship with the Intermediary. If achievable, the second course lays a far sounder foundation for future relationship.

Ultimately, the various procedures described up to this point result in a quoted price for a particular contract of Business Interruption Insurance. If acceptable to the Owner, a policy is issued on the terms proposed.

It is suggested that such a policy should be delivered by the Intermediary in person to the Owner and the opportunity for a face to face meeting should be used to explain once more to the Owner the protection and the limitations to protection afforded by the policy and the need for midterm review of developments.[24] Experience shows that when a loss occurs a great deal of unhappiness on the part of the Owner and dissatisfaction with the efforts of the Intermediary can be avoided by such a preparatory explanation, especially when accompanied by a letter of transmittal along the lines already discussed.

The function of the Intermediary does not cease when the completed policy is delivered to the Insured and its terms are discussed with him. The Intermediary must stand prepared to service the policy throughout its duration. The most important aspect of this service consists of guidance and advice when some incident causes an interruption of operations. "Am I covered?" is the question usually addressed to the Intermediary. Sometimes the answer is to be found in the provisions of the Gross Earnings form, or in the underlying policy or even in endorsements annexed to that policy. The Intermediary must be knowledgeable about the coverages and the exclusions of the contract to advise the Insured whether various causes of interruption are included in the policy coverage. (Now he must know about the new BIC Form.) Then, as renewal time approaches, the Intermediary should again take all steps necessary to provide himself with adequate information to be able to reassess the Insured's needs.

C. The Underwriter

Since the function of the Underwriter, representing the Insurer, is to attach the proper price to the risk of loss assumed, it is critical that he know the obligations that are being assumed under a particular contract of insurance. This is not always the case in practice. It is not unusual for an Underwriter to understand the true nature of the loss he has assumed only after a loss has occurred. In such instances, liability may be imposed on the Insurer far beyond the limits that he believed existed. A whole new series of uncertainties may open up with the writing of policies in the BIC Form. (See Ch. 8.)

There are explanations for such developments. In part, it is due to the inadequate understanding in the insurance community of the exact nature of the coverage afforded. To some extent, this lack of understanding has, in the past, been shared by Adjusters. In an environment of limited understanding, they have often been able to take arbitrary positions and escape challenge from Insureds who have even less understanding. On the other hand, it has been the "front line" experience of Adjusters that has helped flesh out the provisions of the Business Interruption Insurance contract and, in many cases, resulted in changes and improvements. Most of the literature on the subject has been written by persons involved in the loss end of the coverage.

A lack of knowledge on the part of lawyers and jurists has contributed to the results. Nevertheless, it is the responsibility of the Underwriters and those who appoint them to have a sufficient grasp of the nature of the Owner's operations to form an intelligent opinion as to the extent of the possible risk that is being assumed and the price that should be charged.[25]

Class rating is probably an unavoidable necessity in the case of small business enterprises, as it is in the case of such property insurance as Homeowners Insurance or small package policies. It is when dealing with larger limits of coverage that something more than standard operating procedures should prevail. While the frequency of loss may lend itself to the discipline of collected data, the severity of possible loss is another matter altogether.[26]

Just as an Owner or Intermediary has the obligation of uncovering possible "bottlenecks," so does the properly concerned Underwriter. A proper interrogation of the Intermediary can develop a knowledge of potential interruptions of unusual length or even disclose that the Intermediary has not the information or ability to make an adequate determination of their existence. In those instances, the Underwriter should require a survey by a company engineer before accepting a risk. He should make sure that the engineer understands and checks into the types of potential loss situation covered by the Business Interruption Insurance coverage.[27] A problem can arise when the engineer asks for copies of the plan of installation, which the Insured considers as a trade secret. A non-disclosure agreement from the Insurer often closes this gap.

It is particularly in those cases where a departure from standard policy

provisions or the drafting of a manuscript policy is involved that the Underwriter is charged with the responsibility of knowing the underlying conditions;[28] possibly the potential exists for extended interruption due to the presence of radioactive materials or dependence on computerized materials. As
requests for even more esoteric types of coverage appear, the need for full
understanding will expand further.

Despite the growing dependence on rating manuals and fixed procedures in
the process of underwriting, good underwriting still remains an art and not a
science. As one underwriter put it, "When I feel a pain in my left shoulder, I
decline the risk." Nowhere is this more clearly illustrated than in the underwriting of Business Interruption Insurance.

In those cases where the rate to be charged is more or less controlled by
the rating structure, the decision to accept a risk must be based not only on a
thorough knowledge of the factual situation but also on an imaginative understanding of the potential risk exposure. One area for investigation is the Disaster Plan adopted by the Insured. If adequate and effective, it might well be the
basis for accepting a risk or for price reduction. However, some plans have
proved ineffectual because not properly thought through. An example was the
lack of available water to cool the substitute computer.

Since each Insurer makes its own determination as to the modifications in
rating schedules and procedures it will adopt with regard to Business Interruption Insurance writings, no detailing of rating schedules need be included
herein.[29] Historically, no serious complaint about the adequacy of rates has
arisen in this field. As a competitive tool in the writing of additional volume,
this branch of the insurance business is experiencing, at the time this is written,
some of the erosion in profitable underwriting that other areas of underwriting
are experiencing. But such fluctuation in insurance company attitudes are
beyond the scope of this volume.

Some potential rules for what the Underwriters should include were given
in Best's Review some years back:

1. Check that Insured figured his insurance needs on the sales price of his product,
   not the cost to him.
2. Make sure Insured knows that insurance value is figured on gross earnings not
   on gross profits.
3. If not certain of the valuation procedures used, call for help from well-estab-
   lished appraisal services and make use of published indices of building and
   equipment costs.
4. In inflationary times, a more frequent review of values is desirable. It should be
   done every six months or even every three months.
5. If inventory is based on LIFO, the higher priced merchandise has already been
   removed from inventory when there is a period of inflation; consequently under-
   stating the values. In case of loss, the Insured is going to ask for current replacement values on merchandise carried in inventory on earlier lower prices.

D. Summary

This ends the first section of the second part. Hopefully, the exposure to financial loss due to the interruption of the Earnings Stream has been disclosed through the efforts of the Owner and the Intermediary. The latter has put together a contract which, to the fullest extent possible under the present state of the art and the Owner's financial commitment, will minimize the shrinkage in the Earnings Stream, should damage result to the described property by specified perils.

The Intermediary has located an Underwriter who will assume the risk on behalf of his principal and who has issued a policy containing the agreed upon provisions. The policy has been delivered to the Owner (now the Insured) with an explanation of its provisions. The Insured has put the policy away in his safe and, regretfully, gives it no further thought until he gets notice that it is time to renew the policy.

If such were the universal experience, this book would end here. Not before this point, because peace of mind, which is what every Insured buys whether he has a loss or not, requires an understanding of what has been written up to this point. But losses do occur. The policy, then, has to be removed from its safe resting place and the process of remuneration for loss gets under way.

Chapter 10 Notes

1. When cash flow is interrupted for a substantial period of time, a business enterprise can succumb even though it has substantial fixed assets such as buildings, equipment or inventory, and even though it has substantial orders on hand for future delivery. For a time, a business enterprise can subsist by eating up its liquid assets, usually consisting of cash and accounts receivable; but if these are depleted to an excessive amount, the lack of liquidity will weaken the enterprise to a point where it can no longer survive, certainly not at its former level of operation. Even if the interruption of cash flow continues for a less extended period of time, the impact on business activities can still be negative when operations are renewed.

2. *Business Interruption Insurance*, Klein, p. 19-29. See also: *Business Insurance Bottlenecks—Interesting Examples*, Henry C. Klein. (Indianapolis: Rough Notes Co. Inc., 1948).

3. See: "Insuring the Data Processing Risk," Mark T. Haack, *Best's Review* (P & C), Vol. 84 (January, 1984), p. 44.
   "Computer Failure Could Pull Plug in Many Firms," Ellis Simon, *Business Insurance*, (August 11, 1980). p. 1.
   "Computing Coverage," Wm. H. Rodda, *Business Insurance* (June 16, 1980), p. 17.
   "Companies Have Several Options After a Computer Disaster," Len Strazewski, *Business Insurance* (March 28, 1983), p. 24.
   "*Anatomy of a Disaster.*" Jim Davis, *Business Insurance.* (September 26, 1983), p. 3.

4. " 'Maximum Loss Expectancy' Method," Wm. H. Pritchett in 4/26/74 edition of the *National Underwriter*, p. 26.

5. "The accountant is consulted relative to his client's Business Interruption insurance more often than in connection with most other forms of commercial insurance. His connection with it, moreover, is not merely transitory. His advice properly should be sought at the inception of the policy term, at least once during this period, and certainly again should a claim occur under the policy." *Buying and Administering Business Interruption Insurance*, 16 N.Y. C.P.A. 552 (1946). See: "Insurance on Business Profits." Maurice H. Straus, *Journal of Accountancy* (August, 1946).

6. See: American Alliance Ins. Co. v. Keleket X-Ray Corp.

7. One possible choice would have been to measure the potential Earnings Stream at the inception of the policy and let that figure govern the amount of insurance

required by the Coinsurance Clause throughout the life of the contract. This comes close to how the amount would be calculated for a valued policy. It is also the method provided for in the BIC Form. Another possible technique would be to use the method often employed in determining the premium under Workers Compensation Insurance, by auditing the figures at the end of the policy term. Where an Insured did not start up again after the damage, an immediate audit would be required. A third alternative would be to determine the amount of the Earnings Stream at the time of the damage, as is done with actual cash value under a fire policy, and use that figure. A fourth possible method would be to project the Earnings Stream into the future for a specific period starting with the date of the damage, just as though the policy had its inception at that time. The length of time into the future to be chosen could be equal to the period of interruption; or equal to the period until the end of the Insured's next fiscal year; or for a full year into the future, thus setting up an artificial fiscal year. There are defects and deficiencies in each of these alternatives, as there would be in others that might be selected. The decision of the drafters of the form was to establish, as the base from which the adequacy of the amount of the policy would be determined, the period of "12 months immediately following the date of damage to or destruction of the described property."

8. It makes a difference, whether the Intermediary acts as an Agent or Broker. Wright Body Works Inc. v. Columbus Interstate Ins. Agency.

9. An unscrupulous competitive technique to be guarded against is a lower quote based on a higher percentage of coinsurance. See: Industro Motive Corp. v. Morris Agency, Inc.
    Availability and Use of Business Insurance by Urban Small Business: A Survey. (Bethesda, Maryland: All Industry Research Council, July, 1982).

10. "Computers Face Problems," new item in *Business Insurance* (February 9, 1981), p. 3.

11. See article in *Business Insurance*, (May 16, 1983), p. 20, entitled "Business Interruption Covers Lacking" by Stacy Shapiro. See also article by Shapiro and LeRoux about use of robots in *Business Insurance* (March 28, 1983), p. 3. Also *Business Insurance* (June 28, 1976), p. 3.

12. The respective obligations of the parties to repair damages as described in lease should also be examined. See: Mayfair Fabrics v. Henley.

13. For example—the contract requirement of a bakery to deliver products to a fast-food chain would be a basis for buying Extra Expense Insurance. See article in *Business Insurance* (5/28/79), p. 36, entitled "Extra Expense Keeps Presses Rolling" by William H. Rodda.
    See: "Insuring Against Business Interruption," *The Conference Board Record*, Vol. 3, No. 11 (November, 1966).

14. See: Nat'l Union F. Ins. Co. v. Anderson-Pritchard Oil Corp.

15. Lewis Food Co. v. Fireman's Fund Ins. Co. For case involving blanket policy, see: Swedish Crucible Steel Co. v. Travelers Indemnity Co.

16. See article in *Business Insurance* (November 2, 1981) entitled "Bomb Threats Force Business Interruptions." Threats of sabotage of product by outsiders and by employees have recently occurred.

17. See reference to article in *New York Times* in *The Chronicle*, Vol. XXV, No. 13 (March 25, 1880), p. 297.

18. See: *Outline of U & O Insurance*. C.D. Minor, Royal Liverpool Group Publication (March 1, 1941), p. 4.

19. See: Address by Clark Hudson before Kansas City Insurance Society. Reported in *Mid-America Insurance* (October 1973), p. 52.

20. There have been many articles written on the use of the valued policy. See: "Pros & Cons of Valued U & O," Leyton B. Hunter, President, The London Agency— Atlanta, Georgia (February 5, 1968). (Files of the author)

21. It has been stated that the valued form is satisfactory for adjusting a total loss but offers no benefit in case of a partial loss. See: *American Mutual Study Course, Time Element Coverages*, Lesson 2.D., p. 22 (Undated). In one very early decision, the court held that the policy was so worded that it was valued as to a total loss and open as to a partial loss. Lite v. Fireman's Ins. Co.

22. There is a great deal of law dealing with the responsibility of the Intermediary both to the Insured and to the Insurer. (See: "The Anamolous Position of the Insurance Agent," Robert M. Morrison, *Villanova Law Review*, Vol. 12 No. 3 (Spring, 1967.) For cases involving Business Interruption Insurance, see American Home Assn Co. v. Harvey's Wagon Wheels, Inc.; Consolidated Sun Ray Inc. v. Lee; Fliback Company, Inc. v. Philadelphia Mfgs. Mut. Ins. Co.; Greenfield, et al v. Insurance, Inc.; Lauhoff v. Automobile Ins. Co.; Wright Body Works Inc. v. Columbus Interstate Ins. Agency.

23. The reader is referred to: FC&S Bulletins, Fire Volume, Business Interruption Insurance; F.C. Bardwell, *Business Interruption Insurance*; Frank S. Glendening, C.P.A., *Business Interruption Insurance* (National Underwriter Co.: 1980); Henry C. Klein, *Business Interruption Insurance*; K.W. Withers, *Business Interruption Insurance*. (Supra.)

24. For an article on the impact of inflation and recession see: "*Business Interruption Coverage*," Daniel Grady, Accountant, *Best's Review*. (September, 1980), p. 42.

25. An early discussion of underwriting rules can be found in *Bulletin on U & O Insurance*, V.M. Johnson (Improved Risk Mutuals, 1928).

    Johnson listed six types of risk which while good for fire insurance are not necessarily good risks for I.R.M. to accept for U&O. While underwriting has progressed far beyond the simple situations with which he dealt, there is still a lot of basic common sense in what he set as guidelines:

1. *Business should be well established in a staple line, not a new venture, or style or novelty intensive.*
2. *Operating at a good margin of profit.*
3. *Not subject to frequent interruptions due to labor troubles, litigation or rapid fluctuation in volume.*
4. *Management not subject to frequent change of personnel or policy.*
5. *Thoroughly efficient and complete system of business records established and vital records well protected against destruction by fire.*
6. *Production, in case of a manufacturing business, not dependent upon special machinery or equipment which cannot quickly be duplicated. Also production of active plant not dependent entirely upon any one unit of production.*

The rate in Dalton's policy on the Newton Mills was at 80¢ and 90¢ per annum, the same rate which was paid for fire insurance to the manufacturers mutual insurance companies.

26. See: *Interruption Reports—Their Uses and Abuses*, S.J. Justice, F.C.I.I. (Insurance Institute of London: Feb. 16, 1977).

27. See news item re: Tylenol suit, reported in *Business Insurance*, Vol. 17 (January 10, 1983), p. 1.

28. "Principle of Rates," E.C. Bardwell, *Business Interruption Insurance* (1973 Ed.), p. 68.

29. "Business Interruption Coverage," Daniel Grady, address to Special Risk Underwriters reported in *Best's Review*, Vol. 81, (Sept. 1980), p. 42.

11

First Steps When Loss Occurs

Acts of Insured. Acts of Loss Manager. The Adjuster.
Determination of Damage.

A. Introduction

When damage caused by an insured peril interrupts normal operations, a proper understanding and interpretation of the provisions of the Business Interruption Insurance policy becomes a matter of immediate importance. This chapter deals with the early procedures to be followed in the event a loss occurs.

During the century and more that has elapsed since various forms of Business Interruption Insurance were first written in the United States, substantial progress has been made toward the development of rules for applying this coverage to loss situations. A substantial number of court decisions dealing with such policies are on the books. As indicated earlier, several volumes analyzing the application of policy provisions, at least from the Insurer's point of view, have been written.

Policy forms have been replaced and policy wording has changed over that time span. Even the understanding of the subject of the insurance has changed. Nevertheless, the fact remains, that the whole field of Business Interruption Insurance loss settlement has remained an arcane subject. There is no wide spread dissemination of knowledge among the insurance fraternity of how the coverage really works when a loss occurs. This applies not only to Intermediaries who seek to advise their Insureds, but even to some of those appointed by Insurers to adjust and settle such losses. The result is that, in the case of some losses, a settlement, made in good faith but with lack of understanding, may not have been in all respects in conformity with the provisions of the contract. This is more likely to occur in the case of losses of substantial size.

B. Preliminary Acts by the Insured

The usual practice, when damage is suffered, is for the Insured to notify the Intermediary that he has "had a loss." Where the policy was sold to him by the representative of a "direct writer," the communication might be to the sales person or to the local office of the Insurer. The notice is frequently given over the telephone. Such action sets in motion the process of loss adjustment. Almost never is this method of communication challenged by the Insurer.

As soon as the process of adjustment has been set in motion by the giving of notice, the Insured must make a decision as to whether he will rely on the Adjuster sent out by the Insurer to work up the figures showing the amount of his loss or whether the Insured desires to prepare his own figures. In those situations where the interruption will be of short duration and the amount of damages suffered is small, Insureds, historically, have accepted the Adjuster's calculations. Even substantial losses were formerly handled in the same way.

Today, most Adjusters are equipped to apply the policy provisions adequately to the small loss situation. In the case of a loss of substantial size, Insurers typically call in highly skilled Adjusters to represent them. These Adjusters may well be qualified to develop proper figures on behalf of both parties to the contract. But there is so much of a judgmental nature and so many subjective factors involved in determining the amount of a loss of any consequence, that an Insured is well advised to prepare his own figures, independent of the activities of the Adjuster.

The development of the loss figures should be assigned by the Insured to one person, who will be responsible for taking all the steps required by the policy including those necessary to prepare figures for presentation to the Insurer. These figures will serve as a basis for negotiating a settlement of the loss. For the purposes of the following discussion, that person is referred to as the Loss Manager.

In the case of a small business operation and a small amount of damage, the Insured can put on a new hat entitled "Loss Manager" and handle the work himself. In a larger business or where the loss will run into substantial figures, a special individual should be assigned to this role. The term "substantial" is relative to the size of the business of the Insured. When it appears that the ultimate loss might run to $10,000 or more, the expense and effort of having a specific individual appointed would be justified. The person appointed would normally be selected from among the operations staff. He should have sufficient knowledge and managerial ability to handle both the determination of the amount of loss and the arranging for the repairs necessary to restore operations. He should normally be the person responsible for setting into motion and maintaining the Disaster Plan; the usual action under a plan often coincides with duties required by the policy. He may well need assistance in his work but he has ultimate authority and responsibility, subject only to the approval of the chief operations officer and the chief executive officer of the Insured. In the case of very substantial damage, the chief operations officer himself may fill the role of Loss Manager.

The Loss Manager should optimally be relieved of all other duties in connection with the business operation. He should be set up in a separate operations center with a separate set of financial books and a separate filing system. His becomes the command post from which emanate all actions and all negotiations. That is not to say that he acts alone. But his should be the responsibility of seeing that all policy requirements are complied with, that all necessary financial figures are secured or projected and that proper relations are established with the Adjuster. He should have the authority to call upon the comptroller or treasurer of the Insured for all necessary help in working up the pertinent figures. All interim correspondence should go out over his name and all negotiations with the consultants called in to assist the Insured should be monitored by him.

Sight should be not lost of the fact that the business interruption loss usually arises out of physical damage covered by property insurance. When a Loss Manager is appointed to determine the business interruption loss, he should take full control of the property damage loss situation as well.

C. Preliminary Acts of the Loss Manager

1. Becoming Acquainted with Policy Provisions

The discussion will proceed on the assumption that a Loss Manager has been selected and empowered to act. There are certain policy requirements which must be complied with promptly.

The first step to be undertaken by the Loss Manager is to become acquainted with the provisions of the pertinent insurance policies. He may come to the conclusion that he needs expert help in their interpretation, but he should read and become completely familiar with their content. It often happens that with his practical knowledge of the operations of the business, he can spot applications of the text to situations that are unique to this business enterprise and not obvious to whomever may be advising him.

The obvious person to whom to turn first for technical assistance in policy understanding is the Intermediary. On some matters, the Loss Manager may also want to consult the Lawyer for the business entity. Unfortunately, the large majority of Lawyers have had insufficient exposure to the interpretation of these insurance contracts to be of much assistance. Insurance law is a specialty with its own peculiar rules. Where a substantial amount of money is involved, it is not unusual for the Insured's business Lawyer to recommend enlisting the services of a Lawyer who has had experience in handling large business interruption losses. They are usually found in law firms specializing in insurance law.

Many Insureds have found it highly advantageous to engage the services of such an experienced Lawyer as Consultant to guide their activities through all the stages of adjusting and settling a loss. Normally, such a resource person remains in the background until a technical problem requiring his or her service comes to issue.

The increased utilization of computers and the importance of highly specific conditions for their effective performance suggests that, where a computer or software is damaged, a computer engineer be among those experts whose help is co-opted.

There has grown up, particularly in the large metropolitan centers, a special group of persons who have set themselves up as representatives of Insureds in the handling of insurance losses. They are known as Public Adjusters. Usually they must be licensed by the Insurance Department of the state to carry on this activity. A preliminary inquiry as to the level of their expertise and their experience in handling substantial business interruption losses is strongly recommended.

The practice has grown up of compensating Public Adjusters by an amount equal to a percentage of the amount they recover. As their activity has become more professionalized, compensation on a time basis is becoming a preferable alternative, especially in the case of a substantial loss. Sometimes a combination of the two is the basis for compensation.

The position of the Intermediary in the event of a business interruption loss, other than that of receiving and transmitting the notice of loss and discussing policy provisions, varies. The Intermediary may, by a course of conduct in the past, have established the practice of partaking in the activities of the Insured following the occurrence of damage. This may be sufficient to give the Insured a rightful expectation that he will be assisted in the present situation.

Short of such developed practice, it is open to the Intermediary to decide whether he will intervene on behalf of the Insured in the settlement of disputes. Some do, some do not. Many Intermediaries are conscious of their lack of knowledge about the method of determining the amount of loss under a Business Interruption Insurance policy and limit their help to guiding the preliminary steps. Others have staff who are trained in loss handling and who supplant the sales and marketing staff of the Intermediary's office in assisting with the handling of a loss. Still others recommend the services of a Consultant or a Public Adjuster. While there is no legal obligation on the part of the Intermediary to participate in the settlement procedure, other than that based on a prior course of conduct, the retention of good client relations would indicate the advisability of rendering all of the assistance of which the Intermediary is capable. In the case of minor losses, where the Adjuster alone does the calculations, the Intermediary should be ready to act on behalf of the Insured to elicit an explanation from the Adjuster as to how he reached certain conclusions and to transmit to the Adjuster the Insured's reasons, if any, as to why he believes those conclusions are erroneous.

2. Conforming with Policy Requirements in Case of Loss

Equipped to undertake his responsibilities, the Loss Manager proceeds to comply with the requirements of the policy. There are two sections in which these requirements are set forth—one in the underlying policy and one in the Business Interruption Insurance form. They contain, basically, the same provisions. The language concerning losses in the form was adopted in large part from the policy, with those changes deemed necessary to adapt it to the special requirements of a time element contract. The language of the form, where differing from the language of the policy, supersedes the latter. However, in any case where the provisions of the policy have not been superseded, they still continue in force, not only with respect to the property damage but also as regards the business interruption loss.

The question arises as to whether the insertion in the form of the provision about "Requirements in Case Loss Occurs" completely supplants the correspondingly entitled provision in the underlying policy, or whether those requirements in the latter which are not specifically excluded by the form are still to be applied to the business interruption loss. There can be little doubt that a complete substitution was intended.

It should be emphasized that giving oral notice of loss is not in compliance with the provision of the Standard Fire Insurance policy to which the Business Interruption form is usually attached. This could be significant, if it were claimed that no notice of loss ever actually reached the Insurer or its agent and no Adjuster ever was sent out to settle the loss. The policy requires that in case loss occurs "the Insured shall give immediate *written* notice to this Company. . . ." The Gross Earnings form, following the language of the Standard Fire Insurance policy, also requires immediate *written* notice in case of a business interruption loss. (The provisions of the BIC Form are discussed in Ch. 8.)

The words "immediate" and "forthwith" have been interpreted many times by the courts. In general, they interpret the words to mean "reasonable under the circumstances." Knowledge of the damage must have reached the Insured and he must be physically able to react to such knowledge to trigger the running of time.

Notice to its Agent constitutes notice to the Insurer. But the Intermediary with whom the Insured dealt may have acted as a Broker. The Broker, at law, is held to represent the Insured alone. Notice to such person would, therefore, not constitute notice to the Insurer. In the case of a policy issued by an Agent for a direct writer, such person may not have authority to receive notice of loss on behalf of his or her employer. It would be the course of wisdom in the case of damage of any extent to confirm any oral notice with one in writing sent to the Agent who signed the policy, with a copy to the Insurer at its home or regional office. Failure to give notice within a reasonable time could be set up as a defense to any liability on the part of the Insurer.

A careful reading of the provisions of the underlying Standard Fire Insurance policy and of the Gross Earnings form attached to it reveals that, while the title assigned to the provision is the same in both, i.e., "Requirements in Case Loss Occurs," the requirements are not precisely the same as far as they concern the duties of the Insured.

In the Fire Insurance policy, the applicable language requires that the written notice include an inventory of all property, showing in detail actual cash value and amount of loss claimed. In the Gross Earnings form, there is a requirement for immediate notice of any business interruption loss. Neither policy nor form requires that this notice be given under oath. This preliminary statement is to be distinguished from the sworn proof of loss which must be furnished in 60 days.

The Fire Insurance policy calls for the protection of the property from further damage. The Business Interruption Insurance form adds the words "which might result in extension of the period of interruption." This fact becomes of importance when it comes to allocating the cost of protection against increase of loss between the two coverages. If there is any expense for such protection over what it would cost to comply with the requirements of the Fire Insurance policy, it could possibly be allocated to the Business Interruption Insurance policy. This might be helpful if there was insufficient Fire Insurance.

The next requirement of the policy is to separate the damaged from the undamaged property. This is not repeated in the form. All of these costs should be allocated to the Fire Insurance policy.[1]

If the Insured fails to take adequate steps to protect the property from further damages or to separate the property and as a result, further damage is suffered by an Insured's stock of merchandise resulting in a longer interruption before operations can be restored to normal, the violation of the terms of the underlying policy would probably serve as a defense against that part of the business interruption loss resulting therefrom. But if, on the other hand, it were not possible to take adequate steps to prevent further damage then, on theory, the Insured should be compensated for the additional ensuing loss.[2] This should not be classified as an "other consequential loss" to be excluded under the terms of the form.

The next requirement in the Fire Insurance policy, namely "put it in the best possible order," is intended to facilitate the process of investigation by the Adjuster. To comply may require the removal of the debris that resulted from the damage. But the policy contains no requirement as to the time span within which such "putting it in the best possible order" must take place. The Insured could do it at his leisure and be in compliance with the terms of the Fire Insurance policy. (Compare the provisions of the BIC Form, Ch. 16.) There can be little doubt, however, that the "due diligence and dispatch" provisions of the Business Interruption Insurance policy would require a prompt removal of the debris under appropriate circumstances.

Since the Fire Insurance policy will pick up the cost of normal debris removal, is any part of such cost attributable to the business interruption loss? It could be. If the Insured, instead of relying on the efforts of his own work force and his own equipment (which would have been his normal course of action) resorted to heroic measures to clean up the debris, such as working around the clock, engaging additional workmen, hiring special equipment, etc., to expedite the resumption of operations, then the expediting expense incurred could be charged against the Business Interruption Insurance contract.

It would be the function of the Loss Manager to keep track of such extra expense and record it in his loss book. He should also note the amount of time saved by the expediting efforts, in order to have a basis for recovering the expediting expense at the time of loss settlement. The record should show the entire cost, the cost if no expediting activity were carried on and the difference chargeable to the business interruption loss.

It is also desirable for the Loss Manager to make a survey of all leases, labor union contracts and other contracts to which the Insured is a party, which may be affected by the interruption of operations. They may contain provisions which will affect his decisions as he plans for the steps which he will take to restore operations.[3]

D. The Adjuster Arrives

1. Requirement to Send Adjuster

An Adjuster representing the Insurer will usually appear promptly after the giving of notice of damage. A delay in his arrival should not hold up the Loss Manager from proceeding with his duties. After a major catastrophe affecting a wide territory, it is sometimes impossible for the Insurer to send an Adjuster to reach the scene promptly. The Insured should clear the matter of the delay with the Insurer and then take steps to contain the loss.

It has to be accepted as a fact of life that there are degrees of expertise to be found among Adjusters. Where the amount of potential loss appears to be small, the Insurer may have assigned the matter to a local independent Adjuster who may have had limited experience in handling business interruption losses. He may thus lack an adequate understanding of the provisions of such a policy. In the case of a substantial loss where the normal practice is to send in an Adjuster experienced in such losses, he may come from some distance away and may be unfamiliar with local statutory provisions. If so, a co-adjustment would be logical.

There is no provision in the policy or the form requiring the Insurer to send an Adjuster to survey the damage or negotiate a settlement of the loss. The policy provides that the Insured shall furnish the Insurer with the details of his claim and certain circumstances surrounding the property and the damage. The Insurer can sit back, wait until the proof of loss is filed and then decide what course of action to take. Of course, the absence of information from its own sources would be a great handicap in making a judgment. So the practice is almost universal for the Insurer to send an Adjuster to the scene of the damage.

2. Non-waiver Agreement

An exception does exist where the circumstances are such that the Insurer may eventually have to consider denying liability for the loss. Sending an Adjuster under such circumstances might be deemed to constitute a waiver of its rights to deny liability later. Under such circumstances, the Adjuster will request a written statement from the Insured that the appearance of the Adjuster and his activities in the loss adjustment will not constitute a waiver of any defenses the Insurer may have. Some Adjusters have made it a practice of requesting such a "non-waiver" on every loss to which they are assigned.[4]

Neither the Insurer nor the Adjuster is entitled by the policy or the form to require the Insured to sign such a non-waiver. The latter can refuse to do so and continue on his own to prepare his claim. In the usual case, there is no reason why the Insured should refuse to sign and to refuse might seriously complicate the progress of loss settlement. However, it is recommended that the non-waiver agreement specify what defenses the Insurer is not waiving.

3. Meeting the Loss Manager

Upon his arrival, the Adjuster should meet the Loss Manager and present his credentials to the latter. In addition to his business card, these should include the letter appointing him as Adjuster. This is to enable the Loss Manager to ascertain which of the Insurers on the risk are represented by the Adjuster. If not all of them are so represented, special care must be taken by the Insured to preserve his rights against the companies not so represented.[5]

One measure of protection the Insured might take, where the Adjuster claims to represent companies from whom he has no written evidence of authority, is to write to such Insurers, report the arrival of the Adjuster and ask for a statement that such authority exists or that, in the absence of a reply to the contrary, it will be assumed that the Adjuster's statements are correct and that such authority does exist.

4. Preliminary Forms

There are two measures the Adjuster should take as soon as he is ready to go to work. One is designed to overcome an anachronism that still lurks in the Standard Fire Insurance policy and is not eliminated by the Gross Earnings form. That is the provision that the Insurer has thirty days time after receipt of the proof of loss to notify the Insured that it intends to exercise its option to make the repairs or the replacement A strict interpretation of this provision would prohibit the Insured from starting to make repairs until the thirty days had run or the option had been waived. This provision might be read to extend the time which constitutes due diligence and dispatch. To eliminate such possibility, the Adjuster should waive this option on behalf of the Insurer. In one case, the court ruled that since the Insured could not, because of this option, start to make repairs for 30 days, interest was allowable to the Insured for an additional 30-day period.[6]

The second measure is to present the Insured with a form of proof of loss and a written request that it be furnished in accordance with the policy provisions. The Adjuster should ask the Insured whether there is insurance applicable to the loss other than that carried by the Insurers whom he represents. This information will ultimately be set out in the proof of loss, but it should be brought to the surface early.

5. Relationship with Loss Manager

It is important at this juncture to point out a vital distinction between losses under Fire Insurance and under Business Interruption Insurance policies. In the case of the former, it is understandable how the parties may consider themselves in an adversary position. Disputes can arise concerning factual matters: was this fur coat contaminated by smoke or not?; how much will it cost to repaint the kitchen?—to cite very simple examples. Honest differences of opinions can arise but they are about issues which are objective in nature and conflicting attitudes can be accepted with the understanding that an objective test can solve the dispute in most cases.

This is not the case with a Business Interruption Insurance policy. As has been noted in the first part, a great deal of subjective input is called for by the wording of the contract. Such terms as "due diligence," "probable future experience," "do not necessarily continue," and "same quality of service," to name just some of them, can by no stretch of the imagination be considered as denoting objective criteria. There is no absolute right or wrong with such guidelines.

Only by establishing a dialogue based on mutual respect and a desire to understand the constraints under which the other party is acting, can a mutually acceptable settlement be reached. The Insured must accept the restraints of the policy wording which control the decisions of the Adjuster. The Adjuster must accept the need of the Insured to replace the earnings that would have been earned had no damage been suffered.

It is impossible to lay too much stress on the need of both parties to approach the adjustment of the loss on a basis of mutual cooperation. The Adjuster may, at times, be irked by what he considers, rightly or wrongly, to be an incorrect reading of the policy by the Insured, because it is done in a way different from that to which the Adjuster is accustomed. The Insured may consider the Adjuster unnecessarily obstructive in requiring objective proof of speculations which the Insured considers legitimate. Given a proper attitude toward the process of loss settlement, such irritants can be dealt with successfully.

Purely from a psychological point of view, the Adjuster must not approach the Insured with an attitude of superiority. He may know more about Business Interruption Insurance policies, but he knows far less about the intricacies of the Insured's business. For either to try to establish superiority in the relationship in his initial approach can only serve to raise the hackles of the other and poison the relationship. The desirability of such an ongoing relationship will become apparent from time to time as the parties progress through the settlement of the loss.

The Adjuster should secure from the Loss Manager an explanation of the nature of the financial loss records he is keeping. The Adjuster may suggest changes that will make it simpler for him to confirm the ultimate settlement to the Insurer. It also is desirable for the Loss Manager to exchange information with the Adjuster about the engineers and other technicians that he will be using.

6. Examine Policies

With the preliminaries over, the Adjuster should ask to be shown the insurance policies held by the Insured. While these normally will conform to the records in the Insurer's file, occasions have existed where endorsements or other changes have been attached by an authorized Agent to the Insured's policies without being reflected in the Insurer's records. The Adjuster makes a note of all the pertinent parts of the policies for transmission in his preliminary report to the Insurer.

Where more than one policy exists, many of the issues that arise in the case of multiple Fire Insurance policies could occur. Non-concurrencies conceivably could occur where several Business Interruption Insurance policies exist; e.g. valued and non-valued policy or blanket and specific policies. At least one case exists involving cancellation by substitution;[7] also one involving the proration of loss.[8]

At the same time, the Adjuster should secure from the Loss Manager whatever information the latter has about the nature and extent of the damage. If

possible, he should also get some rough estimate of the length of the anticipated business interruption, whether it will be total or partial, and any other
information which will assist the Insurer in setting up a reserve against the loss.
Of course, none of this information is final and binding on either party.

As soon as practicable, the information gathered should be forwarded by
the Adjuster in a written report to the Insurer's Claim Department.[9] Included
in that report should be an expression of opinion as to whether the damage had
been caused by an insured peril. The Adjuster should be careful in any estimate
of loss he makes in his early reports. It makes a Claims Manager very unhappy
to face the need of having to increase a reserve substantially because of an
improper early estimate.

7. Maintain Log Book

Where the amount of loss is substantial, a considerable amount of time
may be required in arriving at a final adjustment and settlement. It is highly
advisable that the Adjuster set up a log book from the very beginning of his
work. This should contain not only a listing of dates and hours spent, but
should also contain notes of the matters discussed and the agreements reached
or disputes unsettled with the representatives of the Insured.

E. Determination of the Physical Property Damage

1. Nature of Survey

These preliminary matters should take but little time and should not delay
the Loss Manager in proceeding with the first of his basic tasks—determining
the parameters of the period of interruption which the operations face. To this
end, he must proceed to determine the full nature and extent of the damage to
the physical plant.

The chemical plant explosion mentioned earlier in the text provided a most
intricate example of the possible contingencies the Loss Manager may face. As
the plant had grown, new equipment had been added replacing parts of the
original installation. Some of the remaining equipment was rapidly becoming
obsolete. To replace the damage with necessary new equipment would require a
change in footings, piping and connections. Drawings for the change in piping
would take two months to complete. At the date of the explosion, there was a
shortage of available electricians and electrical contractors. No one would
undertake a job of this complexity except on a cost plus basis and with no
guarantee of performance time. One piece of equipment—a spray drier—was of
unique, individual design. Because of its size, it could only be field erected from
large sections. The size of the sections depended on road limitations. The
research and development records and calculations for using the spray drier
had been destroyed by the fire. The employee who had developed them had left

his job six months before the explosion. Many experimental runs and analyses would be required before production could be considered normal. The freezing of various lines—water, steam, raw materials, in-process materials and finished product lines (the damage happened in winter)—meant that the lines would have to be stripped of insulation, tested, and damaged parts replaced. Reactors with chemicals in them had overreacted as a result of the explosion and would have to be X-rayed and possibly replaced. There had possibly been damage to the integrity of the explosion proof electric switches due to the blast. The rebuilding of a structure probably would require input from an architect or contractor or both. Since a violent explosion had occurred, it will be necessary to engage the services of a vibration engineer to determine whether the structure had been knocked out of plumb, with the resultant weakening of its elements. This type of situation imposed responsibility on the Loss Manager to call in outside experts to provide him with a basis for and to support the validity of the decisions which he made.

That all these developments and others would have to be taken into consideration was recognized by the Loss Manager as he laid out his plans for proceeding with repairs as well as estimating the length of the interruption This task may be within the competence of the Loss Manager, but he most likely may require help from others. These could include the suppliers or manufacturers of the machinery that was damaged or destroyed. Where a special type of equipment is involved, the question may arise as to whether it can be repaired in place or whether it has to be sent back to the factory which manufactured it for repairs.

Where experts are engaged in this process, they should serve as the means of determining how long it will take to repair or replace. Usually they are more knowledgeable in this area than is the Loss Manager. Their independent opinion will also be of value in the process of establishing the amount of the loss. Whereever feasible, the experts should render two opinions—what will be the time of interruption if normal procedures are followed, and what time can be saved if extraordinary measures are taken to expedite the process. They should also estimate the cost of each of the alternative actions.

2. Additional Areas for Decision

Not only does the determination of the nature and extent of the physical damage provide the Loss Manager with information as to how long it will be, under normal conditions, to restore total productivity, but it supplies him with a basis for making certain subsidiary decisions. It underlies a decision as to what intermediate steps, if any, can and should be undertaken to reduce the Insured's loss. These can include such matters as how to continue the operations of the remainder of the plant or store or service, if only part of them has been stopped by the damage; what alternate facilities of the Insured or of others could be utilized to restore the Earnings Stream that has been interrupted by the damage; which employees are to be retained on the payroll during the period of interruption; and what extraordinary expenditures should be made to speed up restoration of operations.

These decisions must be made whether or not repair or replacement will ever be undertaken. They lie at the base of any claim for loss to be made by the Insured. As has been stated many times, the Insured can establish his claim on a theoretical basis.[10]

This would appear to be an appropriate point in the overall process of loss adjustment for the Loss Manager to discuss with the Owner, after he advises them as to the physical facts and the contractual provisions found in the insurance policies and various other pertinent contracts, just what steps the Owner will decide to take. Does he want to rebuild or replace the damaged property; in what form and in what location; on what time schedule and with what expenditure of funds? Such decisions are vital at this stage of the proceedings. The Loss Manager must be given authority to proceed with whatever course of action top management determines.

3. Removal of Debris

The first step that the Loss Manager normally plans is to arrange for removal of the debris resulting from the damage so that restoration can commence. Taking this first step can be complicated where a different Adjuster is assigned to the property damage loss and to the business interruption loss.

The Adjuster assigned to investigate the damage to the physical property may ask to have the site of the damage left undisturbed to help him in his investigation as to the cause and origin of the damage. Adjusters have been known to serve a notice on the Insured not to disturb anything until they have completed their investigation of the property damage. There is nothing in either type of insurance policy which extends this right to the Adjuster. Many Insureds, however, acquiesce, either through ignorance or because they do not want to tangle with the Adjuster on that matter. Such acquiescence may delay the time when the Insured can get back into production. It has been held that such delay is permissible and can be added to the time involved in "due diligence and dispatch."[11] A fire marshal investigating a claim of arson may also require the maintenance of the status quo until he completes his investigation.

4. In Case of Controversy

Whenever a controversy cannot be resolved, the Adjuster should refer the matter back to his principal. The furnishing of full and timely reports, though time consuming, is the trademark of a good Adjuster.

A special problem can be created—particularly in cases of lesser damage—when the same Adjuster represents both the property Insurer and the business interruption Insurer. A dispute concerning the physical property loss can create a problem of interpersonal relations that can upset the cooperative attitude that should prevail in handling the business interruption loss.

Chapter 11 Notes

1. Anchor Toy Corp. v. American Eagle F. Ins. Co.

2. See: Port Murray Dairy Co. v. Prov. Washington Ins. Co.; Simon v. Girard F&M Ins. Co.

3. In one case, the lease required that the tenant give notice to the landlord within 10 days if he wanted the damage repaired. Harper v. Dampier.

4. For a case where a non-waiver had been signed see: DiLeo v. U.S.F.&G. Co. (1964).

5. Tomar v. National Union F. Ins. Co. One early statement made by an Adjuster reads "They (the Insureds) attempted to shift the responsibility of preparing their claim from their own shoulders, where it properly belongs, to mine. My duties, as you are aware, are to check-up, verify or disprove their claim; but I am not obliged in any way to prepare it for them."
   Thrasher Hall, *Use & Occupancy, Excess Floater & Betterments Ins. Eclairased* (1920).

6. Right of Insurer within 30 days of filing of proof of loss to undertake the rebuilding itself was mentioned but not exercised in Amusement Syndicate Co. v. Milwaukee Mechanics Ins. Co. (1913).

7. Nelson v. American Reliable Ins. Co.

8. Hawkeye Chemical Co. v. St. Paul Fire & Marine Ins. Co.

9. Failure of the Adjuster to take prompt and proper action in cases of business interruption loss was said to necessitate more overpayments than any other single cause. "Problem Claims under Business Interruption Policies," Geo. W. Clarke, Esq., Section of Ins. Law. American Bar Ass'n Annual Meeting in New York, July 9, 1957.

10. Amusement Syndicate Co. v. Milwaukee Mechanics Ins. Co. (1911)

11. A & S Corp. v. Centennial Ins. Co.; Saperston v. American & Foreign Ins. Co.; Bradford v. Canadian F. Ins. Co.

12

Early Decisions of Loss Manager

Resumption of operations. Additional information. Critical Path Management. Writing a memorandum.

A. Temporary Resumption of Operations

1. Constraints on the Loss Manager

The survey of the physical damage will have given the Loss Manager a basic grasp on what he has to do to fulfill his next important mission—that of limiting the amount of reduction in the Earnings Stream, while he restores the plant to the condition it was in prior to the damage. As he faces this task, he must keep in mind the constraints under which he must function.

The ever present possibility that there will be no adequate objective test for determining the amount of a particular loss incurred under a Business Interruption Insurance policy is responsible, in large part, for the mystique that has developed around the loss adjustment and loss settlement procedures. The wording of the contract—"due diligence and dispatch" and "resumption of operations"—are merely guides for conduct rather than measurements of amount. They rely for their foundation on the fundamental duty of an injured party to mitigate the loss which he has suffered and for which he expects to be compensated. In the case of a business interrruption loss, mitigation means minimizing the amount of diminution to the Earnings Stream brought about by the damage to or destruction of the described physical property.

Such minimization effort is possible in at least two areas. The first area is the time it takes to restore operations to normalcy. The second is the utilization of other means for keeping the Earnings Stream flowing during the period of restoration. Both involve the efforts of the Insured. The standard for such effort rests upon another fundamental concept underlying insurance contracts—the parties are to act in good faith. As discussed elsewhere, this implies the same course of conduct that the Insured would have followed had he had no Business Interruption Insurance.

To establish some criteria for what constitutes good faith under this type of contract, the Insurers have introduced the terms noted above. To the effort regarding time they have attached the language "due diligence and dispatch" and to the effort regarding the continuance of the Earnings Stream they have attached the language "resumption of operations." But because of the inherent indefiniteness of these terms, the Insurer has not attempted to define "due diligence and dispatch" and in the case of "resumption of operations" has limited its definition to the types of alternate property that might be used—not about how to use it. Instead, the Insurer has transferred the joint burdens of decision and proof to the shoulders of the Insured.

The Insured must establish that what he has done complies with what constitutes good faith in these two areas. The Insurer will not pay the loss that the Insured has actually sustained—no matter how clear the evidence that the Insured can muster in its support. It will pay only that amount which the Insured can prove he would inevitably have had to suffer if he had properly and adequately applied the two constraints of due diligence and resumptions of operations.

The practical effect of this approach to recovery imposes on the Loss Manager the obligation to monitor all of his decisions and all of his acts in the light of these two constraints. They do not bind his freedom of action; but they do set up boundaries as to the percentage of the dollar loss suffered that he can collect under the insurance contract. (For provisions of due diligence requirement in BIC Form, see Ch. 8.)

2. Impacts of the "Resumption of Operations" Clause

a. Use of Property Described. The provisions of the various Gross Earnings forms differ. The policy that was issued should be carefully read to see just what are its provisions. In the manufacturing forms, the requirements are set out in three categories. The first category requires making the best possible use of the property described in the policy whether it has been damaged or not. Innumerable examples of situations falling within this category could be cited, but a few should give a general idea of the impact of this requirement.

The simplest situation is where there is standby equipment or spare parts for machinery. Where the building housing the business enterprise has been damaged, temporary repairs might be made which would permit operations to continue—the roof could be closed-in temporarily or broken store windows could be boarded up. In the case of a manufacturing operation, where machinery has been damaged but can still operate to some extent, the best possible use of it must be made. If part of the machinery is totally unusable, the remaining machines might be able to take up the slack by the Insured working his help overtime or by putting on a second shift to operate the undamaged machines. (For provisions of Resumption of Operations Clause in BIC Form, see Ch. 16.)

Since finished goods are not covered under the manufacturing form, the matter of a fire sale is applicable only to policies in the mercantile form. There is nothing in the form which requires that the gross earnings received during the period of interruption result from the normal operation of the Insured's business activities as long as it is the same kind of business. The form merely refers to "operations of business."

A prime question is whether proceeding to have a fire sale is a "resumption of operations of the property." A sale of damaged goods, whether or not in conjunction with the sale of undamaged goods, would seem to be such an operation for a mercantile establishment.

A technique sometimes used in connection with a fire sale, where legal, is to use the opportunity to dispose of obsolete merchandise carried in inventory at a low value or, more frequently, to bring in cheaper (and usually inferior) merchandise and to sell it to customers looking for a "bargain." If such a sale takes place during the period of interruption, the sale may benefit the Insurer by reducing the gross earnings loss.

Suppose that the gross earnings are not reduced at all because of the success of the sale. Is there any loss for which the Insured can collect? The question that has to be answered is not whether the Insured has suffered a loss in value—this was taken care of by the Fire Insurance policy—but whether, as a result of the interruption of normal operations due to the fire, there was a diminution of gross earnings. The answer is clear. There was no diminution and therefore no loss under the policy.[1]

The problem becomes stickier when the damaged goods are disposed of in bulk. This could be to the salvage branch of the fire insurance company, which pays the Insured for the remaining value above the amount of the damage. Or it could be by the sale of the damaged goods by the Insured, in bulk to a third party. In both cases, it could well be argued that this was not the normal process of the Insured's operations and that the amount received in the bulk sale should not be included in gross earnings.

If an entirely different type of operation is carried on at a new location than had been the previous business of the Insured, no credit is given in calculating the ongoing Earnings Stream for profits earned therefrom.[2] A parallel can be drawn to the manufacturing cases where the temporary activity was not considered to be normal operations.[3]

b. Use of Other Property. (See Comment #5, p. 309). The second category in the manufacturing form refers to the use of other property whether at the location described or elsewhere. The meaning of the wording of this provision is somewhat ambiguous. Does it mean using—*at the location*—other property which is located at the location or elsewhere, or does it mean using—*at the location or elsewhere*—other property? It would appear that the first is the proper reading of this provision. The word "other" undoubtedly—means other than that damaged, rather than—other than that described, but the place of usage has to be that described in the policy.[4]

One example of the use—at the location—of other property involved the use of a makeshift electrical generator installed to keep operations going until a permanent replacement could be procured for the generator that had been damaged by lightning. The temporary generator, not being appropriate for the task, ran the plant for three days when it burned out. The plant was then shut down for four and one-half days more until the permanent replacement was received and installed. In that case, it was agreed that the cost of the burned out temporary generator was a proper expense to reduce loss. It was also agreed that the loss due to the four and one-half days of additional interruption was covered by the policy, being attributable to the original lightning damage.

Where damage to a building housing a business operation has been substantial, the question usually arises as to whether the Insured should set up temporary operations elsewhere in available space until the original building is restored. In the case of a retail establishment, a shoe store for example, the question can usually be answered in the affirmative if the time of restoration will be extensive, as long as the new store is within the same retail district and the costs involved are within reason. In the case of a manufacturing plant, an affirmative answer is possible if the anticipated expenses will be reasonable and the substitute operation can be conducted on a profitable basis or, at least, that the cost of goods sold will not exceed their sales price. Where profits are earned at another location by continuing the usual operations at that location, they are applied in reduction of the loss just as if partial operations were carried on at the original plant.[5]

c. Use of Stock. The third category in the manufacturing form refers to the use of stock (raw, in process, or finished) at the location described or elsewhere. This is paralleled by the second stage of the two categories in the non-manufacturing form, which refers to the "... merchandise or other property at the location(s) described or elsewhere." A retailer may be able to locate goods of a similar nature with which to stock his shelves until his regular suppliers can replace the damaged merchandise. A manufacturer, whose production had been halted by damage to his inventory of a particular component of his finished product, may purchase a similar component from another source and use it until he replaces the supply whose damage caused the interruption. The goods or component may have to be secured at a higher price than would normally be his cost and thus reduce profitability. However, if the product when finished would still produce enough of a mark-up to reduce the amount of loss that would have been suffered if all operations had stopped until replacement could be procured from the original source, the Insured's loss is calculated on the basis of the savings that could have been achieved.

One additional situation may be of interest in connection with the use of other materials. In one case, the Insured bought the replacement material from a sister corporation at the latter's retail price. The Insurer claimed it should have been charged in at *cost* to the supplier, since both corporations had the same officers and directors. But not all of the stockholders in the two corporations were the same. There was no justification in depriving the non-concurrent stockholders of what was their normal profit to benefit a sister corporation.[6] The Insurer had to reimburse the Insured for this higher cost of the substitute material.

A question arises with regard to the use of the inventory of goods which an Insured normally keeps on hand to meet demands for his product or merchandise. Under usual conditions, the use of such inventory is considered necessary under the Resumption of Operations provision. This is certainly the case where the diminution in size of inventory can be restored after production starts up, without any loss having been suffered by the Insured.

For example, if an Insured normally carried 4,000 widgets in stock, representing ten days of production, and normally shipped 400 widgets a day out of inventory to customers, he could claim no loss as a result of a five day interruption during which period he continued to ship the same 400 widgets a day and reduced his inventory to 2,000 widgets. This is the case provided that, when the interruption comes to an end, he can increase his production to 600 widgets a day without extra cost and gradually bring his inventory back to 4,000 widgets. The temporary reduction in that inventory would not cause loss. If on the other hand, it could be established that because certain items no longer were available in inventory, the sale of other items was reduced and gross earnings were lost, recovery for that loss should be possible.

It has been argued that, since loss of "sales value of production" is the basis for a claim under the manufacturing form, if during shut down, there is no capability to create products which have a sales value, the Insured has indeed suffered a loss under the terms of his contract; that this is the result even though sales continued to be made out of inventory, and even though such inventory could ultimately be restored to normal. The lost hours of productivity were permanently lost. Other hours might be added later but they are not the lost hours.

If one focuses attention on the Earnings Stream and not on the operations themselves, the answer to that argument should be relatively clear. A recoverable loss depends on whether there ever will be a reduction to the Earnings Stream as a result of the damage. If the Insured can replace the inventory he has used up in time to meet future requirements, the Earnings Stream continues undiminished and he has suffered no loss; except for any extra expense he may incur to refill the inventory.

Under the terms of the policy the Insured's loss continues until he is able to resume operations "with the same quality of service which existed immediately preceding the loss." This suggests that it is not the unit size or dollar value of the inventory that must be considered, but rather its adequacy for filling orders when setting the time for resumption of operations. In practice, such composition of the inventory is seldom, if ever, considered in putting together financial figures for the loss. That is a matter worth considering, especially if one is dealing with seasonal or high-style merchandise.

The Insured's argument that he has lost the sales value of the production, even though sales were not lost, has not been answered. The answer lies in the fact that the concept that profit is earned when goods are produced, being an artificial one to start with, is applied only up to a certain point and then other concepts take over. Where no reduction in the Earnings Stream has been sustained, there can be no recovery.

A grey area that remains open is the claim that additional orders which could have been procured during the period of interruption were lost—either as a result of sales personnel slowing down their efforts to find new orders knowing that they could not be filled, or as a result of regular customers transfering their orders to competitors believing that because of the damage they could not be filled by the Insured in time to meet their needs. Such additional orders could have been worked on during the period of interruption had no damage occurred and would have created additional value although it would not be reflected in the financial figures until after the loss was settled and then would show up only indirectly in the overall results. The evidence behind such a claim would have to be very substantial to be creditable.

d. Common Sense Approach. The limitations and requirements spelled out in the Resumption of Operations Clause are not absolute in their effect on the amount of recovery. Despite the availability of some means of resuming operations within the categories outlined, there are situations where the Insured would be justified in disregarding them, without an adverse effect on the amount of his recovery.

Returning to the first category—the continuing use of the property whether damaged or not—a measure of common sense must be applied. The continued working of usable but damaged machinery may result in further damage to it. Nor is there justification for undertaking the trouble and expense of locating and training a second shift of employees if the interruption will last only a few weeks. Also, an uncustomary steady diet of overtime might result in a reduction of the efficiency of the workers and a lowering of the quality of their output.

If a second plant owned by the Insured takes up the slack in production, there could still be an item of loss caused by the extraordinary wear and tear in the second plant. Dies and tools have a limited life usage which could be shortened through the additional use.

Then, there are those situations where the advisability of using other property temporarily is a matter of judgment. An example of the type of problem that can arise is found in the case of one manufacturer who did set up temporary production facilities elsewhere to continue production during the year it would take to rebuild his destroyed plant. He ran into so many unexpected difficulties that the cost of his product at the temporary location was greater than the price he could get for it. In other words, he experienced a net loss. Since he had not reduced the insured loss, the entire cost of the disastrous decision came out of his own pocket.

Take two examples from the third category. Where the Insured has built up his trade and goodwill on the basis of the quality of his merchandise or has featured a particular brand of merchandise, the use of other merchandise could result in damaging consequences. By taking in a competing line and selling it to his regular customers, the retailer might maintain his sales volume, but such action could have a serious impact on the goodwill he had built up for his favorite brand. This loss of good will might not show up in his sales volume until after the business interruption loss had been settled. It would appear that such potential loss of future sales would justify refusing to sell the competing line while waiting for a new stock of his usual brand. (Goodwill is not a part of the described property.)

In the case of a manufacturer who is using components of his own manufacture in the assembly of his final product, a similar result might ensue. To require him to buy components of other manufacturers, when his production of components was interrupted, could prove disastrous to all the credibility he had built up for his finished product. There might be no way he can guarantee the performance of the components produced elsewhere. In addition, he would be building up his competition and be destroying his claim for producing a better product.[7]

One situation involved a maufacturer whose operations were divided into stages, with the early stages resulting in products for which there could be a market if they were not used by the manufacturer as components in his final product. He was a manufacturer of Christmas tree ornaments. One of his subsidiary operations was the production of a special electric bulb which he used as part of the ornaments. His assembly plant was damaged so he could not produce ornaments, but his bulb manufacturing facility was undamaged. Competitors would gladly buy the superior bulbs he was still able to produce. Must the Insured continue to manufacture bulbs and sell them to competing ornament manufacturers under the terms of the Resumption of Operations Clause? To do so would be building up the business of his competitors and could very definitely result in a diminution of the goodwill and reputation for superiority he had built for his own product.[8] Of special interest is the fact that the financial damage resulting from this loss of goodwill might not be realized until well after the business interruption loss was settled.

Along similar lines, is the case of the manufacturer whose plant was damaged, but who could arrange to have another manufacturer produce the product for him. However, this would require the disclosure of his secret formulations to the other manufacturer and information about the secret processes employed in the manufacture. In both of the foregoing situations, the answer would depend upon the course of action the Insured would take if he had no insurance. Though purely a subjective test, it would be the only fair one in the given situations.

e. Differences in Opinion. Not infrequently a difference of opinion will arise between the Loss Manager and the Adjuster as to whether or not a suggested measure will succeed in reducing the loss. If a Loss Manager sincerely believes that a certain step in resuming operations would not, even if successful, reduce the loss sufficiently to justify taking the risk of additional loss, it would be appropriate for him to refuse to take the step urged upon him by the Adjuster. He should set out his reasons in writing sent to the Adjuster. If the latter still insisted that he was right and that the step should be taken, it would seem only proper that the Adjuster should assume the risk of possible enhancement of the loss. In other words, the Insurer should agree that if the Insured takes the steps being insisted upon by the Adjuster, the Insurer will be responsible for any further loss that may result from that course of action. Such a decision should be confirmed by an officer of the Insurer before the Insured should proceed to act on it, since it may be beyond the authority of the Adjuster to agree to it.

There is a problem lurking in the wording of the Resumption of Operations Clause as found in the Gross Earnings form. The wording is, "if the Insured could reduce the loss. . . ." Note that it does not say "could have reduced the loss." Had this latter language been used it would have indicated that hindsight could be applied. As actually worded, however, it suggests that the decision as to whether loss would be reduced by taking or not taking certain actions has to be judged in advance.

This matter of the impact of the Resumption of Operations Clause has been given extended treatment at this point in the discussion because it portrays the practical problems facing the Loss Manager as he decides on what courses of action to take. He wants to avoid any move which would serve as a basis for reducing the amount which the Insured can collect on his loss; any basis for a claim on the Adjuster's part that if the Loss Manager had done certain things that loss would have been smaller.

For that reason, decisions should be carefully considered. Wherever possible, decisions of substantial matters should be made only after consultation with the Adjuster. The reasons for taking a particular action should be carefully documented and recorded. In the last analysis, however, it would appear that a decision made in good faith by the Loss Manager and supported by reasonable business judgment must be the basis for judging his actions under the Resumption of Operations Clause. He should not be penalized if, on hindsight, it should appear that had he taken a different course of action the amount of loss suffered by the Insured for which the Insurer is liable would have been reduced.

3. Steps to Restore Earnings Stream

a. Meaning of Due Diligence and Dispatch. While using his best judgment about keeping as much as possible of the usual Earnings Stream flowing by temporary substitute measures, the Loss Manager must at the same time turn his attention to the task of restoring the normal preexisting Earnings Stream. He must keep in mind that, while the Insurer of the physical property has no concern about what is done with the proceeds of the Fire Insurance policy, such is not the case with the Insurer against interruption of the Earnings Stream. The latter expects the funds collected for the property damage as well as the other capital and credit resources of the Insured to be devoted to mitigating its ultimate loss by the restoration of operations to normalcy with due diligence and dispatch.

That expectation has been incorporated into the language of the contract. Not that the Insured must use due diligence and dispatch; he is under no obligation to do so. But the Insured will be paid for the loss of earnings incurred only during such period of time as would have been required to restore operations to normalcy had the Insured used such due diligence and dispatch.

This raises two questions for the Loss Manager. First, what is meant by due diligence and dispatch? Second, what will constitute due diligence and dispatch under the existing circumstances? Or, put another way, how does one *define* the term and how does one *determine* its application to a particular loss situation?

Assuming an intention on the part of the Loss Manager to use the highest good faith in restoring operations as promptly as possible, there still may exist a wide range of possible courses of action that face him, especially in the case of a substantial loss. Assuming that he is prepared to use diligence, what is *due* diligence? Turning to the dictionary for help, he finds that the word "due" is defined in this context, as "owed or owing because of a moral or natural right." That is nothing more than a restatement of the fact that the diligence has to be in accord with the underlying standards of insurance dealings already mentioned. It would appear that "due" is whatever the person using that term expects it to mean. Well, not quite. "due" cannot appropriately be stretched to include "extraordinary." One of its characteristics must be speed combined with determination, but this does not rule out due deliberation and discretion. Basically, the Loss Manager must be prepared to defend the appropriateness of the action which he does take. If appropriate when measured in the light of the existing conditions, it is *due* diligence.

One other generality should be stated. In passing judgment on the adequacy of actions taken by the Insured, the standard used should be that of the

Insured. Someone else might have been able to do a better job. Someone else might have been able to secure from some other sources the funds to start rebuilding promptly rather than being obliged to wait for funds emanating from the property loss settlement. Someone else might have more political clout. What someone else could or might have done is not the test. All that counts is that this Insured did the best he could with the resources and business ability that he possessed.

It is to the realm of experience and the standards of common sense that the Loss Manager must turn for guidance. Here, the decisions handed down by various courts considering this matter can be of some help and the advice of the Lawyer can be sought. But no two cases are ever exactly the same; so such judicial decisions must be applied with discretion. It may be of help to the Loss Manager to understand the thrust of them, while keeping in mind the vagaries of fact situations and judicial temperaments.

Where there has been extensive damage, the most frequent problem presented to the Loss Manager involves the kind of replacement he should make. Should the replacement building or machinery be the same as that which was destroyed? While he has the opportunity, why not install equipment more modern than that previously in place? Improvements in construction techniques may suggest that the rebuilt structures differ from the old building which housed the operations. What about the additional time necessary to hire an architect to redesign the old plans or to install air conditioning for the first time?

If the making of these improvements in no way extends the period of interruption, the business interruption Insurer will not concern itself with such decisions. But, if restoration of the old could be done more speedily than installation of the new, the issue of due diligence is squarely raised.

At one extreme, it is clearly established that the Insured is not obliged slavishly to restore the damaged or destroyed property with identical counterparts.[9] At the other extreme, an Insured cannot build an eighteen-story building in place of the two-story structure that was destroyed and maintain that the time required to build the larger structure fell within the coverage of the policy.

The line of decision must fall within such extremes. To the extent that the Insured is changing the nature of the property described or is adding an entirely new dimension to it, the additional loss due to any extra time required would not be covered. To the extent that in the course of repairing the damage, the Insured is upgrading his operations or his building to conform to changes in the art, and the steps taken are what he probably would have done had there been no insurance, there probably would be coverage. Once again, the issue cannot be painted black or white. There is an area of grey that depends on the characteristics of the particular situation.

b. Examples of Due Diligence and Dispatch. The court in the Anchor Toy case approved the inclusion within the period of interruption of eleven weeks for the architects, six weeks for drawing plans and specifications, two weeks for the bidding process and two weeks for approval from the authorities. Actual construction time would be twenty-two weeks. Installation of machinery was another eight weeks. The total was 38 weeks. The court then added, "This is the time it would take to replace the structure, providing the building was put up by the experts in the courtroom. But buildings seldom are. In the field, it snows and men fall off girders, and the wrong size window glass is delivered. An estimate of eight weeks for contingencies is not believed to be excessive. To this is to be added two weeks . . . to supply goods in the same state of manufacture as those on hand at the time of the fire. A total, therefore, of forty-eight weeks is found."

The additional time taken when a structure that is readily repairable is torn down and a new structure is erected in its place is unreasonable within the application of the due diligence provision; only the time to repair would be covered. Insistence by the Insured that he would employ only highly qualified mechanics to repair delicate machinery and that their workmanship would deteriorate if they worked overtime was reasonable even if it extended the time for making the repairs.

Where roadblocks are placed in the path of restoring the property before operations can start up again, the due diligence provision can be interpreted to require that the Insured exert all the pressure of which he is capable to break the deadlock rather than sit back and let things drag along. This is what he would do if he had no insurance. The Insurer has a right to expect no less from him.

When a Contingent Business Interruption Insurance policy is held by the Insured, he is subject to the decision of others as to the steps that they will take to restore their own operations. Another person—the Loss Manager of the other property—is involved in the decision making process.

In the Anchor Toy case, the Insured decided to rebuild at another location. After extended negotiations, the purchase of the other plant had fallen through. The Insured then decided not to have its plant rebuilt. From what date does due diligence start to run? Insurer: from the date of damage; Insured: from the time when the negotiations to buy the other plant ceased; Court: The Insurer is right; especially since the Insured did not start to rebuild when the deal was cancelled. If he had, a different result might have been reached.[10]

Where the Loss Manager and the Adjuster have been working in close cooperation, this type of problem is discussed in advance and agreement is often reached. Where it is not possible to agree on what should be done to comply with the requirement of due diligence and dispatch, it might still be possible to agree on the time span that would be required for each of the alternative courses of action. This would narrow the issue for future settlement discussion.

Needless to say, decisions of the type under discussion are usually made at the highest level. It is the function of the Loss Manager to acquaint top management personnel with the provisions of the due diligence clause so that they can be taken into consideration in deciding on a course of action.

Also at a higher echelon would be the decision to discontinue operations at the site of the damage. A reasonable amount of time to reach such a decision should be allowed and ongoing expenses during that period should be included in the loss settlement.

4. Expenses to Reduce Loss

a. Criteria. As the Loss Manager plans the steps he will take to restore operations, the provisions of the section of the Gross Earnings form entitled "Expenses Related to Reducing Loss" require some attention. Their main thrust is to provide that such expenses can be recovered, even though the dollars involved are outside of the procedures that would normally be used.

It could be argued that the due diligence provision clearly places the onus on the Insured of spending whatever monies are necessary to get back into operation; that the recovery is limited to what would be the loss if he spent all monies that due diligence requires and that, therefore, there can be no such thing as "extraordinary" expenses.

But due diligence is at best a nebulous concept. Also, it makes good sense so to frame the insurance contract that certain types of expenses are recoverable rather than limiting recovery only to the loss of earnings. It creates an incentive for the Insured to act "beyond the call of duty."

It is important to note that to be recovered, each item of expense must meet certain criteria: the expense must be related to a loss covered by the policy; the amount of expense attributable to the covered loss must be determinable; the expense must have been incurred for the purpose of reducing loss; and it must have been necessarily incurred for that purpose. The words "necessarily incurred" are not to be read to mean that the job could not have been done without incurring such expenses. Their meaning is that what was achieved by the expenses was necessary to the task of restoring operations and was not collateral thereto.[11]

If the expense is to acquire finished goods, at an above normal price, the excess of price is covered, provided all of the above criteria are met. In the appealed case of *N. W. States Portland Cement Co. v. Hartford F. Ins. Co.*, the court stated that it is not necessary for the Insured to actually replace the inventory used up to file a claim; it can be based on computation of amount consumed when use of inventory ceases. The case points out that the provision applies only to replacing of finished stock, not to ingredients that go into it.

It is also important to note that the aggregate of such expenses laid out could, in an extreme case, exceed the Insured's total loss. The Insured can collect only such amount of his total extraordinary expenses which meet the above criteria up to the amount by which the loss payable under the policy is reduced by the incurring of such expenses.

It is the aggregate expenditure that must result in savings on the loss, not any particular item of expense. However, it seems clear that each individual item in the aggregate would also have to measure up to the criteria listed above. The fact that the interruption of operations may be only partial does not affect the provision concerning expense to reduce loss.

b. Extra Expense Insurance. A distinction is to be drawn between the types of extraordinary expense considered herein above and the kinds of extra expense compensable under an Extra Expense Insurance policy. The latter policy defines Extra Expense as "the excess (if any) of the total cost incurred during the period of restoration chargeable to the operation of the Insured's business, over and above the total cost that would have been incurred to conduct the business during the same period had no damage or destruction occurred." These are extra expenses incurred to *keep* going rather than to *get* going. There is no intention or requirement that the expenditures have the effect of reducing the loss of earnings due to the interruption; rather they are made to prevent the loss of values such as contracts, goodwill and other positions of importance to the Insured. To protect these, he must keep going even though that can be done only at a greater cost than normal. He buys Extra Expense Insurance to recover this greater cost.

c. Retention of Personnel. Another decision frequently required of the Loss Manager involves labor policy. It depends to a large degree on the preliminary estimate of the length of the interruption. If he expects the plant to be back in operation after an interruption of twenty-four hours, it would certainly be folly to discharge employees and then seek to rehire them a day later. At the other extreme, if the shut-down will last for a year, it would be economically unsound to keep ordinary employees on the payroll for that length of time; it would be less expensive to hire and train a new crew a year later. If the interruption is expected to last for a month, then a judgment factor enters the picture. A decision should be made as soon as possible. Payroll is one of the "continuing expenses." Whether it is "necessarily" continuing is the question.

Even though the ordinary payroll is insured without limit of time, it is important for the Loss Manager to balance the pros and cons of continuing to pay such help. Every dollar paid to employees is charged against the total amount that can be collected from the Insurer. Funds not employed for ordinary payroll remain available to apply to other items of loss. This becomes vital when the face amount of the policy may prove inadequate to meet the entire loss suffered by the Insured.

Inherent in the same decision may be the question of which of the employees should qualify as important or "key" employees. Here we have another of those areas for subjective interpretation with which the Business Interruption

Insurance contract abounds. Executives and administrators are easily included. When it comes to sales personnel, distinctions have to be drawn. A salesperson at a retail store counter may or may not be a key employee. One who has a "following"—a group of customers who shop at the store because of a relationship with the salesperson—would probably qualify as a key employee. One who deals solely with casual customers might be easily replaced and should not be considered a key employee. Often the telephone operator-receptionist can qualify as a key employee, particularly one with special knowledge of the companies and individuals with whom the firm does business.[12]

One interesting case involved several managerial employees of a large manufacturing plant which was destroyed in an explosion. They had been kept on the payroll pending a lengthy period of reconstruction. When they complained about the boredom of prolonged idleness, they were given desks and odd jobs with other business enterprises owned by the same business entity. They received no separate salary from the other enterprises. Their activities were in no way required in their temporary positions and they added nothing of real value to the conduct of those other operations. It was purely a psychological and not an operational move. It was successfully maintained by the Insured that their full salaries should be included in the loss.

d. Decision Not to Repair Damage. If the Insured decides not to restore the previous level of operations but to operate the undamaged portion of the described property without repairing the damage, can an Insured be found to have sustained an actual loss? The policy provides that the Insurer's liability extends "to such time as *would be* required, etc. . . ." It does not say "is required." Nor does the Resumption of Operations Clause restrict the right of the Insured to change the extent of business operations. Where an Insured decides that he will not repair the damaged property but will continue operations with the undamaged portion, his time of loss will run until the damaged portion could have been restored with due diligence and dispatch to the same quality of service which existed immediately preceding the damage. This same measure of loss would be applied if the Insured decided not to use the undamaged portion of the property.

e. Decision to Sell. What about a positive act by the Insured which makes it impossible to renew operations; e.g., a refusal to comply with bureaucrats who set conditions precedent to granting a permit to rebuild where litigating the question of compliance could result in a delay of a year or more before the method of rebuilding could be determined?

Selling off the business in its damaged condition is another example of such voluntary action. Several variations could exist in the facts surrounding such selling, including the very important factor of timing. The decision to sell could have been made before or after the loss occurred, and, if after the loss, it could have been made almost immediately or only after the Insured had himself taken steps to investigate the restoration of the damage or the possibilities of relocation. Then, too, the decision might have even been made after steps to restore had already been begun.

The timing of these decisions would have a material effect on the liability of the Insurer. If the decision had already been made before the damage had occurred, and if the time of its implementation would have been prior to the expiration of the time when with due diligence and dispatch operations could have been restored, a cut-off date for sustaining loss would seem relatively simple to determine. It would be the time when the decision would have gone into effect.

But is it so simple? How positively can the time be identified? A notice of intention not to renew a lease, for example, does not mean the inability to stay on as a tenant at will or at sufferance. A corporate motion to liquidate and sell off its assets could be rescinded; and even a contract with an auctioneer to sell the building and equipment could be postponed. Barring very positive objective evidence, it would be most difficult to establish the fact of when the business enterprise would actually have been transferred.

An even more subtle problem arises where the decision not to restore operations is arrived at after the damage occurs. If it can be established that the occurrence of the damage had no influence on the arrival at such decision, the matter should be dealt with on the same basis as if the decision had been made before the damage. For example, the further production of an item could be abandoned due to an adverse court decision; or the further production of a product could be barred by the Federal Trade Commission; or the cost of the Insured's product could skyrocket due to the fact that two of the five worldwide plants that produce the necessary raw materials go out of production making continuing production non-profitable. If, however, the damage triggered the decision not to restore operations, there seems to be little doubt but that recovery for the full period determined on a theoretical basis would be covered.

It is not even certain that the consummation of a sale will terminate all of the Insured's rights to collect from the Insurer for ongoing expenses. In the event that the named Insured remained liable for expenses after he sold off his business venture, expenses which would have been paid for by the Insurer had the business not been sold, the Insured can collect for them as well. This could be the case where a corporate Insured sold off assets but retained liabilities, or where an individual or partnership disposed of the business operation but remained personally responsible under ongoing contracts. This could well extend to outstanding contracts with key employees whose terms of employment were not terminated.

Could the Insured's loss under his policy be measured by the reduction in the purchase price made between him and the Buyer as a result of the damage? The answer must be "No," because the result of the bargaining between Buyer and Seller is not the method of measuring loss provided for in the policy.

Nor can the Insured assign to the Buyer any right to collect for loss of income or expenses incurred by the latter during the period between his acquisition of the damaged property and restoration of operations. This suggests the possible desirability of naming the prospective Buyer as an Insured under a Business Interruption Insurance policy when a letter of intent to buy the business assets is executed before any damage occurs. A release of interest can be held in escrow against the possibility that the transaction is not consummated. Unless specifically added as a named Insured, the Buyer is not a party to the contract. After the commitment to buy is made, the Buyer should consider taking out his own policy. Of course, such action is not necessary when it is the corporate stock and not assets that are being sold.

5. Time Frame of Claim

The Loss Manager must be aware of the time frame within which his claim must fall. It starts at the moment in time when any part of the capacity of the described property to produce an Earnings Stream is inhibited.[13] (Some policies contain a deductible clause; e.g. "waiting-time" under coverage for off-premises power shut-down.) There are circumstances under which such effect could be progressive; in which case, each time period may have to be separately calculated. The period normally ends when the described property could, by due diligence and dispatch, be put back into such physical condition that operations could be resumed with the same quality of service which existed before the damage occurred. (See Comment #12, p. 327, and provisions of BIC Form, Ch. 8.)

Where, by the use of other property, an Insured was able to restore what were normal earnings before the damage at a date earlier than the described premises could have been restored to normal operations, there arises the question of whether the period of loss is thereupon terminated. A number of court decisions say "no." It is the time it would have taken to restore the described property to normal operations that controls. If the claim was settled on the basis of theoretical time to repair and the actual time later proved to be shorter, the settlement could not be reopened, absent fraud or mutual mistake.[14]

It might be argued that the provision about "resuming operations with the same *quality* [italics added] of service" means a duplication of what existed before. This is not practical. An obsolete item might take forever to replace. A practical interpretation must be applied.

B. Requirement to Provide Additional Information

The Business Interruption Insurance policy gives the Insurer certain optional rights in connection with investigating factual matters connected with the Insured's operations both before and after the loss. They are set forth in the

Fire Insurance policy under the heading "Requirements in Case Loss Occurs." Identical provisions are found under the same heading in the Gross Earnings forms. (These are in addition to the right to inspect premises in the Gross Earnings forms.)

Basically, these provisions include the right to examine property, individuals and records. Compliance shall be under oath where appropriate. Where the Insured refused to answer questions about profits earned during the period of interruption or submit copies of a tax return—both of which might shed some light on the Insurer's claim of arson—recovery under the policy was denied, despite the Insured's argument that he was not seeking to recover lost earnings, but only continuing expenses.[15]

On the other hand, where after suit was brought, the Insured "took the Fifth Amendment" and refused to answer questions, the court held he was within his rights.[16] The rationale for the decision was that, while before suit was initiated the parties were dealing on a non-adversary basis and the Insured cannot refuse to cooperate fully under the fraud and concealment provisions of the contract, this relationship changed when suit was brought.

The duty to produce witnesses for examination under oath does not apply to a Public Adjuster who helped prepare the proof of loss, because he is an independent contractor and not an employee of the Insured.[17]

C. Critical Path Management

As he completes his preliminary survey, the Loss Manager should prepare a calendar setting forth the time schedule on which he anticipates restoring the operations to the condition they were in prior to the damage. In it, the various factors that play a role in such restoration are plotted timewise. Where a Period of Indemnity Extension Endorsement or "Lag" exists, the time schedule should also show when the Earnings Stream is expected to be restored to normal.

This exercise is known as Critical Path Management. Basically this consists of making a flow chart of the various factors that will have to come together in order for the work of restoration to proceed on an orderly basis.

In operation, it schedules all of the various stages of the work that have to be undertaken and plots them on a time line that shows when each can start and when each one should finish so that the next stage of work can begin. Take the replacing of steel beams in a building damaged by fire as an example. All ordering of replacement steel must await the clearing of the slab, the determination of the degree of damage to pre-existing steel and the calculation by an engineer of the steel requirements. When the specifications of the structural steel needed is determined, the chart will show the date when it can be ordered from a rolling mill and when it can be delivered to the finishing mill. Then, and not until then, can the finishing mill start the job of preparing the steel for erection. It shows when this stage will be completed and the steel can be shipped to the building site. Only then can actual erection be scheduled. This same procedure is followed for all the materials and labor necessary in the process of construction. By laying out all of this information on a time chart the Loss Manager can schedule all the stages of rebuilding so that they flow together smoothly.

This may seem to be a lot of work but it saves countless hours of futile "hurry up and wait." It also helps decide whether a given extra expense should be incurred in expediting effort. It gives management a tool with which to control the work being done, since it offers a quick facility for changing plans when something goes wrong. For example, a severe winter which prevents outside repair work could eliminate a whole selling season and change the type of merchandise ordered for the "grand opening." The time schedule will show when partial operations can be brought on stream, as well as when the entire work of restoration will be completed.

One of the most useful functions of Critical Path Management is to assist the Loss Manager and the Adjuster to come to a mutual understanding of what constitutes due diligence on the part of the Insured and what will probably be the length of interruption.

It should be apparent that this procedure, while likely to be more accurate than rough calculations, still leaves ample room for differences of opinion. Since a knowledgeable Adjuster will also use the technique of Critical Flow Management in making his own calculations, it behooves the Loss Manager to be equally conversant with the technique. If the charts indicate differing lengths of time for various stages to be completed—based necessarily in part on judgment—there will be an underlying factual question that is subject to objective input.

As indicated, this time schedule is monitored constantly. Changes in the time required for any aspect of the work are incorporated therein and all resultant effects are noted. Where changes in circumstances require a change in scheduling or a reappraisal of the amount of loss, this fact should be communicated promptly to the Adjuster in order to minimize future disagreements. Many of the losses which ended up in long and expensive court procedures could have been adjusted amicably if such a schedule, made available to the Adjuster, had been utilized. The nature of the Business Interruption Insurance policy points unequivocally to the advantage of bringing controversial matters to the discussion table before action is undertaken rather than when the amount of the loss is being settled.

D. Writing a Memorandum

One piece of advice, which runs like a thread throughout this entire process, is that all decisions should be documented in writing. Thus, misunderstandings of what was agreed upon will be reduced in number. Such a writing will protect both parties. The Adjuster can transmit it to the Insurer before agreeing to it, so as to protect himself against future criticism. The advantage to the Insured is obvious.

Either an agreement initialled by both parties or an exchange of letters can be used. The careful drafting of such documents and the choice of appropriate language can frequently be aided by the services of the Insured's Lawyer. Actually, in a loss of large size, he should be standing at the elbow of the Loss Manager in all such negotiations. He and the other experts employed are used to bolster the Insured's position as to why certain measures have to be undertaken.

E. Summary

The steps outlined and discussed above are designed to arrive at an understanding and agreement as to the length of time during which total operations will be interrupted, the time span within which partial operations can be instituted and the extent to which such partial operations can reestablish the Earnings Stream. This composes the first part of the task of the Loss Manager.

The problems that may arise in the course of the physical restoration are outside the scope of this volume except as they exist as the subject of controversy in the court cases collected in Addendum III. Attention will be directed in the next section to the determination of the amount of loss which the Insured has sustained.

Chapter 12 Notes

1. See: Howard Stores Corp. v. Foremost Ins. Co. where claimed diminution was to anticipated future sales volume.

2. Gordon Chemical Co., Inc. v. Aetna C. & S. Co.

3. Hartford F. Ins. Co. v. Wilson & Toomer Fertilizer Co.

4. Omaha Paper Stock Co., Inc. v. Harbor Ins. Co. (Jan, 1978); Gordon Chemical Co. v. Aetna C&S Co.

5. Beautytuft, Inc. v. F.I.A. (1970); Hawkinson Tread Tire Service Co. v. Indiana Lumbermen's Mutual Ins. Co.

6. See: Gordon Chemical Co. Inc. v. Aetna C & S Co.

7. N.W. States Portland Cement Co. v. Hartford F. Ins. Co.

8. See: Gordon Chemical Co. Inc. v. Aetna C & S Co.

9. Anchor Toy Corp. v. American Eagle F. Ins. Co.

10. Not everyone agrees with the court's reasoning. Some feel that when the new location fell through, a whole new chapter opened for decision making.

11. The honest opinion of the Insured must, in the last analysis, set the limits as to which is necessary. See: Eastern Associated Coal Corp. v. Aetna C & S Co.

12. In DiLeo v. U.S.F.&G. Co., the fact that key employee's wages were not paid, did not foreclose showing that they were a continuing expense, in spite of the fact that the business operations never did start up again. Followed in National Union F. Ins. Co. v. Scandia of Hialeah, Inc.

    It may be possible under the State Unemployment Security law for employees who are receiving compensation during a period of interruption (to induce them to standby until operations are renewed) to collect Unemployment Compensation payments. (In Massachusetts, under Gen. Laws c. 151A, §1, 11, (3).) Employers should indicate to employees that application for such compensation will lead to the standby pay being discontinued. An Insurer "buying-back" the increase in taxation resulting from Unemployment Compensation payments should provide for protection against double payment.

    This regulation runs contrary to an opinion expressed in 1939 by J. Victor Herd writing on "Use and Occupancy" in *American Management Ass'n. Insurance Series*

#34 where he said that such employees were not legally entitled to unemployment compensation. The higher rate of tax caused by the layoff of help who collect Unemployment Insurance was stated not to be a recoverable expense under a business interruption loss on the ground that since the expense is payable over an indeterminate period of time, it is both remote and consequential.

This position has been abandoned by the insurance industry.

13. "Time frame includes first day because fire was on that morning and excludes last date because Insured resumed business on that day." Policy ran from "noon to noon." Maple Leaf Motor Lodge Inc. v. Allstate Ins. Co.

14. Steel Products Co. Inc., v. Millers National Ins. Co.

15. Trader d/b/a Pump Tavern v. Indiana Ins. Companies

16. In-Towne Restaurant Corp. v. Aetna C & S Co.

17. Palace Cafe v. Hartford Fire Insurance Co.

13

Process of Adjustment: Determination of the Insured's Loss

The Accountant. Calculating loss. The Adjuster's calculations. The Intermediary.

A. Introduction

In its broadest scope, the process of adjusting a loss follows the general pattern of applying the six P's and the six E's—this time to a new fact situation, a business operation which has already been interrupted in whole or in part. The six P's form the basis of determining the amount of loss the Insured will suffer and the six E's form the basis of determining how much of that loss the Insurer will be called upon to pay.

The representatives of the Insured and of the Insurer pursue parallel paths during the adjustment stage. But, since no strictly objective tests are available to arrive at a conclusion, quite different conclusions may be reached. Due to the speculative nature of the Business Interruption Insurance contract, such differences can be more extreme than in the case of insurance on physical property where a much higher degree of objective evidence is available.[1]

1. Determination of Production-Time Units

The first goal of the adjustment process is to determine the number of "production-time units" that were lost because of the damage. The term "production-time unit" is adopted to represent that portion of time—be it month, week, day, or otherwise—which the Insured customarily uses to measure and control his financial experience. It could be used to measure sales dollars or sales-value-of-production dollars.

There can be total or partial or both kinds of production-time units involved. They are counted from the time the damage occurs until the time when operations of the Insured could be resumed with the same quality of service which would have existed had no damage occurred. It is in accumulating these units that the requirement of due diligence and dispatch is applied.

The number of lost production-time units that are to be considered total and those that are to be considered partial or neutral can be affected by the substitute measures introduced during the period of interruption. Production-time units which would otherwise be totally lost may be changed into partial or neutral, and those that would otherwise constitute partial loss can have the loss reduced or neutralized. This is the area in which the requirement for resumption of operations prevails. ("Neutral" means no loss in earnings even though production or sales is not possible.)

2. Determination of Earnings Dollars per Unit

The second aim of the adjustment process is to determine the number of earnings dollars to be attributed to each totally lost production-time unit. The format outlined in the work sheet is the starting point for such calculations. The percentage of the dollar of gross income that represents gross earnings is established. Seasonal and existential factors are considered in these calculations. Here the policy provision about the past experience and probable future experience of the business comes into play.

Early policies, usually in the valued form, would spell out how the value assigned to a full production-time unit was to be prorated if there was partial production. With the open policy, a different type of procedure gradually evolved. In the case of the Gross Earnings form, one compares the actual financial results of operation during the period of both full and partial operation, with the results anticipated—before the damage had occurred—for the same period.[2]

Whenever an attempt is made to adjust a loss before operations are restored, or when they are not restored with due diligence and dispatch, or when the Insured decides not to repair or replace and thus restore prior operations, it becomes necessary to resort to a counting of theoretical total and partial production-time units lost. One multiplies such theoretical units of time, whole or partial, that were lost by the dollars that would heve been earned per unit (as estimated), to arrive at an adjustment figure.

B. The Accountant

1. In General

The important role played by the Accountant in the purchase of a Business Interruption Insurance Policy has been dealt with from time to time in the previous pages. The same importance exists in dealing with a loss. As one writer put it, "the work of an accountant in setting up a statement of loss under a regular replacement form of coverage pales into insignificance when compared to the work necessary for preparing a proper statement of facts for a Use and Occupancy Loss."[3] The need for the Accountant to apply somewhat different formulations of financial material has been mentioned. So has been the requirement that he be able to lift his eyes from the pages of figures and use a little imagination, both as to the underlying factors which produced past financial results and as to the potential future operations during the life time of the policy and for a year thereafter.[4]

a. Must be Knowledgeable. Except in the case of an extremely large Insured that does a major portion of its accounting work in-house, or an extremely small Insured, who handles all of his own bookkeeping, the Loss Manager should usually call on the services of the independent outside accounting firm which has acted as Accountant for the Insured and is totally familar with the Insured's books and records. The Accountant may even have participated in the preparation of the work sheet before the insurance was purchased. As a general rule, the Loss Manager will enlist the services of such an Accountant in formulating his loss figures, as well as in determining the Business Interruption Value for purposes of the Coinsurance Clause. Where a Public Adjuster or Consultant has been employed and the bookkeeping is simple, he sometimes functions in lieu of an Accountant. The Accountant may also be involved in determining the amount of the property loss.

It is important, however, to ascertain whether the Accountant is familiar with the somewhat different treatment of financial calculations required in the handling of a Business Interruption Insurance loss.[5] Lacking such knowledge, the Accountant should seek help from someone who has it. This is particularly applicable to the past experience of the business. (The future experience calls as much for the use of a crystal ball as it does for accounting techniques.)

The following discussion of the Accountant's activities will touch first on the factors which he must take into consideration as he proceeds with his financial analysis. Later, there will be a brief discussion of the tax consequences of a Business Interruption Insurance loss settlement.

The activities of the Accountant assisting the Insured are paralleled by those of the Accountant that the Adjuster would typically have called in to help him. (For the sake of clarity, the Adjuster and all of his associates and experts will be usually referred to collectively as the "Adjuster.") It is to everyone's advantage for the various Accountants to develop sufficient rapport so that the material they examine in reaching their conclusions is the same for all parties. Discussions as to what information is pertinent and appropriate, carried on at the beginning of their work, can save hours of possible argument and reworking of figures later. The conclusions from the available material may not be the same, but the factual basis for opinions will be understood by all.

b. Areas of Operation. There are three main areas for the Accountant to explore. The first area involves gross earnings. It serves as the basis on which the loss is figured and also for determining the application of the Coinsurance Clause. Not only must he determine what were the Gross Earnings during the period of interruption but also what they would have been had no damage occured as well as the expected gross earnings for the 12 month period following the damage. (See Ch. 8 for provisions of the BIC Form.)

The second area involves a determination of what items of charge or expense incurred by the Insured in the normal operation of his business were discontinuable during the period of interruption, keeping in mind the need of the Insured to start up normal operations when his plant again becomes operable.

Thirdly, the Insured's Accountant should collect from the Loss Manager the figures of expenses paid in the attempt to reduce the loss. These should be supported by figures indicating the savings that were achieved by the expenditures. The figures should be reviewed by the Accountant and put into proper form for presenting a claim. It will be remembered that the Coinsurance Clause does not apply to these items.

There are two more factors that the Accountant must take into consideration in order to anticipate future discussions with the Adjuster. The first factor involves items of loss which are excluded under the terms of the policy. These have been discussed at length earlier and will not be repeated here. Questions may develop in this area which require assistance from the Lawyer.

The second factor involves the impact of the Coinsurance Clause on the liability of the Insurer. The theory behind this provision has also been discussed earlier and will not be repeated. The Insured is in a bind as a result of this clause. In any case where the interruption is for a shorter period than twelve months, the higher the amount of loss claimed during the period of interruption, the higher is the required amount of insurance likely to be to meet the requirements of the Coinsurance Clause. Where the face amount of the policy is on the meagre side, thought must be given to this dilemma in the organization of the claim.

2. Types of Problems

The program facing the Accountant has so far been dealt with on a fairly simplistic basis, more as a means of indicating to the other parties involved in the adjustment what the role of the Accountant should be than as an aid to a person skilled in that profession. The actual compilation of the required figures in a business enterprise of any size and complexity is far from a simple task. This is particularly so when the Accountant finds himself confronted by an Adjuster with a fixed set of ideas of how the figures should be compiled. The outcome often depends on the skill of the Accountant in finding a theory upon which he can rest his calculations which makes good, practical, common sense. This becomes of primary importance when only part of the property was damaged. The allocation of fixed charges to the ongoing sales or production is just one aspect of this situation.

In the usual manufacturing operation, some goods are in the processing pipeline at the time of damage and would have been finished within the period of interruption had no damage occurred. The sales value of such goods should be included in the calculations. Some goods would have been put into the pipeline and been finished within the period of interruption; such goods are included in the calculation. And some goods would have been put into the pipeline and would have been only partly finished during the period of interruption. If the increment in value of this third class is greater than would have been their cost up to the time operations were restored, then the difference should be includable in the calculations.

There are a number of reported cases where the theory for calculating loss upon which the Insured relied was not accepted by the Insurer. A brief reference will be made to some of these cases, primarily as background information rather than to suggest a specific theory to be adopted.

3. Tax Consequences of Loss Payment

The third matter involves the tax consequences of the receipt by the Insured of the proceeds of his Business Interruption Insurance policy. While consideration of this question is beyond the scope of this book, it is suggested that the Accountant should be familiar with the cases and the regulations applying to this area of tax law. For his convenience a list of the more important cases on the subject is made a part of Addendum III.

Among the possible areas for concern are:

- the application of the law concerning involuntary conversion of property to such insurance proceeds;
- the question of the year in which taxes must be paid on the proceeds; and
- the effect of a liquidation of a corporate Insured before payment is received.

Knowledgability of the impact in these sophisticated areas may have some influence on the advice given by the Accountant in connection with the final settlement of the loss.

4. Research and Development Interruption

The business interruption seminar at the 20th Annual Risk Management Conference brought into focus the problem encountered in determining the loss involved when research and development processes are destroyed. (The research may have already yielded results which have been recorded and introduced into production.) Written formulae and test samples used to guide and check production may have been lost. Until the work is repeated and new determinations made, it may not be possible to renew operations. Hopefully much of the information will be stored in the minds of the operator. This will shorten the period for replacement. But a difficult problem of anticipating time requirements exists. (See Ch. 8 for provisions of the BIC Form.)

A much more difficult problem exists where the research and development has reached the stage of pilot trial operations. The validity of the new process has not yet been established. Yet, if established, it would have been in operation earning profits before the damage can be repaired. Since the burden of proving the effectiveness of the new process is on the Insured, it would seem that he would have a hard time establishing this aspect of the amount of his loss.

Where the research has not yet reached fruition and the probability of a successful conclusion is still in doubt, the chances of an Insured collecting for the profits he would have made if the research had not been interrupted are practically non-existent. Should the Insured base his claim on the time it would take to get the research up to the point where it was when the damage occurred, he would still have to prove that the research would have produced profits during the period of interruption—a well-nigh impossible task.

If the work of the Insured is in the field of research and development, and he gets paid for his work on an hourly basis, then his inability to operate and earn income during the interruption could be the basis of a claim on his part.

C. Calculating Amount of Insured's Loss

1. Introduction

The procedures discussed up to this point will have laid a foundation upon which the measurement of the amount of loss can ultimately be based. At the same time that they are being carried out, the actual steps to measure the amount of reduction in the potential earnings are going forward.

To determine the amount of loss under a Business Interruption Insurance policy, two questions must be answered. The first is—how many production-time units of full or partial operation or both will pass before operations are restored to the quality of service which existed immediately preceding the loss, assuming that the Insured uses due diligence and dispatch? The second is—what is the Business Interruption Value of each such production-time unit?

The measurement technique which is used to answer the first question depends on whether the Insured did, in fact, restore operations. If he did, then consideration must be given to surrounding circumstances that existed or would exist during the period of restoration which extended the time for accomplishing the restoration and thus increased the number of production-time units involved. If he did not restore operations, then the theoretical time for accomplishing the physical work of restoration is the basis for calculating the production-time units, without giving any consideration to surrounding circumstances which might extend the time of restoration.

The second question is answered by taking into consideration both the historical record of earnings developed by operations and the projected Earnings Stream that would have been developed had no damage occurred and then determining the number of dollars of gross earnings that would have been earned during each production-time unit of total or partial interruption, assuming that the Insured takes the required steps to minimize loss.

The wording of the Gross Earnings form provides no clear indication of when the historical record ends and of what date the projection of future gross earnings is to be made. More specifically, should the historical record include only those events that occur prior to the date of the damage with the projection of future earnings to be made on the basis of the facts known at that time—in which case the projection is made on the basis of foresight—or does the historical record include all of the historical events that occur up to the time that operations are restored—in which case the projection is made on the basis of hindsight?

As indicated earlier, it would appear that a strong theoretical argument can be made for foresight. In practice, as developed by Adjusters and in court decisions, hindsight has been used. The reasons for this latter approach in large part stem from the fact that at the time of loss settlement the later developments are known to the parties. This is certainly the case by the time the issue reaches the courts.

The authors of this book have split in their opinion. The material presented herein is based on the theoretical approach, though it is recognized that the point of view would be of material importance only in an exceptional situation. (See Comment #9, p. 317.)

At its simplest level, the measure of loss sustained is the difference between the gross earnings that would have been received during the period of interruption had no damage occurred—which can be called the "probable" gross earnings—and the gross earnings which the business enterprise did receive during the period of interruption—which can be called the "actual" gross earnings. Under the provisions of the Gross Earnings forms, the *probable* gross earnings are determined by taking into consideration past experience and probable future experience, while the *actual* gross earnings involve present experience; with the date of damage as the starting point in time for both.

There may be built-in biases as the Accountant and the Adjuster approach their task. The Adjuster will be more inclined to rest his calculations on the actual financial records. These would include not only the financial books, but also tax returns, annual reports, and 10-K statements of publicly owned companies. The Accountant will go a step further and reinterpret past statistics whenever, in his opinion, they fail to give a true, informative picture of what past performance was really like.[6]

2. Ease of Calculation

Some business interruption losses can be disposed of by relatively simple calculations. They occur in business operations which are relatively stable, where sales and production fluctuate but slightly through the year and costs follow a relatively fixed pattern. In such cases, estimates for the future can be extrapolated quite simply from past experience. Trends established by past results can be projected into future results. The percentages of gross income that filtered down to gross earnings can be determined with relative ease. External forces which may affect future results, such as inflation or recession, can be translated to a percentage and be applied to what would otherwise be the expected results.

In more complex situations, there are numerous factors which can fluctuate. Unusual conditions may have prevailed in the past which distorted results. Future results, also, may be skewed by anticipated developments. This situation makes it mandatory for the Accountant to work closely, not only with the Insured's financial officer, but also with the Loss Manager. He must keep an open mind with regard to all past financial figures even though he may have relied upon them in preparing the Insured's earlier financial reports and tax returns.

Actual profits from operations may have been treated by charging off as expense items which should have been capitalized. This is particularly true in a new plant or where substantial physical changes had taken place prior to the damage.

In one case, involving a Boiler and Machinery Insurance policy with a Gross Earnings form attached, the period of interruption was utilized for making the annual repairs, thus avoiding the necessity of the customary shutting down later for 13 days to carry out this chore after operations were resumed. Credit was given against the period of interruption for this 13 days of normal "annual turnaround."[7]

3. Past Experience

As one approaches the matter of past experience, a first question is how far back into the past does one go. The normal practice is to go back one calendar year from the date of damage. The probable reason for this practice is to establish a base from which to make a projection for the twelve month period following the date of damage. But there is nothing in the policy which states how far back "past experience" is to be extended. Given a situation where conditions during the past twelve months were not usual, examination extending two or three years back may be warranted. More rarely, the comparable figures from the prior year covering just the limited period of the interruption are used for purposes of calculating the loss.

Alternatively, the figures for the past full *fiscal* year may serve as a starting base. The date of the fiscal year makes a difference. The nearer the end of the fiscal year is to the date of damage, the more feasible it is to use the fiscal year figures as a base and bring them up to the time of the damage by normal accounting procedures. This is particularly the case with inventories. Where a perpetual inventory is kept, this problem is avoided. Substantial reliance can be placed on perpetual inventories.[8]

His inventory is one place where an Insured sometimes finds it convenient to let imagination control. When used for tax return calculations, inventories have a way of shrinking in value. A good example can be found in the case of inactive inventory or surplus merchandise lying on the shelves. If sold they would have substantial value, but since the likelihood of their being sold is questionable, their value is written-down for tax purposes. On the other hand, when the inventory is being presented in connection with a bank loan, their maximum potential value is sometimes included in the balance sheet.

The courts have been most understanding of this weakness in businessmen's nature. When it comes to calculating a business interruption insurance loss, they hold that it should be adjusted in a "practical" way.[9] The true facts should prevail and the real value of the inventory should be used.[10] What is "real value" can be a matter of judgment in certain situations. But the Insured is not limited to the figures used to prepare his income tax return.[11]

Sometimes the reported figures, other than those of an inventory, have to be "interpreted" to conform to the practical aspects of the business operation. Unusual circumstances may have distorted the prices at which goods were sold. Shortages, over-production, changes in style, unusual competitive pressures or temporary variations in the business climate may have been the cause. It is not possible to list all of the causes that may make it necessary to adjust the actual record of gross earnings. The Accountant must raise with the Insured the possibility of such causes of variation having existed and use his judgment as to how to adjust for them in his calculations.[12]

Other earnings may have come from collateral operations which tie into the operations of the business. Thus, one court found that in calculating the income of a mine, the earnings from rent of company houses occupied by the miners and the profits of the company store selling goods to the miners should be included.[13]

Except for the task of unearthing the unusual factors that may have distorted the figures of past experience, the process of establishing these figures should raise no problem. A convenient method of calculating the result is to follow the format set out in the work sheet.

One caveat may be in order. It should be remembered that in the case of a manufacturing plant, it is not the dollar value of production lost that is material but the sales value of the products that were not manufactured. This approach is not always reflected on the Insured's financial records.

Where the past operation of the business had extended over a period of less than one year, or where the particular operation that is interrupted was still in process of being made ready to start up when damage occurred, the reference to past experience has little relevance.[14]

4. Probable Future Experience

Except for business operations that are relatively stable, past experience does not necessarily reflect probable future experience. The entire matter takes on added significance where the Insured takes the position that the past is not representative of what the future would have been had no damage occurred. Insureds have been known to regard such future with rose-colored glasses.

The term "probable experience" would appear to be clear and simple to understand. "Probable" eliminates sure knowledge; if the true facts were known the word "actual" would be appropriate. The paradox is thus created of the "*actual* loss sustained" being arrived at by considering "*probable* experience."[15]

As discussed earlier, "probable" would appear to indicate that it is foresight and not hindsight that is to be applied. Under the wording of the policy it is foresight "thereafter" to which the calculations are to be applied. "Thereafter" clearly refers to the time after the damage occurs. If the dollar amount of probable future business is to be calculated commencing with the time of damage, it can strongly be argued that such calculations should be carried out within the context of the knowledge available at that time. (See Comment #9, p. 317.)

"Probable experience thereafter" refers to what is likely to have taken place. What is likely to have taken place depends to some degree on what the Insured had in mind to do. The more volatile the business operation, the more importance could be placed on such subjective conjecture. Hence, the need for the development of objective criteria by the Accountant to support the position taken by the Insured.

The Accountant must, as part of his investigation, determine that the interruption resulting from the damage will result in financial loss to the Insured. If no Earnings Stream would have existed during part or all of the period of interruption, there would have been no gross earnings during that time and so, no loss.

5. Continuing Expenses

As every Accountant knows, in the operation of any business enterprise there are expenses which continue even though no business activity is being carried on. These are *fixed* expenses. Payment on a mortgage is an example of

this kind of expense. Then there are expenses that are directly related to production or sales activity: no activity—no expense. These are *variable* expenses.
An example of such expenses would be the cost of materials that went into the
finished product. In between these definite examples, there are expenses and
charges that may or may not continue if the operations are shut down due to
damage to the described property.[16]

Since the Business Interruption Insurance policy will reimburse the Insured
only for those expenses and charges which necessarily continue, the Accountant
must examine each item of expense and every charge incurred and decide into
which category it falls. In the case of items that do not clearly fall into fixed or
variable categories, he is called upon to make a determination.

Certain expenses may arise out of contracts that the Insured has entered
into which cover the period of the interruption; e.g., leases, employment contracts, and advertising contracts. Each contract must be examined to see if it
contains any provisions excusing the Insured from continuing to make payments in the event of a shutdown of operations of the type that has occurred. A
penalty payment to get out of such a contract may well be an expense to reduce
a greater loss that would be experienced if the contract were to continue in
force.[17]

Items which go through the journal rather than the cash book can raise
some problems. Suppose a considerable amount of inventory had been donated
to a charity. By journal entry, the inventory is reduced. This would have the
effect of increasing the cost of the goods that were sold. Only, there is no cash
or account receivable to offset such goods. Instead there is a record of a charitable donation. Past experience has to take such transactions into consideration.

a. Depreciation. In the course of loss adjustment, three questions arise with
regard to the expense item of depreciation and how much remains a continuing
expense. (Depreciation will not continue on property which has been destroyed
and has been converted into cash under the Fire Insurance policy.) On most
business books, depreciation is treated as a charge against gross earnings. It has
been argued that since it is only a fictitious charge and no cash is expended, the
amount charged off really becomes additional surplus. Those who take this
position say that depreciation should be considered as a special kind of gross
earnings which is sheltered against taxation.[18] In the adjustment of a business
interruption loss, this argument has no direct impact. If part of the property
retains value, that value can continue to be depreciated and is treated as a
continuing expense during the period of interruption.[19]

The second question that sometimes arises is with regard to a change in the
rate of depreciation previously used by the Insured. In one case, such a change
was not permitted by the court.[20]

The depreciation or amortization figure that was used could have been tied
into the actual usable life of the property. An example is a die for a punch

press that can be used to make 1,000 stampings before it becomes too worn to be used further. If, at the time of the damage, the die had been used 800 times, it can be used only 200 times more. Assume that had the business continued to operate instead of being shut down and 100 stampings were made each week those 200 stampings would have completely depreciated the die in two weeks time. If the interruption will continue for four weeks, this particular item of depreciation would have stopped after two weeks. So much for depreciation tied directly into the actual usable life of property.

However, that is a rare example of depreciation. Usually, the depreciation is spread over a number of years. The number selected is the result of several interacting factors. One important factor is the length of time that the Internal Revenue Service will accept as reasonable. Another factor is the various tax laws that permit the Insured to accelerate depreciation as an inducement to him to buy more property and aid the economy. Another factor is the profitability of the Insured's business operation and his conflicting desires to shelter bottom line profits from income taxes or to show that he is making a greater profit.

Whatever the influences that operate on him, the particular depreciation practice followed by the Insured is part of his operations policy just as is his policy concerning the type of equipment he will buy and the scale of wages he will pay. The Insurer accepts this as part of the risk it assumes when it issues the insurance policy.

Withers states that, "If saved depreciation expense is involved, it is necessary that the method used in insured's books be corrected. Actual depreciation may include a proper allowance for obsolescence, if any. The basis of depreciation used in fixing values for insurance purposes is usually a good guide where adjustment of the insured's books is necessary."[21]

This statement probably has its roots in the accepted principle that, after a loss, it is the actual facts and not the facts that appear on the Insured's books that prevail; the contract of insurance is entered into on the basis of the facts as they actually exist.[22] If the books of account fail to reflect the actual facts, the books do not control. But, where the theory on which the Insured calculates depreciation and the Insured's books do coincide, then the books do reflect the true state of affairs. The Adjuster may be able to point out, in some cases, that the Insured will benefit in the loss settlement from a change in the method he has used for figuring depreciation.[23]

A third question involving depreciation may arise in connection with the establishment of the Business Interruption Value for the next twelve months. The Insured may be able to prove that he was about to change his method of depreciation to take advantage of changes in the tax law. Under the Gross Earnings form, problems regarding depreciation impact primarily in the area of continuing charges. For Business Interruption Value it really doesn't matter, because expenses and profits are both included in gross earnings.

In a coal mine fire, it was held that the depletion allowance no longer occurs when operations cease and, therefore, may not be a continuing charge.[24]

b. Discretionary Expenses. One of the more difficult types of expense to evaluate are those of a discretionary nature which the Insured has determined were beneficial to the operation of his enterprise. Charitable or political contributions might fall into this category. Unless continued, the good will they have engendered may be gone. They could be classed as normal expenses necessary to resume operations with the preexisting quality of service.

Under a policy with a payroll endorsement excluding or limiting the amount of "ordinary payroll," a determination of who are "important employees" whose compensation will continue to be covered, presents the same type of problem. Payroll includes compensation insurance, vacation and sick pay, union contributions, pension and retirement funds, group insurance, Social Security taxes and other employee benefits. Bonuses that were more or less regularly earned could be an important item of compensation in some companies; so, too, profit sharing. Where key employees earn substantial commission or bonuses on sales in addition to their base pay, the employer may have to compensate them for loss of these extras, if he wants to keep them during interruption. Is this a new charge incurred because of the interruption and hence not collectible?[25]

The continuing receipt of materials during the period of interruption may necessitate the incurring of extra storage charges for them until they can be used in the restored operations. One would expect the Loss Manager to request a suspension of deliveries until the plant was back in operation. But, where such suspension might result in the materials being sold elsewhere and thus not being available when needed, it could be good business judgment to continue accepting delivery without suspension despite the additional expense of storing them until needed. If not taken in, expense would have been encountered after the plant was back in operational condition but could not actually operate because it would not have the needed materials to work on. While it might be argued that this would fall in the class of situations covered by an Extra Expense Insurance policy, this is not the case, nor is the storage charge an extra expense incurred to keep operations going during the period of interruption. It is rather an expense to avoid a condition that would reduce the Earnings Stream after the damaged property was back in usable condition.

If it were necessary to find contractual support for liability for these expenses, it might be considered ". . . an expense necessary to resume operations of the Insured. . . ." Although the physical plant is ready to resume operations, without the sales people or the materials, the Insured is not ready to resume operations with the same quality of service. More likely, however, it would be considered a new item of expense and not be covered.

c. Techniques for Calculating. The usual procedure in calculating continuing fixed charges and expenses is to prepare two columns of figures, one itemizing the various expense items and their amounts, the second setting out—opposite the first—the amount of savings in expense in that item that will result from the suspension of operations. The amount of the *second* column is deducted from gross earnings that will be be lost during the period of interruption. Under previous types of contract, the approach was a little different. A third column showing ongoing expense was constructed representing the difference between column one and column two. This latter amount was added to the profits that would have been earned to calculate the amount of the loss.

6. Insurance required by Coinsurance Clause Calculation

From the calculations that he has made, the Accountant can now start to establish the amount of insurance that should have been carried by the Insured to meet the requirements of the Coinsurance Clause.

There are three methods by which the potential gross earnings for the twelve months succeeding a loss may be estimated. The first is to project prior trends of the Insured's gross earnings on the same curve into the future. This assumes that neither external influences nor the impact of the interruption itself will have any effect on the trend.

The second is to assume that the experience of the Insured will parallel that of the industry as a whole. On hindsight, industry figures are available; on foresight, judgment has to be used to evaluate the opinions of experts.

The third is to depend on the plans and projections of the Insured. Where such planning is a regular part of the Insured's operations, this is probably the best way of making the necessary calculation, keeping in mind all of the previous discussion about calculating future results.

It should be kept in mind that, while the application of the Coinsurance Clause is based on looking twelve months ahead (from date of damage under the Gross Earnings form; from date of policy under BIC Form), there is nothing in the contract which limits the Insured's right to recover only for loss suffered in that period of time if, in fact, the interruption continues for more than one year.

7. Valued Policy

There is no reason, apart from issues such as fraud, misrepresentation or arson, why an Insurer should have access to the Insured's books in case of a valued policy. It opens the Insured to a possible claim by the Internal Revenue Service that he was basing his loss on a non-valued theory and that might subject him to a different tax treatment of the amount collected. As stated, a contrary position can be taken when access is sought to support the defense of arson.[26]

Under a valued policy, increased earnings at another plant, owned by the

Insured but not mentioned in the policy, do not affect amount of loss at damaged plant.[27]

D. The Adjuster's Calculations

1. Nature of his Task

While the Accountant is making his investigation, the Adjuster is following a parallel course of action. A great many of the matters heretofore discussed in connection with the Loss Manager are of equal relevance to the work of the Adjuster. His first order of business will be to form his opinion as to the nature and extent of the physical damage. This will be done whether he has been appointed to adjust the loss under both the physical damage insurance policy and the Business Interruption Insurance policy or only under the latter policy. His investigation will serve as the basis for two types of opinion—the length of time it would probably take, with due diligence and dispatch, to get operations back to normal and those measures, if any, which the Insured might take to minimize his loss.

The Adjuster's task is twofold. Like the Accountant, he must calculate the Insured's loss, but then he must take the next step and calculate the Insurer's liability.

Assuming that he and the Accountant can come to an agreement as to the past experience of the business, he must next address three areas of calculation where even less solid ground for agreement exists.

2. Determining Length of Interruption

Area number one involves the length of interruption, both partial and total. Where the repair has not been completed or hindsight is not possible, an agreement must be sought. The matter of whether due diligence and dispatch had been used, and, if not, what would have been the time of interruption had it been used, must be resolved. The Adjuster should keep in mind that if an agreement cannot be reached between himself and the Loss Manager, the determination will be made by arbitration or litigation. An equitable solution should actively be sought.

3. Resumption of Operations

There are times when the business situation requires careful analysis on the part of the Adjuster to determine what is appropriate action to request in order to resume operations. Such a situation arose in the case of damage at a manufacturing plant. This plant, A, and another plant, B, both were under the same management, but were owned by different corporations with some divergence in stockholder ownership. Both produced resin. Plant A converted all of its own resin into plastic piping. Plant B sold part of its resin to Plant A, at a discounted price, for converting and sold part at full price to other converters. A fire knocked out Plant A's resin producing capacity. At this time, Plant B was in the process of expanding its product line capacity to meet increased customer orders.

The management sent a certain undamaged piece of equipment from Plant A to Plant B, which enabled the latter to increase its production at once. (The similar machine that Plant B had ordered from the manufacturer was not to have been ready for three months. When it was finished, it was redirected to Plant A as a replacement for the equipment sent to Plant B.)

The Adjuster of Plant A's loss requested that Plant B send all of its resin product to Plant A to be converted into plastic piping, so that Plant A could maintain its Earnings Stream. He also believed that the price should be fixed at the previous discounted price. After arguments pro and con, the following equitable arrangement was reached: Plant B would continue to ship its previous quota of resin to Plant A at the discount price; it would ship the extra productive capacity made possible by the transferred equipment to Plant A at a discount price for three months (the time gained) and thereafter at full price; it would cut back on its outside customers as far as it could without destroying goodwill and ship the amount saved thereby to Plant A at full price. The key to this compromise was the diversity in ownership—there was no reason why those who were only stockholders in the corporation that owned Plant B should reduce their profits to help those among them who were stockholders in the corporation that owned Plant A to reduce their loss. The Resumption of Operations Clause imposed no such obligation on them. (The result would have been different if the stockholder lists had been identical.)

4. Measuring Amount of Insured's Loss

Area number two involves the amount of the Insured's loss. This is determined by what would have been the gross earnings of the business had not damage occurred, less non-continuing charges and expenses. As mentioned earlier, the Adjuster should be prepared to present evidence in support of his position. If he runs into difficulty agreeing with the Loss Manager, he should exert maximum effort at this point in the proceedings to prove his point, rather than wait for future proceedings before exerting his best efforts. However, if he senses that the Insured has no intention of being reasonable or of trying to reach a fair result, the Adjuster may deem it expedient to reserve his heavy artillery until later in the battle.

Many factors can be weighed by the Adjuster in appraising the soundness of the Insured's prognostications. They include such things as the capacity of the plant, the capability of the work force and staff, trends in the Insured's line of business, past achievements of management, availability of necessary resources, economic trends in general, plans and experience of others in the same line of business activity and many others. The end being sought is not definite proof that such development would or would not take place, but rather what was the probable future course during the period of interruption of the Insured's business operation as of the date of the damage.

As stated earlier, information learned from such diverse sources as trade journals, trade associations, weather reports, government statistics, as well as from knowledgeable individuals, can shed light on the matter. But while these are helpful, they are not controlling. The determining factor is the condition within the Insured's own business enterprise, even though it may have deviated from the norm of his industry.

Measuring the probable future experience of the Insured's gross earnings by what was the experience of other firms engaged in a similar business enterprise during the period of interruption falls into the category of knowledge gained from using hindsight. The drafters of this Business Interruption form saw fit to base the obligation of the Insurer on probability—and that means measurement by foresight and not by hindsight. (See Comment #9, p. 317.) Theoretically, to live up to the strict terms of the contract, the Adjuster should focus on the fact situation as it existed at the moment the damage occurred.

Having said all that, it still has to be recognized that, as a practical matter, the damage frequently has been repaired and the interruption has ceased by the time that the ultimate amount of the loss becomes a matter of discussion between the parties. Under such circumstances, it is usually possible to work out an agreement based on hindsight, making due allowance for any changes that are now historically known to have occurred during the period of interruption. By then, the Insured has a pretty good idea of what he has lost and will be satisfied with an adjustment based on that knowledge. The impact of the Coinsurance Clause also may have a dampening effect on too ambitious a claim of future gross earnings.

The Adjuster should keep in mind the possibility that operations were not going to be carried on during part or all of the period of shutdown. It could have included the annual repair period or other planned procedure which would have affected the Earnings Stream.[28]

5. Preliminary Discussion with Insured

Where the Adjuster has reached the conclusion that the Insured's projection as to probable future experience is not reasonable under the circumstances, this should become the subject matter of a "gloves off" conference. Most Insureds are tractable if the Adjuster can marshall a solid set of arguments. There will be an occasional Insured who cannot be shaken from his unrealistic position. In such a case the Adjuster, if convinced of his grounds, must stick to his guns and not shrink from the possibility of litigation.

Where the controversy raises questions of policy interpretation or other questions of law, the Adjuster should take action only upon advice of the Lawyer for the Insurer.

6. Loss Items Not Covered

In computing the losses which the Insured has suffered, the Adjuster must keep in mind the policy language which excludes coverage for "any other consequential or remote loss." As a result of the damage to property, not only may the Earnings Stream be diminished during the period of interruption but other economic damage may be suffered. Goodwill might be impaired as a result of alienation of customers. Raw materials which cannot be used during the period of interruption may deteriorate in quality or usability. Productivity of employees may be impaired by residual fear of another explosion. These are not recoverable losses.[29] While items of this type may truly cause financial loss to the Insured, the loss is separated from the original cause of damage by the intervention of a new factor. In other words, the interruption of operations has resulted in a certain situation being created and it is that situation which is the source of the financial loss which followed. The line is a very close one and should be carefully explored.

Where the Adjuster reaches the conclusion that the Insured has not complied adequately with the requirements of resuming operations and using due diligence, it becomes necessary to determine by how much he could have reduced the loss by proper compliance. The development of evidence which will sustain the burden of proving such failure, and the extent thereof, is the responsibility of the Adjuster and is often a most difficult task.

7. Destruction of Books and Records

It has been assumed in the foregoing discussion, that the books and records dealing with prior experience are available for examination. In the case of major damage, it is not unusual for the books and records to have been destroyed. This requires a reconstruction of the past history by investigation and inquiry among suppliers and customers. The Gross Earnings form specifically provides for the production of books and records, or of certified copies if the originals are lost, for examination by the Adjuster. It also provides for the submission "to examinations under oath by any person named by this Company."[30] Such examinations can be utilized in the process of reconstruction and verification of financial facts. It is usually advantageous for the Adjuster and the Accountant to work together in such reconstruction.

There is also the matter of the effectiveness of the extra expenses incurred in actually reducing the amount of the loss. This is usually the least difficult issue to resolve.[31]

8. Cost of Goods

A short summary of the procedure for establishing costs of goods sold during the period of interruption would read as follows:

a. if inventory is adequate to meet ongoing requirements during interruption—fill orders out of inventory and recover only the extra cost, if any, of replacement to inventory;

b. if other goods can be purchased to meet requirements—recover only the extra cost of other goods;

c. if customers can be held off until finished goods can be supplied after restoration of operations—recover only extra cost, if any, of producing those goods;

e. if provable sales are lost permanently because finished goods are not available—recover value of gross earnings lost on such sales;

f. if receipt of incremental value of goods in pipeline is delayed—recover only so much of the cost of completing them as in excess of what would have been the cost if no damage had occurred.

9. Determining the Impact of the Coinsurance Clause

The Adjuster has one further step to take and that is to determine whether the terms of the Coinsurance Clause are triggered. This is area number three. Usually this involves only a mathematical computation. It is possible that the Insured made a miscalculation in the amount of insurance he was required to carry. Experience shows that in order to reduce the amount of premium paid, Insureds have a tendency to underestimate their future income when buying the insurance. On the other hand, an Insured who is intent on maximizing the amount of his claim by projecting increases in future profit sometimes forgets the impact of such a position on the requirement to carry adequate insurance or be subject to coinsurance. In any event, the Insurer's liability is calculated at this point by the Adjuster by applying the result of the calculations under the Coinsurance Clause to the total amount the Adjuster believes the Insured is otherwise entitled to collect.

There can be other factors limiting the amount of the Insurer's liability. The portion of a loss beyond two weeks duration caused by action of civil authorities is not covered. Another limitation would exist where the Insured had other insurance policies covering the loss, in which case the loss has to be apportioned between the participating Insurers. Then, too, the amount of loss suffered may have been affected by strikes, loss of orders or other causes excluded from the protection of the policy.

E. The Role of the Intermediary

When all efforts to reach a compromise between the Adjuster and the Loss Manager have failed, it is sometimes possible to call upon the good offices of the Intermediary to help bring the parties into agreement. Both the Adjuster and the Loss Manager are obliged to operate within the strict limits of the written contract. As with every such contractual structure, there may be extraneous considerations that can be brought to bear. Some of these fall within the relationship between the Intermediary and the Insurer. Given appropriate conditions, the former may be able to effect some relaxation in the strict application of the contract provisions. There is no reason why such efforts should not be made to prevent a resort to litigation.

At this point, the claim is ready to move to the settlement stage.

Chapter 13 Notes

1. "The calculation of indemnity with *approximate* accuracy is the only kind of accuracy contemplated by all the parties to the contract." Buffalo Forge, Co. v. Mutual Security Co.

2. A weighted average selling price had to determine where product was sold at different price in different markets. Nat'l Union F. Ins. Co. v. Anderson Pritchard Oil Corp.

3. "U & O Insurance," J. Wolfe, *Journal of Accountancy* (April, 1925).

4. See address of Ambrose B. Kelly, Esq. entitled *The Role of the Accountant in Business Interruption Insurance* at meeting of National Accountants Ass'n, Portland, Maine. May 17, 1962.

    As pointed out in a discussion at one RIMS Annual Risk Management Conference "the cost of goods sold" used by the Accountant to determine gross profits includes items—especially labor items for other than in-process inventory—not deductible as cost of materials and supplies consumed in the production, as used under the terms of the policy to determine insurable gross earnings for business interruption insurance. Reported by Paul Dudey in *National Underwriter* Vol. 86, No. 18 (April 30, 1982), p. 52.

5. Article by Paul Dudey (supra).

6. See: Fidelity Phenix Ins. Co. v. Benedict Coal Corp.

7. Hawkeye Chemical Co. v. St. Paul Fire & Marine Ins. Co.

8. Miner-Edgar Co. v. North River Ins. Co.

9. American Alliance Ins. Co. v. Keleket X-Ray Corp.; Fidelity-Phenix Ins. Co. of N.Y. v. Benedict Coal Corp.; National Union F. Ins. Co. v. Anderson-Pritchard Oil Corp.; Studley Box & Lumber Co. v. National F. Ins. Co.; Washington Restaurant Corp. v. General Ins. Co. (minority opinion).

10. Use of method of valuation widely used in the industry. See: Mt. Royal Assurance Co. v. Cameron Lumber Co. Ltd. (Canada)

11. See: Fidelity-Phenix Ins. Co. of N.Y. v. Benedict Coal Corp.

12. By writing down the inventory to eliminate cost of raw materials considered to be obsolete, Insured raised cost of goods used and reduced profit for income tax

purposes. For insurance purposes, Insured wanted to reverse the process, thereby reducing the percentage of the selling price which recaptured the cost of the goods used and increasing the percentage that was gross earnings. The majority accepted the finding of the Master it had appointed to the effect that the original reduction properly reflected costs of goods used in normal production activities and met the policy provisions in a practical way. A strong minority opinion claimed that the reduced figure represented "value" and not "cost" as required by policy. American Alliance Ins. Co. v. Keleket X-Ray Corp.

13. Fidelity-Phenix Ins. Co. v. Benedict Coal Corp.

14. Nat'l Union F. Ins. Co. v. Anderson-Pritchard Oil Corp.

15. Probable experience thereafter does not mean actual experience. Hawkinson Tire Tread Service Co. v. Indiana Lumberman's Mut. Ins. Co.

16. In 1974, Bardwell stated that non-continuing expenses amount to between 25-45% of gross earnings for manufacturing and mercantile firms and about 5% for service companies. Op. cit., p. 29.
    Extensive discussion of such items can be found in Klein, Glendening and Withers (Ops. Cit.); Miner-Edgar Co. v. North River Ins. Co.

17. This point was inherent but not actually raised in Supermarkets Operating Co. v. Arkwright Mut. F. Ins. Co.

18. Carmen G. Blough, *CPA Journal of Accounting* (July, 1958), p. 78.
    "Depreciation & Corporate Profits," Murray Brown, *Survey of Current Business*, Vol. 43:5-12 (U.S. Dept. of Commerce: Oct. 1963).

19. The depreciation in the value of the manufactured product or goods on hand were not "fixed" charges. Standard Printing & Publishing Co. v. Bothwell. But what about a stock of seasonable merchandise, when sales operations cannot be carried on? Destroyed property does not depreciate any longer, so it is not a continuing charge. Fidelity Phenix Ins. Co. v. Benedict Coal Co.

20. An attempt by the Insured to reduce a depreciation factor of 10.73% used before the fire, to 1.84% afterwards, on the basis of the President's feeling that it was proper, was not accepted by the court. General Ins. Co. v. Pathfinder Petroleum Co.

21. Withers, *Business Interruption Insurance*, p. 136. No depreciation is allowed on the property that has been destroyed. American Ins. Co. v. Pickering Lumber Corp. See: American Alliance Ins. Co. v. Keleket X-Ray Corp. and cases cited.

22. An accellerated depreciation rate which has been applied to production property can affect the Insured adversely if the property is destroyed and acceleration depreciation stops; for then the discontinued expense is greater in amount and gross earnings less discontinued expense is lower.

23. Jack Jones, a former veteran adjuster for the G.A.B., stated in 1964 that they refigure at a truer percentage so that net gross earnings are not reduced so much. The business operations would have earned more that way.

24. Fidelity Phenix Ins. Co. v. Benedict Coal Corp.

25. See: Palace Cafe v. Hartford F. Ins. Co.

26. Trader v. Indiana Insurance Companies.

27. Omaha Paper Stock Co. Inc. v. Harbor Ins. Co.

28. Hawkeye Chemical Co. v. St. Paul F. & M. Ins. Co.

29. For other specific examples, see Klein. op. cit. p. 264, ¶2. (The details of the story about cows mentioned by Klein is found in "Sidelines and Loss Ratios," an address by William J. Greer to the Western New York Field Club, March 7, 1924.) See also: Pacific Coast Engineering Co. v. St. Paul F. & M. Ins. Co.; Withers, op. cit. p. 20.

30. For a case where the Insured took the Fifth Amendment and refused to answer questions, see Intowne Restaurant Corp. v. Aetna C. & S. Co.

31. The question is raised whether the Coinsurance Clause is applied to set a ceiling on the total amount the Insured can collect including the expenses to reduce the loss. Suppose a loss of $60,000, but Insurer's share is reduced to $48,000 because that was the amount of the policy. By spending $10,000, in expediting expense, the Insured reduced the loss from $60,000 to $42,000. Does he collect $42,000 plus $10,000 or only $42,000 plus $6,000 to reach a ceiling of $48,000?

    George S. Jones said $48,000 is the ceiling on recovery. Geo R. Blum said "No." Since it is the extent to which the Insurer's loss is reduced that creates a new ceiling on recovery—it would appear that Jones is correct.

14

Process of Settling the Claim: Determination of Insurer's Liability

---

Submitting proof of loss. Conference to settle claim. Ancillary matters.

A. Submitting Proof of Loss

1. Necessity for Filing

The Proof of Loss called for by the Gross Earnings forms is made up of two parts. One is a recitation of facts which establish the Insurer's liability for the loss, and two is a statement of the Insured's claim. The discussion herein deals primarily with the second aspect. Usually the Insured submits such a claim prepared by his financial officer or by his Accountant. That claim presentation is then reviewed by the Adjuster and his related Accountant. At the same time, the Adjuster and his Accountant present figures indicating their opinion as to the amount of loss sustained by the Insured and the amount which the Insurer is obligated to pay. Where a loss is of substantial size, a discussion often takes the place of a preliminary Proof of Loss with an extension of time for filing a formal Proof of Loss.

By the terms of the underlying policy, the loss is payable 60 days after submission of such a Proof of Loss and agreement of the parties as to the amount of loss or that amount has been developed by an Appraisal.[1] While the requirement can be waived by the Insurer or the Adjuster,[2] an Insured who relies on a claim of such waiver has the burden of proving that it took place. For that reason, the Insured should seek a written statement of waiver where possible.

It should be borne in mind by all parties involved that the provisions written into the Standard Fire policy and into the Business Interruption Insurance

233

policy forms are not always the final word in the matter. Statutes have been adopted in many states overriding the provisions of the insurance contracts. By and large they were adopted to protect the Insured from technical traps which would bar his recovery under the policy.

A number of courts have held that, when the Insured's contract consists of a Business Interruption Insurance form attached to a Standard Fire Insurance policy, there is no applicable provision requiring the Insured to file a Proof of Loss. As stated by one court in holding that a failure to file a Proof of Loss did not create a forfeiture of the policy: "the standard (fire policy) proof of loss provision has no applicability to a rent loss caused by a fire."[3] Another case stated that "a casual reading of these policy provisions shows their inapplicability to damage (sic) sustained by interruption of business."[4]

Other courts have held that the rendering of Proofs of Loss is unnecessary. As stated in the Telesky case, "the proof of loss provisions . . . are not adapted to claims for use and occupancy."[5] While these cases may be of use to the Lawyer in a situation where the Insured has failed to file a Proof of Loss, it is strongly advised that a Proof of Loss be filed in every case. It is also suggested that a written extension of time be secured if one is required, or a written waiver of the requirement for filing a Proof of Loss if that is the agreement reached with the Adjuster.

The question arises as to which of the two varieties of Proof of Loss the Insured is obliged to submit—the one provided for in the underlying Fire Insurance policy or the one provided for in the Business Interruption Insurance policy form. There is no statement in the form that its provisions are a substitute for the policy provisions. Where the two differ, the provisions of the form would apply to a business interruption loss. Where nothing in the form contradicts the requirements of the underlying policy, the question remains open as to what extent the latter must also be complied with in view of the statement in the form that "all provisions and stipulations of this form and policy shall apply separately to each such item." For discussion of requirements for Proof of Loss under BIC Form see Ch. 16.

2. Contents of Proof of Loss

Both the policy and the form set out the requirements with regard to the contents of a Proof of Loss. The one in the form is obviously an attempt to adapt the provisions in the Fire Insurance policy to the type of coverage provided. The attempt is not one hundred percent successful.

There are some aspects of the requirements set out in the form which are worthy of comment. By its terms, the "origin" of the property damage is requested, not the "cause." Origin could mean either of two things, but it is clear that here the type of peril which caused the damage is asked for, not the place in which it originated.

The form calls for a statement as to the interest of the Insured and of "all others in the business." This is another instance of the problems that result from use of the word "business." If the word means the business enterprise which owns the damaged property, its potential is wide indeed. Suppose the business enterprise is a corporation; then all the stockholders have an interest in it. It is much more likely that, in this instance, reference is to the business operation. The party operating the property, i.e., the corporate entity, would be listed. Neither mortgagees, lessors or other parties having an interest in the physical property would be listed.

Notice of changes is required. The form calls for notice of change "of said business," while the underlying policy calls for notice of changes regarding the described property. These can be quite different matters, and if the requirements of the policy still apply, it may be necessary to comply with both.

An early issue was raised by the provision calling for estimates upon which the amount of loss claimed is based. To what extent must the Proof of Loss indicate the individual items of property damage and the interruption caused by the time to repair or replace each one of them. Looking at the underlying Fire Insurance policy the answer is blurred by the use of the word "property." If it refers to *insured* property, there would be no application to a business interruption loss. However, if it refers to *described* property, then that would clearly bring all references to "property" in the underlying policy within the scope of the Business Interruption Insurance policy form requirements.

It is fortunate that in earlier years, when the Gross Earnings forms contained no separate provision for filing a Proof of Loss, that practical common sense prevailed in the industry and appropriate adjustment was made by Adjusters in settling business interruption losses. The Gross Earnings forms issued in more recent years attempt to clear up this issue by including a provision about requirements in the event of loss indicating that the word "property" applies to the physical property described. The BIC Form clarifies the matter by stating that the Insured must "send us a signed sworn statement of loss containing the information we request to settle the claim."

3. Time for Filing

The time requirement for filing a Proof of Loss is explored in depth elsewhere. At this point it should merely be pointed out that the policy and the Gross Earnings form call for filing it within sixty days after the damage. Under the BIC Form it is "within 60 days after our request." Where state statutes intervene to limit the responsibility of the Insured to file a Proof of Loss, they overrule policy provisions.

This due date should be conspicuously diaried by the Loss Manager on his calendar. If he cannot have a Proof of Loss ready by that time, he should ask for the extension provided for in the policy. But unless such an extension, properly executed, is in his hands before the time runs out, he would be well advised to file a temporary Proof of Loss including therein the best information then available. An extension signed by the Adjuster would be sufficient to protect the Insured. It could be argued that the latter may have no authority to sign an extension, but it would appear that he has apparent authority in the usual situation.

In the case of an interruption that will extend beyond sixty days, it is clear that a compliance with the time requirement would have to be based on estimates. But there are many situations where the Insured is not in a position to reach even an estimate of his final loss within sixty days of the damage. In such circumstances, a preliminary Proof of Loss is an appropriate tool. However, a Proof of Loss which contained only a single statement to the effect that, "I believe that I have lost, and feel that I will continue to lose $2,250 per month until I am back in business," was held not to be an adequate compliance with the requirement for filing a Proof of Loss.[6]

4. Reservation of Rights

It is suggested that when submitting a preliminary Proof of Loss before the final amount of the claim has been ascertained, the Loss Manager should state that according to his "present knowledge and belief" the amount of his loss is so-and-so much but that he reserves the right to amend the figures up to the time that a final claim is presented or agreement is reached in settlement of the loss. Then, as new knowledge is received which establishes the fact that the first figures were too high or too low, an appropriate adjustment can be made by filing an amended Proof of Loss.[7] Of course, such action is obviated when the parties agree on the amount of the loss before the Proof of Loss is filed.

The Insured can later claim an amount of loss greater than that set out in the Proof of Loss provided there has been no award by appraisal.[8] The Proof of Loss on record would certainly be produced as evidence against the enlarged claim but, if the evidence is available to justify the increase, based on later information, the Insured would not be limited to the amount in the Proof of Loss. After all, the policy does say that the Proof of Loss is to be based on "knowledge and belief."

In *Fidelity Phenix Ins. Co.* v. *Benedict Coal Co.*, the court said, "The proofs are not part of the contract of insurance. The contract requires that they be made, but then they are only declarations of the Insured, admissible in evidence as such, but not conclusive as to the facts they state. If they contain false statements, upon which the company relies, and so acts or refrains from acting that injury would result, an estoppel would result therefrom if the statement were denied. But no estoppel arises in the ordinary cases of erroneous statement in Proof of Loss, where the company is not induced to admit a liability it would otherwise not have admitted or was otherwise misled into changing its position." This is different than the defense of false swearing in Proof of Loss which must be intentional and provable by clear and unequivocal evidence.

There are times when such a reservation of the right to amend is appropriate even when the Insured believes that all of the pertinent information is at hand. Such a reservation would have to be withdrawn when final agreement on amount is reached, but at least it keeps the door open until that time. The letter of submission could well contain a statement that the Insured believes he has furnished all of the information required by the policy but that he is ready to repair any deficiencies or omissions that come to his attention.

The Proof of Loss is usually submitted to the Adjuster. He should accept it only for transmittal to the Claims Manager of the Insurer, who normally retains the right to accept or reject the claim. The authority of an Adjuster to whom a loss is assigned is normally limited to making a computation of the amount of the loss the Insured has suffered and the amount of loss for which the Insurer is responsible. Where the amount of the loss is relatively small, the Insurer will normally accept the decision of its Adjuster. Nevertheless, where an Adjuster proposes to enter into a firm and binding agreement as to the amount that the Insurer will pay, provided the Insured will agree to that amount, it is appropriate for the Insured to request proof of the Adjuster's authority. Where an Insurer denies that the Adjuster had authority to bind it to a settlement figure, the courts are inclined to find that the Adjuster had apparent authority for that purpose.

When transmitting the Proof of Loss to his Claims Manager, the Adjuster usually accompanies it with his own "Statement of Loss". Frequently the Adjuster will send along an opinion as to the desirability of taking subrogation and also some comment on the nature of his dealings with the Insured and whether the Insurer should continue on the risk.

B. Conference to Settle Claim

The existence of a difference of opinion as to the amount of the loss calls for the parties to sit down together to determine wherein the differences lie. Again at this point, the relationship achieved between the Loss Manager and the Adjuster can affect their ability to work out a compromise which is acceptable to both. If a final agreement can be reached, the claim can be settled and the matter proceed to a close.

In the case of the small businessman who has relied on the Adjuster to prepare the Proof of Loss, it is customary for the Adjuster to sit down with the Insured and go over the calculations in detail. From experience it can be stated that these calculations are usually accepted as presented, with the possible exception of the deduction under the Coinsurance Clause. Shifting a part of the loss to the Insured's shoulders is often accomplished painfully.

It should be borne in mind that even at the negotiation for settlement stage, the parties should not be acting as adversaries. The Insured is dealing with his Insurer; they are bound together by a contract that requires good faith on both sides. Unfortunately, the adversary frame of mind often invades the settlement negotiations. It can be engendered by a Proof of Loss in which the claim has been padded to allow room for compromise. Despite such purpose, if this exaggeration is lacking in any support so that it can be proved to have been intentional, it may provide a basis for a defense of fraud and a denial of all liability.[9]

On the other side of the coin, reference can be made to the requirement that Insurers, to protect their rights, must reject the Proof of Loss when it represents a claim larger than they consider reasonable. Sometimes it is returned with the letter of rejection and sometimes it is "retained awaiting further instructions from the Insured."

Assuming once more that a proper relationship has been established, the rejection is recognized as a formality and is merely a prelude to a face to face conference at which the differences of opinion are explored in depth. Where the Adjuster is dealing with the Loss Manager or a Public Adjuster, differences in calculations and compilations are taken up one by one. This is where the earlier cooperation between the parties pays off. At least, they have been traveling along the same track in reaching their respective conclusions.

The responsibility rests with the Adjuster to possess the necessary skill in the art of negotiation to be able to bring the parties into agreement.[10] After all, dealing with business interruption losses is a matter with which he has experience, while the average Insured or even his representative other than a Public Adjuster seldom has equal experience. A knowledgeable Adjuster is a real asset under such circumstances. The more he knows about the rights of the parties and the legal interpretations of the contract, the wider his experience in the way business enterprises are conducted and the more skillful he is in bringing home to the Insured the cost and trouble attendant upon pursuing an unwarranted amount of compensation, the greater will be the benefit to both parties. Moreover such an Adjuster should be open to demonstration that his original assumptions and calculations were not necessarily correct and that he needs to make changes and concessions.

C. Ancillary Matters

There are a number of ancillary matters which are also taken care of during the settlement stage of the proceedings.

1. Partial Payment on Account

In case of an interruption of long duration, it frequently is necessary for the Insured to receive funds under his contract to keep his business enterprise alive until he is back in operation. To this end, he will ask the Adjuster to arrange partial interim payments against the amount of the ultimate loss. Assuming that there is no question of the ultimate liability of the Company for a loss in some amount, the making of such interim payments should be a normal procedure.[11] Obviously, the Adjuster's opinion as to the likely amount of the ultimate loss is relevant as to what the Adjuster will recommend by way of partial advances. It has been suggested that there might be a monthly audit following the monthly closing of the books, and a monthly calculation of loss; then a monthly payment until the loss stops running.

Indeed, there is reason to believe that an unjustified refusal to make partial payments—whether for the purpose of putting pressure on the Insured or otherwise—which results in the Insured being unable to continue his operation, could be grounds for holding the Company liable for "bad faith." After all, the insurance is sold and bought on the theory that it would provide to the enterprise such funds as the enterprise itself would have provided had there been no interruption.[12]

2. Subrogation Receipt

There are instances where the damage that caused the interruption resulted from the acts of a third party and were of such nature as to impose legal liability on such third party in favor of the Insured.[13] Under the terms of the policy, the Insurer has a right to request from the Insured an assignment of his rights against the third party. The subrogation receipt conferring such assignment is usually presented for execution before final payment is made. Where the Insured was not fully compensated for his loss this must be given consideration out of any subrogation recovery. (For discussion of subrogation under the BIC Form, see Ch. 16.)

3. Interest and Costs

Whether an amount for interest should be paid in addition to the amount agreed upon for the loss frequently becomes a matter for consideration. With the presentation of a proper Proof of Loss, the claim becomes due and payable. If not paid within sixty days therefrom, the Insured is entitled to interest on the amount owed. The rate of interest would be that set as the legal rate. Tender by the Insurer of the amount it admits to owing stops the running of interest on that amount.[14]

All of the costs incurred by the Company Adjuster in working out an adjustment, such as fees for experts as well as the cost for his own services, are the liability of the Insurer. Costs incurred by the Insured for similar services of specialists and experts in arriving at the amount of the loss and preparing the Proof of Loss are normally absorbed by the Insured.[15] Of course, if it can be shown that they were incurred to reduce the loss, they are collectible to the extent the loss was thereby reduced.

4. General Release

At the time of final payment, the Insured is usually asked to sign a general release. Where the amount paid has been arrived at by compromise, such a request is in order. If the amount paid has been agreed upon as due to the Insured, it would not appear that the refusal of the Insured to sign such a release would be in order. There is nothing in the policy that requires it.[16]

5. Payment by Mistake

Where payment was made through and on the recommendation of an Adjuster who incorrectly thought that there was coverage for the loss under the policy, the amount paid could not be recouped.[17] In another case, a settlement made in good faith was not allowed to be reopened because of later developments.[18]

D. Summary

This brings to a conclusion the discussion of the practice and procedures to be followed in settling a loss under a Business Interruption Insurance policy. The diminution in Gross Earnings per production-time unit, multiplied by the number of units during which operations would be interrupted in whole or, proportionately in part, is the basic process in fixing the amount of loss. Efforts on the part of the Insured to reduce the loss are required to comply with certain criteria; the Insurer's liability reflects the benefits that are achieved by such efforts. The Insured's actual loss suffered may be more than the Insurer's liability if adequate actions were not taken by the Insured or an insufficient amount of insurance is carried.

When the amount of loss is agreed upon, the filing of appropriate papers and the payment of the claim finally close the case. Where the amount of loss payable by the Insurer cannot be agreed upon between the parties, an exchange of correspondence is in order. The Insurer should formally notify the Insured in writing of its refusal to accept the Proof of Loss. A statement of the reason for the refusal should be included in such writing. This may be an appropriate time for the Insurer to put on record defenses which it may have against payment of any loss.

The Insured having filed his Proof of Loss under oath needs no additional formal presentation. However, a statement of the Insured's position on the items objected to by the Insurer should be sent to the Insurer. Ultimately, these positions will have to be disclosed by the parties and such disclosure before legal action is instituted might save a lot of later trouble and expense. Both parties in their correspondence should make it clear that they are not waiving any rights or claims that have not been specified in their writings.

If all attempts to reach an agreement fail, then the parties must resort to other means to determine the amount to which the Insured is entitled under the terms of the contract.

Chapter 14 Notes

1. Gross Earnings form under "Requirements in Case Loss Occurs"; Victory Cabinet Co. v. Ins. Co. of North America. See also: Standard Fire Insurance policy under "When loss payable."

2. See: DiLeo v. U.S.F.&G. Co. (1964) Ebert v. Grain Dealers Mut. Ins. Co.; Cf: Victory Cabinet Co. v. Insurance Co. of North America. The Insurer by its action or lack of action can effect a waiver of the need to file a proof of loss. Arcadia Bonded Warehouse Co. Inc. v. National Union Fire Ins. Co.

3. Budrecki v. Fireman's Ins. Co. In the Budrecki case (a standard policy with rent insurance rider attached) the court said, "We find nothing either in the contract of insurance or the statute . . . which makes for a forfeiture of the policy because of non-compliance (in filing proof of loss) in this particular. The penalty, in both instances, to be visited upon the assured, is that he cannot maintain an action upon the policy until such proof of loss is forthcoming, and then not unless such action is commenced within 12 months next after the fire."

4. Local custom may play a role. A&S Corp. v. Centennial Ins. Co.

5. Telesky v. Fidelity Guaranty F. Corp.

6. Trader v. Indiana Insurance Companies.

7. Proof of loss should not be too vague. See: Mudrick's Inc. v. National Surety Corp.
   A preliminary proof of loss was filed in General Ins. Co. v. Pathfinder Petroleum Co.

8. See: Dileo v. U.S.F.&G. Cf: Anchor Toy Corp. v. Am. Eagle F. Ins. Co.

9. Palace Cafe v. Hartford Fire Ins. Co.; Lykos v. Am. Home Ins. Co.

10. Edwin W. Whitmore, General Adjuster, is quoted as saying "Art, not Science, adjusts Interruption claims." *Business Insurance*, Vol. 21 No. 9 (May 1, 1978), p. 37.

11. See: Omaha Paper Stock Co. Inc. v. Harbor Ins. Co. (January 11, 1978).

12. See: District Court decision in United Nuclear Corp. v. Allendale Mut. Ins. Co. reprinted in *Business Insurance*, June 6, 1983, where punitive damages of $25 million were imposed. Associated Photographers Inc. v. Aetna C. & S. Co.

13. See: Rempfer v. Deerfield Packing Corp. (not business interruption); International Service Ins. Co. v. Home Ins. Co.; Palatine Ins. Co. v. O'Brien (second case, 1908).

14. See: Lewis Food Co. Inc. v. Milwaukee Ins. Co.

15. Puget Sound Lumber Co. v. Mechanics and Traders Ins. Co.

16. See: Ebert v. Grain Dealers Mut. Ins. Co.

17. National Insurance Company v. Butler.

18. American Ins. Co. v. Parker.

15

The Process of Litigation

The lawyer. Appraisal. Bringing suit. Interest. Post-judgment items. Lawyer's fees and costs.

A. Introduction

This section of the second part deals with the subject of litigation, where one party or other to the contract of Business Interruption Insurance goes to court to establish his rights under the policy. Such action is normally instituted by the Insured based on the refusal of the Insurer to pay monies to which the Insured believes he is entitled.

The refusal of the Insurer to pay usually finds its justification in at least one of five principal reasons: 1) No valid policy of insurance exists; 2) there was no coverage for the loss under the existing policy; 3) the Insured did not sustain any actual loss; 4) the amount claimed by the Insured is excessive; 5) by some act or failure to act the Insured has lost his rights to collect for his loss.

Similar reasons for refusal to pay could arise under the Fire Insurance policy. They form the subject matter of a vast number of decided cases, making up a large part of the body of insurance law. It is assumed that the Lawyer is familiar with these cases, as well as with the practices and procedures involved in handling cases based on a policy of Fire Insurance. Reference will, therefore, be made in the text primarily to those cases involving policies of Business Interruption Insurance. The discussion will not deal with the first two reasons for refusal noted above, namely that no valid policy of insurance exists or that the policy did not provide coverage for the loss which was suffered. These topics are considered outside the scope of this book.

The Lawyer searching for cases which deal specifically with the interpretation of Business Interruption Insurance contracts will find a surprisingly small number. Great caution should be taken in depending on these reported cases for authority. Not only has the language of the policies been modified over the years, but also the underlying contractual theory upon which this type of insurance is based has undergone change. Decisions based upon an interpretation of the language of earlier policies may not be relevant today.

To add to the problem, it is apparent that the courts which handed down those decisions did not always clearly understand the role played by this type of insurance. As a result, some decisions fall far short of the mark.

Statutory provisions beyond those establishing the form of the Standard Fire Insurance policy often affect a particular situation. The possible impact of such statutes must be kept in mind both in studying the decided cases and in preparing a given case for trial. (No analysis of such state regulations will be attempted.)

Addendum III contains a collection of almost all of the cases decided in the state and federal courts dealing with all types of time element insurance. A few English and Canadian cases are also referenced. The collection also includes cases involving tax matters. There are cases which deal with collateral matters referred to in the text. Still others deal with matters not referred to in the text.

Any analysis herein of the cases is limited in scope. It is intended to give direction in research rather than to represent a full development of the legal aspects of this kind of insurance. Often the case that is cited in the notes is not cited as authority for the legal point being discussed, but as a source of greater understanding of the issues. A study of the cases themselves should be undertaken by the Lawyer.

B. The Lawyer

1. Enters the Case on Either Side

The material in this section of the book, dealing with the function and activities of the Lawyer, is presented in a more direct and staccato manner than is used in previous sections. It is intended to be read in conjunction with earlier chapters and their chapter notes which often contain reference to the same court decisions. After reading and acquainting himself or herself with the textual material in the rest of the book, he or she may find a case that opens the door to further constructive research. While limited in scope, this section does cover most of the practical matters of concern to a Lawyer litigating a claim in connection with a Business Interruption Insurance policy.

Ideally, the Lawyer for the Insured has been involved, at least to some extent, in the handling of the loss adjustment and the settlement discussion. Certainly, this should have been the procedure in the case of a substantial loss.

The Loss Manager would be well advised to call upon the Lawyer's advice in connection with many areas of his dealings with the Insurer. This includes not only the signing of forms and agreements but also the actions to be taken by the Insured during the period of interruption which have a bearing on the provisions of the insurance policy.

While the Lawyer should play an active role in guiding the actions of the Loss Manager, it is usually preferable that such guidance be from behind the scenes rather than taking the form of actual participation in the discussions. Experience suggests that the presence of the Lawyer tends to inhibit the progress of negotiations. This is a matter for judgment, however, depending on the relationship that develops between the Adjuster and the Loss Manager.

Under normal circumstances, the Insurer's Claims Officer is capable of handling most of the legal questions that come up in the course of loss settlement, both questions involving liability and questions involving coverage. In situations where some legal problem arises with which he is unfamiliar, he would do well to call in the Company Lawyer for advice. Rather than demonstrating weakness, this sharing of decision making in matters that may later involve considerable litigation expense is sound corporate practice.

Usually when an appraisal is held, and always if suit is actually brought, legal representation becomes necessary. Just as in the case of the Loss Manager and the Adjuster, the selection of legal representation by the Claims Officer should be on the basis of experience with the type of insurance policy involved.

2. Preliminary Inquiry

If the Lawyer has been called in only when negotiations for the settlement of the loss have broken down, his first step is to become fully acquainted with both the facts and the legal implications involved. This applies to the Lawyer for either party.

The policy, the correspondence, the form of notice, the proof of loss and any other forms signed by the parties should be examined to establish whether there has been compliance with the technical requirements of the policy. This investigation should also shed light on the reason or reasons given by the Insurer for not meeting the Insured's request for payment.

It is suggested that a careful reading of each word of the insurance policy may prove of value. A slightly different wording may have been used which changes the nature of the rights of the parties under the contract. This was much more important before standard forms were adopted, but even today standard forms may vary from Insurer to Insurer, nor are they always used. A change in the wording of a standard form sometimes opens the way for new interpretation.[1]

In one situation, the owner of Massachusetts property was insured under a policy written on the New York standard form. The entire insuring transaction took place in Massachusetts. An inquiry at the office of the insurance commissioner disclosed that permission had never been given by the commissioner to the Insurer to use the New York form in Massachusetts. Under those circumstances, the provisions of the contract were to be read to conform with those of the Massachusetts Standard Fire Insurance policy. This resulted in a substantial difference in after-loss requirements and procedures.

A determination also should be made as to whether the policy is a valued or a non-valued one. This determination is not always simple where special language has been used to take care of the Insured's special requirements.

It is a mistake for the Insured's Lawyer to limit his preliminary investigation to the obstacles raised to date. The Insurer's Lawyer will review the same record with a fine tooth comb seeking out other issues, previously overlooked, which can be raised as obstacles to the Insured's success. A dispute about the amount of recovery at the negotiation stage often is accompanied by a denial of liability at the lawsuit stage. To be forewarned is helpful.

The examination by the Insured's Lawyer of the written material should be followed by a conference with all of the Insured's personnel who dealt with the Adjuster or Claims Officer. This preliminary conference should deal solely with things said or done which might serve as a basis for claiming that the Insured has complied adequately with contract requirements or that the Insurer has committed itself to a certain position. This could serve as a basis for setting up a claim of waiver or estoppel, in the event that certain technical defenses are raised. Full details of any such transactions should be documented. This step is of the utmost importance especially where there has already been an indication that the Insurer is or will be claiming that it is not liable under the policy.

Preliminary inquiries will follow one or both of two routes, depending on the known grounds for the Insurer's position. A claim that no liability exists because of the failure of the Insured to meet the requirements of the policy would call for exploration in depth with the Loss Manager as to the steps which he did take. A claim that no liability exists because the Insured breached the terms of the contract, whether by increasing the risk or attempting to defraud the Insurer or otherwise, calls for investigation into other specific channels.

It is also advisable for the Insured's Lawyer to acquaint himself with the pertinent legal decisions at this early stage of the proceedings. To wait until it is necessary to file a brief with the court can result in overlooked opportunities for making an authoritative presentation to the representative of the Insurer or for assembling a well-founded case. Worse, it could result in the giving of unsound advice for the Insured's conduct.

A similar responsibility rests upon the Lawyer for the Insurer. He should set up interviews with the Adjuster and any Claims Manager who has been involved in the adjustment process. By assuming an objective stance, he can evaluate the Insurer's position and the chances for ultimate success in litigation. Supposedly, he is already adequately aware of the state of the law on the subject but, if not, he should bring his knowledge up to date.

It is to no one's advantage to allow matters involving business interruption claims to go to litigation if an understanding and compromising attitude can avoid it. The hearings and trial can be long drawn out and costly. From long experience, it can be said that results are often highly unpredictable. With the exception of situations where fraud of some kind is involved, a conciliatory attitude is usually well-advised.

3. Conference between Lawyers

Assuming that the preliminary homework and investigation have been undertaken by the Lawyer for each of the parties to the dispute, a conference between them, without waiving any of their clients' rights, is highly recommended. This stage in the course of the proceedings, rather than the meeting on the courthouse steps, is the proper place to try to effect a settlement. The Insured presumably is hurting because the substitute Earnings Stream that he expected to be receiving under his policy has not been forthcoming. Insurers, in general, must feel under pressure to avoid the appearance of refusing to meet just claims; the development of punitive damage, liability for extra-contractual damage and consumer protection statutes awarding double or triple damages for improper delays in paying claims suggests such action.

Experienced lawyers can assess fairly accurately their chances of success in pressing their respective claims. Most disputes are ultimately settled by a compromise at some time in the course of the proceedings. Final victory is often an expensive undertaking for Insureds, particularly if their time and the effort required are calculated. Making law by pressing matters to a decision before a court of record is generally of little benefit to Insurers. Even if not all issues in dispute can be resolved, a narrowing of the issues is to everyone's benefit.

Given the elaborate pre-trial disclosure procedures adopted by most states, there is little to gain by not laying the cards on the table at such a preliminary conference. Such a process could go a long way toward eliminating the need for a trial.

The words of appreciation spoken by one judge are appropriate here. In *Anchor Toy Corp. v. American Eagle Fire Insurance Company*, Justice Steuer commended counsel for their negotiations prior to going to trial. He said, "such questions as the estimated amount of business during the period and the percentage of profit were not only of great complexity due, among other factors, to the means of administering the corporate business, but also were at best matters of opinion. It is therefore greatly to the credit of counsel that many of these questions were resolved by agreement. It is in the best professional tradition that such facts could be stipulated even though wide varying opinions could have been supported by expert opinion."[2]

Even when the Insurer has what appears to be sound technical defenses against any payment, making an appropriate compromise settlement should not be ruled out by its Lawyer. He should approach the problem free of any emotional bias that the Company Adjuster or Claims Supervisor may have developed in the course of their dealings with the Insured or his representatives. The focus should be on the dollar cost to the Insurer.

However, if the defense is based on any type of fraudulent action on the part of the Insured, of which the Insurer's Lawyer is independently convinced, then dollar cost should not enter into his consideration. If arson, a highly exaggerated claim or other type of intentional fraud is involved, then no level of exertion is too great to defeat the claim. It is the duty of every Insurer to make fraudulent action just as unprofitable for an Insured as it can. This is a responsibility it owes to the insurance community as well as to the public at large.

C. Appraisal

1. In General

Where the dispute involves the amount that the Insured is entitled to collect, the appraisal process offers a desirable procedure for settling the issue. The decisions concerning appraisals fall within the sphere of general insurance law. As such, the subject would not normally be one for discussion in this volume. An exception will be made in this instance, however, because the procedure could play such a satisfactory role in disposing of disputes as to the amount of the business interruption loss.

A preliminary inquiry should be made as to whether, in the particular state, the courts hold that an appraisal falls within the statute governing arbitration. Some do; others do not. The majority treat the provisions for appraisal in the Standard Fire Insurance policy as falling outside of the arbitration statute. This has a very definite impact on the manner in which the appraisal is conducted. "The distinction between an arbitration award enforcible through court confirmation and an appraisal subject only to enforcement in a separate plenary action depends upon whether the award encompasses the entire controversy between the parties and whether the appropriate degree of formality attended the proceedings."[3]

Statutes in the various states outline the procedures to be followed and obligations of the parties. They should be read in connection with the policy.

Although there is no specific reference to an appraisal in the Business Interruption Insurance form, it has been generally held that the appraisal provisions of the underlying Fire Insurance policy apply to losses under this type of coverage. The language used in the Standard Fire Insurance policy as appropriate for property losses has to be "adapted" to make it conform to the requirements of a business interruption loss, but this process does not appear to have been seriously questioned. The BIC Form does contain a provision about appraisal. (See: Ch. 16.)

2. As a Condition Precedent to Bringing Suit

The New York Standard Fire Insurance policy, by its terms, contains no such limitation. The provision merely states than in case of a failure to agree as to the actual cash value or the amount of the loss, "on the written demand of either, the process of an appraisal shall be undertaken" and that "an award in writing . . . shall determine the actual amount of cash value and loss." This is to be compared with the Massachusetts policy which states . . . "such reference, unless waived by the parties, shall be a *condition precedent* to any action in law or equity. . . ."[4] A later clause in the policy provides that the loss shall be payable after ". . . ascertainment of the loss is made either by agreement . . . or by the filing . . . of an award. . . ."

The issue was raised in the *Hawkinson Tread Tire Service Co.* case where the court said, "It is generally held that where a policy provides that, upon disagreement as to the amount of the loss, the amount of the loss shall be appraised . . . upon the written demand (or request) of either, the provision does not make the appraisal a condition precedent to a plaintiff's action on the policy. The written demand or request, however, has been held to be a condition precedent to an award upon appraisal. . . ."[5] But in that case the court held that the issues in controversy did not include the *amount* of the loss.

The refusal of the Insurer to participate in an appraisal has been held to be a waiver of the requirement. It has also been held that the Insurer cannot raise as a defense the failure of the Insured to ask for an appraisal when the Insurer itself did not ask for one: "If an arbitration (sic) is really desired, no reason is apparent why it might not be had after an action is brought; the proceedings being stayed in the meantime. . . ."[6] Failure to demand an appraisal does not penalize the Insurer by depriving it of its defenses under the policy.[7]

3. Getting Started

Appraisal proceedings are instituted by a demand of either party. The procedure to be followed and the time constraints are set out in the policy, but state statutes frequently bear upon the process. These should be checked by the Lawyer.

The New York Standard Fire Insurance policy contains specifications regarding the qualifications of the Appraisers. They must be "competent" and "disinterested." The BIC Form requires that they be competent and impartial. State statutes sometimes establish the same type of qualifications.

4. Agreement for Appraisal

A written form of agreement for submission to Appraisers is sometimes prepared, which defines the agreement between the parties, the scope of the appraisal and the names of the Appraisers and Umpire.[8] There is no obligation resting on either party to sign such preliminary agreement. If properly drawn, there should be no objection to signing such an agreement and it does serve to establish the parameters for the appraisal procedure. The policy eliminates any suggestion that by participating in the appraisal the Insurer is waiving any of its rights to deny liability under the policy.

5. Hearings

The Appraisers usually sit as a panel to hear evidence from the parties and their witnesses. The Umpire does not serve as a member of such panel. His only function is to solve differences between the Appraisers. If he is present, it is only as an observer.

There is no requirement that the Appraisers take an oath, as would be the case if the procedure constituted an arbitration. To quote from *In the Matter of Delmar Box Co., Inc.*, "There is thus no indication whatever that the legislature intended to make applicable to fire insurance appraisals the more formal practice prevailing in arbitration with regard to such matters as oaths, notice and hearings, the sittings of the arbitrators, the entry of judgment upon confirmation of award or the consequences following upon the *vacatur* of an award."

6. Evidence

The concept behind an appraisal also delineates the type of evidence that is relevant to the hearings. Any information bearing on the amount of the loss falls into that category. At the same time, questions of liability and questions of law clearly do not fall within the scope of the Appraisers' duties.[9]

Unfortunately, the line of demarcation is not always that clear. It is sometimes necessary for the Appraisers, in determining what profits were lost, to decide on incidental or preliminary questions of law or accountancy.[10] Questions as to which operations of the Insured were included in the "described property" may have to be made before gross earnings can be determined.[11] Whether the depreciation of the destroyed property should be considered in determining insurable value must also have to be decided as a precondition to determining amount of loss. While depreciation on the damaged property was excluded in determining the amount of the loss, it was not be to deducted in figuring business interruption value.[12]

The *Delmar Box* case offers language which succinctly describes the rules applying to the kind of evidence that can be offered. It reads in part, "Appraisers proceedings are, moreover, attended by a larger measure of informality and appraisers are not bound by the strict judicial investigation of an arbitration ... Appraisers ... are likewise not obliged to give the claimant any formal notice or to hear evidence; and they may apparently proceed by *ex parte* investigations, so long as the parties are given an opportunity to make statements and explanations to the Appraisers with regard to the matters in issue."[13] This relaxed approach would appear to fulfill the underlying purpose of the process, which is to obviate court proceedings and speed the equitable settlement of claims.

It is important that all of the evidence upon which the parties base their position should be made available to the Appraisers. It is only under rare circumstances that additional evidence on the matters of value and loss will be accepted by a court after the Appraisers have made their final report.

7. Award

Each of the Appraisers acts independently to appraise the loss. After all the evidence is in, each Appraiser, as a preliminary matter, prepares his own figures as to the "actual cash value and loss to each item." Translating this language to a business interruption loss, he sets down his opinion as to the Business Interruption Value and the amount of the Insured's loss. Where the amount of the Insurer's payment after the application of the Coinsurance Clause has to be determined, some statutes delegate the authority to the Appraisers to make a decision. The term "loss," as it appears in the appraisal provision, could theoretically refer either to the Insured's loss or the loss the Insurer must pay. Since the award represents the number of dollars to be paid the Insured, if he prevails, the latter meaning is the appropriate one.

The two Appraisers then meet and attempt to come to an agreement on each of these matters. The natural bias that is built into being selected by one of the opposing parties will tend toward the acceptance by the Appraiser of his party's approach to the calculation of the amount of loss. Which means that the Appraisers frequently represent a second level for negotiation and compromise. Even in the absence of any such bias, agreement will usually represent a give and take process until there is a meeting of the minds. Those items concerning which the Appraisers can agree are then established as part of the base for the final figure. The Umpire can have no influence over them. Those on which they cannot agree are submitted to the Umpire for his decision. Where the two Appraisers agree completely, it is not necessary to submit anything to the Umpire.[14]

When a dispute is submitted to him, the Umpire seeks to come to an agreement with at least one of the Appraisers. The Umpire may not find the position of either Appraiser acceptable. He is not limited to approving one or the other and may suggest his own form of award.[15]

If the Umpire agrees on the amount of loss with one of the Appraisers, a form of award, properly itemized, is signed by the two who agree. It is filed with the Insurer and becomes binding on the parties as to the amount of loss that the Insured will collect, assuming no defense exists to its payment.[16]

Since two persons must agree for an award to be valid, either of the Appraisers has the choice of agreeing with the Umpire. If neither is willing to do so, there is no award, and the entire matter of the amount of loss must be determined in court.

There is a strong tendency in the courts to uphold an award signed by two persons. There is a reluctance to examine the process by which the final figure was reached. Absent strong evidence of fraud or a clear error of law, the award will stand. However, awards have been successfully attacked when they were patently erroneous.[17]

8. Effect of Award

Absent any reason to overrule the appraisal award, the filing of that award with the Insurer should bring the controversy over amount to an end. If other matters of defense exist, however, they will have to be litigated in court, unless the parties had agreed to submit such matters to arbitration. This would be a true arbitration subject to all of the regulations which are not relevant to an appraisal. Usually, when such arbitration is agreed upon, the matter of amount is incorporated in the same proceeding rather than being resolved by appraisal techniques.

9. Refusal to Pay Award

If the Insurer refuses to pay the amount of the award, the Insured must proceed by way of a suit on the policy to collect the amount awarded, rather than by bringing a suit on the award itself.[18] In defense of such suit, the Insurer could raise all defenses against liability under the policy. As stated earlier, the fact of entering into the appraisal process would not constitute a waiver of any right to such defenses.

10. Payment of Appraisers

Under the terms of the policy, each party pays the fee for its own Appraiser while the expenses of the appraisal and the fee of the Umpire is split between them. The same formula is provided under the BIC Form. Statutes sometimes provide that if no award can be agreed upon by two persons, the Umpire is paid by the Insurer, who can reimburse itself for half from any other monies it is paying to the Insured.

D. Bringing Suit

1. In General

If the Insurer refuses to pay the amount claimed by the Insured, whether it be in the absence of an appraisal award or after an appraisal has fixed the amount of the Insured's loss, the only recourse available to the Insured is to bring suit. An appeal to the insurance commissioner has sometimes been successful, but usually that official will not step in if the refusal is based on a denial of liability or a legal defense against payment. By statute in some states, the Insurer may be subject to a fine, for refusing unjustifiably to pay the award.

2. Time for Bringing Suit

A suit should not be brought prematurely. All of the necessary preliminary steps must first be taken. This includes meeting the policy requirements unless they have been waived by the Insurer. Altogether too often the claim of waiver is an after thought, made necessary by the Insurer's defense that the suit was brought prematurely. This is a poor substitute for having complied with the requirements before bringing suit. On the other hand, the Insured is sometimes able to plead a waiver or an estoppel based on the position or action taken by the Insurer and proceed to institute suit without full compliance.[19]

Similarly, the suit must be brought within the time stipulated by the applicable limitations period.[20] Reference to the time for bringing suit is contained in the underlying Fire Insurance policy. Sometimes, this varies from the usual period for bringing other types of contract action provided for by state law. No reference to the bringing of suit is contained in the Gross Earnings form, so that the provisions of the underlying Fire Insurance policy prevail. (For reference to the provisions of the BIC Form see Ch. 16.) The time of the damage is clearly the inception of the loss.[21]

The conduct of the Adjuster or of the claims personnel in dealing with the Insured can sometimes be construed as an extension of the time available for bringing suit.[22] Variations exist. In one case, no specified time limit on bringing suit was found to be the result where the underlying property coverage had been cancelled, leaving only the business interruption coverage.[23]

Sometimes damage occurs before the written policy has been received by the Insured. Usually, he holds a written binder or Certificate of Insurance, though it is possible that only an oral binder exists. These conditions do not bar a suit on the contract of insurance. There are numerous decisions confirming the rights of the Insured in such a situation.[24]

3. Parties

Since an Insured can recover only to the extent of his insurable interest, it is desirable to name as plaintiffs all those who have such an interest.[25] Conversely, all Insurers whose policies cover the loss should be joined as defendants. Where 31 of the 33 Insurers were out-of-state corporations and were named as plaintiffs in a federal court action, while the two domestic corporations were named as plaintiffs in a suit for a declaratory judgment in the state court, the federal action was dismissed because all indispensable parties were not included.[26]

A mortgagee to whom the proceeds of the fire policy may have been made payable does not have to be joined as a party in a suit to collect for the business interruption loss. A mortgagee has no insurable interest in the Earnings Stream. The receiver or trustee of an Insured who has filed in bankruptcy is the proper person to bring suit under a policy running to the bankrupt. The executor of the estate of a deceased Insured may be named as party plaintiff.[27]

A holding company, which is the sole stockholder of a subsidiary corporation that was named as Insured, has no right to bring suit in its own name. Corporation A controlled B, and B controlled C, while C controlled D and E, of which the latter corporation owned the described property. The policy covered C and all subsidiary and affiliated "companies . . . on premises situated . . . in Louisiana." Only D and E were located in Louisiana. A suit brought in the name of C was dismissed. Since C was not operating in Louisiana, it had no Earnings Stream there; the interruption was to the Earnings Stream of E which was also an Insured. As a stockholder, C had no insurable interest in E's Earnings Stream.[28]

Where several operating companies are named as coinsureds in a single policy, it is important to determine whether their interests are identical. If they are, the matter of loss sustained is evaluated blanket over all of the operations. The profits of one may be used to offset the losses of another.

Where several corporations have the same management and are engaged in a related operation, but the holders of stock vary between the corporations, the profit gained by one does not have to be applied to offset a loss sustained by the other.[29] This position is not defeated by naming all of the different parties as joint plaintiffs in a suit.

An Insured who sold his property after it was damaged and was paid for his loss up to the date of the sale, then assigned his policy to the buyer. Since the assignment was not agreed to by the Insurer, the assignee could not maintain an action on the policy for losses subsequently accruing.[30] However, if the Insured continued to have an interest in any loss occurring after the sale, the purchaser, to whom the claim had been assigned, could collect the amount due to the Insured in a suit brought in the name of the Insured.

4. Pleadings

The pleadings should set up a case in contract based on the policy of insurance. That is the contract between the parties which the Insured is trying to enforce. An Appraiser's award merely establishes *prima facie* the amount that the Insured is entitled to recover.

Again, no attempt will be made to discuss the details of the pleadings available to both parties. The cases cited in Addendum III include some in which questions of pleading were involved.

5. Master

The complicated nature of the evidence that may have to be presented has sometimes led a court to refer the matter of a business interruption loss to a court appointed Master; usually in cases where the amount of the loss has not previously been agreed upon or has not been determined by Appraisers. The report of the Master may or may not be final on such matters, depending on the terms of the court's reference to him.[31]

6. Evidence for the Insured

a. In General. In general, no analysis in depth of the evidence that must be presented to establish the Insured's case will be attempted; certainly none of that basic evidence which is necessary in every suit on an insurance policy. The burden of proving a loss within the provisions of such policy rests upon the Insured and it must be established within the rules of evidence applicable to a civil suit based on an insurance contract.

In the case of a Business Interruption Insurance policy, the Insured is called upon to establish, as a minimum, the existence of a valid contract and his compliance with the terms thereof (the facts that fulfill the requirements of the six P's described in the first part), the dollar amount of his claim with supporting calculations, and the failure of the Insurer to pay.

There are some aspects of the evidence related to a business interruption loss, however, that are worthy of special consideration and they will be touched on briefly in the following pages. Although the references will be made in connection with the trial, they are also applicable to both the adjustment and the appraisal procedures. At least one case in which the specific matter has been considered will be noted in most instances. Again the caveats are repeated: Early cases may have been decided under a policy containing different language; different states vary in their application of rules of law to this type of contract; the court may have been wrong in its decision, as determined by later decisions, or may be out of step with the weight of authority.

Reference will sometimes be made in the pages that follow to some of the issues decided by the courts in connection with cases involving Use and Occupancy and other types of time element coverage in addition to Gross Earnings policy forms. These may serve as a guide to the Lawyer preparing his evidence.

b. Practical Approach. It should be constantly kept in mind that the nature of the Business Interruption Insurance contract is such that tight, strict lines cannot be drawn for determining the amount of the loss.[32] A business approach rather than a legal approach should be taken. The court should be made to recognize that a practical solution of the issue of amount of loss is to be sought.[33]

This was expressly stated by the court in *Hutchings v. Caledonian Ins. Co.* as follows: "Many arguments as to the elements which should be taken into consideration in fixing the exact amount to be allowed as the recovery are stressed by plaintiffs and defendants alike. Many of these arguments are in the nature of cross-currents, and would lead us into the realm of speculation and sophistry. We are faced here with the practical matter of doing justice between the parties and not with a problem in sophistry." The method employed in reaching a determination is one which must result in a reasonably sound conclusion.[34]

   c. Background Information. In those cases where the amount of loss is in dispute, the Insured's Lawyer is usually well advised, as a preliminary matter, to provide the trier of the facts with background information about the industry in which the Insured is engaged and the niche that he occupies in it. Any material difference between the Insured's methods and those of the competition should be brought out at this time.

Background information about the Insured's business operation should be presented, including the history of his growth and development, his planning, promotion and sales policies, as well as a full description of how operations are conducted. This information will create a framework on which to support the calculations and figures used to develop the Insured's claim. Where the amount of the loss is not in dispute, much of this background detail can usually be omitted.

Some situations exist where establishing the amount of the loss at the trial is relatively simple. This could occur where the amount of loss has been agreed upon and the only issue revolves around the obligation of the Insurer to pay; where there has been an agreement of the amount of loss by the Appraisers, but their award is being challenged;[35] or where the Insured holds a valued policy.[36]

Evidence as to the amount of the loss suffered by the Insured should be fairly certain after the completion of loss adjustment and the filing of the proof of loss. However, in his suit, the Insured can claim a larger amount of loss than claimed at any earlier stage of the loss settlement.

A copy of his proof of loss can be offered by the Insured at the trial for the purpose of establishing the fact that one was filed and the date thereof. The proof of loss filed by the Insured does not constitute evidence of the information contained therein; such evidence must be presented by witnesses who have knowledge of the facts or can qualify to give an opinion as an expert.[37] A proof of loss can be filed after suit has been started.[38]

The Insured is not absolutely bound by erroneous statements in his proof of loss in all cases.[39] The fact that no proof of loss has been furnished, may not be a bar to recovery by the Insured if its filing has been waived.[40] An admission made by the Insurer's Adjuster concerning the amount of the Insured's loss, not made in the course of attempted settlement and not made under a stipulation that it may not be used, is admissible in evidence.[41]

d. Intention of the Parties; Ambiguity. Extrinsic evidence as to the intent of a party in entering into the contract can be introduced if the court finds the wording ambigious and one party claims that, as interpreted by the other party, it does not express his intent.[42] The question is one of fact to be determined by the court. The general legal rule about finding for the Insured when ambiguities exist in a contract prevails in cases of Business Interruption Insurance; but where the policy was prepared by a broker for a sophisticated Insured, ambiguities were interpreted against the Insured.[43]

Some courts seem to have little trouble in finding ambiguities. Witness the majority in the *Washington Restaurant* case which found that "due consideration" is a vague, ambiguous expression as was the reference in the policy to "saved expenses." Another court said common sense required them to find that "due consideration" means "rational consideration."[44]

Where appropriate circumstances exist, reformation of the policy may be sought as a preliminary step.[45]

e. Damage but no Loss. There are a substantial number of cases where it was found that while the Insured had suffered physical damage to his property, he had not suffered a loss under the Business Interruption Insurance policy because, during the period of interruption, the business would have operated at a net loss, without earning either profits or money to cover any part of continuing charges and expenses.[46] Other cases are to be found which hold that there was no loss which fell within the terms of the policy.[47] A reading of these cases provides background on this major issue as well as guidance on how to present the evidence.

Normally where sales are made out of inventory, the normal profit on sales shows up on the books. If there is enough inventory to fill all orders until operations resume, the amount of sales would remain constant, though there would be a depletion of the inventory. Provided that a catch-up game had been played and the depletion refilled without extra expense, there would be no loss shown on the Insured's books. If it would cost more to fill the hole in inventory than it would have cost to produce the same amount of goods absent any damage, this extra cost is a cost incurred to reduce loss and, to the extent that it can be shown to have done so, it can be recovered; even though it might not show up in the figures for the period of interruption.[48] (See Comment #12, p. 327.) Only after operations are restored will the cost of replacing the consumed units in inventory be experienced and determined. If it cannot be shown that there was a need to refill the inventory, no extra cost of production need be undertaken, and, therefore, no loss suffered by the Insured can be established.

It is necessary for the Lawyer and the Accountant to adjust their presentation of the pertinent data so as to parallel the requirements of the policy. There is no single method that has to be followed. Addendum IV portrays one format in which the evidence of the amount of loss can be presented. It tracks closely with what is accepted as a standard approach. The advantage of following such an approach is that the evidence will go in smoothly, with fewer objections as to form being raised by the Lawyers. Examples of different ways in which calculations have been presented in court are found in the cases.[49]

f. Establishing Amount of Loss. Earlier sections of the book have indicated how the factors of experience before and probable experience after the damage are to be treated. This area of the case should have been thoroughly explored before the Lawyer is called upon to take legal action. It would not be amiss, however, to mention some of the situations where these two factors were considered by a court.

In presenting evidence of the past experience of the business, neither party is bound by the facts as shown in written reports. Usually, it is the Insured who wishes to introduce facts other than those recorded for income tax purposes or for dealing with stockholders. However, it is possible to envision a situation where the profits picture was inflated by the Insured to keep lenders happy. In such case, the Insurer will be able to introduce conflicting facts. The Insured is not bound by his own testimony as to physical facts and objective matters which could have been observed as well by other witnesses and is entitled to their more favorable testimony.[50]

Past experience is normally compiled on the basis of the Insured's occupancy of the described premises. The use of past experience figures when projecting future experience ordinarily would be substantiated by evidence indicating operations at the same location and calculated on sound business judgment.

Evidence of probable future experience must similarly be based on sound thinking. Various techniques for calculations have been accepted by the courts. The experience for other firms engaged in the same line of business "was given great weight" in one case.[51]

In another case it was suggested that, where production had historically gone forward on a fairly steady basis, an estimate of probable production during the period of suspension could be tested for correctness by using a moving average covering a reasonable period immediately preceding the damage to indicate the trend of the operations at time of damage. (In that case, a four month period.)[52]

Among the pertinent decisions are those considering the length of the prior period to be taken into consideration. Though the usual practice is to consider the preceding twelve months, this is not the time element always used. Some of the differing time frames used have been:

1. "The average daily production of the last twelve months of full production" in the case of a manufacturer of forges and other heavy machinery.[53]
2. Where prices have been declining steadily, one court did not allow the Insured to go back and take an average of the prices in effect during the 8 months of its existence.[54]
3. The period of January 1 to March 5 was used in the case of a fire on March 4 because there were inventories on both of those days, although the latter inventory was taken after the fire.[55]
4. Figures for the two month period preceding the fire.[56]
5. A policy provision establishing the dates of April 30, May 1 and 2, as setting the average production of electricity, was controlling.[57]
6. A period from 6/8/58 to 1/28/59 best represents what the gross earnings and profits would have been from 6/8/60 to 11/28/61.[58]

Cases dealing with the meaning and application of the word "probable" are also fairly numerous.[59]

g. Period of Recovery. Evidence as to the length of the period of recovery can be a substantial source of controversy. Even where the damage has been repaired by the time the case is ready for trial, there is always a possible dispute as to whether due diligence and dispatch have been employed. The Insured is not obliged to use the shortest time offered in contracts or estimates in calculating length of suspension. Here again a common sense approach must be taken. Contractors do not always live up to their promises. Financial reliability of the contract must also be considered by the Insured.

Earlier sections contain much discussion on the setting of an appropriate time frame around the period of suspension. This is one of the areas where a preliminary explanation of the Insured's operations and the business atmosphere in which it is conducted can be of great help to the trier of the facts.

With the possible exception of the time necessary for finding suppliers of replacement equipment and supplies, information regarding time for restoring production is usually not in the hands of the Insured or his employees. Outside experts are needed. Their evidence can deal with the nature of the damage and the extent of repair and replacement that will be necessary, as well as to the length of time necessary to rebuild or repair.

Where the damage was repaired, it would appear that the controlling factor is the time necessary to restore operations at the premises described, taking into consideration all factors that would impinge on the restoration to a physical condition reasonably similar to that which would have existed had no damage occurred. Where damage was not repaired, theoretical time measure is used and gives no regard to the season of year, weather conditions, or other accidental fact that may delay construction.[60] Reported decisions frequently draw no distinction as to whether or not the damage was repaired, whether or not a similar structure was rebuilt or whether or not future operations were carried on at the same premises.

The Insured's Lawyer should introduce evidence concerning the length of time required to rebuild or repair using due diligence and dispatch. This is accomplished by estimate, if the property is not rebuilt or repaired; by estimate, if the property is to be rebuilt or repaired but renewed operations have not yet started; and from actual experience, if the damage was repaired and operations resumed. This latter suggestion is the practical way to deal with the issue in the usual situation. The time required with the exercise of due diligence to restore operations may or may not coincide with the time actually taken to get back into operation. The Insured should deal with this issue in his original presentation to the court.

If reconstruction at the actual site of the damage had taken less time than the parties had estimated, the loss is usually settled on the actual time that it took because that is the best evidence. Where the loss has been closed before completion of the rebuilding and then it is found that less time than figured was necessary to restore operations, the matter remains settled except in the case of fraud or the like. In one case, where full production volume was restored even before physical repairs were completed, it was the theoretical period necessary to make the repairs that still controlled.[61]

h. Fixed Charges and Continuing Expenses. The Business Interruption Insurance policy form requires coverage only for those expenses and charges that necessarily continue during the period of suspension. The Lawyer for the Insured would do well to scrutinize ongoing expenses and fixed charges very carefully and eliminate in his evidence all those that do not necessarily continue.

A definition of the term "fixed charges" and its application to a given fact situation has also been considered by the courts in cases where the policy contained those words.[62] The term "fixed charges" does not appear in current Gross Earnings forms. They refer to "normal charges" which continue. For provision in BIC Form see Ch. 16 hereafter.

The "fixed charges" in one case were defined as "those expenses necessarily incurred in maintaining the organization in such a state of efficiency as would enable it to resume normal production without substantial delay after the strike was ended, or as the strike might be broken by a gradual return of employees".[63] Another court said: "The term 'Fixed Charges' has no well defined meaning ... depending somewhat upon the connection in which it is used. ..."[64]

Specific items constituting fixed charges have been discussed in many cases. Fixed charges do not include interest on the money owed for the burnt portion of the plant where the policy limited reimbursement for fixed charges to those "due to the disablement of the power plant, etc."[65] Club and associations dues were deemed proper fixed charges by one court, as was the maintenance of a branch office in New York City.[66]

The terms "continuing expense" and "necessarily continuing expenses" have been discussed by the text book writers as well as having been discussed in a number of cases.[67] One typical issue involves the charge for rent. In such cases, the wording of the Insured's lease is often of major importance.[68]

The continuance of depreciation as an expense item also has been the subject of legal decisions. As stated previously, where the property is entirely destroyed, depreciation does not continue as a fixed charge, though it is still included in calculating the insurable value.[69] Similarly, depreciation on inventory which could not be used while operations were suspended has been held not to be a fixed charge.[70] Where no evidence of the depreciation charge is introduced by the Insured, a court cannot consider it, though it is normally a continuing expense.[71] Depletion, as contrasted with depreciation, ordinarily stops when production stops.[72] (See Comment #10, p. 323.)

i. Payroll Maintenance. The burden of proof rests with the Insured to justify as necessary the continued maintenance on the payroll of people for whom there is no productive work available during the period of suspension. The existence or non-existence of a labor pool from which a successor could be hired, the amount of investment in training, the possession of specialized knowledge or a relationship with customers or suppliers are among the guides for considering an employee as a person whose continued maintenance on the payroll is a necessary continuing expense. The burden of proof is also with the Insured to establish the fact of his continued employment and the value of his services. Some cases require that for coverage of payroll charges, the Insured does, in fact, continue the individual on his payroll while others allow recovery as long as they would have continued had the Insured proceeded to restore operations.[73]

If the employee is utilized elsewhere in some productive capacity, there is a presumption that the Insured is gaining some value from the services rendered and not all of the paycheck is unproductive and can be recovered from the Insurer. The Insured has the burden of proof of overcoming this presumption.[74] The fact that an employee is a key person in his old job does not per se render him a key person under the provisions of the policy.[75]

Where the partners in a firm were key employees, they could not put in a claim for the continuation of their draw during the period of suspension as a continuing expense and at the same time claim to have lost the same amount in profits, where their profits in prior periods included their draw.[76] A contrary result would be to grant them a double recovery.

According to the regulations interpreting Massachusetts General Laws c.151(a)§1-R(3) dealing with unemployment compensation, a key employee who is continued on the payroll to keep him from trying to find work elsewhere is entitled to collect unemployment compensation insurance as well, if he or she is not working. No attempt has been made to check the provisions in other states.[77] (See Comment #10, p. 323.)

j. Setting Prices and Amounts. Questions about the criteria to be used in setting prices and amounts have been considered in various cases. Different approaches have been taken in different cases. The following examples provide an idea of the variety of approaches which may be used in an appropriate case: the cost of raw stock used in production is based on inventory figures adjusted for obsolescence of materials for future use;[78] the Office of Price Administration ceiling price for each grade of lumber (established at a time when price control existed) adjusted for freight differential is to be used;[79] when several processes are carried on before the final product comes out, the product must be charged into each next operation at its then market value;[80] in one case, the court made an off-hand reference to the fact that there was a 15% downward trend in the tire retreading industry, . . ." but it is not clear what effect this had on the final outcome.[81] In the case of a policy insuring *profits* where the language read: "Profits . . . that would have been receivable by the insured on the data (sic) of the fire from the sale of the damaged merchandise in the ordinary course of the Insured's business," the court interpreted this to mean the going market price as established by evidence of actual sales about the time of the fire.[82] The depreciation in value of the manufactured product or goods on hand was not a fixed charge.[83]

k. Exclusion Involving Termination of Third Party Relationship. The Lawyer for the Insured should be aware of the implications involved in this exclusion. Properly interpreted, it may not necessarily limit the area of the loss.

This exclusion provides that in order for an increase in loss resulting from a suspension, lapse or cancellation of a lease, license, contract or order to be covered under the policy, such event must result *directly* from the interruption of business. The effect of the use of the word "directly" is to make certain that the event is not one that stems from the damage to the described property – or even to the described premises. Rather, it must stem from the interruption of business. In all probability, the term "business" in this context refers to the business operations. Thus, the additional diminution in the Earnings Stream must result directly from the fact that because the Insured could not operate, the lease, license, contract, or order was suspended, lapsed, cancelled, or, alternatively, that the continued existence of the lease, license, contract, or order depended on the Insured being able to operate and when he could no longer operate, the relationship was terminated.

It would be necessary to examine the terms of the lease, license, contract or order to see whether the third person's right to suspend, lapse, or cancel it rested on the inability of the Insured to continue his operations. If it did, then we have a direct result and the additional loss is covered. If it did not, then the additional loss is not covered. Under such an interpretation, a cancellation of a lease of real estate based on the extent of the physical damage to the property would not result directly from the interruption of business. Similarly, the cancellation of a license to operate a chemical plant, which was cancelled because of a severe explosion, would not result directly from an interruption of business.

On the other hand, a decision by a buyer, made in good faith, that the Insured could not get back into operation soon enough to deliver the ordered goods within the specified delivery date, which led the buyer to cancel his order and place it elsewhere, could well be considered to stem directly from the interruption of the business operation.

For example, if the goods to fill an order to be shipped on September 10th were to be produced during the first week of September, and a fire on August 1 put the plant out of operation for three months, it is reasonable to expect that the buyer would cancel the order and place it elsewhere.

There is still another string attached to this third type of special exclusion, before the Insurer will be liable for the additional loss. This limits the liability to "such loss as affects the Insured's earnings during, and limited to, the period of indemnity covered under this policy."

The period of indemnity is the time it would take with due diligence and dispatch to rebuild, repair, or replace the damaged or destroyed property. A fire might interrupt operations for three months. The contract that is cancelled might call for production spreading over the next year. There might be sufficient cause to justify cancellation of the entire contract with the resultant loss of a full year's earnings. This special exclusion clause, however, limits the Insurer's liability to the loss of earnings that would have been earned during the three month period of shut-down.

It sometimes happens that, because of the damage and consequent interruption of operations, the Insured will lose the chance to secure a reasonably anticipated contract for future production. This loss of future income is taken into consideration under the contract provision dealing with the probable experience thereafter and not under the special exclusions clause.

l. Expenses to Reduce Loss. After all evidence of the diminution in gross earnings resulting from the interruption has been introduced, thought must be given to the existence of expense that may have been incurred to reduce loss. The Lawyer for the Insured should secure from his client and introduce into evidence any bills that fit into the category of expense related to reducing loss. He has the burden of establishing that such expenses were necessary if the reduction was to be achieved, and also that the Insurer's loss was reduced by a specific amount as the result of the expenditures.[84] (Under the provisions of the BIC Form, the Insured is required to keep a record of such expenses.)

Where only one of the two perils which caused the damage was covered by the policy, the Lawyer must establish how much of the expense was incurred in connection with the covered loss.[85]

7. Evidence for the Insurer

a. No Loss Sustained. The reasons underlying the Insurer's refusal to pay the claimed loss obviously determines the course taken by the Insurer's Lawyer in presenting evidence for the defendant. At least one of the five reasons mentioned earlier must be established if a successful defense is to be maintained. (As stated, the first two—no valid policy and no coverage for the loss—are beyond the scope of this text.)

The defense that the Insured has suffered no loss for which he is entitled to compensation has been presented to the courts on a number of occasions. The policy language controlling such limitation lies in the words "Actual Loss Sustained." These words, or the earlier wording, "not exceeding the Actual Loss Sustained," have been present in the Use and Occupancy Insurance forms and later in the Business Interruption Insurance forms since the early days of this century. While sometimes challenged and sometimes misinterpreted, they usually have been useful in reinforcing the principle of indemnity in this type of insurance contract.

One line of possible defense would be to establish the fact that although there was damage, no diminution in the Earnings Stream developed as a result of the interruption. This is the type of situation which can exist when sales can continue out of inventory or where the damage has been repaired and production has resumed once more and the lost production has been recovered without extra cost.

A different line of defensive evidence would be appropriate where it can be established that no Earnings Stream would have been produced during the period of interruption and, therefore, the advent of the interruption did not cause any diminution of the Earnings Stream for which the Insurer is liable. This defense can be asserted where repairs have been made as well as where the Insured opts not to rebuild.

An example of this approach is the *Washington Restaurant* case which involved a restaurant operating at a loss; there was no profit and the operating expenses of $10,800 a month exceeded gross earnings by $3,400. In other words, the gross earnings paid for only a part of the operating expenses and the restaurant owner had to dig into his pocket for the balance, to the tune of $3,400 a month. After a fire damaged the restaurant, gross earnings disappeared but so did a major portion of the operating expenses, with the result that the monthly loss that the restaurant owner had been sustaining was reduced from $3,400 to only $2,900 during the period of rebuilding.

This Insured had a Gross Earnings form of Business Interruption Insurance with a limit of liability of $3,000 per month for three months. The Insurer denied liability on the grounds that the Insured had not suffered a loss with regard to continuing expenses, but had actually benefited by the reduction in his out-of-pocket loss. The court split; a majority finding for the Insured; the minority writing a very strong dissenting opinion.

Unfortunately, neither side actually came to grips with what appears to be the real question raised by the facts, namely which particular dollars of operating expense that had been incurred before the damage occurred had been covered by the earnings. Should one start with the first dollar of expenses or the last? Did the first dollar of earnings pay for the first dollar of expense? Or put another way, did the income received from the operations pay for the first $7,445 of the $10,845 of expenses, leaving the last $3,400 to be paid by the Insured or was the first $3,400 of expenses paid for by the Insured and the balance met out of earnings? If expenses were first paid out of earnings, then there were always enough earnings to pay at least $2,900 of the expenses. When the fire stopped all of the earnings, this $2,900 of expenses, previously earned, was no longer earned. So the policy did cover this diminution in earnings. However, if the earnings are deemed to have been applied starting with the last dollar of expense–then there never was enough earnings to pay for $3,400 of expense and the Insured picked this up. The $2,900 of expenses that continued was part of this $3,400, not previously earned; it had always been part of the Insured's responsibility not the Insurer's. As a result of the fire, the Insured's out of pocket loss had been reduced from $3,400 to $2,900, as the Insurer claimed. He was better off than before.

This second approach seems unconscionable since the $3,000 limit in the policy would never have been at risk prior to the fire. This could hardly be the contract which the parties intended. Thus, the majority were right, in result at least.

The controversy cannot be left, however, without a glance at the *Goetz* case, an earlier Wisconsin decision which the minority opinion in the *Washington Restaurant* case referred to as "a case very much in point." The *Goetz* case was a decision under an earlier form of contract, in which the Insurer was to pay the "net profits . . . and such fixed charges and expenses . . . as must necessarily continue."[86]

What is significant in the *Goetz* case is that the jury found that, had the operations continued during the 49 days of interruption, there would have been a loss sustained of $4,062.64,–"an excess over the fixed charges and expenses of $3,820.30. . . ." In other words, not one penny of the fixed charges and expenses would have been earned. This fact apparently impressed the dissenting judge in the *Washington Restaurant* case because he stated, concerning the Goetz case: "The insured . . . could not have received from the conduct of the business (had operations been uninterrupted) *anything* [italics added] to be devoted to the payment of such fixed charges. . . ." This statement clearly separates the two sets of facts.

b. Underlying Factors. Technical defenses are also available to the Insurer. They can be advanced with justification in cases of arson, fraud and the like as well as in cases where the Insured is unreasonable. Where no such situation exists and the failure to comply with policy conditions has not prejudiced the Insured, they should be and usually are waived by the Insurer.

Overzealousness in seeking to find technical grounds for not paying otherwise honest losses is one reason for the development of extra contractual liability upon Insurers. Today the possibility of such exposure often inhibits the Insurer from refusing to pay in cases where such refusal would be proper. Reliance upon technicalities also adds impetus for the general tendency of judges and juries to torture the facts and distort the law in order to provide recovery for Insureds. That tendency is damaging enough without providing it with any justification.

c. *Areas and Types of Defense Tactics.* Within these general observations, there are specific cases which can guide the actions of the Lawyer for the Insurer. Most of them involve Business Interruption Insurance policies.

They include cases demonstrating a variety of defense tactics. For example, the Lawyer for the Insurer can sometimes make a sharp and telling attack on items of expense and fixed charges which were non-continuing and which had not been removed from the calculations. While a judgment factor exists for the Insured in this area of consideration, it is not nearly as flexible a standard as in some of the other calculations that must be made.

In some circumstances, the proof of loss may be used by the Insurer as a ground for a defense of fraud or false swearing. Being made under oath, the seriousness of misstatements in the document can carry substantial impact.[87] Because of the large scope for differences in opinion as to amount of loss made possible by the wording of the Business Interruption Insurance policy, one would expect that fraud in exaggeration of the dollar amount of loss suffered would be a frequent item of defense. A review of the legal decisions indicates that such is not the case. This probably results from the fact that the policy's very indefiniteness permits wide variations in opinion honestly concluded. The courts have also been quite reticent to affix a label of fraud on excessive claims.[88] But depending on the facts, that defense is still available and can be maintained if the circumstances are appropriate.[89]

Claiming an excessive amount of loss is not fraud where the Insured insists his is a valued policy, even if he is found to be wrong.[90] On the other hand, acceptance by the Insurer of a proof of loss and the making of partial payment of the loss, especially when based on ignorance of pertinent facts, will not bar the Insurer from subsequently raising the defense of no liability under the coverage of the policy.[91]

Where a proof of loss was furnished in connection with the Fire Insurance, this met the requirements of the Business Interruption Insurance policy form when the basic information applicable to both claims was identical and the same company was involved.[92]

If there has been inadequate compliance with the obligation of the Insured to produce his books and records when demanded, a ground for denying recovery exists.[93] Similarly, the Insured's refusal to comply with a request to submit to an examination under oath can be fatal to his claim. However, the employee of a Public Adjuster is not an employee of the Insured who has to be produced by the latter for examination by the Insurer, since the Public Adjuster is an independent contractor.[94]

Those defenses, available under the underlying Property Insurance policy, which are based on changes in the nature, condition, or extent of the described property or which act to terminate or suspend the liability of the Insurer thereunder, also apply to the Business Interruption coverage. They have been raised, sometimes successfully, in a number of cases.[95]

d. Application of the Coinsurance Clause. Substantial reference has been made previously in this text to the impact and workings of the Contribution or Coinsurance Clause. The burden of proof is on the Insurer to establish that the Insured carried an inadequate amount of insurance and that the Coinsurance Clause applies. The rationale behind the usage of this provision in any insurance contract, is sometimes hard for the jury, or even a judge, to understand. It may be a little easier to explain with respect to a Business Interruption Insurance policy.

In addition to the fundamental reasons for coinsurance in the case of business interruption coverage, it is impossible at the time the policy is written to establish with any degree of certainty what will be the amount of Business Interruption Value at the time that damage may occur. The parties, therefore, agree in the policy that the standard for measuring the Insurer's exposure is an amount equal to the amount of gross earnings that will be earned by the operations during the twelve months following the damage. (The time frame is changed under the BIC Form.) The parties may agree that the Insured will buy and pay for 100% of that amount or for only a part of the potential gross earnings—say 50 or 75%—and that percentage then becomes the established base. Any failure on the part of the Insured to have paid for an amount of insurance equal to that base will make him a coinsurer for the deficiency. Since the Insured is in the better position to know the facts about the amount and extent of his potential future gross earnings and has the right to decide as to how much insurance he will buy and pay for, it is quite fair to place upon him the burden of making the proper calculations.

E. Interest

1. In General

In general, where any claimant has to go to court, a substantial period of time can elapse before the plaintiff can receive any money. To protect plaintiffs from losing the benefit of the use of the money during the period of delay, the states have adopted statutes imposing prejudgment interest from the time the amount became payable until the date of final judgment in the legal action. Claims resulting from losses under insurance policies come within the terms of such statutes.

2. Liquidated vs. Unliquidated Claims

Most state statutes draw a distinction between situations where the amount of the claim is liquidated, and situations where the claim is unliquidated.

This general rule extends to Business Interruption Insurance losses. If the amount that would be due the Insured, assuming the Insurer will be found liable under the policy, has been agreed upon by the parties in writing or has been determined by Appraisers, or can be determined with reasonable accuracy from truthful evidence made available to the Insurer, interest will be allowed to the Insured, calculated from the time the amount of the loss is due and payable under the policy terms up until the time of judgment.

It should be kept in mind that the proof of loss is only a claim made by the Insured; it does not fix the liability of the Insurer. An agreement which will bind the Insurer must be *in writing*, which means that the Insurer must signify in writing for just what amount it is willing to be liable. There may be statutory provisions in a particular state which would affect this rule.

3. When Did Loss Occur

One interesting aspect of this matter of interest arises in connection with the question of when a business interruption loss occurs. If, as maintained at an earlier point in this text, the entire loss occurs at the time of damage and is only *measured* by the running of time and the acts of the parties, there should be no problem with the calculation of interest after the filing of the proof of loss.[96] Where the amount of loss was in dispute and was determined by the results of the court action, one court dealt with this amount retroactively, carrying the award back to the time when interest would have run under the policy terms if the amount had then been agreed upon.[97]

In opposition to the general point of view is only (apparently) the case of *Charles Dowd Box Co. v. Firemen's Fund Ins. Co.* which held that interest did not start to run until a year had elapsed. Only then was it possible, by hindsight, to determine what was the full extent of the loss due to interruption. To understand the result in that case, it should be noted that interest was sought on the amount of extra expenses incurred under the Resumption of Operations clause. Since no part of such expense is recoverable until after it has been established that the extra expenses have actually reduced the amount of loss, no amount can be said to be payable until the interruption is terminated and production has been reestablished and a definite assessment of the effectiveness of the extra expenses can be made. In this context, the decision was correct. It is unfortunate that the court did not make this distinction clear in its opinion.

A somewhat parallel situation existed in *Standard Printing and Publishing Co. v. Bothwell*, a case involving a policy of strike insurance. Since there was no means of determining when the strike would terminate, no way of determining the total amount of loss existed until after the strike was settled.

4. Continuing Loss

Suppose some part of the loss had not yet been suffered as of the date when interest on the claim began to run. This could be the case where the date established as a starting point for the running of interest antedated the time when the period of interruption ended. It would seem appropriate to make some adjustment to accommodate this fact. The parties themselves did this in effect in one case where they agreed upon what would be an appropriate median point for their calculations of interest.[98]

It should again be mentioned that the various court decisions are based on policies with varying wording. For example, with regard to a pre-July, 1953 form, the New York Supreme Court commented in the *Anchor Toy* case: "The ambiguity and uncertainty as to the proper date from which to compute interest arises by reason of the carelessness of defendants and their agents in assembling the several policies."

5. Cases on Interest

In one case, interest was allowed on the amount of the property loss, but not on the amount of fixed charges covered by the Business Interruption Insurance policy.[99] In another, where the Insured appealed the decision of a lower court, he was allowed no interest during the period of his appeal.[100] Where the Insurer had paid into court the amount that was ultimately awarded, interest did not run on the award.[101]

F. Post-Judgment Items

Several additional post-judgment items have been raised in the reported cases. One involves costs of suit; another, attorney's fees. Local customs and statutory provisions govern both of these areas.

In the case of *Fidelity Phenix v. Benedict Coal*, the matter of a return premium was raised. It was held that the statute requiring refund of a portion of the premium in case of a partial loss was not applicable to Use and Occupancy insurance. A contrary opinion was expressed in the case of *Eisenson v. Home Ins. Co.* The payment by the Insurer of a loss under a Business Interruption Insurance policy does not reduce the amount of the policy. The Loss Clause in the Gross Earnings policy form provides: "Any loss hereunder shall not reduce the amount of this policy." This language does not appear in the BIC Form itself.

Even though the face amount of the policy is exhausted by the loss resulting from a particular incident of damage, the automatic reinstatement clause provides that the full amount is available to pay for another loss resulting from other damage caused by an insured peril during the policy term. Such would be the case even though the first loss had not yet been settled.

An interesting case involves a loss settlement based on certain representations made by the Insured as to the impossibility of finding another source for replacing lost productive capacity. Shortly after receiving payment in settlement of his claim and prior to the time agreed upon for restoring production, the Insured found such capacity. The Insurer sought to reopen the case and reclaim the payment on the ground of fraud. It was unsuccessful in its attempt; the settlement being final.[102]

G. Lawyer's Fees and Costs

1. In General

The case for the allowance of lawyer's fees and costs to the prevailing party in a suit can be argued on three grounds. It reimburses the winner to some extent for the expense to which he has been put in gaining that to which he was rightfully entitled. It punishes the loser where he acts in an unjustified manner. Finally, it tends to reduce the number of frivolous actions which the court must hear.

The right to order such payments is ordinarily provided by statute, with broad discretion being typically granted to the court. In practice, the assessment of such charges is often made in the case of unjustified appeals.

2. Lawyer's Fees

A number of cases in which lawyer's fees were allowed in cases involving Business Interruption Insurance can be found.[103] In most such instances, the award was made to the Insured. But there are cases where the Insurer was awarded such fees. The amount awarded was usually determined by the court.

3. Costs

The costs allowed are generally statutory costs. These are far less than the actual expenses incurred by the parties in maintaining their respective positions in the suit.

H. Summary

The somewhat vague language of the Business Interruption Insurance forms, the lack of conformity of their language with that of the underlying Fire Insurance policy and the subjective and speculative standards they set for reaching certain important factual conclusions offer a fertile opportunity for Lawyers representing both Insured and Insurer to achieve the settlement of claims under such policies.

It is the responsibility of the Lawyer for the Insured to be sufficiently acquainted with the theory and practice applicable to this coverage to be able to bring to the bargaining table and, if necessary, to the courts, a broad understanding of the protection offered under a Business Interruption Insurance policy. It is similarly the responsibility of the Lawyer for the Insurer to preserve the concept of indemnification for loss sustained in the payment to Insureds who are entitled to collect under the terms of their policies.

Chapter 15 Notes

1. A good example of this type of situation can be found in Omaha Paper Stock Co. v. Harbor Ins. Co. (March, 1979 decision)

2. Even though lawyers have been introduced into the scene, an adversary situation has not yet been established at this point in the proceedings.

3. See: In the matter of Delmar Box Co. Inc.; Elberon Bathing Co. Inc. v. Ambassador Ins. Co. Inc.

4. See: Employers Liability Assurance Corp. v. Traynor.

5. Hawkinson Tire Tread Service Co. v. Indiana Lumbermens Mut. Ins. Co.

6. Amusement Syndicate Co. v. Prussian Nat'l Ins. Co. (Rent Ins.); Miner Edgar Co. v. North River Ins. Co. "The task of the referee . . . was roughly analogous to that of an appraiser. See N.Y. Consolidated Laws, Art. VII §173.

7. See: General Ins. Co. v. Pathfinder Petroleum Co.; Cf. Cohen v. American Ins. Co.; reported in Insurance Advocate (Feb. 22, 1947), p. 15.

8. See: Lewis Food Co. v. Fireman's Fund Ins. Co. for example of agreement.

9. Feinbloom v. Camden Fire Inc. Ass'n.

10. American Ins. Co. v. Pickering Lumber Corp.

11. See: Lewis Food Co. v. Fireman's Fund Ins. Co.

12. American Ins. Co. v. Pickering Lumber Corp.; Elberon Bathing Co. Inc. v. Ambassador Ins. Co. Inc.

13. ". . . appraisers are not confined to a single method of valuation but, in the absence of bad faith, misconception of duty or mistake, may employ any reasonable method." Miner Edgar Co. v. North River Ins. Co.; Union Lake Associates, Inc. v. Commerce and Industry Ins. Co.

14. Nickals v. Ohio Farmers Ins. Co.

15. Union Lake Associates Inc. v. Commerce and Industry Ins. Co.

16. The parties are not bound by the award of the appraisers if their figures are

changed by legal issues not within their jurisdiction. Cf: Lakewood Mfg. Co. v. Home Ins. Co.

17. See: Palatine Ins. Co. v. O'Brien, (1907); Elberon Bathing Co. Inc. v. Ambassador Ins. Co. Inc.

18. If a party sets up the award in its pleadings, it cannot later assail the same. Gray v. Merchants Ins. Co. (1906)

19. See: Thorrez Maes. Mfg. Co. v. American Central Ins. Co.; Cf: Victory Cabinet Co. v. INA.

20. C.A. Enterprises Inc. v. Employers Commercial Union Ins. Co.; Cf: Leung v. Dornberge Ins. Inc.

21. Becker v. Merchants Mut. Ins. Co.

22. Hebert Mfg. Co. v. Northern Assur. Co. Ltd. See: Anderson & Middleton Lumber Co. v. Lumberman's Mut. Cas. Co.

23. Eureka Security F&M Ins. Co. v. Simon, The majority held that this was a complete contract of insurance by itself, and since it contained no special limitation on bringing suit, none existed; the normal period for bringing a contract action under state law controlled.

24. Lauhoff v. Automobile Ins. Co. of Hartford; Parlier Fruit Co. v. Fireman's Fund Ins. Co. Industro Motive Corp. v. Morris Agency, Inc.; Cf: Consolidated Sun Ray Inc. v. Lea.

25. See: Kassner v. Travelers Ind. Co. where same parties had different interests.

26. American Ins. Co. v. Bradley Mining Co. Suit should name receiver of insolvent Insurer. See: Fleet-McGinley Co. v. Bothwell. For a case dealing with service of process and venue see Beautytuft, Inc. v. F.I.A.

In the case of Hart-Bartlett-Sturtevant Grain Co. v. Aetna Ins. Co., it was held that there is no joint liability between the several Insurers and no joint cause of action.

27. See: Michael v. Prussian National Ins. Co.

28. Unijax, Inc. v. F.I.A..

29. Gordon Chemical Co. Inc. v. Aetna Cas. & Surety Co.

30. Holt v. Fidelity Phenix Fire Ins. Co.

31. Newark F. Ins. Co. v. Bisbee Linseed Co. An accountant was appointed as Master. Am. Alliance v. Keleket X-Ray Corp. (Master was called an "Auditor".)

Auditor's report was prima facie evidence of the facts therein. New England Gas & Electric Ass'n v. Ocean Acc. & Guar. Corp.

32. Standard Printing Co. v. Bothwell; Travelers Indemnity Co. v. Kassner.

33. National Union F. Ins. Co. v. Anderson-Pritchard Oil Co.; Am. Alliance Ins. Co. v. Keleket X-Ray Corp.; Fidelity Phenix Ins. Co. v. Benedict Coal Corp.; Studley Box & Lumber Co. v. National F. Ins. Co.

34. Hart-Bartlett-Sturtevant Grain Co. v. Aetna Ins. Co. (reasonable); Puget Sound Lumber Co. v. Mechanics and Traders Ins. Co. (unreasonable); See: Rempfer v. Deerfield Packing Co. (a tort case for negligence).

35. Tomar Co. Inc. v. National Union F. Ins. Co. The Adjuster had apparent authority to agree to the amount of loss. Gray v. Merchants Ins. Co.

36. Unton v. Liverpool London & Globe Ins. Co.

37. A reading of the cases suggests that adequate preparation of witnesses to answer questions asked at the trial was overlooked by counsel.

38. The fact situation has great bearing on the matter of the proof of loss. The provision for one is not part of the basic contract for coverage.

39. Fidelity Phenix F. Ins. Co. v. Benedict Coal Corp.; A&S Corp. v. Centennial Ins. Co.

40. A&S Corp. v. Centennial Ins. Co.; Ebert v. Grain Dealers Mut. Ins. Co.; Cf: Victory Cabinet Co. v. Ins. Co. of N.A.

41. Maple Leaf Motor Lodge Inc. v. Allstate Ins. Co.

42. See: Lewis Food Co. v. Fireman's Fund Ins. Co.; See: Studley Box & Lumber Co. v. National F. Ins. Co.; Burdett Oxygen Co. v. Employers S.L. Ins. Co.; Farmers Chemical Assoc. v. Maryland Cas. Co.

43. Eastern Asso. Coal Co. v. Aetna C&S Co.

44. General Ins. Co. v. Pathfinder Petroleum Co.

45. Allowed: Hutchings v. Caledonian Ins. Co.; Gray v. Merchants Ins. Co.
    Denied: Lasker v. Am. Ins. Co.; World F&M Ins. Co. v. Palmer.

46. No evidence was introduced in National F. Ins. Co. v. Hutton. See Withers, *Business Interruption Insurance*, p. 134.

47. Great Northern Oil Co. v. St. Paul F & M Ins. Co. (1975); National Children's Exposition Corp. v. Anchor Ins. Co.; Port Murray Dairy Co. v. Providence

PART TWO

Washington Ins. Co.; Rogers v. American Ins. Co.; Rothenberg v. Liberty Mutual Ins. Co.; Scher v. Hartford F. Ins. Co. (Rent ins.); Finer Amusements Inc. v. Citizens Ins. Co. The court in Howard Stores v. Foremost Ins. Co. stated, "There was no actual *suspension* [italics added] of business operations." Suspension is not the basis for a claim; a reduction in operations due to damage which results in a diminution of the probable Earnings Stream is sufficient. See: Rothenberg v. Liberty Mut. Ins. Co.

48. This is accomplished when settlement figures are finalized.

49. See: Hawkeye Chemical Co. v. St. Paul F&M Ins. Co.; National Union F. Ins. Co. v. Anderson-Pritchard Oil Co.; Chas Dowd Box Co. v. Fireman's Fund Ins. Co.

50. Chas Dowd Box Co. v. Fireman's Fund Ins. Co.

51. Hutchings v. Calidonian Insurance Co.

52. Profits on intercompany sale of products at various stages of completion are frequently calculated at that level. Miner Edgar Co. v. North River Ins. Co.

53. Buffalo Forge Co. v. Mutual Security Co. (supra).

54. General Ins. Co. v. Pathfinder Petroleum Co.

55. Miner Edgar Co. v. North River Ins. Co.

56. National Filtering Oil Co. v. Citizens Ins. Co.

57. N.E. Gas & Elec. Ass'n v. Ocean Ass. & Guar. Corp.

58. A & S Corp. v. Centennial Ins. Co.

59. Hawkinson Tread Tire Service Co. Inc. v. Indiana Lumberman's Mut. Ins. Co..

60. Amusement Syndicate v. Milwaukee Mechanics Ins. Co. (1913); A & S Corp. v. Centennial Ins. Co.; Anchor Toy Co. v. Am. Eagle F. Ins. Co.; DiLeo v. U.S.F.&.G.

61. Steel Products Co. v. Millers Nat'l Ins. Co.

62. Standard Printing & Publishing Corp. v. Bothwell.

63. Buffalo Forge Co. v. Mutual Security Co. (strike ins.) See also: Fleet McGinley Co. v. Bothwell.

64. Miner Edgar Co. v. North River Ins. Co.

65. Nusbaum v. Hartford Fire Ins. Co.

66. Puget Sound Lumber Co. v. Mechanics & Traders Ins. Co.

67. Bardwell *New Profits*, pp. 17-25; Withers, *Business Interruption Insurance*, pp. 107-109; Klein *Business Interruption Insurance*, pp. 286-288. See: Eastern Associated Coal Corp. v. Aetna C. & S. Co. Note #15. See: Standard Printing and Publishing Co. v. Bothwell.

68. Supermarkets Operating Co. v. Arkwright Mut. Ins. Co.

69. American Ins. Co. v. Pickering Lumber Corp.

70. Standard Printing & Publishing Co. v. Bothwell.

71. See: Miner Edgar Co. v. North River Ins. Co.

72. Fidelity Phenix Ins. Co. v. Benedict Coal Corp.

73. National Union F. Ins. Co. v. Scandia of Hialeah Inc.; DiLeo v. U.S.F.&G. Co.; Cf: Royal Indemnity Co. v. Little Joe's Fish Inn, Inc. (involving charge for rent); Hutchings v. Caledonian Ins. Co.; Salary of $1,000 a month never actually paid to president was an abateable expense. A & S Corporation v. Centennial Ins. Co.

74. William F. Foley, Jr., V. P. Johnson & Higgins, at RIMS meeting New Orleans, *Business Insurance*, Vol. XXI, No. 9 (May 1, 1978), p. 37.

75. Hawkinson Tread Tire Service Co. v. Indiana Lumberman's Mutual Ins. Co.

76. Eisenson v. Home Ins. Co.

77. Since amounts paid to unemployed employees results in an increase in the rate of taxation charged against the employer in the future, it would be well for an employer to secure an agreement from the employee not to seek such payments as long as the employee remains on the payroll.

78. American Alliance Ins. Co. v. Keleket X-Ray Corp.

79. American Ins. Co. v. Pickering Lumber Corp.

80. National Union F. Ins. Co. v. Anderson-Pritchard Oil Corp.; Gordon Chemical Co. Inc. v. Aetna C&S Co.

81. Hawkinson Tire Tread Service Co. v. Indiana Lumbermen's Mut. Ins. Co.

82. General Ins. Co. v. Pathfinder Petroleum Co.

83. Standard Printing & Pub. Co. v. Bothwell.

84.   American Alliance Ins. Co. v. Keleket X-Ray Corp.

85.   Hart-Bartlett-Sturtevant Grain Co. v. Aetna Ins. Co.

86.   Goetz v. Hartford F. Ins. Co.

87.   Lykos v. American Home Ins. Co.; Cf: Eisenson v. Home Ins. Co. The false swearing by the Public Adjuster in executing a proof of loss on behalf of the Insured will be attributable to the Insured.

88.   Palace Cafe Co. v. Hartford F. Ins. Co.

89.   The defense must be pleaded. Sam Snead School of Golf v. Anchor Casualty Co. But it can be raised after appraisers' award. Elberson Bathing Co. Inc. v. Ambassador Ins. Co. Inc.

90.   Eisenson v. Home Ins. Co.

91.   Bower & Kaufman v. Barthwell.

92.   Telesky v. Fidelity Guaranty Corp.

93.   Trader v. Indiana Insurance Companies.

94.   Palace Cafe Co. v. Hartford F. Ins. Co.

95.   For defense of Statute of Limitations, see: Hebert Mfg. Co. v. Northern Assurance Co.

96.   See: Becker v. Merchants Mutual Ins. Co.

97.   DiLeo v. United States Fidelity & Guarantee Co.

98.   Anchor Toy Corp. v. Am. Eagle F. Ins. Co.

99.   Nusbaum v. Hartford F. Ins. Co.

100.   Quality Molding Co. v. Am. National F. Ins. Co.

101.   The Insured has opted to deprive himself of the interim use of the funds; so the purposes of equity have been served.

102.   American Ins. Co. v. Parker. See also: National F. Ins. Co. v. Hutton.

103.   Amusement Syndicate Co. v. Prussian Nat. Ins. Co.; Eisenson v. Home Ins. Co.; Omaha Paper Stock Co. Inc. v. Harbor Ins. Co. (1978/1979 cases)

16

Handling of a Loss
Under the BIC Form

Common policy conditions. Commercial property conditions. Appraisal.
In the event of loss. Limitation. Loss determination. Loss payment.
Resumption of operations.

A. Introduction

Section D of the BIC Form is entitled "Loss Conditions." It incorporates by reference such conditions as may appear in the Common Policy Conditions and the Commercial Property Conditions. It then deals with the matter of losses in six sections, namely: Appraisal, Duties in the Event of Loss of Business Income, Limitation—Electronic Media and Records, Loss Determination, Loss Payment and Resumption of Operations.

B. Common Policy Conditions

The Common Policy Conditions include a number of provisions, most of which are similar in kind to those found in earlier forms. One new provision gives the Insurer the right to examine the Insured's records for the period of the policy and for three years after its expiration.

Such a provision would be of possible help in the event of litigation. Whether the discovery of facts in conflict with those advanced in connection with the loss settlement (other possibly than facts showing fraud) would be of avail in reopening a loss is very questionable.

C. Commercial Property Conditions

The Commercial Property Conditions contain provisions which are material parts of the overall contract. Most of them fall into areas that deal with administering the ongoing arrangement with the Insured and fall outside the scope of this volume. Two relevant requirements deal with conditions that must be complied with before suit can be brought. These are:

1. There must have been full compliance with all of the terms of the Coverage Part. This is a repetition of a condition in the BIC Form itself.
2. Suit must be brought within 2 years after date of the damage. This provision, of course, is subject to the provisions of statutory limitations.

D. Appraisal

1. The language appearing in the BIC Form generally follows that in the New York Standard Fire Insurance policy. Either party may ask for an appraisal. Compliance with the request appears to be mandatory: "if requested each party *will* [italics added] select .... an Appraiser." The Insured cannot unilaterally waive the requirement if the amount of loss cannot be agreed upon—an appraisal would under such circumstances be a condition precedent to bringing suit. If the Insured requests an appraisal, the Insurer must participate in one. Of course, the parties could mutually waive the requirement, thereby permitting the Insured to bring suit without an appraisal.

2. Arrangements for paying the costs of the appraisal are set forth. These are similar to the conditions in the previous forms.

3. Participation in an appraisal does not constitute a waiver by the Insurer of the right to deny liability.

E. Duties in the Event of Loss of Business Income

Most of these duties have been discussed in the first part. They are briefly repeated here.

1. There is the duty to notify the police if a law may have been broken. This provision is discussed in Ch. 8.
2. Prompt notice must be given of the direct physical loss (*sic*) or damage. Included must be a description of the property involved.

The BIC Form does not require that the notice be in writing; though the Insured would still be well-advised to confirm any oral notice to his Agent or Broker in writing to a representative of the Insurer. Just how detailed must the description be? A repetition of the language of the "property described" in the policy would probably suffice. It would indicate that the damage was suffered by the property producing the business income.

3. The Insured is required to give the Insurer a description of how, when, and where the damage occurred. This relates to the peril involved and is to provide information showing that the ensuing loss is covered under the terms of

the policy. The description is to be given as soon as possible. Whether the timing thus described is different from "prompt notice" under *2.*, above, is not clear.

4. The Insured must also take steps to protect the property from further damage. The language used is appropriate to a property insurance policy. It does not say damage which "might result in extension of the period of interruption" as does the Gross Earnings form. To the extent that only an increased loss of value to the physical property occurred with no additional loss of business income, it would appear that the requirement is not relevant. However, most Business Income Coverage Insurance would be written in conjunction with a Property Insurance policy; under that policy there would be relevancy and the increased interruption resulting from such failure would not be covered.

The Insured is also required to keep a record of his expenses, for consideration in the settlement of the claim. It is highly improbable that failure to record a particular expenditure would exclude it from consideration in settling the claim.

5. The Insured must permit the Insurer to inspect the property and records proving the *loss* [italics added]. Inspection of the property would prove the damage, not the loss. Past records would not prove the loss, but would be a factor in its calculation. Once again, the need to distinguish between "loss" and "damage" is indicated.

6. The Insured, if requested, is required to answer and sign under oath, questions about the insurance, the claim, and the books and records. The policy reads "permit us to question you." Whether this extends to employees of the Insured is not indicated. It undoubtedly would extend to *corporate* officers and employees where the Insured is a corporation.

7. The Insured must submit a signed, sworn statement of loss on necessary forms supplied by the Insurer within 60 days after it is requested. Is the furnishing of the necessary forms by the Insurer a condition precedent to the obligation of an Insured to submit the statement? If no request is made need a sworn statement be furnished? Apparently yes, unless it is waived—because of the payment of loss provisions making it a condition precedent to recovery.

It is to be noted that the term "proof of loss" is no longer used. This makes sense because the document is only a claim of loss and not final proof of the amount of the loss.

8. The Insured must cooperate with the Insurer in the investigation or settlement of the claim. Presumably the Insured must cooperate in both aspects. If so, the word "and" could well be substituted for "or." A great deal of emphasis has been placed in earlier chapters on the desirability of such an attitude on the part of the Insured. Here it is stated as an obligation of the Insured.

The Insured has the duty of resuming all or part of his "operations" as quickly as possible. The impact of this new obligation has been discussed elsewhere.

F. Limitation—Electronic Media and Records

Electronic media and records are defined as consisting of three kinds of property. First are the items of physical property on which data can be stored. This would fall into the class popularly known as "hardware" or "peripherals," being peripheral to the computer itself. The second is the data stored on this property. The third are the programs which are designed to make use of the stored data. The latter two fall into the class of "software."

Physical damage could affect the objects on which the data is stored, as well as the data which is stored thereon, and also the writing by which the programs are first inscribed. Nothing is said about damage to the computer itself. Such damage would not fall within the limitation of this section.

In spite of the fact that two examples are included in the BIC Form illustrating how this limitation works, it is not easy to understand its effect. In the first place, although it is classed as a *limitation*, it offers a choice between the *longer* of two periods. The first period runs for 60 days from the date of the physical damage; this applies to damaged media and records. The second period apparently begins at the same time and runs for as long as is necessary, using reasonable speed, to replace other property which had been damaged so that the media and other records, which have already been replaced, can now be used.

If this is a correct interpretation of the language describing the second period, it is not easy for the average reader to understand. It is likely that after further consideration the syntax of this sentence will be modified to make it more easy to read and understand.

G. Loss Determination

1. This section sets out the information upon which the calculation of the amount of the loss will be based. It replaces the *prior* and *probable future* experience of the business provision found in the Gross Earnings form. Business Income and Extra Expense are treated separately. The first information required is based on the Net Income of the business before the direct physical damage occurred. It is to be noted that no time limit is attached to "before."

    a. The word "business" is used by itself. This could be misleading. The Accountant's report of a business enterprise could show a profit or loss due to activities other than "operations." An example would be interest earned on investments.

    b. The reminder, found elsewhere, that it is income before income taxes that should be used, is not repeated here.

2. Next is a calculation of the likely net income of the business if no dam-

age had occurred. As mentioned earlier, the use of the word "likely" in place of "probable" does not appear to have changed the thrust of this provision; particularly in determining whether hindsight or foresight is to be used. Presumably this means during the "period of restoration," but it is not so specified.

3. Next to be considered are operating expenses necessary to resume operations.

    a. The earlier definition of Business Income in the BIC Form includes "continuing normal operating expense." Here the requirement of *continuing* is eliminated. Such change in language would extend coverage to include a situation where the Insured did not rebuild. The expenses, though not "continuing," would still be ones necessary to resume operations if operations were to be resumed. The language is broad enough to include such interpretation.

    b. The word "normal" has also been omitted. If operations were in fact restored, would unusual operating expenses necessarily incurred in resuming operations be included here rather than under Extra Expense? This is answered in the negative by the provisions about Extra Expense that follow.

4. Other relevant sources of information will also be included. These include the Insured's "accounting procedures." This would appear to answer the question raised elsewhere in the book as to whether the Insurer is bound by the Insured's method of accounting, including the way of taking depreciation. Apparently it is. No outside sources of information, such as general information in the trade, are mentioned. However, such sources are not excluded, either.

5. Extra Expense.

    a. This is the second item entering into calculation of the amount that the Insured can collect.

    b. It includes expenses that exceed those normal operating expenses that would have been incurred during the period of restoration and which have been discussed earlier. Two deductions will be made from that amount:

        • The salvage value of property bought for temporary use, and no longer needed when operations are resumed.

        • Extra Expense paid for by another and different type of insurance.

    c. It also includes necessary expenses that reduce the Business Income loss that would otherwise have been incurred.

H. Loss Payment

1. Payment will be made in 30 days after sworn statement of loss is received. There can be little doubt that unless the amount of loss has been agreed upon, the Insured could and should request a form as soon as he

believes he will, within the next 60 days, have his figures together. Query, if the Insured does the requesting, does the 60 days limit no longer apply? If no form is forthcoming from the Insurer, the Insured can compose his own form.

What is written elsewhere in this book about filing a *preliminary* proof of loss would still be relevant in connection with the 60 day limit here, but probably would not trigger the running of time for payment of the loss.

2. Payment will be made, provided the Insured has complied with all the terms of the Coverage Part, and an agreement in settlement of the loss has been reached or an appraisal award has been made.

I. Resumption of Operations

This section follows in a general way the wording of the similar section in the Gross Earnings form. It does not place an obligation on the Insured to act but it reduces the recoverable portion of the loss he has actually suffered if part of that loss could have been avoided by taking proper action. This applies both to resuming operations and to ongoing Extra Expense.

It is based upon the extent to which the Insured can use other property to resume operations and to the extent to which he can return operations to normal and make unnecessary any more Extra Expense. The latter provision would apply to replacing at the described premises temporary operations with normal operations as the latter became available.

This section is also discussed elsewhere.

17

Special Types of
Business Interruption Insurance

---

*Rent and Leasehold. Extra Expense. Earnings. Profits.
Strike. New ISO Forms.*

A. Introduction

The special needs for protection against the interruption of the Earnings Stream possessed by certain types of business enterprise, has led to the preparation of special forms of contract. In most respects, such contracts follow the form used for the usual business interruption policies. However, where necessary, changes have been introduced to meet the special needs.

It has been decided not to explore those changes to any extent in this volume. The nature of the changes from the basic Gross Earnings form can be determined by a careful reading of the form.

In the list of cases an attempt has been made to indicate an example(s) of a special form, by using a letter to denote the form. For example, R = Rent Insurance. It should be kept in mind that cases involving special forms deal with issues that are common to all business interruption issues; this results in their appearing throughout the volume as reference to the more general issues.

B. Special Forms

1. Rent Insurance and Leasehold Insurance

This type of policy preceded the policy of Business Interruption Insurance in the United States. The *Leonardo* case was tried in 1842. The flow of earnings is the production of rents by property. Several forms exist, depending on whether the owner or the tenant's interest is being protected. A flow of monthly rentals can be necessary for the protection of the owner's interest in property; the stability of rental expense can be vital to the continuation of a business enterprise. Cases are substantial in number and a representative few are marked with the prefix (R).

2. Extra Expense Insurance

This type of insurance reimburses the owner for the increase in the "pay-out" stream, rather than for any decline in the Earnings Stream. A business which must keep on operating instead of closing, despite the expense entailed, is a candidate for this type of insurance. The letter "X" is prefixed to some cases involving this type of insurance.

3. Earnings Insurance

For smaller businesses or situations where the Owner does not want to get involved with a Coinsurance Clause, this type of insurance has evolved. It is relatively new and few cases have been brought concerning this type of policy. Some of those cited in the index bear the prefix "E".

4. Profits Insurance

The American type covers the potential profit on finished goods that have not yet been sold and delivered. As such, it is insurance on past rather than future production. However, there are American cases and literature which apply this term to what is called Business Interruption Insurance herein. Also in England, the term can refer to this latter type of coverage. The reference prefix is "P."

5. Strike Insurance

A strike is not the type of peril dealt with in policies of Property Insurance, yet strikes can interfere with the normal flow of the Earnings Stream. Problems arise somewhat similar to those that arise under Business Interruption Insurance. Several cases are included in the list of cases, marked with the prefix "S".

6. Other Types

Numerous other types have been developed over the years. Some have been developed through manuscript policies. Most of them have not been the subject of a court decision. No attempt has been made to attach a prefix to them.

7. New ISO Forms

A revision and redrafting of all these forms has been undertaken by ISO.

They are included in the package of new forms filed with the various Insurance Departments. As indicated above, some have been incorporated by reference in the Business Income Coverage Form which has been analyzed.

Addenda

Addendum I

Comments

For the benefit of those readers who find in the matter of Business Interruption Insurance policies fertile soil for raising challenging philosophical problems, there follow a number of comments and hypothetical questions that may challenge their thinking.

293

Comment #1

Two Boston Letters

The conflict in opinion in Boston about Dalton's undertaking is exemplified in the letters of two Boston correspondents of New York insurance publications.

1. *The Chronicle*, Vol. XXV (March 25, 1880), p. 196.

"Boston underwriters are at last in possession of the philosopher's stone and are now engaged in transmitting of "something that glitters" into pure gold.

"It is understood that the stone was picked up by two gentlemen of the Bay State, the one the treasurer of the _____ Manufacturing Company and the other a prominent lawyer; but both being philanthropically disposed, handed over to the underwriters without expectation of fee or reward the following little memorandum, which really amounts to nothing, as anyone can see at a glance, only being required. In fact, it is all done as a matter of Form:

'The _____ Insurance Company, in consideration of _____ dollars, do insure the _____ Manufacturing Company against loss or damage by fire to the amount of $_____ on the use and occupancy of _____ mill buildings _____ situate _____.

'It is a condition of this contract of insurance, that if said buildings or machinery therein, or either of them, or any part thereof shall be destroyed or so damaged by fire occurring during the term or conditions of this policy, that the mill is entirely prevented from producing _____, this company shall be liable at the rate of _____ dollars per day, for each working day of such prevention; and in case the building, or machinery, or any part thereof, are so damaged as to prevent the making of a full day average product of _____ this company is to be liable per day for that proportion of _____ dollars which the product so prevented from being made

295

bears to the average daily yield previous to the fire, which for the purposes of this insurance is agreed to be _____, not exceeding in either case the amount insured. Loss, if any, to be computed from the day of occurrence of any fire to the time when the mill could with ordinary diligence and dispatch be repaired, or rebuilt and machinery replaced therein, and not to be limited to the day of expiration named in this policy.

'Permission is granted to make necessary alterations and repairs; to run machinery extra hours but not later than ten o'clock p.m.; to use kerosene oil for lights, and to have and make other insurance, without notice, until requested.'

"The coffers of our insurance companies are beginning to grow plethoric as these 'blessings in disguise' are showered upon them.

"All insurers, as a rule, you know, are governed entirely by feelings of philanthopy, and it is really pleasant to feel that in case of any overflow of their generosity they can prudently provide a way by which underwriters can keep up the supply.

"It may be called a beneficient provision, whereby the assured secures all the benefits arising from the destruction of his property.

Boston—March 22, 1880."

2. *The Spectator,* Vol. XXIV, No. 5 (May, 1880), p. 187

"Boston—The latest novelty in underwriting in Boston has been profit insurance. The originator of the idea was Edward Atkinson, of the Manufacturers Mutual Ins. Company, a man of wonderful fertility of invention. It occurred to him that the large mills he was insuring were not properly protected, and that this additional could not for the present be taken up by the mutual companies. He therefore suggested to some of the stock insurance companies the desirability of getting up a form of policy which would allow them to pay, in event of fire loss, the profits in the business during the time that the mill machinery was not in operation. The hint was gratefully received—at least it has been followed out in a very large number of instances. For the purposes of a contract the estimated daily income of the manufacturing corporation is fixed at a certain stated amount, and the company insuring this for say $10,000 agrees to pay $33.33 per diem, until the machinery is again put in operation or the sum insured has by repeated payments been exhausted, when the loss is a total one, or a proportionate part of this amount when the loss is a partial one. . . . These mills are owned by large impersonal corporations, and the moral hazard is therefore reduced to a minimum. But, more than this, they are in all cases manufacturing establishments that are under the constant and minute supervision of the inspectors of the mutual insurance companies. These officials do not hesitate to point out and insist upon their removal. How efficacious their supervision is may be judged by the reports of the mutual companies, which show that cotton and woolen mills have been made less hazardous, from an insurance point of view, than churches, or even warehouses. If the same low

average of loss can be kept up, as it has been for eight or ten years past, there is no reason why insurance should not be in every way desirable to stock companies. The trouble will come, if it comes at all, by applying the same system to mills that are owned by private individuals, or to those that the mutual companies will not insure. If this is done, the risk will be greatly increased, and the opportunity for making a scientific estimate of chances will be wholly removed. I have not yet heard of any-one who has made this departure, though, as time goes on, the temptation to do so will grow stronger. Within the past month our Boston underwriters have taken in more than $100,000 in premiums for profit insurance."

3. The volume entitled *The Factory Mutuals 1835-1935*, which is primarily the history of the Manufacturer's Mutual Fire Insurance Company, speaking about Use and Occupancy insurance, states that the only contemporaneous account gives credit for the initial thought to Edward Atkinson and refers to *The Spectator,* Vol. XXIV, No. 5, (May 1880), page 187, for an account of Mr. Atkinson's attitude toward this type of insurance. It indicates that the suggestions were passed along to Henry R. Dalton, a Boston broker and a friend of Mr. Atkinson. Mr. Dalton discussed the question with A.W. Damon.

Clyde M. Kohler, in his book on Business Interruption Insurance, is quoted as saying that the first policy was issued to the Newton Mills, the Webster Mfg. Co., the China Mfg. Co. and the Pembroke Mills. In 1880, F.M. Weld was the Treasurer of the China Mfg. Co. and a director of the Arkwright Mutual Fire Insurance Company, one of the factory mutual insurance companies. He may have been the "Treasurer" referred to in the Boston letter.

Inquiries at the Clerk's office of the Supreme Judicial Court of Massachusetts indicate that neither Henry R. Dalton, A.W. Dawson or Edward Atkinson was a member of the bar in Massachusetts at the time in question.

The identity of the "lawyer" remains a mystery. E.C. Bardwell, in *New Profits—Business Interruption Insurance* writes on page 7, "Credit is given to Henry R. Dalton of Boston and Edward Atkinson, *New England Textile Mill Operator*, for simultaneously but independently developing the per diem form about 1880" (emphasis added).

George Harrington in the Insurance Education Course of U&O Insurance given under the auspices of the Insurance Society of New York, 1934-1935, states: "Edward Atkinson, then a cotton mill operator, is more generally considered as the father of U&O Insurance, but it was not until August, 1895, that he, as President of Boston Manufacturers Mutual Fire Insurance Company, secured approval of his directors to issue a policy." An extended discussion of the reason for the delay is set out in *The Factory Mutuals.*[1]

In the May, 1917, issue of the *Insurance and Commercial Magazine* appears

---

1. Atkinson is credited with being the drafter of the Massachusetts Standard Fire Insurance policy. Edward Atkinson, *The Prevention of Loss by Fire* (Boston: Daurell & Upham, 1900). He died on December 11, 1905.

a report including a letter sent in 1916 by Mr. Damon who was by then president of the Springfield Fire & Marine Insurance Company to Henry R. Dalton, Jr. which reads:

> *"The first Use and Occupancy insurance taken out by your father was for the four mills of B. Rodman Weld's office—Webster Mfg. Co., China Mfg. Co., Pembroke Mills and Newton Mills, rates same as paid annually to Manufacturers' Mutuals (Boston, Arkwright) on the Plant's fire insurance—80¢ and 90¢ per annum. Have a strong impression that these four placings were dated March 3, 1880, but can not verify this date. Our little office [Washington F&M Insurance Company at the corner of State and Exchange Streets, Boston] took in some premiums in the months we were placing this kind of insurance. Mr. Dalton probably talked the form over before having any printed."*

The reporter of the magazine continues, *"After all the risks had terminated without many renewals, Mr. Dalton conceived the idea of writing policies on a 3 year term and secured a number of mills on that basis, but competition soon appeared and things changed in many ways, rates, companies, etc."*

A footnote to the well established belief about the originality of the 1879 policy attributed to Dalton is found in a news report appearing in the April, 1880, issue of the *Insurance Times*, p. 232. After reporting on Dalton's type of insurance and quoting the language of the policy of use and occupancy for $5,000 with a daily value of $16.66. The reporter goes on to say:

> *"This piece of insurance is not altogether new in this country, very similar policies, though not so carefully worded, were in use "down East" (in New England) many years ago; but the companies were afraid of them and they were soon dropped. The following is a specimen form then used, viz:*
> *"To cover in all his factory buildings known as the .... mill, situate .... against the loss arising from the damage and destruction of his buildings or machinery by fire, either or both of which damage or destruction may prevent the manufacture of goods. And the amount insured is to be $21,235 to be reduced $137 for each working day. In the event of any loss or damage of the buildings or machinery by fire, which the daily manufacture is prevented, then the loss under this policy is to be calculated at $137 per day, to ...."*

This article goes on to say: *"The whole system is the same as that long practiced here under the form of rent and lease policies, being simply an insurance of consequential damages to which there can be no reasonable objection under proper limitations."*

This was the form that undoubtedly served as the model on which the 1879 policy was framed; an insurance of productive capacity. The idea of insuring productivity also carried over to the early use and occupancy policies.

Comment # 2

Insurable Interest

Michael v. Prussion National Insurance

One would think that a knowledgeable court would have seen behind the language of the policy—behind the words "use and occupancy"—to the purpose of the parties in entering into that particular contract. The availability to the Insured of the financial reward he would have received if the use to which the described property had been put had continued uninterrupted—that and that alone had a financial interest for the Insured sufficient to motivate him to pay a premium to buy the policy.

To hold, as this court did, that the words "use and occupancy" were ambiguous, that their meaning was not clear to an ordinary person in the position of this Insured—a business firm operating a grain elevator—strains the imagination. To reach out and find a meaning in the kind of property right that it did—the availability of the material property to its owner for whatever purposes he might want to put it to—destroyed the whole validity of the agreement on which parties had had a meeting of minds.

The court apparently was anxious to avoid saying that it was insurance of profits because then this would be a violation of the unconditional ownership provision of the underlying fire policy. One can imagine that the judges believed there was some broad public policy in protecting the price-fixing pooling agreements of the grain elevator operators in western New York. (This was before the anti-trust laws were adopted.) But there would appear to be other routes the court could have taken to accomplish the same result.

First they could have declared, as did the court in the *International Boiler*

Works case that there was no such thing as a right to earn profits that could be the basis of an insurable interest. Then they could have held that the inchoate property right in use-value was based on the availability of the property to produce an Earnings Stream. They would have still been talking about availability—which differs from profits. Or, following the course taken by later courts with respect to the requirement about filing a proof of loss within a specific time, the court could have held that the provision about sole and unconditional ownership was not applicable to insurance of such an inchoate right in property as the right to have the property available for the generation of an Earnings Stream.

Suffice it to say that the *Michael* decision served as a basis for many problems both for the insurance industry and the courts.

In their ruling following the *Shakertown* case, (Rev. Rul. 74-444,) the I.R.S. carried the game of defining use and occupancy one step further. The right to availability of the physical property for such use as the owner might want to make of it, was now a recompense for the right to use the property and, hence, was like rent. The differentiation between rental value and rents was brushed aside. The fact that a lessor has a right to rents but not a right of use and occupation which has been transferred to the lessee was disregarded.

The final result that has been reached is the sound one—that this type of insurance insures the Earnings Stream despite the presence of the words "use and occupancy," but it was a long trail before the effects of the *Michael* decision were overcome.

The case of *Steel Products Co. v. Millers National Ins. Co.* provides a good example of the problems created by the *Michael* decision. In the *Steel Products* case where Gross Earnings Form #4 was involved, the Insured was able to restore his full Earnings Stream some months prior to when the damaged property was restored to use. Once he got operating, the Insured made a profit, so that, by the time of restoration, he had recouped part of his potential maximum loss. The Insured wanted to establish the time over which loss was calculated from the time of damage until the time when the Earnings Stream was restored to normal; thus collecting the shortage of income at its maximum. The Insurer sought to establish calculations as of a later time, when operations were restored. The court accepted the position of the Insurer.

In reaching its decision the court followed the authority of the case of *Nickols v. Ohio Farms Ins. Co.* and of the statement in 4 Appleman, *Insurance Law & Practice* (§2329), to the effect that "a business interruption policy provides *use and occupancy coverage* tied to the insured premises." In the *Nichols* case the policy did contain the words "use and occupancy." Pyramiding on the fact that Appleman says the two terms—use and occupancy and business interruption are interchangeable—the *Steel Products* court read the concept of use and occupancy into a contract where that term and all the vestiges of meaning it may have retained from its definition in the *Michael* case no longer appeared.

The adoption of the Gross Earnings form was in part a recognition that any of the philosophical meaning that may have been attached, rightly or wrongly, to the term "use and occupancy" no longer was to play a part in this kind of insurance. The interest that was insured, without equivocation, was to be the Gross Earnings, i.e., profits that would have been produced by continuing operations plus continuing expenses.

The court continues with the following gobbledy gook, "it is the effect of interruption of such use and occupancy or gross earnings of the business which is insured" and later ". . . the dates on which use and occupancy of the insured premises was restored." Nothing of the kind. The "loss resulting directly from necessary interruption of business," referred to in the first paragraph of the Gross Earnings form, refers to the diminution in the ability of the business operation to produce gross earnings of the type described in paragraph four. Any possibility that it is the availability of the property to be put to any use that the Insured may desire which is insured has been removed.

As discussed elsewhere, the interposition of the words "actual loss sustained by the insured resulting directly from such interruption of business," in an attempt to parallel the actual cash value language of the underlying Fire Insurance policy, does not constitute a method of setting a value, before and after the damage, on the insurable interest insured. They provide a measurement for calculating the loss and derive their applicability from the language which follows about reduction in Gross Earnings.

In the *Steel Products* case, the issue was not that of amount of loss; the parties had agreed to that amount. It involved the question of the period over which the loss was to be calculated. Do the words "*only* [italics added] for such length of time" mean that that is the only way of measuring time or does it mean that that is the maximum time that can be measured? The court decided that the words provided the measure that was to be used, giving no special effect to the insertion of the word "only." The loss was to be measured from the date of the damage until operations were actually restored in those areas where there was a use of due diligence and dispatch. A theoretical time measurement would be used where due diligence was not used or the property was not restored.

Termination of Insurable Interest

Where the Insured sells his business entity following the damage but during the time that the interruption would have continued had he repaired the property, does the sale cut off his right to collect for diminution of the Earnings Stream until repairs would have been completed?

It would appear that two criteria must co-exist positively. First, that the Insured continued to have an insurable interest and second that he had the intention, at the time of the damage, to continue to dedicate his property to the production of an Earnings Stream. If this is correct, then it would make a difference as to when he contracted to transfer ownership. If done before the damage, his right to collect for diminution of the Earnings Stream would terminate at the time the transfer took place. If done after the damage, then it could run further up to the date the replacement or repair could have been effected.

What if a decision to abandon the operation by a certain date had been reached prior to the damage but no actual steps had been taken to carry it into effect by the time of damage? In the *DiLeo* case, the Insurer failed to produce evidence sufficient to prove that the Insured would, in fact, have moved out at expiration of a notice to vacate. Therefore, there was the requisite insurable interest left to support a claim. Absent any better evidence as to when the Insured would have been forced out or when he had intended to leave, thus terminating this thread of interest, the court allowed recovery until the time the property could have been rebuilt.

Comment #3

Valuing Availability for Use & Occupancy

The two *Freundlich* cases threw out a challenge—in the absence of a pre-agreed value, how does one put a value on use and occupation as defined by the *Michael* case and adopted by the *Freundlich* cases. It is a challenge that probably could not be met. In 1913, Leo Levy, a leading insurance lawyer in New York, said that use and occupancy policies would have to be valued.

The log jam was broken by inserting in most policies a provision stating how a loss was to be measured. For those "pure" use and occupancy policies that have continued to be issued, the problem still remains—they must be valued.

There are some interesting theoretical questions that come to mind as one contemplates the calculation of loss figures under a pure use and occupancy policy that was open. Suppose, for example, there was a large plant of which only a small part was damaged, but a part which was crucial to the operation of the entire plant. Under a Gross Earnings policy the loss would be measured until repairs were made. But under the *Michael* decision, would there be a total loss of the right to use the described property for any use the insured may want?

Suppose there is insurance for each of the lessees in a large manufacturing structure. Under Gross Earnings forms, different amounts of loss could be found for each of the tenants. Must the same value be placed on the right to availability for desired use for all of the tenants?

Reaching far out, the following question might be posed: Does the exclusion in the standard fire policy for "loss resulting from interruption of business or manufacturer" apply with equal force to the loss of the right to have the property available for any use that the insured may want to put it to? Or was this right actually covered under the Fire Insurance policy?

Comment #4

Civil Authority Clause:
Must The Described Property Be Damaged?

In 1957, Hurricane Dianne destroyed the water mains in the City of Scranton, Pennsylvania, creating the danger of a conflagration should a fire break out. The Mayor declared a state of emergency and ordered all stores closed. In the case of *Cleland Simpson v. Firemens Ins. Co.*, the Insured, who held a fire policy with a business interruption rider sought payment for loss of gross earnings during the time his store was thusly closed. The Supreme Court of Pennsylvania upheld the decision of a lower court that the loss of earnings, resulting from an apprehension of fire when no property had been damaged by fire, was not covered.

Despite the semantic argument of Justice Musmanno in his dissenting opinion, one can follow the argument of the court. What is unfortunate is that the author of the headnote, when the opinion was published, did not understand the issue involved. As a result he included the following inaccurate statement in the headnote: "The policy restricts the loss to that following a direct invasion of the *property* by fire ... and the subsequent prohibition by civil authority of access to the *property*." The second referral to "property" is accurate. The first is the product of the writer's imagination. The court said no such thing. This illustrates the pitfalls to the unwary lawyer who relies upon headnotes in conducting legal research.

In 1970, the District of Columbia Court of Appeals, in the case of *Bros. Inc. v. Liberty Mutual F. Ins. Co.* dealt with a curfew on the sale of alcoholic beverages imposed during the civil disorders of 1968 which followed the assassination of Martin Luther King, Jr. The Insured held a policy of Fire Insurance with extended coverage and a Gross Earnings Form #3. There was no physical damage to the Insured's premises nor to any adjacent building. The trial court found no liability.

On appeal, the court stated that the Insured did not allege physical damage to his property, nor did the curfew prohibit access to the premises "because of damage to or destruction of *adjacent property*" (italics added). The summary judgment of the lower court was confirmed.[1]

In a similar case, *Two Caesars Corp. v. Jefferson Ins. Co.*, counsel for the Insured pointed out that in their policy the limitation to "adjacent property" did not appear, so that the *Bros. Inc.* case was not controlling. In its opinion, the court missed completely the thrust of the Insured's argument. It states, "we are unable to follow appellant's reasoning." The court then quotes the above language of the *Bros. Inc.* case and then goes on to state that "no such consideration (about no adjacent property being damaged) could have influenced the court in its decision." This misreading of its own earlier decision is then followed by this statement: "The inescapable fact is, however, that by the clear provisions of this policy, the loss is compensable only when the Order of Civil Authority, which prohibits access, is predicated upon damage to or destruction of the business property." Citing as authority the *Cleland Simpson* case from whose erroneous headnote the language was lifted. It also cites as authority for its statement the case of *Bros. Inc.*

The culmination of this distortion can be found in *Adelman Laundry & Cleaners Inc. v. Factory Insurance Association* handed down by the Wisconsin Supreme Court in 1973. Here the former language (not mentioning "adjacent property") appeared in the policy. The case arose out of a curfew in Milwaukee due also to riots following King's assassination.

Citing the *Two Caesar's* case as construing the policy provisions to make loss compensable only when the Order of Civil Authority which prohibits access to the premises is predicated upon damage to or destruction of business property, this court takes the next step and concludes in effect that the words "the property" means the described property. In other words, there must be damage to the property described in the policy. Then, as if not realizing what they had done, the court concludes, "We agree with the District of Columbia Court of Appeals in the *Two Caesar's* case."

One could write at length of the fallacy of this ultimate conclusion, but the facts speak for themselves.

There has been a revolt against the fallacious thinking involved in the above line of cases. In *Sloan v. Phoenix of Hartford Ins. Co.*, the Court says flatly that it does not agree with the conclusion reached in the *Two Caesar's* case. In that case the court said, in part: "paragraphs one and two (of the

---

1. It should be noted that the revised form of the Civil Authority clause existed here—the one adding the word "adjacent."

Gross Earnings form) refer to coverage for business losses caused by physical damage, while paragraph seven (the Civil Authority Clause) covers business interruption losses caused by denial of access to the property. A similar conclusion was reached by the same court in *Southland Bowls, Inc. v. Lumbermen's Mutual Insurance Co.*

This latter line of reasoning will undoubtedly be adopted in interpreting the BIC Form in which the coverage afforded under the Civil Authority Clause is listed as an additional coverage. The word "adjacent" does not appear in this form.

Comment #5

Use of Other Property

The term "property" in the Business Interruption Insurance–Gross Earnings form is used in two different connotations. One is its use in connection with the property *described*. The second is its reference to *other* property that the resumption of operations provisions requires be *used* in case of damage to the described property.[1]

Do the two uses refer to the same physical objects?

There are several bases on which to seek an answer. The *described* property is used in connection with operations at described premises. The property to be *used* is not so limited.

The first refers to property in which the Insured must have an insurable interest at the time of damage. No such limitation applies to the other because of the reference to "property of the Insured or others." (The wording in the BIC Form is "at the described premises or elsewhere." For discussion, see Ch. 8.)

If the conclusion is reached that the property to be used extends beyond the limits of the property described, how far outside is the Insured required to reach? The form establishes no limit.

It is necessary to turn to the intention of the parties to answer the question. After weighing arguments pro and con, the best conclusion is that the basic test should be applied: What would the Insured have done if he had had no insur-

---

1. Both of these are to be distinguished from the use of the word Property in this book as one of the six P's.

309

ance.[1] This opens up the decision to matters of judgment, of policy, of good will, of competition. All of these considerations would be in an Insured's mind in making a decision.

The courts seem to follow the same rule. The *Gordon Chemical* case is one in point. There the court said in part: "The purpose of the policy is to preserve the continuity of the insured's earnings. The policy does not accomplish that purpose if the insured manufacturer is required to act as a distributor of its competitors in order to reduce its business interruption loss."

One negative aspect of this provision is that an Adjuster may make demands on the Insured specifying other property he wants used and thus place the burden on the Insured to prove that its use would not have helped or would have caused other negative results. It would seem that only such steps taken as will reduce the loss will be considered compensible.

---

1. K.W. Withers *Business Interruption Insurance* (Berkeley: Howell-North Press, 1957), p. 19, deals with the question as follows: "The Insured is called upon to do what he normally would do to protect the net profits of the business . . . ." If "normally" means when he has no insurance, there is no argument. Withers also says "any expedient that could be used to reduce loss without *undue* or *unilateral* risk should be employed." The exact meaning of the italicized words is not clear.

Comment #6

Loss

A close examination of the way the word "loss" is used in the underlying Standard Fire Insurance policy clearly indicates that it is used in two different ways. It is used first to denote the happening of an *event* which causes economic harm to the Insured. This can be deduced from such phrases as "time of loss," "whether before or after a loss," "preserve the property at or after a loss," "for loss occurring while" and "within two years from the time the loss occurred." In each of these examples, the word "fire" could be substituted for "loss."

But, in the same policy, "loss" is used to denote the *amount* of economic harm that is caused. This second meaning can be deduced from such phrases as "a greater proportion of any loss," "time when the loss shall become payable," "to recover for such loss," and "the amount of the loss." In these examples an amount of money could be substituted, but not the word "fire." There is even one instance where both meanings appear in a single clause, to-wit, "In case of loss under this policy and a failure of the parties to agree as to the amount of loss . . . ."

In the Fire Insurance policy provisions regarding proof of loss, there appears the phrase "for loss or damage." What is the meaning of "loss" in this phrase? What is the effect of linking the two words together? Ordinarily such usage indicates that the two words connote the same thing. Such an interpretation makes sense in the Fire Insurance policy and would limit "loss" to the event—to the physical happening. The proof of loss must be filed within a certain number of days after the occurrence of the fire.

Turning to the Business Interruption Insurance rider, it is clear that the same double usage permeates. While in most instances, the word is used to denote the amount, there still are examples of where it denotes an event, as in "immediately preceding the loss" and "experience thereafter had no loss occurred." As discussed in the text, such a usage can only create misunderstanding.

The chapter on the BIC Form notes the continuation of this usage in that form. For example, in the first paragraph entitled Coverage, the word "loss" is used to mean both diminution of financial income and physical damage to the property and also a third, blurred use, in the phrase Cause of Loss, as a reference to the *peril* which causes the damage, from which damage the suspension of operations flows, which is the cause of the financial loss. And finally, in the first subparagraph thereunder, "loss" is used to describe the result of the application of accounting principles to the result of the entire business enterprise, extending beyond operations.

There is no doubt that the double usage of this word will continue. The point is that the practicioner must keep the distinction in mind when dealing with actual situations.

Comment #7

Cancellation and Loss of Contracts

The Gross Earnings form, in effect, excludes any increase in loss that results from a cancellation of any contract unless it results directly from the interruption and then only for the period of the interruption. Three types of situation could be involved.

One is where, because of the damage and resultant stoppage of work under a contract now in production, the Insured will not be able to complete performance within the time specified and his customer cancels the entire contract in keeping with contract provisions and refuses to take tardy delivery and pay for any of the product. Under this situation, the Insured suffers a loss of the entire cost of the raw materials and labor (even undamaged goods) plus the loss of his prospective profit, less any salvage amount he might recover.

Would it make any difference whether the notice of cancellation from the customer were received during the period of interruption or at a later date, after production had been renewed? In particular, what about the loss that resulted in connection with the specialized raw materials that the Insured had taken in for this contract and now had no use for; the materials would lose much of their value at the moment of cancellation, which might not occur during the period of interruption?

Two is where the customer, believing that the Insured will not be able, within the time schedule, to complete an order which is not yet in production, cancels the order and transfers his business elsewhere. This would appear to be the type of situation specifically dealt with in the policy and recovery would be limited to the Earnings Stream that would have resulted during the period of interruption.

313

Three is where the customer does not place his usual order with the Insured because he believes the Insured will not be able to produce during the necessary time frame. This is really the loss of a business opportunity. In the much cited case of *Rogers v. American Insurance Company*, involving a bowling alley whose league customers did not believe the damage to the bowling alley would be repaired in time for the opening of the bowling season, and who, contrary to their expressed plans, did not sign seasonal contracts but took their business elsewhere, the court did not allow recovery of anticipated profits that would have been earned after the restoration of operations date. The language of the exclusion was unambiguous, said the court.

Some try to explain the broadness of the *Rogers* decision on the basis that the future income from the league business was still speculative at the time the business opportunity was lost. Others emphasize the fact that all bowlers, even those on the league teams, pay on a nightly basis for the use of the lanes. There is no season's contract. But the language of the court makes it apparent that it was merely construing the terms of the policy conservatively. Even though the facts might be construed as a cancellation or a lapse of the contract, recovery for loss from such cause was limited under the terms of the policy. And this is not an unreasonable interpretation since tuition coverage and similar policies have long been available to insure just these type exposures.

A somewhat similar fact situation is encountered in the case of a warehouse which lost its normal seasonal business because it was not in condition to receive apples for storage when the crop became ripe. In that case, however, the loss of income claimed was not the loss of storage fees, but the loss of the profit that the Insured would have enjoyed if he were holding apples in storage when the high price season arrived. This was a speculative loss, not a rental loss. The investor could have hired other premises to store apples.[1]

In such cases of lost business opportunity, the question is always present—for how long into the future would the Insured be able to claim a diminution in his Earnings Stream? Suppose the leagues liked their new arrangement and never returned. A common sense approach must be taken. Undoubtedly, any loss of business beyond the present season should be attributed to insufficient business ability or loss of good will rather than as a consequence of the damage.

Note that the form excludes any *increase* of loss. Such an increase would not begin until the time the property would otherwise be ready to resume operations. Thus, if a contract which would have continued operations for nine months is cancelled because there will be a delay of three months to repair the fire damage, the insured can collect for the loss suffered by the cancellation for the first three months, but not for the last six months. This cost income would be a part of the normal gross earnings loss calculation.

---

1. See: George W. Clark "Problem Claims under Business Interruption Policies," address delivered at American Bar Ass'n Convention, New York on July 9, 1957.

Comment #8

Friendly Fire

An interesting problem that sometime presents itself in fire insurance cases involves a "friendly fire," i.e., a fire which burns only in the area where it is intended to burn but causes damage to insured property. This can be either property left in the vicinity of the fire or property outside of the fire zone which is affected by the heat or smoke from the combustion. By well established law, the Insurer is not liable for such damage, although it is generally accepted that a fire ceases to be "friendly" when it exceeds its intended heat even though it remains within its intended confines.

Thus the fire in a stove is not "hostile" to the pearl necklace voluntarily hidden in the fire pit of the stove for safekeeping. Neither is damage caused by smoke emanating from a fireplace when no flames escaped.

The theory behind this legal position is that the parties intend to cover only the peril of "hostile" fires. Apart from the justification for this theory or possible changes in it, the question arises whether the same requirement of hostility should be applied to Business Interruption Insurance losses?

At first glance, the answer is "why not." The Business Interruption Insurance form tracks with the Fire Insurance policy. It is possible to argue, however, that in the case of Fire Insurance, the parties are dealing with damage to the materiality of the described property. The fire has to be hostile toward that materiality.

In the case of Business Interruption Insurance, however, the parties are not dealing with materiality of property but with an intangible—the Earnings Stream resulting from the use of the property. A fire—whether hostile or friendly—doesn't directly affect the Earnings Stream. This approach gives rise

315

to an argument that loss resulting from damage caused by even a friendly fire might well be compensable under a Business Interruption Insurance policy.

Comment #9

Foresight vs. Hindsight

An unresolved difference of opinion among many practitioners including the authors of this book, as to the point in time from which a decision as to the amount of loss sustained is to be made, presents an opportunity for the reader to reach an independent opinion. Specifically, the issue is—in determining what is the amount of loss, should *foresight* be applied to the facts available at the time of damage or should *hindsight* be applied to the facts available at some later point in time. To phrase the issue even more concretely—does the Insured base his claim on the facts about the probable future of the business as he knew them or should have known them when the damage occurred or must the Insured take into consideration, in preparing his claim, those events which have occurred subsequent to that time and up to the time of settlement of the loss amount. In the first instance the Insured would be relying on "foresight," in the latter instance on "hindsight."

The issue can be considered moot where, as happens in most cases, the interruption has come to an end and operations have been restored by the time the Insured is ready to put his loss figures together. While differences frequently arise as to how the facts are to be interpreted, there is minimal likelihood of a dispute as to what are the facts. As a practical matter, one would expect both parties to take into consideration what has actually transpired. That is not to say that the issue becomes irrelevant. It merely recognizes the practical difficulty of arguing about what probably would have happened when the parties know what actually did happen.

There can be situations where the occurrence of totally unanticipated events played a role in what took place during the period of interruption. The outbreak of war would be an extreme example of such an event. The theoretical issue could make a great difference in such a situation. The probable future experience as foreseen at the time of the damage would not take the impact of this event into consideration, while looking backward at events from the viewpoint of the moment of renewed production, it would be necessary to take the impact of the war into consideration. Many less dramatic events than the outbreak of armed hostilities can be advanced as examples of the problem.

The difference in approach acquires an even more critical status when the matter of settlement is being discussed prior to the restoration of operations. And in those cases where the Insured decides not to restore, rebuild or replace the damaged property, the difficulty is compounded. The speculative element is increased.

The problem relates to the time at which the risk of unknown loss is transferred by the Insured to the Insurer by the terms of the policy of Business Interruption Insurance. That policy provides for such transfer when a stated peril causes damage, which damage causes an interruption of business, which interruption causes a diminution of the Earnings Stream that continues during the period of interruption, and which diminution causes loss to the Insured.

Under the policy, have the parties contracted to transfer the risk of loss on the basis of the facts that are known or should be known at the time of damage or only on the basis of the facts that are known when operations recommence? If the parties settle before operations recommence, would they first have to agree which events that have occurred since the time of damage should be taken into consideration? (Such agreement does not necessarily have to be on the basis of what the contract originally contemplated.)

The proponents of hindsight set up custom as the first support for their position. For many years, adjusters have been adjusting losses on the basis of all of the facts known at the time of settlement. The "foresighters" answer that, unless it can be shown that the Insured knew of the custom and acceded to it, he cannot be bound by it. There must be a meeting of the minds.

Hindsighters argue that it is a basic principle of insurance that the policy is designed to do for the Insured what his business would have done had there been no interruption. The earnings could have been affected by weather conditions that prevailed during the period of interruption, by changes in the Insured's industry and by general financial and economic conditions that existed during that period. These have an impact on what the business operation would have done and, therefore, play a role in what the policy will do in compensating the Insured for the loss that he suffered.

The response to this argument is that it does not meet the issue. All the subsequent events might have affected the earnings, but again they might not have done so. The Insured's factory could have produced and sold an increasing number of gloves even though competitor's volume shrank, or the proposed advertising campaign could have overcome the unfavorable weather conditions.

In other words, it is the Insured's earnings based on his own plans and capacities that would have determined what his business would have done. Even hindsight involves speculation based on assumptions. But hindsighters argue that one cannot ignore historical certainty, i.e., what is known to have occurred and that while some degree of conjecture is involved in both approaches, the use of hindsight reduces such conjecture to a minimum.

The proponents of hindsight place heavy reliance on the presence of the words "Actual Loss Sustained" appearing in the Business Interruption Insurance policy form. There can be no doubt that these words, somewhat parallel to the words "actual cash value" in the underlying fire policy, at the least suggest that the coverage is intended to embrace reality as much as possible, and eschew, where unnecessary, fanciful considerations. Only hindsight makes this possible.

Over the years, a majority of the courts have adopted this practical approach, even though a close reading of some of the cases suggests that this conclusion may not have been necessary. For example in the case of *General Ins. Co. of America v. Pathfinder Petroleum Co.*, it may well have been that the court's opinion that what the president of the Insured company "felt" did not make sense in light of what was happening in the industry. What happened later was used to test the validity of the foresight used by the Insured. Put another way, hindsight can be used to test the credibility of preferred foresight.

Over the years, the adjusting fraternity, faced with the task of placing the marks on the yardstick used in loss measurement, have done yeoman's work in trying to make the Business Interruption Insurance policy operate constructively. The courts have added their thinking to the process. They have taken the position that the Insured must prove that his loss was real. To meet this test some courts have held that the only time when an Insured can meet this criteria is when he is back in production and can apply hindsight. When confronted with the situation where the Insured does not rebuild, the answer is given, "Oh, that is different. In that case we will use a theoretical test."

Foresighters argue that such a standard for determining the contractual rights of the parties, especially where the contract has no provision for such duality of techniques, is open to question. They say that no one can say just what would have happened had future operations not been interrupted when they were. One's imagination can run riot with imaginings. Machinery could have broken down, a strike might have been called, the foreman might have been killed, a later occurrence might have caused the same kind of damage, etc., etc. Countless events could have affected the process of production, none of which will ever be known, because such production was never carried on. There is no *actual* experience. There is no experience which is "real, which exists in reality."

The word "actual" both as defined in the dictionary and as used in common speech represents the antithesis of the hypothetical or potential. And yet the entire process of establishing the amount of loss in the case of business interruption is speculative and hypothetical. The fact that damage has been sustained may be real and actual, but that the amount of the loss can be expressed in an actual, provable amount is almost never possible. There are too many places where subjective and not objective criteria have to be applied to reach such a result, even when the best of expert testimony is available to aid in the task. (As noted elsewhere, even normal accounting practice, is not necessarily followed.) To require the yardstick of reality, of actuality, to be applied to something that never was actual or real is, according to foresighters, to frame a contract based upon an impossibility.

Moreover, they assert that the policy provisions for limiting the amount of loss to what the Insured would have lost during the completely speculative period involved when applying the test of due diligence and dispatch, effectively eliminates any claim that recovery is based on what actually happened.

As is pointed out earlier, this problem was recognized as early as 1918 when the use of the words "Actual Loss Sustained" were first proposed. It is apparent that even before the final adoption of the term "Actual Loss Sustained," the practical application of the phrase was the subject of serious doubt. Those doubts have not been dissipated with time. Nevertheless, hindsighters, acknowledging that a business interruption loss must be based on some degree of conjecture take the position that hindsight reduces that to a minimum.

A second line of attack by the foresighters denies the position that the basic theory of indemnity requires that the Insured should be made whole for his actual loss, no more, no less. It is an established rule of law, they argue, that the parties to an insurance contract can set any rule for measurement of loss that appears appropriate to them. As stated in *Northwestern States Portland Cement Co. v. Hartford Fire Ins. Co.*, "the parties are free to write their own contract and are bound by its terms, whether they make the Insured more or less than whole."

The many cases where an Insured was paid for the time required to build a modernized form of building and those cases where no allowance was made for additional loss resulting from the application of local ordinances or regulations are other examples of where the concept of actual indemnity is more honored in its breach than in its observance.

The valued form of insurance policy is another example of an arbitrary determination in advance of how the unit of time or production will be valued. Except where forbidden by statute, the validity of such a *non-actual* measure is legal. As stated in *Unton vs. Liverpool, London and Globe Ins. Co.*, "a valued policy, or a policy which is analogous thereto, insofar as it prescribes a method for determining the amount of the loss covered, is unobjectionable and binding between the parties." Hindsighters counter that while devices such as replacement cost coverage and agreed value policies are exceptions to the principle of indemnity which underlies all insurance, there are sound public policy reasons for these limited departures from the principle which are inapplicable to business interruption insurance in general.

The foresighters further argue that the policy at no time indicates that hindsight is required, except as it is implied in the completely separate provision for recovery of the amount of extra expense. To determine that amount, one probably has to wait until it is possible to determine to what extent the extra expense reduced the ultimate loss. It can be claimed that such determination can properly be made only after operations are restored. From this approach the otherwise highly questionable decision the court in the case of *Charles Dowd Box Co. Inc. v. Fireman's Fund Ins. Co.* makes some sense. The interest sought to be recovered in that case was interest on the amount of extra expense.

The case of *Hutchings v. Caledonian Ins. Co.* provides another example of how a decision which apparently supports the hindsight approach does not necessarily do so. In that case the Insured had been in operation for only 12 1/2 days and presented to the court a rosy picture of the future growth of the enterprise. There was evidence that at the time of the fire the Insured was "having considerable trouble in making a go of the warehouse." How acceptable were his projections based on foresight?

Under such circumstances, other factors could be reasonably introduced to test the "rosy" claims of the Insured. This would explain why the court stated "the court attaches great importance to the experience of the other tobacco markets in South Carolina." In its words, "we know of no better guide in helping us ascertain the probable experience of the (insured). . . ." This action could well be taken to measure the validity of the Insured's claims based on foresight, without indicating that foresight was not the ultimate basis for the projection. But the fact remains, hindsight was used; whether for itself or to measure credibility. The effect is the same.[1]

Still another line of attack advanced by the foresighters is based on the principal that the intention of the parties must be taken into consideration. As stated in *Bowen & Kaufman v. Bothwell*: "The parties to an insurance contract are entitled to fix their rights thereunder; intention is controlling." The hindsight approach, it is argued, runs directly against the purpose of this kind of insurance. The policy is advertised, bought and sold on the basis that it would do for the Insured what his business would have done had no damage occurred. Certainly a flow of income from the policy, to replace the flow of income from operations, is what the Insured intended and what the Insurer held out as an inducement to buy the insurance. Obliging the Insured to wait for a determination of the amount of his loss until operations are restored does not conform to such an intention.

---

1. See also *Stuyvesant Oil Co. v. Jacksonville Oil Mill* and *State Import and Export Corp. v. Hartford Fire Ins. Co.* for similar situations.

However, hindsight is based upon practicality and real world considerations. In the real world, this contemplated problem is resolved by means of advance payments. While such are arguably not required by the policy, in this time of "bad faith" and extra contractual damage awards, an Insurer which refuses to advance funds runs a terrible risk indeed.

Where operations were never restored, the courts are faced with a problem. In the *DiLeo* case, for example, the court was obliged to adopt the position that the actual loss sustained provision is *obviously* meant to apply only when there is an actual resumption of the Insured's operations. "The measure of loss is based on either of two criteria" said the opinion, "(a) loss of gross earnings for a limited period *as estimated* when there is no resumption of business or (b) actual loss, inferring an *actual* resumption of business." However, while conjecture is more involved where an Insured does not rebuild, hindsight, i.e., taking what actually happens relative to external events into consideration, is still implicit in the adjustment process.

An example of the problem is found in the operation of the Coinsurance Clause. Is the determination of what are the gross earnings that would have been earned during the 12 months immediately following the date of damage to be determined by foresight, based on the facts that are known at the date of the damage, or must they wait for the twelve months to pass so that the parties may have the benefit of hindsight before deciding whether and to what extent the Insured is a co-insurer? Obviously foresight must be used.

The policy provision requiring a proof of loss to be filed within a fixed period of time following damage, even though that date may arrive long before operations are restored, argues for the use of foresight. Hindsighters say that, in practice, a claim form may be filed earlier but that a "proof of loss" cannot be filed until the amount is agreed upon.

As mentioned earlier, the provision for the payment of extra expenses is a separate contractual arrangement incorporated into the Business Interruption Insurance contract. In that separate contract, hindsight must be used under its terms. However, this usage is not *per se* extended to the entire contract and does not provide an absolute answer.

Perhaps the argument is a function of the terms "hindsight" and "foresight." The real question is whether a loss is to be measured wholly on conjecture or rather, upon conjecture where necessary and real facts where known. The truth is that history is hardly ever ignored whether directly considered or just used as a test of credibility. Thus, while "foresight," under the terms of the written policy of insurance, is academically and philisophically justifiable, as a practical matter hindsight will be used so that, in truth, it is a combination of the two approaches which prevails.

The language of the BIC Form shifts the weight of the argument a little more in favor of hindsight, but not enough to cause a change of opinion. See discussion in Ch. 8.

Comment # 10

Continuing Expenses and Charges.

A problem often arises concerning the amount an Insured can recover if he decides not to restore operations. The policy form is drafted on the assumption that operations are restored. In such a case, the policy states that the Insurer shall be liable for the Actual Loss Sustained. How this is to be determined is not stated. A ceiling is imposed—the reduction in gross earnings (as later defined) that the Insured would have enjoyed, adjusted by subtracting any charges and expenses which do not necessarily continue during the period of interruption and still permit the Insured to start up operations "with the same quality of service which existed immediately preceding the loss."

The application of this provision is fairly straightforward when the Insured does restore operations. But a question arises when, for one reason or another, operations are not restored. Can the Insured still recover for any expenses and charges he would have incurred if he had restored operations and while he was so doing?

The policy form inferentially requires that the Insurer pay for expenses *necessarily* incurred but not necessarily for expenses *actually* incurred. Assuming that the expenses and charges would have necessarily been incurred had the Insured restored operations and assuming further that the Insured did not actually incur such expenses and charges because he decided not to restore operations, would compensation for such unincurred expenses and charges violate the theory of indemnity? And if it did, was provision for such violation built into the contract by agreement of the parties?

The courts are divided in the way they deal with the issue. Since the policy form has changed in language over the years, each decision must be viewed in the light of the contract involved. Applying to all contracts is the basic concept that it was drafted by the Insurer and, if deemed ambiguous, will be interpreted most favorably on behalf of the Insured.

With respect to the Gross Earnings forms currently in use, the general comments set forth elsewhere about the effect of the phrase "Actual Loss Sustained" has direct application. In view of the opinion that it does not describe an actual, ascertainable amount of dollars, it can represent indemnity only in an approximate way. Thus there is room for interpretation. Interpreting the contract most favorably to the Insured, recovery can be had for expenses and charges that the Insured, who decides not to restore operations, would have reasonably incurred had he, in the alternative, decided that he would restore operations and had done so. For discussion of impact of wording changes in BIC Form see Ch. 8.

However, such an Insured does not present an attractive case for such unincurred expenses. Accordingly, arguments against such a recovery based upon the general concepts of indemnity and windfalls should prevail.

Comment #11

Consequential Loss?

It is necessary to consider the difference between consequential loss and consequential damage. Where the policy speaks of direct loss, it is referring to direct damage—a chain of physical events that is unbroken by the intervention of an independent other cause nor is stretched beyond the intention or forseeability of the parties when they entered into the insurance contract.

An example of the difference between consequential damage and consequential loss would be that of an automobile sales agency which sold a mix of Cadillacs, Buicks and Chevrolets. If an insured peril prevented delivery of any Cadillacs, on which a larger per unit profit was earned, the sales mix would change and profits would be less. Such a loss of profits is a consequential loss.

All insurance loss is consequential in one respect—it develops as a consequence of damage to property that is insured by a peril insured against. As was pointed out in the early chapters, the rulings of the English judges that loss of income from property was not a loss within the coverage of a Fire Insurance policy was not because there was an intervening cause. Rather, these decisions were based upon the conclusion that the parties did not have loss of income in mind when they entered into the contract of Fire Insurance.[1] As mentioned by the judges, it was possible to buy insurance coverage on profits at the time. This decision, once reached, became the mold which later courts used to form their opinions.

But to make doubly sure there was no room for doubt, there was written into the Standard Fire Insurance policy, when it was drafted, a specific state-

---

1. Identical policies were being written on income producing and non-income-producing property.

ment that excluded compensation for loss resulting from interruption of business or manufacture. Such a loss was called a "consequential" loss. In other words, not only did it follow from the materiality loss (sequential) but its existence depended on that loss (consequential). This raises an interesting question. Does the use-value of property depend from the materiality-value or is it co-existant and coincident with it? If you can have damage to the use-value without damage to the materiality-value then the answer would be clear. It is not dependent.

Then what about a loss under the Civil Authority Clause? There, the diminution in the use-value is not derivative of or a secondary characteristic of any diminution in the materiality-value of the Insured's property. They are both parallel in existence. So, too, when the physical property *is* damaged, the reduction in both the materiality and use values is simultaneous. The impairment of use-value does not flow from the impairment of materiality-value and is not dependent on it.

However, the term "consequential" is well ingrained in usage, and except as a pedantic exercise, there is no chance of changing it.

The English text-book, Welford & Otter Barry gives as the main types of fire consequential loss:

1. Anticipated profit—parallel to the gross earnings of the Business Interruption Insurance form.
2. Continuing expenses—expenses that continue whether the business is operating or not and are normally set-off by earnings made.
3. Increased expense—extra costs of production made necessary by the damage.
4. Depreciation—this could be of other assets that could not be used and which depreciated in condition while waiting for repairs, or could be just a continuing expense under the way the books were set up.
5. Liability to third persons—a drain of assets due to the existing rules of law—not of production.

Comment # 12

Resumption of Operations:
Use of Inventory to Continue Sales.

It is well established that, if inventory on hand when operations are interrupted is used to maintain sales, the Insured is entitled to recover any additional cost that is incurred in replacing the inventory once operations are resumed. (For possible impact of wording of BIC Form, See Ch. 8.) Several questions come to mind concerning the proposition.

First, on what theory is this liability imposed? Bardwell takes the position that the use of the inventory in such circumstances does not reduce or prevent the loss—it merely postpones it. He rests the liability on the theory that the additional cost of restoring the inventory represents extra expense to reduce loss.

Normally, measures to effect such reduction of loss take place during the period of interruption. As such, they fit into the policy provision that the time of loss continues *until* production is restored. But in the case of a manufacturing plant, the restoration of inventory can commence only *after* production is restored.

To meet the provisions of the policy it would be necessary to say that the period of loss remains open until the inventory is replaced. This can be accomplished by the argument that the operations have to be restored to the same quality as before the interruption and that means with the same level of inventory.

If this is a correct answer, the next question arises—how much time does the Insured have within which to refill the inventory? The first answer would be with the use of due diligence and dispatch or, in other words, within a reasonable time. But the frame of mind that constitutes reasonableness when bringing interruption to an end may be quite different from reasonableness which exists after operations are renewed.

How much of a deadline is imposed on the Insured? Suppose, he decides that other use of the equipment or manpower is more important to the business venture than using such to restore inventory; that, even if he had had no insurance, his first steps after restoration of operations would not have been the replenishment of his depleted inventory. So the Insured resumes operations but most of his productive capacity is devoted to producing goods for the new season which is about to open. He stretches out the build up of his old inventory. If the loss period remains open until the cost of replenishing the inventory can be determined by actual cost figures, quite a time might elapse before the inventory is replaced, with all kinds of potential impact on the amount of loss he can collect under his policy. Suppose further that the Insured never really needed the amount of goods he had in inventory in the first place and does not replace all the inventory reduction. Or, as a worse case, the Insured decides to change the character of the products he produces and never reproduces any one of the items sold out of inventory.

It would seem that the Insured's need to have an inventory of a certain size and type should be a condition precedent to any recovery of extra cost of providing such goods. Next, a time which represents due diligence should be fixed by the same process as operated when the damage first occurred. Losses in gross earnings during the extended period, other than those involved in replenishing the inventory should be excluded from the loss.

Under the terms of the BIC Form[1], the Insurer agrees to pay "for necessary expenses incurred during the 'period of restoration' ..... for Extra Expense to replace any property ... to the extent it reduces the amount of loss ...." Does this wording eliminate any claim for extra cost for replacement of inventory effected *after* operations have been restored? A strict reading of the language would so indicate. However, it may be argued that the extra expense to replace inventory was "incurred" when the inventory was used up.[2] Further, this wording is obviously directed towards productive property as opposed to inventory.

Perhaps, the wisest course is to estimate the extra costs and incorporate them into the settlement figures, whether or not the inventory is ever replaced. Such a basis for settlement might create problems for the tax people particularly if the replacement, when undertaken, would have occurred in the following fiscal year. For an accrual basis tax payer, when has the income accrued? But let the tax court wrestle with that one.

---

1. Sections A.3. a. and A.3.a.(3a).
2. This would give to the word "incurred" the further meaning of an obligation created in addition to an expenditure made.

Comment #13

Howard Stores Corp. v. Foremost Ins. Co.

1. Meaning of "Business" as in "Interruption of Business"

The significance of the early discussion in the text about the various possible meanings of the word "business" is exemplified by the 1981 decision of *Howard Stores Corp. v. Foremost Insurance Company.* The question arises in connection with the first paragraph in the Gross Earnings forms which speak of the "interruption of business."

In the decision of the New York Supreme Court and, on appeal, of the New York Court of Appeals, the facts were that following an incident of water damage, there was "no actual suspension of *business operations*" (italics added). There had been physical damage to the described property. The Insured based his claim on an adverse effect on continuing sales in the described store and in two other stores.

The court assumed that the use of the word "business" at this particular juncture means the operation of the business. When this type of coverage was based on productivity, there had to be an interruption of production to constitute a loss. But does this same limitation apply today under the Gross Earnings form? "Business" can also mean the financial results of the activities carried on as in the example of the statement: "business is not good." Now that gross earnings are specified as representing the insurable interest involved, a financial interpretation of this wording may be reasonable. (The BIC Form specifically deals with operations.)

In the *Howard Stores* case, the Insured had projected an increase in the sales volume and the profitability of this store. While there was some increase, it was not as much as had been projected. The growth in the gross earnings that had been anticipated from the operation of the store had not been realized. The Insured attributed this to the water damage to the described property, and filed a claim for the diminution in earnings achieved.[1]

While the decision was in favor of the Insurer on this point, it should be noted that there was another reason for the finding, besides the lack of suspension of operations: there was simply no evidence that the failure to meet the projected increases was directly attributable to the water damage. Such a conclusion was pure speculation. It is not beyond the range of possibility to assume that in a case where there was evidence tying the financial loss to the damage suffered, a loss could be established even when there was no suspension of operations caused by the damage, on the ground that there was credible evidence to show that the projected gross earnings would have been achieved had the damage not occurred.

2. Expenses to Reduce Loss

Another question arises from the *Howard Stores* case. The Insured tried to collect for loss that resulted from the attempts to mitigate damages. The court makes the statement that "expenditures in mitigation of damages must be made in the reasonable anticipation of reducing the recovery below the amount of the loss." Reasonable in whose eyes? If the Insured takes steps that everyone else says are not reasonable and yet succeeds in reducing the loss, is he entitled to be reimbursed under the terms of the contract?

If there is no reduction, there ordinarily would be no recovery. But if the parties agree that the Insured would be reimbursed for any loss that may result from the steps recommended by the Insurer, there should be no reason why the terms of this auxillary contract should not be fulfilled. Yet the *Howard Stores* decision ends with the declaration "expenditures which result in an increased loss cannot be justified. Such a claim strips the business interruption insurance coverage of any rational meaning." While this statement may be true, fairness requires that it not be applied to steps taken at the insistance of the Insurer.

The question arises as to whether the reduction in earnings potential that results when part of the stock in trade of a retail store is damaged by an insured peril and can no longer be offered for sale constitutes a recoverable loss under the Gross Earnings form. Some of the language in the case of *Howard Stores Corp. v. Foremost Ins. Co.* would seem to indicate that the answer is "No." While recognizing that the inability to conduct *normal* business operation and function is the basis for establishing a loss, the two New York courts' statements that there must be an "actual suspension of business operations" seems to imply that the store must be closed. However, a close reading of the cases indicates that the decision was based on a lack of adequate evidence, i.e.,

---

1. The Insured muddled up his claim by including the less than projected growth in two other stores which had divested themselves of merchandise to restock the described store.

the failure of the Insurer "to meet the burden of proving a business interruption loss." The court rejects as "pure speculation" the evidence of loss produced by the Insured.

It is interesting to note that while the policy in that case reads "necessary interruption of business" the court used the words "actual suspension of business operations." This is the wording to be found in the BIC Form which reads "necessary suspension of your operations" and in which "operations" are defined as "type of business activities."

Under this wording, the question still remains unanswered. Does "type of operations" mean "retail sales"? If so, the retail sales of the rest of the stock in trade having continued unabated, there would be no loss. The shutting down of one department in a department store because its stock was damaged would not constitute a suspension of the type of business operations in the store as a whole. But it could not mean that otherwise how could there be a "partial loss"? There would be no recovery if half of the machinery in a factory was damaged by fire, but the other half continued to operate. A more reasonable interpretation would be to include in the meaning of "suspension" the inability of any part of the described property to carry on the function to which it had been dedicated by the Insured. Such an interpretation would consider the shutting down of a single department in a department store as a suspension under the terms of the contract.

Comment # 14

A Few of the Many Questions that are Raised in Connection with Average Issues

1. **Q:** If a dress manufacturer's samples for next season's dresses are destroyed by an insured peril just prior to their showing, resulting in a loss of potential sales, is there a business interruption loss?

   A: If the samples are treated as finished goods the answer is No. But what if it is claimed that showing the samples is part of operations or that they are part of the operative equipment? It would be difficult to include them within the term "patterns" which are more clearly items used in production. If they were specifically named, along with patterns, designs and similar objects used in production, the odds are that the loss of sales resulting from their destruction could be covered. That destruction could cost the manufacturer an substantial part of next season's sales.

2. **Q:** A and B were insured under the same policy, A's finished product was sold to B as raw material, A gave B price concession as a volume discount (price was lower than price to third persons). After B's plant is destroyed, A finds customers for the goods usually sold to B and at the higher price. Is A's extra profit to be credited to B's business interruption loss?

   A: Yes, if all of the goods that A is previously produced are marketed. If A can sell only part of the goods B used to take, then consideration must be given to the increased cost of goods sold that would be loaded on every

333

unit of production sold by A. This would show up on his profit and loss statement ultimately.

3. **Q:**   Even though extra expense is not affected by co-insurance, do operations of the Coinsurance Clause affect the ceiling on total recovery? Suppose the total of the amount payable for loss of income, when added to the extra expense recoverable, is more than would have been paid if no additional expense had been incurred? Example: Insured with $100,000 policy is a co-insurer for 50%. Loss of $80,000 would have been settled at $40,000. By spending $15,000, Insured reduces loss to $60,000. Insurers liability for loss of income is 50% or $30,000, plus $15,000 additional expense = $45,000. This is more than Insurer would have paid if no additional expense had been laid out.

A: The question really is—which takes precedence, the Coinsurance Clause or the Extra Expense Clause? The Gross Earnings Clause uses the language "the amount by which the *loss* otherwise payable under this policy is thereby reduced." The Coinsurance Clause reads "... liable, in the event of *loss*, for no greater percentage...." If the word "loss" in both clauses is applied to the same stage of calculation, the Insured would collect $45,000. If the words *"otherwise payable"* apply to a time after the Contribution Clause is applied, then a ceiling of $40,000 applies. There is a split of authority on this point. (For possible impact of wording of BIC Form see Ch. 8.)

4. **Q:**   A competitor agreed to provide Insured with part of his production of a raw material. To make this possible, Insured shipped to competitor a piece of undamaged equipment and took in its place the competitor's order for later delivery of a similar piece of equipment from the manufacturer. Additional expense was involved in transferring equipment and buying the new machine. It reduced Insured's loss. Is additional expense recoverable?

A: Yes; to the extent that it reduced amount payable by Insurer.

5. **Q:**   Should the continuing salary allowed to the president, who owns all of the stock of the insured corporation, include the "perks" he normally gets, such as an automobile country club expenses, etc.?

A: If it is fair compensation, it can be recovered as part of continuing expenses; if it is more than the job is worth on the market, then it could be considered as a transfer of profits and not as an expense. A partner's draw may represent past salary and past withdrawal of profits. Only amounts fairly attributed to salary should be part of continuing expense.[1]

6. **Q:** Key personnel are kept on while the Insured decides whether or not to continue the business enterprise. They are later let go, when he decides to sell out except for those necessary to be retained if the business is to be sold at the best price. To what extent are such salaries part of continuing expense?

   A: All, until the decision to sell business. Then none, because those retained are not necessary to renew operations, but to obtain a buyer. A reasonable time is allowed in this connection to decide on a course of action.

7. **Q:** A power failure caused a temporary shutdown of operations. Workers on the next general shifts were told to report for work, but are sent home on arrival because power is not yet restored. They collect pay for the shift under their contract. Is this pay part of continuing expense?

   A: Yes, if, in the good faith judgment of Insured, the power was going to be restored during their shift.

8. **Q:** If the Insured by his own actions makes restoration of operations impossible—example: discards a machine that could have been repaired and used temporarily and orders a new model which takes time to deliver— can he still collect under his policy?

   A: Yes; to the extent he can establish a recoverable loss. Insurer is protected under the Resumption of Operations Clause; no forfeiture for such action can be read into the policy.

9. **Q:** Is there any obligation on the Insured to arrange for key employees to apply for unemployment insurance compensation during the period of interruption and only make up the difference in income, thereby cutting the expense of ongoing salaries.

   A: No. It would adversely affect the unemployment insurance rate against the Insured.

10. **Q:** A manufacturer, in order to avoid losing markets, shipped a final product with an inferior part but with warranty to replace it if necessary, and charged his regular full price. He thereby reduced the loss. Should the

---

1. See *Eisenson v. Home Insurance Co.*

gross earnings received during the period of interruption be reduced so as to set up a reserve against possible costs of such a warranty?

A: It is an undetermined cost of doing business. Maybe it is additional expense to reduce loss. How to measure potential cost is a difficult question.

11. **Q:** The Insured's plant produced a large percentage of the world production of a particular chemical product. The destruction of the plant caused a severe shortage in the available market supply and, as a consequence, a substantial rise in the world selling price. Is the Insured's loss to be measured by the price that existed during the shut down?

A: No. Had there been no damage to the Insured's plant, the price would not have gone up.

12. **Q:** While the Insured's plant is shut-down for repair of fire damage, a strike is called at a competitor's plant which increases the market price of the Insured's products. Can the Insured base his business interruption loss on the higher market price that developed?

A: No, under the foresight approach. The probable future experience is based on the situation that existed when the damage took place.

13. **Q:** A valued policy reads: "Total suspension—if the buildings. . .shall be destroyed. . .so as to necessitate a total suspension of business, then this Insurance shall be liable at a rate of $4,000 (100%) per working day for such total suspension.

"Partial suspension—this insurance shall be liable for such proportion of $4,000 (100%) per working day which the proportion of reduction in output bears to the total production which would, but for such partial suspension, have been obtained during the period of total suspension." The Insured's plant is working at 80% of capacity at the time of total suspension—what is valued amount that he can collect?

A: "At a rate of" is not necessarily defined to mean proportionately to its then usage. So, $4,000 a day would be collected.

Addendum II

Forms

TEXT OF
STANDARD FIRE POLICY

IN CONSIDERATION OF THE PROVISIONS AND STIPULATIONS HEREIN OR ADDED HERETO AND OF the premium, this Company, for the term of *years* from *inception date* At 12:01 A.M. (Standard Time) to *expiration date* AT 12:01 A.M. (Standard Time) at location of property involved, to an amount not exceeding the amount(s) specified in the Declarations, does insure *the insured named* in the Declarations and legal representatives, to the extent of the actual cash value of the property at the time of loss, but not exceeding the amount which it would cost to repair or replace the property with material of like kind and quality within a reasonable time after such loss, without allowance for any increased cost of repair or reconstruction by reason of any ordinance or law regulating construction or repair, and without compensation for loss resulting from interruption of business or manufacture, nor in any event for more than the interest of the insured, against all **DIRECT LOSS BY FIRE, LIGHTNING AND BY REMOVAL FROM PREMISES ENDANGERED BY THE PERILS INSURED AGAINST IN THIS POLICY, EXCEPT AS HEREINAFTER PROVIDED,** to the property described herein while located or contained as described in this policy, or pro rata for five days at each proper place to which any of the property shall necessarily be removed for preservation from the perils insured against in this policy, but not elsewhere.

Assignment of this policy shall not be valid except with the written consent of this Company.

This policy is made and accepted subject to the foregoing provisions and stipulations and those hereinafter stated, which are hereby made a part of this policy, together with such other provisions, stipulations and agreements as may be added hereto, as provided in this policy.

1 **Concealment,** This entire policy shall be void if, whether
2 **fraud.** before or after a loss, the insured has wil-
3 fully concealed or misrepresented any ma-
4 terial fact or circumstance concerning this insurance or the
5 subject thereof, or the interest of the insured therein, or in case
6 of any fraud or false swearing by the insured relating thereto.
7 **Uninsurable** This policy shall not cover accounts, bills,
8 **and** currency, deeds, evidences of debt, money or
9 **excepted property.** securities; nor, unless specifically named
10 hereon in writing, bullion or manuscripts.
11 **Perils not** This Company shall not be liable for loss by
12 **included.** fire or other perils insured against in this
13 policy caused, directly or indirectly, by: (a)
14 enemy attack by armed forces, including action taken by mili-
15 tary, naval or air forces in resisting an actual or an immediately
16 impending enemy attack; (b) invasion; (c) insurrection; (d)
17 rebellion; (e) revolution; (f) civil war; (g) usurped power; (h)
18 order of any civil authority except acts of destruction at the time
19 of and for the purpose of preventing the spread of fire, provided
20 that such fire did not originate from any of the perils excluded
21 by this policy; (i) neglect of the insured to use all reasonable
22 means to save and preserve the property at and after a loss, or
23 when the property is endangered by fire in neighboring prem-
24 ises; (j) nor shall this Company be liable for loss by theft.
25 **Other Insurance.** Other insurance may be prohibited or the
26 amount of insurance may be limited by en-
27 dorsement attached hereto.
28 **Conditions suspending or restricting insurance. Unless other-**
29 **wise provided in writing added hereto this Company shall not**
30 **be liable for loss occurring**
31 (a) while the hazard is increased by any means within the con-
32 trol or knowledge of the insured; or
33 (b) while a described building, whether intended for occupancy
34 by owner or tenant, is vacant or unoccupied beyond a period of
35 sixty consecutive days; or
36 (c) as a result of explosion or riot, unless fire ensue, and in
37 that event for loss by fire only.
38 **Other perils** Any other peril to be insured against or sub-
39 **or subjects.** ject of insurance to be covered in this policy
40 shall be by endorsement in writing hereon or
41 added hereto.
42 **Added provisions.** The extent of the application of insurance
43 under this policy and of the contribution to
44 be made by this Company in case of loss, and any other pro-
45 vision or agreement not inconsistent with the provisions of this
46 policy, may be provided for in writing added hereto, but no pro-
47 vision may be waived except such as by the terms of this policy
48 is subject to change.
49 **Waiver** No permission affecting this insurance shall
50 **provisions.** exist, or waiver of any provision be valid,
51 unless granted herein or expressed in writing
52 added hereto. No provision, stipulation or forfeiture shall be
53 held to be waived by any requirement or proceeding on the part
54 of this Company relating to appraisal or to any examination
55 provided for herein.
56 **Cancellation** This policy shall be cancelled at any time
57 **of policy.** at the request of the insured, in which case
58 this Company shall, upon demand and sur-
59 render of this policy, refund the excess of paid premium above
60 the customary short rates for the expired time. This pol-
61 icy may be cancelled at any time by this Company by giving
62 to the insured a five days' written notice of cancellation with
63 or without tender of the excess of paid premium above the pro
64 rata premium for the expired time, which excess, if not ten-
65 dered, shall be refunded on demand. Notice of cancellation shall
66 state that said excess premium (if not tendered) will be re-
67 funded on demand.
68 **Mortgage** If loss hereunder is made payable, in whole
69 **interests and** or in part, to a designated mortgagee not
70 **obligations.** named herein as the insured, such interest in
71 this policy may be cancelled by giving to such
72 mortgagee a ten days' written notice of can-
73 cellation.
74 If the insured fails to render proof of loss such mortgagee, upon
75 notice, shall render proof of loss in the form herein specified
76 within sixty (60) days thereafter and shall be subject to the pro-
77 visions hereof relating to appraisal and time of payment and of
78 bringing suit. If this Company shall claim that no liability ex-
79 isted as to the mortgagor or owner, it shall, to the extent of pay-
80 ment of loss to the mortgagee, be subrogated to all the mort-
81 gagee's rights of recovery, but without impairing mortgagee's
82 right to sue; or it may pay off the mortgage debt and require
83 an assignment thereof and of the mortgage. Other provisions

84 relating to the interests and obligations of such mortgagee may
85 be added hereto by agreement in writing.
86 **Pro rata liability.** This Company shall not be liable for a greater
87 proportion of any loss than the amount
88 hereby insured shall bear to the whole insurance covering the
89 property against the peril involved, whether collectible or not.
90 **Requirements in** The insured shall give immediate written
91 **case loss occurs.** notice to this Company of any loss, protect
92 the property from further damage, forthwith
93 separate the damaged and undamaged personal property, put
94 it in the best possible order, furnish a complete inventory of
95 the destroyed, damaged and undamaged property, showing in
96 detail quantities, costs, actual cash value and amount of loss
97 claimed; **and within sixty days after the loss, unless such time**
98 **is extended in writing by this Company, the insured shall render**
99 **to this Company a proof of loss,** signed and sworn to by the
100 insured, stating the knowledge and belief of the insured as to
101 the following: the time and origin of the loss, the interest of the
102 insured and of all others in the property, the actual cash value of
103 each item thereof and the amount of loss thereto, all encum-
104 brances thereon, all other contracts of insurance, whether valid
105 or not, covering any of said property, any changes in the title,
106 use, occupation, location, possession or exposures of said prop-
107 erty since the issuing of this policy, by whom and for what
108 purpose any building herein described and the several parts
109 thereof were occupied at the time of loss and whether or not it
110 then stood on leased ground, and shall furnish a copy of all the
111 descriptions and schedules in all policies and, if required, verified
112 plans and specifications of any building, fixtures or machinery
113 destroyed or damaged. The insured, as often as may be reason-
114 ably required, shall exhibit to any person designated by this
115 Company all that remains of any property herein described, and
116 submit to examinations under oath by any person named by this
117 Company, and subscribe the same; and, as often as may be
118 reasonably required, shall produce for examination all books of
119 account, bills, invoices and other vouchers, or certified copies
120 thereof if originals be lost, at such reasonable time and place as
121 may be designated by this Company or its representative, and
122 shall permit extracts and copies thereof to be made.
123 **Appraisal.** In case the insured and this Company shall
124 fail to agree as to the actual cash value or
125 the amount of loss, then, on the written demand of either, each
126 shall select a competent and disinterested appraiser and notify
127 the other of the appraiser selected within twenty days of such
128 demand. The appraisers shall first select a competent and dis-
129 interested umpire; and failing for fifteen days to agree upon
130 such umpire, then, on request of the insured or this Company,
131 such umpire shall be selected by a judge of a court of record in
132 the state in which the property covered is located. The ap-
133 praisers shall then appraise the loss, stating separately actual
134 cash value and loss to each item; and, failing to agree, shall
135 submit their differences, only, to the umpire. An award in writ-
136 ing, so itemized, of any two when filed with this Company shall
137 determine the amount of actual cash value and loss. Each
138 appraiser shall be paid by the party selecting him and the ex-
139 penses of appraisal and umpire shall be paid by the parties
140 equally.
141 **Company's** It shall be optional with this Company to
142 **options.** take all, or any part, of the property at the
143 agreed or appraised value, and also to re-
144 pair, rebuild or replace the property destroyed or damaged with
145 other of like kind and quality within a reasonable time, on giv-
146 ing notice of its intention so to do within thirty days after the
147 receipt of the proof of loss herein required.
148 **Abandonment.** There can be no abandonment to this Com-
149 pany of any property.
150 **When loss** The amount of loss for which this Company
151 **payable.** may be liable shall be payable sixty days
152 after proof of loss, as herein provided, is
153 received by this Company and ascertainment of the loss is made
154 either by agreement between the insured and this Company ex-
155 pressed in writing or by the filing with this Company of an
156 award as herein provided.
157 **Suit.** No suit or action on this policy for the recov-
158 ery of any claim shall be sustainable in any
159 court of law or equity unless all the requirements of this policy
160 shall have been complied with, and unless commenced within
161 twelve months next after inception of the loss.
162 **Subrogation.** This Company may require from the insured
163 an assignment of all right of recovery against
164 any party for loss to the extent that payment therefor is made
165 by this Company.

IN WITNESS WHEREOF, this Company has executed and attested these presents; but this policy shall not be valid unless countersigned
by the duly authorized Agent of this Company at the agency hereinbefore mentioned.

© 1982

BUSINESS INTERRUPTION

Gross Earnings Form for Manufacturing or Mining Risks

CF 15 04

(Ed. 01 83)

Insurance applies to this item(s) only when "Business Interruption", a specific amount and a coinsurance percentage are specified therefor in this policy, and, unless otherwise provided, all provisions and stipulations of this form and policy shall apply separately to each such item.

SECTION I—DESCRIPTION OF COVERAGES

1. This policy insures against loss resulting directly from necessary interruption of business caused by damage to or destruction of real or personal property, except finished stock, by the peril(s) insured against, during the term of this policy, on premises occupied by the Insured and situated as herein described.

2. In the event of such damage or destruction this Company shall be liable for the ACTUAL LOSS SUSTAINED by the Insured resulting directly from such interruption of business, but not exceeding the reduction in Gross Earnings less charges and expenses which do not necessarily continue during the interruption of business, for only such length of time as would be required with the exercise of due diligence and dispatch to rebuild, repair or replace such part of the property herein described as has been damaged or destroyed, commencing with the date of such damage or destruction and not limited by the date of expiration of this policy. Due consideration shall be given to the continuation of normal charges and expenses, including payroll expense, to the extent necessary to resume operations of the Insured with the same quality of service which existed immediately preceding the loss.

3. Resumption of Operations: It is a condition of this insurance that if the Insured could reduce the loss resulting from the interruption of business,

A. by complete or partial resumption of operation of the property herein described, whether damaged or not, or

B. by making use of other property at the location(s) described herein or elsewhere, or

C. by making use of stock (raw, in process or finished) at the location(s) described herein or elsewhere,

such reduction shall be taken into account in arriving at the amount of loss hereunder.

4. Gross Earnings: For the purposes of this insurance "Gross Earnings" are defined as the sum of:

A. Total net sales value of production,

B. Total net sales of merchandise, and

C. Other earnings derived from operations of the business,

less the cost of:

D. Raw Stock from which such production is derived,

E. Supplies consisting of materials consumed directly in the conversion of such raw stock into finished stock or in supplying the service(s) sold by the Insured,

F. Merchandise sold, including packaging materials therefor, and

G. Service(s) purchased from outsiders (not employees of the Insured) for resale which do not continue under contract.

No other costs shall be deducted in determining Gross Earnings.

In determining Gross Earnings due consideration shall be given to the experience of the business before the date of damage or destruction and the probable experience thereafter had no loss occurred.

5. Definitions: The following terms wherever used in this policy shall mean:

A. "Raw Stock": material in the state in which the Insured receives it for conversion by the Insured into finished stock.

B. "Stock in Process": raw stock which has undergone any aging, seasoning, mechanical or other process of manufacture at the location(s) herein described but which has not become finished stock.

C. "Finished Stock": stock manufactured by the Insured which in the ordinary course of the Insured's business is ready for packing, shipment or sale.

D. "Merchandise": goods kept for sale by the Insured which are not the product of manufacturing operations conducted by the Insured.

E. "Normal": the condition that would have existed had no loss occurred.

SECTION II—EXTENSIONS OF COVERAGE

1. Alterations and New Buildings: Permission granted to make alterations in or to construct additions to any building described herein and to construct new buildings on the described premises. This policy is extended to cover, subject to all its provisions and stipulations, loss resulting from damage to or destruction of such alterations, additions or new buildings while in course of construction and when completed or occupied, provided that, in the event of damage to or destruction of such property (including building materials, supplies, machinery or equipment incident to such construction or occupancy while on the described premises or within 100 feet thereof) so as to delay commencement of business operations of the Insured, the length of time for which this Company shall be liable shall be determined as otherwise provided herein but such determined length of time shall be applied and the loss hereunder calculated from the date that business operations would have begun had no damage or destruction occurred.

This clause does not waive or modify any of the conditions of the Automatic Sprinkler Clause, if any, attached to this policy.

2. Expenses Related to Reducing Loss: This policy also covers such expenses as are necessarily incurred for the purpose of reducing loss under this policy (except expense incurred to extinguish fire) and such expenses, in excess of normal, as would necessarily be incurred in replacing any finished stock used by the Insured to reduce loss under this policy; but in no event shall the aggregate of such expenses exceed the amount by which the loss otherwise payable under this policy is thereby reduced. Such expenses shall not be subject to the application of the Coinsurance Clause.

3. Interruption by Civil Authority: This policy is extended to include the actual loss sustained by the Insured, resulting directly from an interruption of business as covered hereunder, during the length of time, not exceeding 2 consecutive weeks, when, as a direct result of damage to or destruction of property adjacent to the premises herein described by the peril(s) insured against, access to such described premises is specifically prohibited by order of civil authority.

SECTION III—COINSURANCE

This Company shall not be liable for a greater proportion of any loss than the amount of insurance specified for this item bears to the amount produced by multiplying the Gross Earnings that would have been earned (had no loss occurred) during the 12 months immediately following the date of damage to or destruction of the described property by the coinsurance percentage applicable (specified on the first page of this policy, or by endorsement).

CF 15 04 (Ed. 01 83)

Page 1 of 4

© 1982

SECTION IV—LIMITATIONS AND EXCLUSIONS

1. Electrical Apparatus Clause: This Company shall not be liable for any loss resulting from any electrical injury or disturbance to electrical appliances, devices, fixtures or wiring caused by electrical currents artificially generated unless fire as insured against ensues, and then this Company shall be liable for only its proportion of loss caused by the ensuing fire.

2. Finished Stock: This Company shall not be liable for any loss resulting from damage to or destruction of finished stock nor for the time required to reproduce said finished stock.

3. Limitation—Media For Electronic Data Processing: With respect to loss resulting from damage to or destruction of media for, or programming records pertaining to, electronic data processing or electronically controlled equipment, including data thereon, by the peril(s) insured against, the length of time for which this Company shall be liable hereunder shall not exceed—

    A. 30 consecutive calendar days; or

    B. the length of time that would be required to rebuild, repair or replace such other property herein described as has been damaged or destroyed;

whichever is the greater length of time.

4. Nuclear Clause (Not applicable in New York): The word "fire" in this policy or endorsements attached hereto is not intended to and does not embrace nuclear reaction or nuclear radiation or radioactive contamination, all whether controlled or uncontrolled, and loss by nuclear reaction or nuclear radiation or radioactive contamination is not intended to be and is not insured against by this policy or said endorsements, whether such loss be direct or indirect, proximate or remote,

or be in whole or in part caused by, contributed to, or aggravated by "fire" or any other perils insured against by this policy or said endorsements; however, subject to the foregoing and all provisions of this policy, loss by "fire" resulting from nuclear reaction or nuclear radiation or radioactive contamination is insured against by this policy.

5. Nuclear Clause (Applicable in New York): This policy does not cover loss or damage caused by nuclear reaction or nuclear radiation or radioactive contamination, all whether directly or indirectly resulting from an insured peril under this policy.

6. Special Exclusions: This Company shall not be liable for any increase of loss resulting from:

    A. enforcement of any ordinance or law regulating the use, construction, repair or demolition of property; or

    B. interference at the described premises, by strikers or other persons, with rebuilding, repairing or replacing the property or with the resumption or continuation of business; or

    C. the suspension, lapse or cancellation of any lease, license, contract or order unless such suspension, lapse or cancellation results directly from the interruption of business, and then this Company shall be liable for only such loss as affects the Insured's earnings during, and limited to the period of indemnity covered under this policy;

nor shall this Company be liable for any other consequential or remote loss.

SECTION V—OTHER PROVISIONS

1. Control of Property. This insurance shall not be prejudiced by any act or neglect of any person (other than the Insured), when such act or neglect is not within the control of the Insured.

2. Divisible Contract Clause: If this policy covers two or more buildings or the contents of two or more buildings, the breach of any condition of the policy in any one or more of the buildings covered or containing the property covered shall not prejudice the right to recover for loss occurring in any building covered or containing the property covered, where at the time of loss a breach of condition does not exist.

3. Inspection of Property and Operations: This Company and any person or organization making inspections on this Company's behalf shall be permitted but not obligated to inspect the Insured's property and operations at any time. Neither the right of this Company and any person or organization to make such inspections nor the making thereof nor any report thereon shall constitute an undertaking, on behalf of or for the benefit of the Insured or others, to determine or warrant that such property or operations are safe or healthful, or are in compliance with any law, rule or regulation.

4. Liberalization Clause: If during the period that insurance is in force under this policy, or within 45 days prior to the inception date thereof, on behalf of this Company there be adopted, or filed with and approved or accepted by the insurance supervisory authorities, all in conformity with law, any changes in the form attached to this policy by which this form of insurance could be extended or broadened without increased premium charge by endorsement or substitution of form, then such extended or broadened insurance shall inure to the benefit of the Insured hereunder as though such endorsement or substitution of form had been made.

5. Loss Clause: Any loss hereunder shall not reduce the amount of this policy.

6. Pro Rata Clause: The liability under this policy shall not exceed that proportion of any loss which the amount of insurance hereunder bears to all insurance, whether collectible or not, covering in any manner the loss insured against by this policy.

7. Protective Safeguards: It is a condition of this insurance that the Insured shall maintain so far as is within his control such protective safeguards as are set forth by endorsement hereto.

Failure to maintain such protective safeguards shall suspend this insurance, only as respects the location or situation affected, for the time of such discontinuance.

8. Requirements in Case Loss Occurs: The Insured shall give immediate written notice to this Company of any Business Interruption loss and protect the property from further damage that might result in extension of the period of interruption; and within 60 days following the date of damage to or destruction of the real or personal property described, unless such time is extended in writing by this Company, the Insured shall render to this Company a proof of loss, signed and sworn to by the insured, stating the knowledge and belief of the Insured as to the following:

    A. the time and origin of the property damage or destruction causing the interruption of business,

    B. the interest of the Insured and of all others in the business,

    C. all other contracts of insurance, whether valid or not, covering in any manner the loss insured against by this policy,

    D. any changes in the title, nature, location, encumbrance or possession of said business since the issuing of this policy, and

    E. by whom and for what purpose any building herein described and the several parts thereof were occupied at the time of damage or destruction,

and shall furnish a copy of all the descriptions and schedules in all policies, and the actual amount of business interruption value and loss claimed, accompanied by detailed exhibits of all values, costs and estimates upon which such amounts are based.

The Insured, as often as may be reasonably required, shall exhibit to any person designated by this Company all that remains of any property herein described, and submit to examinations under oath by any person named by this Company, and subscribe the same; and, as often as may be reasonably required, shall produce for examination all books of account, bills, invoices and other vouchers, or certified copies thereof if originals be lost, at such reasonable time and place as may be designated by this Company or its representative, and shall permit extracts and copies thereof to be made.

9. Subrogation Clause: This insurance shall not be invalidated should the Insured waive in writing prior to a loss any or all right of recovery against any party for loss occurring to the property described.

EXTENDED COVERAGE ENDORSEMENT

(PERILS OF WINDSTORM, HAIL, SMOKE, EXPLOSION, RIOT, RIOT ATTENDING A STRIKE, CIVIL COMMOTION, AIRCRAFT AND VEHICLES)

This policy is extended to insure against direct loss by Windstorm, Hail, Smoke, Explosion, Riot, Riot Attending A Strike, Civil Commotion, Aircraft and Vehicles as hereinafter provided, only when premium for EXTENDED COVERAGE is shown on the first page of this policy or by endorsement.

CF 15 04 (Ed. 01 83)

SECTION I—PERILS INSURED AGAINST

1. Windstorm or Hail, excluding loss caused directly or indirectly by frost or cold weather, or ice (other than hail), snow or sleet, whether driven by wind or not.

A. This Company shall not be liable for loss to the interior of the building(s) or the property covered therein caused:

(1) by rain, snow, sand or dust, whether driven by wind or not, unless the building(s) covered or containing the property covered shall first sustain an actual damage to roof or walls by the direct action of wind or hail and then shall be liable for loss to the interior of the building(s) or the property covered therein as may be caused by rain, snow, sand or dust entering the building(s) through openings in the roof or walls made by direct action of wind or hail; or

(2) by water from sprinkler equipment or from other piping, unless such equipment or piping be damaged as a direct result of wind or hail.

B. This Company shall not be liable for Windstorm or Hail damage to the following property:

(1) Windmills, wind pumps or their towers;

(2) Crop silos or their contents;

(3) Metal smokestacks; or

(4) When outside of buildings,

(a) Grain, hay, straw or other crops,

(b) Lawns, trees, shrubs or plants.

(c) Awnings of fabric or slat construction, canopies of fabric or slat construction, including their supports,

(d) Signs or radio or television antennas, including their lead-in wiring, masts or towers.

2. Smoke, meaning sudden and accidental damage from smoke, other than smoke from agricultural smudging or industrial operations.

3. Explosion, including direct loss resulting from the explosion of accumulated gases or unconsumed fuel within the firebox (or combustion chamber) of any fired vessel or within the flues or passages which conduct the gases of combustion therefrom.

A. This Company shall not be liable for loss by explosion of steam boilers, steam pipes, steam turbines or steam engines, if owned by, leased by or

operated under the control of the Insured.

B. The following are not explosions within the intent or meaning of these provisions:

(1) Shock waves caused by aircraft, generally known as "sonic boom",

(2) Electric arcing,

(3) Rupture or bursting of rotating or moving parts of machinery caused by centrifugal force or mechanical breakdown,

(4) Water hammer,

(5) Rupture or bursting of water pipes,

(6) Rupture or bursting due to expansion or swelling of the contents of any building or structure, caused by or resulting from water,

(7) Rupture, bursting or operation of pressure relief devices.

4. Riot, Riot Attending a Strike or Civil Commotion, including direct loss by acts of striking employees of the owner or tenant(s) of the described building(s) while occupied by said striking employees and shall also include direct loss from pillage and looting occurring during and at the immediate place of a riot, riot attending a strike or civil commotion. This Company shall not be liable for loss resulting from damage to or destruction of property due to change in temperature or humidity or interruption of operations whether or not such loss is covered by this policy as to other perils.

5. Aircraft or Vehicles, meaning only direct loss resulting from actual physical contact of an aircraft or a vehicle with the property covered or with the building(s) containing the property covered, except that loss by aircraft includes direct loss by objects falling therefrom.

This Company shall not be liable for loss:

A. by any vehicle owned or operated by an Insured or by any tenant of the described premises;

B. by any vehicle to fences, driveways, walks, or when outside of buildings, to lawns, trees, shrubs or plants;

C. to any aircraft or vehicle including its contents other than stocks or aircraft or vehicles in process of manufacture or for sale.

The word "vehicles" means vehicles running on land or tracks but not aircraft. The word "aircraft" shall include self-propelled missiles and spacecraft.

SECTION II—GENERAL EXCLUSIONS—OTHER PROVISIONS

1. Nuclear Exclusion (Not applicable in New York): (This clause applies to all perils insured against hereunder except the perils of fire and lightning, which are otherwise provided for in this policy): Loss by nuclear reaction or nuclear radiation or radioactive contamination, all whether controlled or uncontrolled, or due to any act or condition incident to any of the foregoing, is not insured against by this policy, whether such loss be direct or indirect, proximate or remote, or be in whole or in part caused by, contributed to, or aggravated by any of the perils insured against by this endorsement; and nuclear reaction or nuclear radiation or radioactive contamination, all whether controlled or uncontrolled, is not "explosion" or "smoke".

2. Water Exclusion: This Company shall not be liable for loss caused by, resulting from, contributed to or aggravated by any of the following:

A. flood, surface water, waves, tidal water or tidal wave, overflow of streams or other bodies of water, or spray from any of the foregoing, all whether driven by wind or not;

B. water which backs up through sewers or drains;

C. water below the surface of the ground including that which exerts pressure on or flows, seeps or leaks through sidewalks, driveways, foundations, walls, basement or other floors, or through doors, windows, or any other opening in such sidewalks, driveways, foundations, walls or floors;

unless fire or explosion as insured against ensues, and then this Company shall be liable for only its proportion of loss caused by the ensuing fire or explosion.

3. Volcanic Eruption: This Company shall not be liable for loss caused by volcanic eruption unless direct loss by fire or breakage of glass or safety glazing material ensues. In this event, this Company shall be liable for only the direct loss to the property insured caused by the ensuing fire and if an insured peril, the ensuing breakage of glass or safety glazing material.

Volcanic eruption means the eruption, explosion or effusion of a volcano.

4. War Risk: (This clause applies to all perils insured against hereunder except the perils of fire, lightning and removal which are otherwise provided for in this policy): This Company shall not be liable for loss caused directly or indirectly by:

A. hostile or warlike action in time of peace or war, including action in hindering, combating or defending against an actual, impending or expected attack,

(1) by any government or sovereign power (de jure or de facto), or by any authority maintaining or using military, naval or air forces; or

(2) by military, naval or air forces; or

(3) by an agent of any such government, power, authority or forces, it being understood that any discharge, explosion or use of any weapon of war employing nuclear fission or fusion shall be conclusively presumed to be such a hostile or warlike action by such a government, power, authority or forces;

B. insurrection, rebellion, revolution, civil war, usurped power, or action taken by governmental authority in hindering, combating or defending against such an occurrence.

5. Other Provisions: This endorsement does not increase the amount(s) of insurance provided in this policy.

If this policy covers on two or more items, the provisions of this endorsement shall apply to each item separately.

6. Apportionment: This Company shall not be liable for a greater proportion of any loss less the amount of the deductible, if any, from any peril or perils included in this policy than:

    A. the amount of insurance under the policy bears to the whole amount of fire insurance covering the property, or which would have covered the property except for the existence of this insurance, whether collectible or not, and whether or not such other fire insurance covers against the additional peril or perils insured against hereunder, nor

    B. for a greater proportion of any loss less the amount of the deductible, if any, than the amount hereby insured bears to all insurance, whether collectible or not, covering in any manner such loss, or which would have covered such loss except for the existence of this insurance; except if any type of insurance other than fire extended to cover

additional perils or windstorm insurance applies to any loss to which this insurance also applies, or would have applied to any such loss except for the existence of this insurance, the limit of liability of each type of insurance for such loss, hereby designated as "joint loss", shall first be determined as if it were the only insurance, and this type of insurance shall be liable for no greater proportion of joint loss than the limit of its liability for such loss bears to the sum of all such limits. The liability of this Company (under this policy) for such joint loss shall be limited to its proportionate part of the aggregate limit of this and all other insurance of the same type. The words "joint loss" as used in the foregoing, mean that portion of the loss in excess of the highest deductible, if any, to which this policy and other types of insurance above referred to both apply.

7. Provisions Applicable Only When This Policy Covers Business Interruption, Tuition Fees, Extra Expense, Rent or Rental Value, Leasehold Interest or Other Consequential Loss: The term "direct", as applied to loss, means loss, as limited and conditioned in this policy, resulting from direct loss to described property from the peril(s) insured against. If the business of the owner or tenant(s) of the described building(s) is interrupted by a strike at the described location, this Company shall not be liable for any loss due to interference by any person(s) with rebuilding, repairing or replacing the property damaged or destroyed or with the resumption or continuation of business.

CAUTION

WHEN THIS ENDORSEMENT IS ATTACHED TO ONE FIRE POLICY, THE INSURED SHOULD SECURE LIKE COVERAGE ON ALL FIRE POLICIES COVERING THE SAME PROPERTY.

COMBINATION BUSINESS INTERRUPTION WORK SHEET

(For Use With Business Interruption Forms CF 15 03 and CF 15 04
For Manufacturing, Mercantile or Non-Manufacturing Risks)

CF 15 15
(Ed. 05 77)

COMPANY	POLICY NO.	AGENCY

Name of Insured _____

Location of Risk _____

Date _____

ALL ENTRIES TO BE ON AN ANNUAL BASIS	COLUMN 1 Actual Values for Year Ended.....19__	COLUMN 2 *Estimated Values for Year Ending..........19__
A. Total annual net sales value of production from Manufacturing Operations; and total annual net sales from Merchandising or Non-Manufacturing Operations, (Gross sales less discounts, returns, bad accounts and prepaid freight, if included in sales)	$	$ ....
B. Add other earnings (if any) derived from operations of the business:		
1. Cash Discounts Received (not reflected in the amounts deducted under D)		....
2. Commissions or Rents from Leased Departments	....	....
3.	....	....
C. Total ("A" plus "B")	$	$ ....
D. Deduct only cost of:		
1. Raw stock from which such production is derived .... $		$ ....
2. Supplies consisting of materials consumed directly in the conversion of such raw stock into finished stock or in supplying the service(s) sold by the Insured	....	....
3. Merchandise sold, including packaging materials therefor	....	....
4. Service(s) purchased from outsiders (not employees of the Insured) for resale which do not continue under contract	....	....
5. Total deductions	$	$ ....
E. GROSS EARNINGS ("C" minus "D")	$	$ ....
IF INSURANCE IS TO BE WRITTEN WITHOUT PAYROLL ENDORSEMENTS:		
F. Take 50, 60, 70 or 80% of "E", Column 2, as amount of insurance required, depending upon percentage Coinsurance Clause to be used (......... %)		$ ....
IF INSURANCE IS TO BE WRITTEN WITH ORDINARY PAYROLL EXCLUSION ENDORSEMENT, Deduct From "E" Above:		
G. All Ordinary Payroll Expense	$	$ ....
H. Business Interruption Basis for Coinsurance ("E" minus "G") ...	$	$ ....
I. Amount of Insurance—Take 80, 90 or 100% of H, Column 2, depending upon percentage Coinsurance Clause to be used (......... %)		$ ....
IF INSURANCE IS TO BE WRITTEN WITH ORDINARY PAYROLL-LIMITED COVERAGE ENDORSEMENT, Complete "G" and "H" and the following:		
J. Select the largest Ordinary Payroll Expense for .... consecutive calendar days .... 90, 120, 150 or 180	$	$ ....
K. Business Interruption Basis for Coinsurance ("H" plus "J")	$	$ ....
L. Amount of Insurance—Take 80, 90 or 100% of K, Column 2, depending upon percentage Coinsurance Clause to be used (......... %)	$	$ ....

*INSTRUCTIONS: THE COINSURANCE CLAUSE ALWAYS APPLIES TO THE FUTURE (never the PAST). Column 2 is merely a projection of known past values (shown in Column 1) to the next 12 months from the date the computation is prepared.

Do not inadvertently enter Cost of Sales as Cost of Raw Stock under "D" above. Deduction under "D" above should not include any labor. "Freight in" may be considered as a part of the cost of raw stock.

Business Interruption values should be checked at regular intervals and the agent or broker notified at once of any actual or impending change that would affect values during the next 12 months from the date such change becomes known.

(over)

CF 15 15 (Ed. 05 77)

EXPLANATORY NOTES:

1. To obtain annual net sales value of production from Manufacturing Operations, the following procedure is recommended:

   Net sales of Insured's product during the year (i.e. gross sales less discounts granted, returns, allowances, bad debts, and prepaid freight, if included in sales figures) . . . . $ . . . .

   DEDUCT—Inventory of FINISHED STOCK at beginning of year, priced at sales value . . . . $ . . . .

   Balance . . . . $ . . . .

   ADD—Inventory of FINISHED STOCK on hand at end of year, priced at sales value . . . . $ . . . .

   TOTAL—Annual Net Sales Value of production during the year . . . . $ . . . .

2. To obtain cost of raw stock, merchandise sold, or supplies consisting of materials consumed, the following procedure is recommended:

   Inventory (including stock in process) at beginning of year . . . . $ . . . .

   ADD—Cost of raw stock, merchandise and such supplies purchased during the year (including cartage and transportation charges on said incoming purchases) . . . . $ . . . .

   TOTAL . . . . $ . . . .

   DEDUCT—Inventory (including stock in process) at end of year . . . . $ . . . .

   Amount for deductions 1, 2, and 3 of "D" . . . . $ . . . .

   Note: Adjust for any inventory increase or decrease caused by price fluctuations.

3. Under deduction 2 of "D", the words "supplies consisting of materials" are intended to refer only to tangible or physical supplies (i. e. materials), and the deduction of intangible supplies (such as heat and power) is not permitted nor shall intangible supplies which are not "materials" be deemed to be raw stock.

COMMON POLICY CONDITIONS

All Coverage Parts included in this policy are subject to the following conditions.

A. CANCELLATION

1. The first Named Insured shown in the Declarations may cancel this policy by mailing or delivering to us advance written notice of cancellation.

2. We may cancel this policy by mailing or delivering to the first Named Insured written notice of cancellation at least:

   a. 10 days before the effective date of cancellation if we cancel for nonpayment of premium; or

   b. 30 days before the effective date of cancellation if we cancel for any other reason.

3. We will mail or deliver our notice to the first Named Insured's last mailing address known to us.

4. Notice of cancellation will state the effective date of cancellation. The policy period will end on that date.

5. If this policy is cancelled, we will send the first Named Insured any premium refund due. If we cancel, the refund will be pro rata. If the first Named Insured cancels, the refund may be less than pro rata. The cancellation will be effective even if we have not made or offered a refund.

6. If notice is mailed, proof of mailing will be sufficient proof of notice.

B. CHANGES

This policy contains all the agreements between you and us concerning the insurance afforded. The first Named Insured shown in the Declarations is authorized to make changes in the terms of this policy with our consent. this policy's terms can be amended or waived only by endorsement issued by us and made a part of this policy.

C. EXAMINATION OF YOUR BOOKS AND RECORDS

We may examine and audit your books and records as they relate to this policy at any time during the policy period and up to three years afterward.

D. INSPECTIONS AND SURVEYS

We have the right but are not obligated to:

1. Make inspections and surveys at any time;

2. Give you reports on the conditions we find; and

3. Recommend changes

Any inspections, surveys, reports or recommendations relate only to insurability and the premiums to be charged. We do not make safety inspections. We do not undertake to perform the duty of any person or organization to provide for the health or safety of workers or the public. And we do not warrant that conditions.

E. PREMIUMS

The first Named Insured shown in the Declarations:

1. Is responsible for the payment of all premiums; and

2. Will be the payee for any return premiums we pay.

F. TRANSFER OF YOUR RIGHTS AND DUTIES UNDER THIS POLICY

Your rights and duties under this policy may not be transferred without our written consent except in the case of death of an individual named insured.

If you die, your rights and duties will be transferred to your legal representative but only while acting within the scope of duties as your legal representative. Until your legal representative is appointed, anyone having proper temporary custody of your property will have your rights and duties but only with respect to that that property.

COMMERCIAL PROPERTY CONDITIONS

This Coverage Part is subject to the following conditions, the Common Policy Conditions and applicable Loss Conditions and Additional Conditions in Commercial Property Coverage Forms.

A. CONCEALMENT, MISREPRESENTATION OR FRAUD

This Coverage Part is void in any case of fraud by you relating to it. It is also void if you intentionally conceal or misrepresent a material fact concerning:

1. This Coverage Part;
2. The Covered Property; or
3. Your interest in the Covered Property.

B. CONTROL OF PROPERTY

Any act or neglect of any person other than you beyond your direction or control will not affect this insurance.

If you violate a condition of this Coverage Part, we will not pay for loss or damage at the involved location. But your coverage will continue for other locations at which the violation does not apply.

C. INSURANCE UNDER TWO OR MORE COVERAGES

If two or more of this policy's coverages apply to the same loss or damage, we will not pay more than the actual amount of the loss or damage.

D. LEGAL ACTION AGAINST US

No one may bring a legal action against us under this Coverage Part unless:

1. There has been full compliance with all of the terms of this Coverage Part; and
2. The action is brought within 2 years after the date on which the direct physical loss or damage occurred.

E. LIBERALIZATION

If we adopt any revision that would broaden the coverage under this Coverage Part without additional premium within 45 days prior to or during the policy period, the broadened coverage will immediately apply to this Coverage Part.

F. NO BENEFIT TO BAILEE

No person or organization, other than you, having custody of Covered Property will benefit from this insurance.

G. OTHER INSURANCE

1. You may have other insurance subject to the same plan, terms, conditions and provisions as the insurance under this Coverage Part. If you do, we will pay our share of the covered loss or damage. Our share is the proportion that the applicable Limit of Insurance under this Coverage Part bears to the Limits of Insurance of all insurance covering on the same basis.
2. If there is other insurance covering the same loss or damage, other than that described in 1. above, we will pay only for the amount of covered loss or damage in excess of the amount due from that other insurance, whether you can collect on it or not. But we will not pay more than the applicable Limit of Insurance.

H. POLICY PERIOD, COVERAGE TERRITORY

Under this Coverage Part:

1. We cover loss or damage commencing:
   a. During the policy period shown in the Declarations; and
   b. Within the coverage territory.
2. The coverage territory is:
   a. The United States of America;
   b. Puerto Rico; and
   c. Canada.

I. TRANSFER OF RIGHTS OF RECOVERY AGAINST OTHERS TO US

If any person or organization to or for whom we make payment under this Coverage Part has rights to recover damages from another, those rights are transferred to us to the extent of our payment. That person or organization must do everything necessary to secure our rights and must do nothing after loss to impair them. But you may waive your rights against another party in writing:

1. Prior to a loss to your Covered Property or Covered Income.
2. After a loss to your Covered Property or Covered Income only if, at time of loss, that party is one of the following:
   a. Someone insured by this insurance;
   b. A business firm:
      (1) Owned or controlled by you; or
      (2) That owns or controls you; or
   c. Your tenant.

This will not restrict your insurance.

BUSINESS INCOME COVERAGE FORM

Various provisions in this policy restrict coverage. Read the entire policy carefully to determine rights, duties and what is and is not covered.

Throughout this policy the words "you" and "your" refer to the Named Insured shown in the Declarations. The words "we," "us" and "our" refer to the Company providing this insurance.

Other words and phrases that appear in quotation marks have special meaning. Refer to SECTION G — DEFINITIONS.

A. COVERAGE

We will pay for the actual loss of Business Income you sustain due to the necessary suspension of your "operations" during the "period of restoration." The suspension must be caused by direct physical loss of or damage to property at the premises described in the Declarations, including personal property in the open (or in a vehicle) within 100 feet, caused by or resulting from any Covered Cause of Loss.

1. Business Income

Business Income means the:

a. Net Income (Net Profit or Loss before income taxes) that would have been earned or incurred; and

b. Continuing normal operating expenses, including payroll, incurred.

2. Covered Causes Of Loss.

See applicable Causes of Loss Form as shown in the Declarations.

3. Additional Coverages

a. Extra Expense.

Extra Expense means necessary expenses you incur during the "period of restoration" that you would not have incurred if there had been no direct physical loss or damage to property caused by or resulting from a Covered Cause of Loss.

(1) We will pay any Extra Expense to avoid or minimize the suspension of business and to continue "operations":

(a) At the described premises; or

(b) At replacement premises or at temporary locations, including:

(I) Relocation expenses; and

(II) Costs to equip and operate the replacement or temporary locations.

(2) We will pay any Extra Expense to minimize the suspension of business if you cannot continue "operations."

(3) We will pay any Extra Expense to:

(a) Repair or replace any property; or

(b) Research, replace or restore the lost information on damaged valuable papers and records;

to the extent it reduces the amount of loss that otherwise would have been payable under this Coverage Form.

b. Civil Authority.

We will pay for the actual loss of Business Income you sustain and necessary Extra Expense caused by action of civil authority that prohibits access to the described premises due to direct physical loss of or damage to property, other than at the described premises, caused by or resulting from any Covered Cause of Loss. This coverage will apply for a period of up to two consecutive weeks from the date of that action.

c. Alterations and New Buildings.

We will pay for the actual loss of Business Income you sustain due to direct physical loss or damage at the described premises caused by or resulting from any Covered Cause of Loss to:

(1) New buildings or structures, whether complete or under construction;

(2) Alterations or additions to existing buildings or structures; and

(3) Machinery, equipment, supplies or building materials located on or within 100 feet of the described premises and:

(a) Used in the construction, alterations or additions; or

(b) Incidental to the occupancy of new buildings.

If such direct physical loss or damage delays the start of "operations," the "period of restoration" will begin on the date "operations" would have begun if the direct physical loss or damage had not occurred.

d. **Extended Business Income.** We will pay for the actual loss of Business Income you incur during the period that:

(1) Begins on the date property (except "finished stock") is actually repaired, rebuilt or replaced and "operations" are resumed; and

(2) Ends on the earlier of:

(a) The date you could restore your business, with reasonable speed, to the condition that would have existed if no direct physical loss or damage occurred; or

(b) 30 consecutive days after the date determined in (1) above.

Loss of Business Income must be caused by direct physical loss or damage at the described premises caused by or resulting from any Covered Cause of Loss.

4. **Coverage Extension**

If a Coinsurance percentage of 50% or more is shown in the Declarations, you may extend the insurance provided by this Coverage Part as follows:

Newly Acquired Locations

a. You may extend your Business Income Coverage to apply to property at any location you acquire other than fairs or exhibitions.

b. The most we will pay for loss under this Extension is 10% of the Limit of Insurance for Business Income shown in the Declarations, but not more than $100,000 at each location.

c. Insurance under this Extension for each newly acquired location will end when any of the following first occurs:

(1) This policy expires;

(2) 30 days expire after you acquire or begin to construct the property; or

(3) You report values to us.

We will charge you additional premium for values reported from the date you acquire the property.

This Extension is additional insurance. The Additional Condition, Coinsurance, does not apply to this Extension.

B. EXCLUSIONS

See applicable Causes of Loss Form as shown in the Declarations.

C. LIMITS OF INSURANCE

The most we will pay for loss in any one occurrence is the applicable Limit of Insurance shown in the Declarations.

The limit applicable to the Coverage Extension is in addition to the Limit of Insurance.

Payments under the following Additional Coverages will not increase the applicable Limit of Insurance:

1. Alterations and New Buildings;
2. Civil Authority;
3. Extra Expense; or
4. Extended Business Income.

D. LOSS CONDITIONS

The following conditions apply in addition to the Common Policy Conditions and the Commercial Property Conditions.

1. **Appraisal**

If we and you disagree on the amount of Net Income and operating expense or the amount of loss, either may make written demand for an appraisal of the loss. In this event, each party will select a competent and impartial appraiser.

The two appraisers will select an umpire. If they cannot agree, either may request that selection be made by a judge of a court having jurisdiction. The appraisers will state separately the amount of Net Income and operating expense or amount of loss. If they fail to agree, they will submit their differences to the umpire. A decision agreed to by any two will be binding. Each party will:

a. Pay its chosen appraiser; and

b. Bear the other expenses of the appraisal and umpire equally.

If we submit to an appraisal, we will still retain our right to deny the claim.

2. **Duties In The Event Of Loss Of Business Income**

You must see that the following are done in the event of loss of Business Income:

a. Notify the police if a law may have been broken.

b. Give us prompt notice of the direct physical loss or damage. Include a description of the property involved.

c. As soon as possible, give us a description of how, when, and where the direct physical loss or damage occurred.

d. Take all reasonable steps to protect the property at the described premises from further damage. If feasible, set the damaged property aside and in the best possible order for examination. Also keep a record of your expenses, for consideration in the settlement of the claim.

e. Permit us to inspect the property and records proving the loss.

f. If requested, permit us to question you under oath at such times as may be reasonably required about any matter relating to this insurance or your claim, including your books and records. In such event, your answers must be signed.

g. Send us a signed, sworn statement of loss containing the information we request to settle the claim. You must do this within 60 days after our request. We will supply you with the necessary forms.

h. Cooperate with us in the investigation or settlement of the claim.

i. Resume all or part of your "operations" as quickly as possible.

3. **Limitation — Electronic Media And Records**

We will not pay for any loss of Business Income caused by direct physical loss of or damage to Electronic Media and Records after the longer of:

a. 60 consecutive days from the date of direct physical loss or damage; or

b. The period, beginning with the date of direct physical loss or damage, necessary to repair, rebuild or replace, with reasonable speed and similar quality, other property at the described premises due to loss or damage caused by the same occurrence.

Electronic Media and Records are:

(1) Electronic data processing, recording or storage media such as films, tapes, discs, drums or cells;

(2) Data stored on such media; or

(3) Programming records used for electronic data processing or electronically controlled equipment.

This limitation does not apply to Extra Expense.

Example No. 1:

A Covered Cause of Loss damages a computer on June 1. It takes until September 1 to replace the computer, and until October 1 to restore the data that was lost when the damage occurred. We will only pay for the Business Income loss sustained during the period June 1 — September 1. Loss during the period September 2 — October 1 is not covered.

Example No. 2:

A Covered Cause of Loss results in the loss of data processing programming records on August 1. The records are replaced on October 15. We will only pay for the Business Income loss sustained during the period August 1 — September 29 (60 consecutive days). Loss during the period September 30 — October 15 is not covered.

4. **Loss Determination**

a. The amount of Business Income loss will be determined based on:

(1) The Net Income of the business before the direct physical loss or damage occurred;

(2) The likely Net Income of the business if no loss or damage occurred;

(3) The operating expenses, including payroll expenses, necessary to resume "operations" with the same quality of service that existed just before the direct physical loss or damage; and

(4) Other relevant sources of information, including:

(a) Your financial records and accounting procedures;

(b) Bills, invoices and other vouchers; and

(c) Deeds, liens or contracts.

b. The amount of Extra Expense will be determined based on:

(1) All expenses that exceed the normal operating expenses that would have been incurred by "operations" during the "period of restoration" if no direct physical loss or damage had occurred. We will deduct from the total of such expenses:

(a) The salvage value that remains of any property bought for temporary use during the "period of restoration" once "operations" are resumed; and

(b) Any Extra Expense that is paid for by other insurance, except for insurance that is written subject to the same plan, terms, conditions and provisions as this insurance; and

(2) All necessary expenses that reduce the Business Income loss that otherwise would have been incurred.

5. Loss Payment

We will pay for covered loss within 30 days after we receive the sworn statement of loss, if:

a. You have complied with all of the terms of this Coverage Part; and

b. (1) We have reached agreement with you on the amount of loss; or

(2) An appraisal award has been made.

6. Resumption Of Operations

We will reduce the amount of your:

a. Business Income loss, other than Extra Expense, to the extent you can resume your "operations," in whole or in part, by using damaged or undamaged property (including merchandise or stock) at the described premises or elsewhere.

b. Extra Expense loss to the extent you can return "operations" to normal and discontinue such Extra Expense.

E. ADDITIONAL CONDITION

Coinsurance

If a Coinsurance percentage is shown in the Declarations, the following condition applies in addition to the Common Policy Conditions and the Commercial Property Conditions.

We will not pay the full amount of any loss if the Limit of Insurance for Business Income is less than:

a. The Coinsurance percentage shown for Business Income in the Declarations; times

b. The sum of:

(1) The Net Income (Net Profit or Loss before income taxes), and

(2) All operating expenses, including payroll expenses,

that would have been earned (had no loss occurred) by your "operations" at the described premises for the 12 months following the inception, or last previous anniversary date, of this policy (whichever is later).

Instead, we will determine the most we will pay using the following steps:

1. Multiply the Net Income and operating expense for the 12 months following the inception, or last previous anniversary date, of this policy by the Coinsurance percentage;

2. Divide the Limit of Insurance for the described premises by the figure determined in step 1; and

3. Multiply the total amount of the covered loss by the figure determined in step 2.

The amount determined in step 3 is the most we will pay. For the remainder, you will either have to rely on other insurance or absorb the loss yourself.

Example No. 1 (Underinsurance):

When: The Net Income and operating expenses for the 12 months following the inception, or last previous anniversary date, of this policy at the described premises is $400,000
The Coinsurance percentage is 50%
The Limit of Insurance is $150,000
The amount of loss is $ 80,000

Step 1: $400,000 × 50% = $200,000 (the minimum amount of insurance to meet your Coinsurance requirements)

Step 2: $150,000 ÷ $200,000 = .75

Step 3: $ 80,000 × .75 = $60,000

We will pay no more than $60,000. The remaining $20,000 is not covered.

Example No. 2 (Adequate Insurance):

When: The Net Income and operating expenses for the 12 months following the inception, or last previous anniversary date, of this policy at the described premises is $400,000
The Coinsurance percentage is 50%
The Limit of Insurance is $200,000
The amount of loss is $ 80,000

Step 1: $400,000 × 50% = $200,000 (the minimum amount of insurance to meet your Coinsurance requirements)

Step 2: $200,000 ÷ $200,000 = 1.00

Step 3: $ 80,000 × 1.00 = $80,000

We will cover the $80,000 loss. No penalty applies.

This condition does not apply to the Extra Expense Additional Coverage.

F. OPTIONAL COVERAGES

If shown in the Declarations, the following Optional Coverages apply separately to each item.

1. Maximum Period Of Indemnity

a. The Additional Condition, Coinsurance, does not apply to this Coverage Form at the described premises to which this Optional Coverage applies.

b. The most we will pay for loss of Business Income is the lesser of:

(1) The amount of loss sustained during the 120 days immediately following the direct physical loss or damage; or

(2) The Limit of Insurance shown in the Declarations.

2. Monthly Limit Of Indemnity

a. The Additional Condition, Coinsurance, does not apply to this Coverage Form at the described premises to which this Optional Coverage applies.

b. The most we will pay for loss of Business Income in each period of 30 consecutive days after the direct physical loss or damage is:

(1) The Limit of Insurance, multiplied by

(2) The fraction shown in the Declarations for this Optional Coverage.

Example:

When: The Limit of Insurance
is $120,000
The fraction shown in
the Declarations for
this Optional Cover-
age is   ¼

The most we will pay for loss in each period of 30 consecutive days is:

$120,000 × ¼ = $30,000

If, in this example, the actual amount of loss is:

Days 1-30	$40,000
Days 31-60	20,000
Days 61-90	30,000
	$90,000

We will pay:

Days 1-30	$30,000
Days 31-60	20,000
Days 61-90	30,000
	$80,000

The remaining $10,000 is not covered.

3. Agreed Value

a. To activate this Optional Coverage:

(1) A Business Income Report/Work Sheet must be made a part of this policy and must show financial data for your "operations":

(a) During the 12 months prior to the date of the Work Sheet; and

(b) Estimated for the 12 months immediately following the inception of this Optional Coverage.

(2) An Agreed Value must be shown in the Declarations or on the Work Sheet. The Agreed Value should be at least equal to:

(a) The Coinsurance percentage shown in the Declarations; multiplied by

(b) The amount of Net Income and Operating Expenses for the following 12 months you report on the Work Sheet.

b. The Additional Condition, Coinsurance, is suspended until:

(1) 12 months after the effective date of this Optional Coverage; or

(2) The expiration date of this policy;

whichever occurs first.

c. We will reinstate the Additional Condition, Coinsurance, automatically if you do not submit a new Work Sheet and Agreed Value:

(1) Within 12 months of the effective date of this Optional Coverage; or

(2) When you request a change in your Business Income Limit of Insurance.

d. If the Business Income Limit of Insurance is less than the Agreed Value, we will not pay more of any loss than the amount of loss multiplied by:

(1) The Business Income Limit of Insurance; divided by

(2) The Agreed Value.

Example:

When: The Limit of Insurance
is $100,000
The Agreed Value is $200,000
The amount of loss is $ 80,000

Step (a): $100,000 ÷ $200,000 = .50

Step (b): .50 × $80,000 = $40,000

We will pay $40,000. The remaining $40,000 is not covered.

4. Extended Period Of Indemnity

Under paragraph A.3.d., Extended Business Income, the number "30" in subparagraph (2)(b) is replaced by the number shown in the Declarations for this Optional Coverage.

G. DEFINITIONS

1. **"Finished Stock"** means stock you have manufactured.

   "Finished stock" also includes whiskey and alcoholic products being aged, unless there is a Coinsurance percentage shown for Business Income in the Declarations.

   "Finished stock" does not include stock you have manufactured that is held for sale on the premises of any retail outlet insured under this Coverage Part.

2. **"Operations"** means the type of your business activities occurring at the described premises.

3. **"Period of Restoration"** means the period of time that:

   a. Begins with the date of direct physical loss or damage caused by or resulting from any Covered Cause of Loss at the described premises; and

   b. Ends on the date when the property at the described premises should be repaired, rebuilt or replaced with reasonable speed and similar quality.

   "Period of restoration" does not include any increased period required due to the enforcement of any law that regulates the construction, use or repair, or requires the tearing down of any property.

   The expiration date of this policy will not cut short the "period of restoration."

Addendum III

Table of Cases

*Cases involving Use & Occupancy, Business
Interruption, Rent and Other Time Element Cases Plus
Some Peripheral Matters.*

Legend

R - Rent Insurance Case
X - Extra Expense Insurance Case
E - Earnings Insurance Case
P - Profits Insurance Case
S - Strike Insurance Case

Abbott v. Sebor, 3 Johns. Cas. 39; N.Y., 2 Am. Dec. 139 (N.Y. 1802).

Adelman Laundry v. F.I.A, 59 Wis. 145, 207 N.W.2d 646; 1973 Fire & Casualty Cas. (CCH) 667 (1973).

(P/R) Aetna Ins. Co. v. Martin, 64 Ga. App. 789, 14 S.E.2d 161; 3 Fire & Casualty Cas. (CCH) 159 (1941).

(P/R) Aetna Ins. Co. v. Martin, 2 Fire & Casualty Cas. (CCH) 169; returned without inst., 191 Ga. 458, 12 S.E.2d 633, 2 Fire & Casualty Cas. (CCH)645 (1940).

(P)   American Alliance Ins. Co. v. Keleket X-Ray Corp., 248 F.2d 920 (6th Cir. 1957); 9 Fire & Casualty Cas. (CCH) 348 (1957).

AM. Home Ass. Co. v. Harvey's Wagon Wheel, Inc., 398 F.Supp. 379 (D.Nev. 1975), aff'd 554 F.2d 1067 (1977).

American Ins. Co. v. Bradley Mining Co., 57 F.Supp. 545 (Cal. 1944).

(P/R) American Ins. Co. v. Mattox, 94 W.Va. 766, 120 S.E. 912 (1929).

(P)   American Ins. Co. v. Parker, 181 F.2d 53 (Va. 1950).

(P)   American Ins. Co. v. Pickering Lumber Corp., 87 F.Supp. 512 (N.D. Cal. 1949), aff'd, 183 F.2d 587 (9th Cir. 1950).

Amusement Syndicate Co. v. Milwaukee Mechanics Ins. Co., 136 Pac. 914 (1913).

Amusement Syndicate Co. v. Prussian Nat. Ins. Co., 85 Kan. 367; 116 P. 620 (1911).

(P)   Anchor Toy Corp. v. Am. Eagle F. Ins. Co., 4 Misc. 2d 364, 155 N.Y.S.2d 600 (1956).

Anderson & Middleton Lumber Co. v. Lumberman's Mut. Casualty Co., 53 Wash.2d 404; 333 P.2d 938 (1959).

Apparel City Sewing Machine Co. Inc. v. Transamerica Ins. Group, 129 Cal. App. 3d 400; 181 Cal. Rptr. 64 (1982).

(P)   Arcadia Bonded Warehouse Co. Inc. v. Nat. Union F.I. Co., 206 La. 681, 19 So.2d 514 (1944).

(R)   Arley v. Liberty Mut. Ins. Co., 388 P.2d 576 (Nev. 1964).

(P)   A & S Corp. v. Centennial Ins. Co., 242 F.Supp. 584 (N.D. Ill. 1965).

Associated Photographers Inc. v. Aetna C. & S. & Co., 677 F.2d 1251 (8th Cir. 1982); 1982 Fire & Casualty Cas. (CCH) 1257.

Atlantic Steel Co. v. Hartford F. Ins. Co., 39 Ga.App. 680; 148 S.E. 286 (1929).

(T)   B.C. Fir & Cedar Lumber Co. v. Minister of Nat. Revenue, 1930 Can. Exch. 59 (1930).

Barclay v. Cousins, 2 East 544 (England 1802).

Baroness of Pontalba v. Phoenix Ins. Co., 2 Rob. 131; 35 Am. Dec. 205 (La. 1842).

Beautytuft, Inc. v. F.I.A, 48 F.D.R. 15, 26; (E.D. Tenn. 1969).

Beautytuft, Inc. v. F.I.A, 431 F.2d 1122 (6th Cir. 1970).

(P/R) Becker v. Merchants Mut. Ins. Co., 22 Ins. L.J. 227 (La. 1893).

(T) Berkeley Inn, Inc. v. Centennial Ins. Co., 282 Pa. Super. 207; 422 A.2d 1078 (1980).

Bird v. St. Paul F & M Ins. Co., 224 N.Y. 47; 120 N.E. 86 (1918).

Blascheck v. Bussell, (App.) 33 T.L.R. 51 (England 1916).

Blascheck v. Bussell, 33 T.L.R. 74 (England 1916).

(S/P) Bower & Kaufman v. Bothwell, 152 Md. 392; 136 A. 892 (1927).

(R) Bradford v. Canadian Ins. Co., 150 So.2d, 630 (La. 1963).

(P) Brecher Furn. Co. v. Firemen's Ins. Co. of Newark, N.J., 154 Minn. 776; 191 N.W. 912 (1923).

Bros Inc T/A The Judges Inn v. Liberty Mutual Fire, 268 A.2d 611 (D.C. 1970).

(R) Budrecki v. Firemen's Ins. Co. of Newark N.J., 114 N.J.L. 187; 176 A. 143 (1935).

(P) Buffalo Elevating Co. v. Prussian Nat. Ins. Co., 64 A.D. 182; 71 N.Y.S. 918 (1901).

(S/P) Buffalo Forge Co. v. Mutual Security Co., 83 Conn. 393; 76 A 995 (1910).

(X) Burdett Oxygen Co. v. Employers Surplus Lines Ins. Co., 419 F.2d 247 (6th Cir. 1969).

Burnand v. Rodocanachi Sons & Co., 47 L.T.R. (n.s.) 277; 7 A.C. 333 (England 1882).

C.A. Enterprises Inc. v. Employers Commercial Union Co., 376 N.E.2d 534, 1978 F & C 724 (Ind. 1978).

Canada Sugar Refining Co. v. Ins. Co. of North America, 1900.

(T) Cappel House Furnishing Co. v. U.S., 140 F.Supp. 92 (S.D. Ohio 1956), 56-1 U.S.T.C. 9376; aff'd 244 F.2d 525 (6th Cir. 1967), 57-1 U.S.T.C. 9681.

(P) Lawrence Carey et al v. The London Provincial F. Ins. Co., 33 Hunnewell, 315 (N.Y. 1884).

(T) Carroll Furniture Co. v. Comm'r, 15 T.C. 943 (1950).

(T)   Central Tablet Mfg. Co. v. U.S., 339 F.Supp. 1134 (S.D. Ohio 1972), 72-1 U.S.T.C. 9324; *rev'd,* 481 F.2d 954 (6th Cir. 1973), 73-2 U.S.T.C. 9545; *aff'd,* 417 U.S. 673 (1974), 74-2 U.S.T.C. 9511.

(P)   Charles Dowd Box Co. v. Fireman's Fund Ins. Co., 351 Mass 113; 218 N.E.2d 64; 12 Fire & Casualty Cas. (CCH) 1093 (1966).

Chatfield v. Aetna Ins. Co., 71 A.D. 164, 75 N.Y.S 620 (1902).

Chicago & W.I.R Co v. Englewood Connecting Ry Co., 115 Ill. 375; 4 N.E. 246, 1886.

(P/R)   Chronicle Bldg. Co. v. N.H. Fire Ins. Co., 21 Ga 687; 94 S.E. 1043 (1918).

Citizens Savings & Loan Assn. v. Proprietors Ins. Co., 78 AD(2) 377, 435 N.Y.S. (2nd) 303 (1981).

City Tailors Ltd v. Evans, England, Court of Appeals. England (10/20/21) (12/9/21).

Clearvu Packaging Inc. v. Nat'L Union F. Ins. Co., 434 N.E.2d 365, 1982 Fire & Casualty Cas. (CCH) 1246 (Ill. 1982).

(P)   Cleland Simpson Co. v. Firemen's Ins. Co. of Newark N.J., 11 D. & C.2d 607 (1957).

(P)   Cleland Simpson Co. v. Firemen's Ins. Co. of Newark N.J., 392 Pa. 67; 140 A.2d 41 (1958).

Cohen v. American Ins. Co., N.Y. Sup. Ct. Reported in Ins. Advocate, Feb. 22, 1947, at p. 15.

Comm'r. v. Gillette Motor Transport, Inc., 364 U.S. 136; 80 S. Ct. 1497 (1960).

(T)   Comm'r. v. Glenshaw Glass Co., 18 T.C. 860 (1952); *aff'd,* 211 F.2d 928 (3rd Cir. 1954), 54-1 U.S.T.C. 9328; *rev'd,* 348 U.S. 426 (1955), 55-1 U.S.T.C. 9308; *reh. denied,* 349 U.S. 925 (1955).

Comm'r. v. William Goldman Theatres Inc., 211 F.2d 928 (1954).

(E)   Comm'r. v. Piedmont-MT Airy Guano Co., 3 B.T.A. 1009 (1926).

(T)   Comm'r v. Newcastle Breweries, 12 Tax. Cas. 927 (1927).

Congress Bar & Restaurant Inc. v. Transamerica Ins. Co., 42 Wis. 2d 56; 165 N.W.2d 409 (1969).

Consolidated Sun Ray Inc. v. Lea, 276 F.Supp. 132 (E.D. Pa. 1967), aff'd 401 F.2d 650 (3d Cir. 1968).

Continental Oil Co. v. Nat'l Fire Ins. Co. of Conn., 541 P.2d 1315 (Okla. 1975).

Eureka-Security F&M Ins. Co. v. Simon d/b/a Simon Drugs, 1 Ariz. App. 274, 401 P.2d 759 (1965).

Eyre v. Glover, 16 East 218 (England 1912).

Farmers Chemical Ass'n Inc. v. Maryland Cas. Co., 421 F.2d 319 (6th Cir. 1970).

Farmers Mutual Ins. Co. v. New Holland Turnpike Co., 122 Pa. St. 37; 15 A. 563 (1888).

Febock v. Jefferson County, 219 Wisc. 154, 262 N.W. 588 (1935).

Feinbloom v. Camden Fire Ins. Ass'n., 54 N.J. Super 541 (1959), 149 A.2d 616. See: 30 N.J. 154; 152 A.2d 172 (1959).

Feinman v. Consolidated Mut. Ins. Co., 155 N.Y.S. 2d 326 (1956).

(P)   Fidelity-Phenix Ins. Co. of NY v. Benedict Coal Corp., 64 F.2d 347 (4th Cir. 1933).

(R)   Finer Amusements Inc. v. Citizens Ins. Co. of N.J., 327 F.2d 773 (7th Cir. 1964).

(P)   Firemen's Ins. Co. v. Lasker, 18 F.2d 375 (8th Cir. 1927).

First Investment Co. v. Vulcan Und. of Nor. Brit. & Merc. Ins. Co., 33 F.2d 785 (9th Cir. 1927).

(P/R) First Investment Co. v. Vulcan Und. of Nor. Brit. & Merc. Ins. Co., 129 Or. 688; 278 P. 967 (1929).

Fitzgerald d/b/a F. Bottling Works v. Continental Ins. Co., 275 A.D. 453, 99 N.Y.S. 22 430 (1949).

(T)   Flaxlinum Insulating Co. v. Comm'r, 5 B.T.A. 676 (1926).

(P/S) Fleet-McGinley Co. v. Bothwell, 143 Md. 324, 122 A. 202 (1923).

Fli-Back Co. Inc. v. Phila. Mfg's Mut. Ins. Co., 502 F.2d 214 (4th Cir. 1974).

Flint v. Fleming, 91 N.Y.S. 519 (1830).

Foote Mineral Co. v. Maryland Casualty Co., 277 F.2d 452 (6th Cir. 1960).

(P)   General Ins. Co. v. Pathfinder Petroleum Co., 145 F.2d 368 (9th Cir. 1944), cert. denied, Pathfinder Petroleum Co. v. General Ins. Co., 324 U.S. 844 L.Ed. 1406, 65 S.Ct. 679 (1945).

(T)   Georgia Carolina Chem. Co. v. Comm'r, 3 T.C.M. (CCH) 1213 (1944).

(T)   Glenborg Union Fireclay Co. v. Comm'r, 12 Tax Cas. 427 (1922).

J. Gliksten & Son, Ltd. v. Green, [1929] A.C. 381 (House of Lords 1929).

(P)   Hawkinson Tread Tire Service Co. v. Indiana Lumbermen's Mut. Ins. Co., 362 Mo. 823, 245 S.W.2d 24 (1951).

Hayes v. Milford Mut. Fire Ins. Co., 170 Mass. 492, 49 N.E. 754 (1898).

Hebert Mfg. Co. v. Northern Ass. Co., 108 N.H. 381, 236 A2d 701 (1967).

Hebner v. Palatine Ins. Co., 157 Ill. 144, 41 N.E. 627 (1895).

(P/R) Heim v. American Alliance Ins. Co., 147 Minn. 283, 180 N.W. 225 (1920), reh. *den. Heim v. American Alliance Ins. Co.,* 147 Minn. 290, 180 N.W. 1022 (1921).

(P)   Heller v. Royal Ins. Co., 151 Pa. 101, 25 A. 83 (1892).

(P)   Heller v. Royal Ins. Co., 177 Pa. 262, 35 A. 726 (1896).

Herbert Mfg. Co. v. Northern Assur. Co., 108 N.H. 381, 236 A.2d 701 (1967).

Hillier v. Alleghany County Mut. Ins. Co., 3 Pa. 470 (1846).

Hillyard v. Hartford Fire Ins. Co., 91 App.D.C. 206, 198 F.2d 606 (1952).

(R)   Holt v. Fidelity Phoenix Fire Ins. Co., 187 Misc. 1043, 69 N.Y.S.2d 35 (1946), aff'd. *Holt v. Fidelity Phoenix Fire Ins. Co.,* 273 App. Div. 166, 76 N.Y.S.2d 398 (1948), aff'd Holt v. Fidelity Phoenix Fire Ins. Co., 297 N.Y. 987, 80 N.E.2d 364 (1948).

Home Ins. Co. v. Eisenson, 181 F.2d 416 (5th Cir. 1950).

Howard Stores Corp. v. Foremost Ins. Co., 82 A.D.2d 398 (1981).

Howard Stores Corp. v. Foremost Ins. Co., 56 N.Y.2d 991, 453 N.Y.S.2d 682, 439 N.E.2d 397 (1982).

Hudson Mfg. Co. v. N.Y. Underwriters Ins. Co., 33 Fed. Rep. 2d 460 (7th Cir. 1929).

(P)   Hutchings v. Caledonian Ins. Co., 35 F.2d 309 (4th Cir. 1929).

(P)   Hutchings v. Caledonian Ins. Co., 52 F.2d 744 (D.C.S.C. 1931).

Ice City Inc. v. Ins. Co. of America, 456 PA 210, 314 A.2d 236 (1974).

Industro Motive Corp. v. Morris Agency Inc., 76 Mich. App. 390, 256 N.W.2d 607 (1927).

(T)   Inland Steel Co. v. U.S., 80-2 U.S.T.C. (CCH) ¶9833 (1980).

Insurance Co. of N.A. v. Canada Sugar Ref. Co. Ltd., 87 F. 491 (2nd Cir. 1898), rev'd *Canada Sugar Refining Co. v. Insurance Co. of North America,* 175 U.S. 609, 20 S.Ct. 239 (1900).

Maple Leaf Motor Lodge Inc. v. Allstate Ins. Co., 53 App. Div. 2d 1045, 386 N.Y.S.2d 162 (1976).

(T)   Marcal Pulp & Paper Co. v. Commissioner, 30 T.C. 1345, aff'd 268 F.2d 739 (3rd Cir. 1959), *cert. denied* 361 U.S. 924 (1959).

(T)   Marshall Foods v. U.S., 393 F.Supp. 1097 (D.Minn. 1974), *aff'd per curiam* 75-2 U.S.T.C. [p]9536, *cert. denied* 423 U.S. 928 (1975).

(T)   Maryland Shipbuilding & Drydock Co. v. U.S., 409 F.2d 1363 (Ct. Cl. 1969).

(T)   Massillon-Cleveland-Akron Sign Co. v. Commissioner, 15 T.C. 79 (1950).

(P)   Mayfair Fabrics v. Henley, 97 N.J. Super. 116, 234 A.2d 503 (1967), *aff'd. Natell v. Henley,* 103 N.J. Super. 161, 246 A.2d 749 (1968).

(T)   Mellinger v. U.S., 54-1 U.S.T.C. (CCH) [p]9197 (S.D.Tex. 1953), *rev'd* 228 F.2d 188 (5th Cir. 1954).

(P)   Menzies v. North British Ins. Co., 9 Dunl. 694 (Scotland 1847).

(P)   Michael v. Prussian Nat. Ins. Co., 171 N.Y. 25, 63 N.E. 810 (1902).

(E/T)   Miller v. Hocking Glass Co., 80 F.2d 436 (6th Cir. 1935), *cert. denied Hocking Glass Co. v. Miller,* 298 U.S. 659, 80 L.Ed. 1384, 56 S.Ct. 681 (1936).

(P/T)   Miner-Edgar Co. v. North River Ins. Co., 70 Ins. Law Journal Vol. 70, p. 1084 (NY 1928).

Mt. Royal Assur. Co. v. Cameron Lumber Co., 151 L.T.R. 23 A.C. 313 (Canada 1933), aff'd 47 Brit. Col. 52, 3 D.L.R. 402 (England 1934).

(T)   Moholy v. U.S., 235 F.2d 562 (9th Cir. 1956).

(R)   Moving Picture Co. of Am. v. Scottish Union & Nat. Ins. Co., 244 Pa. 358, 90 A. 642 (1914).

Mudrick's Inc. v. National Surety Corp., 143 App. D.C. 39, 442 F.2d 761 (1971).

(P/R)   National Children's Exposition Corp. v. Anchor Ins. Co., 279 F.2d 428, 83 A.L.R.2d 879 (2nd Cir. 1960).

(P)   National Filtering Oil Co. v. Citizens Ins. Co., 106 N.Y. 535, 13 N.E. 337 (1887).

National Fire Ins. Co. v. Butler, 260 Iowa 1159, 152 N.W.2d 271 (1967).

(P)   National Fire Ins. Co. v. Hutton, 396 S.W.2d 53 (Ky. 1965).

National Union Fire Ins. Co. v. Anderson-Pritchard Oil Corp., 141 F.2d 443 (10th Cir. 1944).

(P)   The Patapsco Ins. Co. v. Coulter, 28 U.S. (3 Pet.) 222 (1830).

(P)   Phillips v. Home Ins. Co., 128 A.D. 528, 112 N.Y.S. 769 (1908).

(T)   Piedmont-Mt. Airy Guano, 3 B.T.A. 1009 (1926).

(P/R) Playhouse Theatre v. U.S.F. Ins. Co., 23 A.D.2d 545, 256 N.Y.S.2d 143 (1965).

Plummer Hat Co. Ltd. v. British Traders Ins. Co., Ltd., 1932 N.Z.L.R. 576 (New Zealand 1932).

(P/X) Port Murray Dairy Co. v. Providence Washington Ins. Co., 52 N.J. Super. 350, 145 A.2d 504 (1958).

Potier v. Perry, 286 Mass. 602, 190 N.E. 822 (1934).

Princess Garment Co. v. Firemen's Fund. Ins. Co., 115 F.2d 380 (6th Cir. 1940).

(P)   Puget Sound Lumber Co. v. Mechanics & Traders Ins. Co., 168 Wash. 46, 10 P.2d 568 (1932).

Quality Molding Co. v. Am. Nat'l Fire Ins. Co., 272 F.2d 779 (7th Cir. 1959).

Raphtis v. St. Paul F. & Marine Ins. Co., 86 S.D. 491, 198 N.W.2d 505 (1972).

Recher & Co. v. North British & Merchantile Ins. Co., [1915] 3 K.B. 277 (England 1915).

Rempfer v. Deerfield Packing Corp., 4 N.J. 135, 72 A.2d 204 (1950).

(T)   Rex v. B.C. Fir & Cedar Lumber Co., Ltd., 1932 A.C. 441, 48 T.L.R. 284 (England 1932).

Riggs v. Commercial Mut. Ins. Co., 125 N.Y. Rep. 7, 25 N.E. 1058 (1890).

(T)   Rite-Way Products v. Commissioner, 12 T.C. 475 (1949).

Roddis Lumber & Veneer Co. v. Am. Alliance Ins. Co., 330 Mich. 81, 47 N.W.2d 23 (1951).

(P)   Rogers d/b/a/ Elmer's Plaza Bowl v. Am. Ins. Co., 338 F.2d 240 (8th Cir. 1964).

(P/R) Roselip v. Raisch, 73 Cal. App.2d 125, 166 P.2d 340 (1946).

Ross v. Travelers Indem. Co., 325 A.2d 768 (Me. 1974).

Rothenberg v. Liberty Mut. Ins. Co., 115 Ga. App. 26, 153 S.E.2d 447 (1967).

Royal Indemnity Co. v. Little Joe's Catfish Inn, Inc., 636 S.W.2d 530, 1983 F. & C. Reports 509 (Tex. 1982).

(P)   Tanenbaum v. Freunlich, 39 Misc. 819, 81 N.Y.S. 292 (1903).

Tanenbaum v. Simon, 40 Misc. 174, 81 N.Y.S. 655 (1903), aff'd, 84 A.D. 642, 82 N.Y.S. 1116 (1903).

Telesky v. Fidelity Guaranty F. Corp., 140 Pa. Super. 457, 13 A.2d 899 (1940).

(T)   Thalhimer Brothers v. Commissioner, 27 T.C. 733 (1957).

(R)   Thorrez & Maes Mfg. Co. v. American Cent. Ins. Co., 32 F.S. 423, 119 F.2d 423 (6th Cir. 1939).

Tomar Co. Inc. v. National Union Fire Ins. Co., 346 F.2d 318 (7th Cir. 1965).

Tonge v. Watts, 2 Strange 1251 (Hilary term 19 Geo. 2) (England 1746).

(T)   Triboro Coach Co. v. Commissioner, 29 T.C. 1274 (1958).

(E)   Trader, et al., d/b/a Pump Tavern v. Indiana Ins. Companies, 1980 Fire & Casualty Cas. (CCH) 269 (Wash. 1980).

Travelers Ind. Co. v. Kassner, 1976 Fire & Cas. Cases 1504 (Fl. 1975).

Two Caesars Corp. v. Jefferson Ins. Co., 280 A.2d 305 (D.C.App. 1971).

Unijax Inc. v. Factory Ins. Ass'n, 328 S.2d 448 (Fla. Dist. Ct. App. 1976), cert. denied, 341 S.2d 1086 (Fla. 1976).

(R)   Union Lake Associates Inc. v. Commerce & Industry Ins. Co., 89 Mich. App. 151, 280 N.W.2d 469 (1979).

(T)   The United Insurance Co. v. Lenox, 1 Johns. Cas. 377 (N.Y. 1800).

(P)   Unton v. Liverpool, London & Globe Ins. Co., 166 Minn. 273, 207 N.W. 625 (1926).

(R)   Van Nest v. Citizen's Ins. Co., 134 Minn. 94, 158 N.W. 725 (1916).

(P)   Victory Cabinent Co. v. Insurance Co. of North America, 183 F.2d 360 (7th Cir. 1950).

Victory Container Corp. v. Sphere Ins. Co., 448 F.Supp. 1043 (S.D. N.Y. 1978).

Waldridge Hosiery Mill, Inc. v. Hartford Steam Boiler Inspection and Ins. Co., 239 Ark. 47, 386 S.W.2d 938 (1965).

(P/E)   Washington Restaurant Corp. v. General Ins. Co., 64 Wash.2d 150, 390 P.2d 970 (1964).

(P/R)   Whitney Estate Co. v. Northern Assurance Co., 155 Cal. 521, 101 P. 911 (1909).

(T)   Williams Furniture Co. v. Commissioner, 45 B.T.A. 928 (1941).

(P)   Wilson & Toomer Fertilizer Co. v. Automobile Ins. Co., 283 F. 501 (D. Fla. 1922), *aff'd sub. nom, Hartford F. Ins. Co. v. Wilson and Toomer Fertilizer Co.,* 4 F.2d 835 (5th Cir. 1925), *cert. denied, Hartford F. Ins. Co. v. Wilson and Toomer Fertilizer Co.,* 268 U.S. 704 (1925).

Womble v. Dubuque F. & Marine Ins. Co., 310 Mass. 142, 37 N.E.2d 263 (1941).

(R)   World Fire & Marine Ins. Co. v. Palmer, 182 F.2d 707 (5th Cir. 1950), *cert. denied,* 340 U.S. 852 (1950).

(P)   Wright v. Pole, 1 A. & E. - Q.B. 621; 3 N. & M. - K.B. 819 (England 1824).

Wright Body Works Inc. v. Columbus Interstate Ins. Agency, 132 Ga. App. 307, 208 S.E.2d 111 (1974), *rev'd,* 233 Ga. 268, 210 S.E.2d 801 (1974).

Wylie Hill & Co., Ltd. v. Profits & Income Ins. Co., 12 Scots L.T. 408 (Scotland 1904).

(T)   Zerweck Jewelry Co., [p]62,085 T.C.M. (P.H.)

Addendum IV

Final Settlement Figures
Business Interruption Insurance
Loss Adjustment
Gross Earnings Form # 4

*(Adapted from a case presented at the annual meeting
of the Society of Chartered Property and Casualty
Underwriters October 12, 1966)*

EXHIBIT A-1
Profit & Loss Statement
Year Ended August 31, 1985

	Amount	Percent to Sales
Net Sales (Exclusive of Returned Sales, Sales Allowances and Sales Discounts)	$12,450,000	100.00%
Less—Cost of Sales:		
Inventory 9/1/84 (raw materials, direct supplies and finished goods)	$ 2,500,000	
Net Purchases (net of purchase discounts return purchases and purchase allowances)	4,000,000	
Freight In	50,000	
Direct Labor (excluding overtime premium)	2,500,000	
Factory Overhead (See Schedule)	1,300,000	
	10,350,000	
Less—Inventory 8/31/85 (raw materials direct supplies and finished goods)	1,100,000	
Cost of Sales	9,250,000	74.3%
Gross Profit	$ 3,200,000	25.7%
Less—Expenses: (See Schedule)		
Selling Expenses	$ 1,225,000	9.8%
Delivery and Shipping Expenses	632,000	5.1%
General Expenses	1,024,000	8.2%
Total	2,881,000	23.1%
Net Operating Profit Before Taxes	$ 319,000	2.6%
Add—Other Income:		
Rent—Leased Area	$ 36,000	
Scrap Sales	$ 12,000	
Total	$ 48,000	.3%
Total Profit Before Taxes	$ 367,000	2.9%

A 10% increase in sales was estimated for year commencing 9/1/85. It is estimated that all expense ratios would remain unchanged for the period 9/1/85. It is estimated that all expense ratios would remain unchanged for the period 9/1/85-86.

Mark-up on finished goods is one-third to obtain selling price.

There was no "Work-in-Progress" inventory as of 9/1/84 or 8/31/85.

EXHIBIT A-2
Schedule of Expenses
Year Ended August 31, 1985

	Amount
Factory Overhead:	
Indirect Labor	$ 284,000
Factory Supervision	248,500
Building Maintenance & Watchman	130,000
Overtime Premium (wages)	65,000
Depreciation	150,000
Factory Supplies	104,000
Heat, Light and Power	65,000
Insurance	30,000
Rent (Chicago Warehouse)	24,000
Miscellaneous (including stationery, etc.)	19,500
Payroll Taxes, Insurance & Employee Benefits	130,000
Taxes (real estate, etc.)	50,000
Total	$1,300,000
Selling Expenses:	
Salaries[1]	$ 205,000
Sales Commissions	550,000
Advertising	150,000
Travel and Entertainment	85,000
Bad Debts	135,000
Samples and Sales Aids	50,000
Miscellaneous Expenses	50,000
Total	$1,225,000
Delivery and Shipping Expenses:	
Salaries—Drivers	$ 55,000
Salaries—Shipping	18,000
Outside Shipping Expenses	505,000
Depreciation—Trucks and Autos	12,000
Insurance—Trucks, etc.	42,000
Total	$ 632,000
General Expenses:	
Executive and Officer Salaries	$ 774,500
Professional Services[2]	13,000
Travel	25,000
Telephone	85,000
Key Man Life Insurance	22,000
Auto Expense	8,500
Stationery, Postage, etc.	96,000
Total	$1,024,000

1. Includes $175,000 minimum guarantee to salesmen.

2. Includes $10,000 retainer to legal counsel.

EXHIBIT B
Business Interruption Work Sheet

Date _____ 11/28/85

ALL ENTRIES TO BE ON AN ANNUAL BASIS	COLUMN 1 Actual Values for Year 8/31 Ended....19_85_	COLUMN 2 *Estimated Values for Year Ending .11/15. 19_86_
A. Total annual net sales value of production from Manufacturing Operations; and total annual net sales from Merchandising or Non-Manufacturing Operations, (Gross sales less discounts, returns, bad accounts and prepaid freight, if included in sales)	$10,810,000.	$12,991,000.
B. Add other earnings (if any) derived from operations of the business:		
1. Cash Discounts Received (not reflected in the amounts deducted under D)		
2. Commissions or Rents from Leased Departments	36,000.	36,000.
3. Scrap sales .... (1.015%)	12,000.	13,000.
C. Total ("A" plus "B")	$10,858,000.	$13,040,000.
D. Deduct only cost of:		
1. Raw stock from which such production is derived	$4,700,000 (43.478%)	$5,648,000.
2. Supplies consisting of materials consumed directly in the conversion of such raw stock into finished stock or in supplying the service(s) sold by the Insured	(Included Above)	(Included Above)
3. Merchandise sold, including packaging materials therefor	---------	---------
4. Service(s) purchased from outsiders (not employees of the Insured) for resale which do not continue under contract	---------	---------
5. Total deductions	$4,700,000.	$5,648,000.
E. GROSS EARNINGS ("C" minus "D")	$6,158,000.	$7,392,000.
IF INSURANCE IS TO BE WRITTEN WITHOUT PAYROLL ENDORSEMENTS:		
F. Take 50, 60, 70 or 80% of "E", Column 2, as amount of insurance required, depending upon percentage Coinsurance Clause to be used (....50....%)	$3,079,000.	$3,696,000.
IF INSURANCE IS TO BE WRITTEN WITH ORDINARY PAYROLL EXCLUSION ENDORSEMENT, Deduct From "E" Above:		
G. All Ordinary Payroll Expense	$	$
H. Business Interruption Basis for Coinsurance ("E" minus "G")	$	$
I. Amount of Insurance—Take 80, 90 or 100% of H, Column 2, depending upon percentage Coinsurance Clause to be used (........%)		$
IF INSURANCE IS TO BE WRITTEN WITH ORDINARY PAYROLL-LIMITED COVERAGE ENDORSEMENT, Complete "G" and "H" and the following:		
J. Select the largest Ordinary Payroll Expense for .... consecutive calendar days .... 90, 120, 150 or 180	$	$
K. Business Interruption Basis for Coinsurance ("H" plus "J")	$	$
L. Amount of Insurance—Take 80, 90 or 100% of K, Column 2, depending upon percentage Coinsurance Clause to be used (........%) ...	$	$

*INSTRUCTIONS: THE COINSURANCE CLAUSE ALWAYS APPLIES TO THE FUTURE (never the PAST). Column 2 is merely a projection of known past values (shown in Column 1) to the next 12 months from the date the computation is prepared.

Do not inadvertently enter Cost of Sales as Cost of Raw Stock under "D" above. Deduction under "D" above should not include any labor. "Freight in" may be considered as a part of the cost of raw stock.

Business Interruption values should be checked at regular intervals and the agent or broker notified at once of any actual or impending change that would affect values during the next 12 months from the date such change becomes known.

(over)

CF 15 15 (Ed. 05 77)   Copyright, Insurance Services Office, Inc., 1977

EXHIBIT C

INVENTORY DATA:		8/31/84	8/31/85	Decrease
Raw Materials		$1,150,000	$ 500,000	$ 650,000
Finished Goods				
Materials		900,000	400,000	500,000
Labor		450,000	200,000	250,000
	Total - - - - -	$2,500,000	$1,100,000	$1,400,000

	Year Ending	
EXPLANATORY NOTES:	8/31/85	8/31/85

1. To obtain annual net sales value of production from Manufacturing Operations, (Item A) the following procedure is recommended:

	8/31/85	8/31/85
Net sales of Insured's product during the year (i.e. gross sales less discounts granted, returns, allowances, bad debts, and prepaid freight, if included in sales figures)	$12,450,000 − 640,000	$13,695,000 − 704,000
	$11,810,000	$12,991,000
DEDUCT−Inventory of Finished Stock at beginning of year, priced at sales value	1,800,000	800,000
BALANCE	$10,010,000	$12,191,000
ADD−Inventory of Finished Stock on hand at end of year, priced at sales value	800,000	800,000
TOTAL−Annual Net Sales Value of production during the year	10,810,000	12,991,000

2. To obtain cost of raw stock, merchandise sold, or supplies consisting of materials consumed, (Item D) the following procedure is recommended:

	8/31/85	8/31/85
Inventory at beginning of year	1,150,000	500,000
ADD−Net cost of raw stock, merchandise, or supplies consisting of materials purchased during the year (including cartage and transportation charges on said incoming purchases)	4,050,000	5,648,000
TOTAL	$ 5,200,000	$ 6,148,000
DEDUCT−Inventory at end of year	500,000	500,000
Amount for deductions 1, 2, and 3 of "D" 43.478% of Net Sales	$ 4,700,000	$ 5,648,000

NOTE: Adjust for any inventory increase or decrease by price fluctuations.

3. Under deduction 2 of "D", the words "supplies consisting of materials" are intended to refer only to tangible or physical supplies (i.e. materials), and the deduction of intangible supplies (such as heat and power) is not permitted nor shall intangible supplies which are not materials" be deemed to be raw stock.

	8/31/85	8/31/85
FIGURES MAKING UP THE DEDUCTION ARE BAD DEBTS	$ 135,000	$ 148,500
OUTSIDE SHIPPING	505,000	555,500

EXHIBIT D
Gross Earnings Computation and Expected Expenses
For 5 1/2 Month Restoration Period Commencing 11/15/85[1]

Net Sales Value of Production		$8,444,000[2]
Deduct Raw Materials & Supplies	(43.478%)	3,670,000
		4,774,000
Add Other Income: 5 1/2 Months Rent	16,500[3]	
Scrap Sales	8,600[4]	25,100
Value of Gross Earnings		$4,799,100

	EXPENSES FOR 5 1/2 MONTH PERIOD HAD NO LOSS OCCURRED	NON CONTINUING EXPENSES
OTHER MANUFACTURING COSTS		
Direct Labor (Excluding Premium Overtime)	1,768,555	$1,503,272
Indirect Labor	200,899	170,764
Factory Supervision	113,813	–
Building Maintenance and Watchmen	59,540	41,678
Overtime Premium (Wages)	45,975	45,975
Depreciation	68,700	13,740
Factory Supplies	73,543	73,543
Heat, Light and Power	45,975	39,079
Insurance	13,740	–
Rent (Chicago Warehouse)	10,992	–
Miscellaneous	13,828	12,455
Payroll Tax, Ins. & Employee Benefits	91,950	68,963
Taxes–Real Estate, etc.	22,900	–
SELLING EXPENSES		
Salaries	93,890	–
Commissions	389,115	–
Advertising	106,130	79,598
Travel & Entertainment	60,155	45,116
Samples & Sales Aids	35,406	26,555
Miscellaneous	35,406	26,555
DELIVERY & SHIPPING EXPENSES		
Salaries–Drivers	38,929	33,090
Salaries–Shipping	12,683	10,781
Depreciation–Trucks & Auto	5,496	–
Insurance–Trucks & Autos	19,236	–
GENERAL EXPENSES		
Executive & Office Salaries	354,721	–
Professional Services	5,954	–
Travel	11,450	–
Telephone	38,930	–
Key Man Life Insurance	10,076	–
Auto Expenses	3,893	–
Stationery, Postage, etc.	67,906	44,139
TOTAL EXPENSES	$3,819,786	$2,235,303

1. 5 1/2 Months includes 2 week building trade strike which would have prevented repairs had work been done immediately.
2. Assumes that 65% of annual sales value of production would have been achieved during these 5 1/2 months.
3. Assumes rent abatable from date of fire.
4. Estimated for restoration period of 5 1/2 months.

EXHIBIT E
Computation of Limit of Recovery
For the 5 1/2 Month Period

Gross Earnings	$4,799,100
Less Non-Continuing Expenses	2,235,303
	$2,563,797

Coinsurance Computation

Insurance Carried $\dfrac{2,500,000}{3,696,000}$ = 67.64% Recovery

Insurance Required

67.64% × 2,563,797 = 1,734,152 (Limit of Liability)

EXHIBIT F
Actual Operating Figures
For 5 1/2 Months of "Distressed Operation"

Sales Value of Production	$6,333,000*
Deduct Raw Materials and Supplies (43.478%)	2,753,462
	$3,579,538

Add Other Income: Rent		
	Scrap Sales 6,500	6,500
Gross Earnings Value		$3,586,038

Manufacturing Cost Accounts Where Expenses to Reduce Loss Were Incurred

Account	Normal	Actual	Expense to Reduce Loss
Direct Labor (incl. Prem. Overtime)	$1,326,400	$1,650,000	$ 323,600
Indirect Labor	150,700	175,000	24,300
Factory Supervision	131,800	142,000	10,200
Depreciation	68,700	65,265	(3,435)
Payroll Tax, Ins. & Emp. Benefits	69,000	82,000	13,000
Total			$ 367,665

Extra Expenses to Reduce Loss (From Outside Vendors)

Premium Cost–Stainless Steel & Die Stamping	$ 84,000
Extra Cost of Heat Treating from Outsiders	14,000
Temporary Warehouse Rental	6,000
Materials and Labor to Temporarily Restore Loading Dock (Net of Salvage)	9,800
Total	113,800
Total Expense Incurred to Reduce Loss	$ 481,465

*Assumes that 75% of normal production was achieved, i.e., 75% of $8,444,000.

EXHIBIT G
Loss and Claim Calculation

Reduction in Gross Earnings Less Non-Continuing Expenses:

Projected Sales Value of Production for 5 1/2 Month Restoration		$8,444,000
Actual Sales Value of Production for 5 1/2 Month Restoration		6,333,000
Reduction in Sales Value of Production		2,111,000
Add Net Loss of Rents and Scrap Sales	$25,100	
	−6,500	18,600
Total Reduction		$2,129,600

Ratio of (Gross Earnings Less Non-Continuing Expenses)
to (Sales Value of Production + Rents & Scrap Sales)

$$\frac{2,563,797}{8,444,000 + 25,100} = \frac{2,563,797}{8,469,100} = 30.272\%$$

Loss of Gross Earnings Less Non-Continuing Expenses:	
$2,129,600 × 30.272% =	$ 644,673
Expense to Reduce Loss Per Schedule (Exhibit E)	481,465
Total Loss	$1,126,138

Determination of Loss Collectible

Annual Gross Earnings Value at Time of Loss	$7,392,000
Insurance Carried	2,500,000
Insurance required (50% of 7,392,000)	3,696,000

Percentage Recoverable:
$$\frac{2,500,000}{3,696,000} = 67.64\%$$

Coinsurance Penalty Applies Only to Reduction in Gross
Earnings Less Non-Continuing Expenses—As Follows:

655,673 × 67.64% =	436,057
Expense to Reduce Loss	481,465
Total Recovery	$917,522

Addendum V

Glossary of Terms

ADJUSTER

The representative of the Insurer to adjust and settle the loss including all of his associates and experts.

AMOUNT OF POLICY

The total number of dollars provided by the contract to cover loss from a particular cause of peril.

ASSIGNMENT OF CLAIM

See: *Holt v. Fidelity Phenix.*

BOTTLENECK

Situation or condition that would extend period of replacement beyond time that would normally be expected.

BUSINESS INTERRUPTION VALUE

The dollar amount of gross earnings to which the Contribution Clause will apply.

BUSINESS NEED

A need for the goods or services produced by utilization of property, such as orders in hand or sales in expectation.

BUSINESS OPPORTUNITY

Results from the need for the products of the Insured's operation which has already led or is reasonably expected to lead to an order for such products.

BUSINESS POTENTIAL

The existence of a need of products of the type produced by the Insured business plus the tools of production available to meet that need.

CHOMAGE

Early type of Business Interruption Insurance under which recovery is based on a percentage of the amount of fire insurance loss.

CONTRIBUTING PROPERTIES

In Contingent Business Interruption Insurance, the source of materials needed for Insured's continuing operations.

DISASTER PLAN

A pre-arranged plan for transferring operations to another location in case of damage to the described property.

EARNINGS POTENTIAL

The ability of the described property to be used to produce an Earnings Stream.

EARNINGS STREAM

The flow of funds produced by the operations of a business.

ENDORSEMENT
A paper containing other contract provisions attached to the underlying policy. See: FORM

FORM—also POLICY FORM
The paper attached to the policy which contains the provisions of the contract of Business Interruption Insurance. See: Endorsement

LAG INSURANCE
Covers retardation in the restoration of flow of Gross Earnings to their pre-damage state.

NON-WAIVER AGREEMENT
Written statement signed by Insured that the participation of Adjuster in loss adjustment does not waive Insurer's defenses against liability under the policy.

OFF PREMISES RISK
Risk of Owner's operations being interrupted by damage to property not on the described premises.

PROFITS INSURANCE
Insurance on profits of goods produced but not yet sold.

PUBLIC ADJUSTER
Represents the Insured in adjustment and settlement of loss.

RECIPIENT PROPERTIES
In Contingent Business Interruption Insurance: Customers whose continued need for Insured's product or services keeps Insured operating.

RENT
Rent is the sum stipulated to be paid for the use and enjoyment of land. *Kennedy v. Boston Continental*

RESERVES AGAINST RISK
Standby equipment and supplies that can be thrown into the breach if primary facilities are put out of commission.

RIDER (also a SLIP)
An endorsement attached to an insurance policy.

RISK MANAGEMENT
The avoidance, reduction, and acceptance of risk and then the laying off of the balance of risk by insurance or similar technique.

SEQUENTIAL APPROACH
Examining Business Interruption Insurance through the activities of the people involved in its functioning in a business setting.

STATIC USE VALUE
The value of the property for property insurance purposes.

UNDERWRITER
The person who acts to assume liability for the Insurer under an insurance contract.

USE POTENTIAL
The potential of property being used as a tool in the production of an Earnings Stream.

USE VALUE
The value attached to the fact that property can function in a particular fashion.

VALUED POLICY
A policy expressing on its face an agreement that the property insured shall be valued at a specific sum.

INCOME STREAM
The flow of funds resulting from the exploitation of a business opportunity. See: Earnings Stream.

RISK
The property which is subject to damage by a peril.

RISK OF LOSS
The potential of the described property being damaged by a peril.

TIME-LOSS UNIT (RATE OF LOSS)
The amount of economic loss the Insured would suffer for each unit of time that production was terminated or curtailed.

USABILITY
Ability to be used or employed in developing an Income Stream.

Addendum VI

Index